A CRITICAL CON
AMERICAN STAGE Ivi Uɔi̇ɔıɔ̣ʌ̣ı̣

Elizabeth L. Wollman is Associate Professor of Music at Baruch College in New York City, USA. She is the author of *The Theater Will Rock: A History of the Rock Musical, from* Hair *to* Hedwig and *Hard Times: The Adult Musical in 1970s New York City,* as well as many articles and book chapters.

Also available in the Critical Companions series from Bloomsbury Methuen Drama:

BRITISH MUSICAL THEATRE SINCE 1950
Robert Gordon, Olaf Jubin, and Millie Taylor

BRITISH THEATRE AND PERFORMANCE 1900–1950
Rebecca D'Monté

DISABILITY THEATRE AND MODERN DRAMA: RECASTING
MODERNISM
Kirsty Johnston

MODERN ASIAN THEATRE AND PERFORMANCE 1900–2000
Kevin J. Wetmore, Siyuan Liu, and Erin B. Mee

THE PLAYS OF SAMUEL BECKETT
Katherine Weiss

THE THEATRE OF ANTHONY NEILSON
Trish Reid

THE THEATRE OF EUGENE O'NEILL
Kurt Eisen

THE THEATRE OF TENNESSEE WILLIAMS
Brenda Murphy

THE THEATRE OF TOM MURPHY: PLAYWRIGHT ADVENTURER
Nicholas Grene

VERSE DRAMA IN ENGLAND, 1900–2015: ART MODERNITY AND
THE NATIONAL STAGE
Irene Morra

For a full listing, please visit www.bloomsbury.com/series/critical-companions/

A CRITICAL COMPANION TO THE AMERICAN STAGE MUSICAL

Elizabeth L. Wollman

Series Editors: Patrick Lonergan and Kevin J. Wetmore, Jr.

Bloomsbury Methuen Drama
An imprint of Bloomsbury Publishing Plc

B L O O M S B U R Y
LONDON • OXFORD • NEW YORK • NEW DELHI • SYDNEY

Bloomsbury Methuen Drama

An imprint of Bloomsbury Publishing Plc

Imprint previously known as Methuen Drama

50 Bedford Square	1385 Broadway
London	New York
WC1B 3DP	NY 10018
UK	USA

www.bloomsbury.com

BLOOMSBURY, METHUEN DRAMA and the Diana logo are trademarks of Bloomsbury Publishing Plc

First published 2017

© Elizabeth L. Wollman and contributors, 2017

British Library Cataloguing-in-Publication Data
A catalogue record for this book is available from the British Library.

ISBN:	HB:	978-1-472-51338-0
	PB:	978-1-472-51325-0
	ePDF:	978-1-472-51388-5
	eBook:	978-1-472-51048-8

Library of Congress Cataloging-in-Publication Data
A catalog record for this book is available from the Library of Congress.

Series: Critical Companions

Cover image: *Crazy for You* (Shubert Theatre, New York, 1992).
(© Joan Marcus Photography)

Typeset by RefineCatch Limited, Bungay, Suffolk

To find out more about our authors and books visit www.bloomsbury.com.
Here you will find extracts, author interviews, details of forthcoming events
and the option to sign up for our newsletters.

For my students and my teachers

CONTENTS

Contents

ACKNOWLEDGEMENTS

I am grateful for the enthusiasm, support, and advice I have received as I have worked on this project. My thanks to the members of the Musical Theater Forum, the Fine and Performing Arts Department at Baruch College, and the Theater Department at the CUNY Graduate Center. Thanks in particular to Shane Breaux, Ryan Donovan, John Graziano, Alosha Grinenko, Stefanie Jones, Jennifer Jones Wilson, Ray Knapp, Brian Murphy, Carol Oja, Gillian Rodger, David Savran, and Stacy Wolf for answering specific questions or directing me to particular sources at various points along the way.

At Baruch, Skip Dietrich, Karen and Bob Freedman, Gil Harel, Leonard Sussman, Anne Swartz, and Zoë Sheehan-Saldaña lent especial support. At Bloomsbury Methuen Drama, my thanks to Mark Dudgeon, Susan Furber, Emily Hockley, Patrick Lonergan, and Kevin Wetmore. I am grateful for Daniel Gundlach, who is a deft and insightful indexer, and for Merv Honeywood, who oversaw production of this volume.

My love and appreciation to my extended family and my friends on the OP. And last but never least, my profound gratitude to Andy, Paulina, and Pip for being so nice to come home to.

INTRODUCTION

As its title might imply, *A Critical Companion to the American Stage Musical* is meant to serve as a companion to the many other fine books that survey the history of the American stage musical as it has developed, mostly on, but also off Broadway and across the United States. To that end, I have written this book to complement, not compete with, the extant musical theater histories that almost overwhelmingly trace the history of the Broadway musical with primary emphasis on the genre's structure, style, and aesthetic development. This book emphasizes instead the American stage musical as an ever-adapting commercial entertainment form that is the product of an endlessly shifting social, cultural, political, and economic environment.

From the Civil War through the early twenty-first century, the American stage musical has remained a vibrant, viable entertainment form. Yet it has not managed to survive devastating economic and political crises, radical sociocultural shifts, and the rise of far more modern, inexpensive, mass-mediated popular entertainments by accident, luck, or inherent brilliance. Rather, like all commercial entertainment forms, the musical theater has by necessity repeatedly reinvented itself to fit the needs of its ever-changing audience. Were this not the case, a war or severe economic downturn would have easily killed it off years ago. Or, even more likely, it would have become extinct with the advent of film, or the record player, or television, or the Internet. But the American stage musical lives on and, in recent years, has even grown in worldwide popularity. This book, then, is more about how the genre has developed, adapted, and survived than it is a study of the various stylistic or aesthetic ingredients that make up its canon.

And yet *A Critical Companion to the American Stage Musical* is hardly a radical departure, nor does it aim to be an alternative history. Like a vast majority of books about musicals, this one follows chronologically, from the genre's earliest influences in the Colonial Era, to its formation in the post-Civil War years and early twentieth century, to the present. Like other histories, too, this one examines the ways the American stage musical has drawn from outside influences, such as blackface minstrelsy, vaudeville, film, television, jazz, rock music, and hip-hop.

Finally, like the others, this book focuses for the most part on musicals that have run on Broadway. There is good reason for this: plenty of musicals have been performed across the country (and increasingly across the globe), but New York's commercial theater district, located in the Times Square neighborhood of midtown Manhattan, continues to house the largest concentration of commercial theaters in the nation. It is also home to the industry that controls them and exerts strong influence on the genre as it is developed elsewhere. New York City's storied theater district, known informally as "Broadway" due to its proximity to the famous avenue that cuts up through Times Square, has since the early twentieth century staged productions that have both mirrored and helped shape American popular culture. The fact that "Broadway" is synonymous with "the American stage musical" is no accident—nor can New York City's influence on the growth and development of the American stage musical be underestimated.

Where this book departs, however, is in its attempt to take more of a bird's-eye view of the genre than most other books do. While most of Broadway's "greatest hits," from *Show Boat* to *Oklahoma!* and *A Chorus Line* to *Hamilton*, are detailed, and while a handful of Off Broadway productions are too, none is necessarily analyzed closely for style, score, or overall aesthetics. Instead, this book turns its lens on the outside forces—whether cultural, political, social or economic—that have helped shape the musical into one of the US's premier mainstream commercial entertainment forms.

A book about the American stage musical that does not devote itself to close readings of landmark Broadway productions might seem an odd departure from the norm, but this is precisely the point of the book: in the roughly two decades that musical theater studies has developed as a vibrant, interdisciplinary field of study, many excellent books about the genre have been published to meet the demand at colleges and universities across the world. These books range broadly in style and approach, but most trace the growth of the Broadway or Broadway-style musical by moving from one important production, composer and lyricist team, or innovative producer or director to the next, pausing each time to analyze representative musical numbers, describe aspects of a show's structure or style, or unpack notable scenes.

There are, in short, plenty of studies of the stage musical that focus on the shows themselves; I have referred to as many as I have been able to get my hands on in the course of researching and writing this book. I am grateful for the insights of fine scholars such as Gerald Mast (*Can't Help Singin': The American Musical on Stage and Screen*, 1987), Gerald Bordman (*American*

Musical Theatre: A Chronicle, 2001), John Bush Jones (*Our Musicals, Ourselves: A Social History of the American Musical Theatre*, 2003), Ray Knapp (*The American Musical and the Formation of National Identity*, 2005; *The American Musical and the Formation of Personal Identity*, 2006), Larry Stempel (*Showtime: A History of the Broadway Musical Theater*, 2010), Stacy Wolf (*Changed for Good: A Feminist History of the Broadway Musical*, 2011), and James Leve (*American Musical Theater*, 2016), among others. These scholars' surveys have served countless undergraduate and graduate students; they have served their contemporaries as well. I have learned a great deal from the books I have turned to while researching this one, and have no desire to attempt to supplant them. Instead, I hope this book will contribute to a growing wealth of knowledge about the musical theater by examining it from different, complementary angles.

In considering the many external factors that have influenced the development of the American musical, I hope to help fill in gaps, as well as to address questions that I regularly field in nearly two decades of teaching. In my experience, most students who take courses on musicals come away with a strong grasp of the genre's most important creators, characteristic structures and stylistic elements. Over the course of a semester, they learn, for example, about 32-bar song form, the plot of *Oklahoma!*, what an "I Want" song is, and the fact that *Cats* is, for the most part, about cats that sing and dance. They know who Richard Rodgers and Ethel Merman were, about the list songs Cole Porter and Stephen Sondheim wrote, and about why George M. Cohan and Lin-Manuel Miranda matter.

Fewer, however, come away with a clear sense of how various forces help keep the stage musical alive and kicking. I am frequently interrupted during lectures about *Show Boat*, George Gershwin, or *Rent* with questions about how the theater industry works, why it is centered in New York, what a preview period is, or how musicals function politically, culturally, or in competition with other forms of entertainment. In an attempt to answer at least some of these questions, this book explores the relationship that the Broadway musical—whether as a fully developed genre or as a series of early influences—has had with American commerce, society, and (popular) culture. The body of the text considers the stage musical's history and development chronologically, with an eye toward the sociocultural, artistic, and commercial trends that have influenced and altered it. The contributed essays at the end of the book provide additional insights about how musicals are conceived and developed, how they function on the amateur, American regional, and international levels, and how they are studied by scholars.

Introduction

No entertainment product exists in a vacuum, and thus, the American stage musical is neither merely a succession of openings and closings nor a series of scripts, stars, and scores. I hope this book will help students engage with larger questions about the American stage musical as an ever-changing art form that is forever adapting to the needs of the world around it.

CHAPTER 1
THE BIRTH OF (THE POPULAR CULTURE OF) A NATION: STAGE ENTERTAINMENT IN A NEW LAND

Over the course of its hundred-plus years of development, the American stage musical has grown into an international entertainment commodity. There are, of course, still always plenty of stage musicals to be found in New York City's Times Square, the commercial theater district located at the intersection of Broadway and Seventh Avenue, and stretching roughly from West 42nd Street to West 48th Street.[1] Since the early twentieth century, this legendary rough-and-tumble neighborhood has cradled the development of the entertainment form that has become known, even as it has globalized, as—the "Broadway musical." For over a century, Times Square has been both spiritual home to the American stage musical and geographical home to the commercial theater industry in the United States, which is one of many reasons why the neighborhood is so world-famous.

The stage musical is distinguished herein from latter-day film, television, and Internet musicals, all of which are mass-mediated entertainments. Part of the appeal of stage musicals is their very liveness: they are performed by actors on a stage before live audiences, who often pay handsomely for the experience.

Yet the advent of mass media has allowed the American stage musical to grow well beyond the physical confines of Times Square. Today, many stage musicals are conceived, developed, and performed not only in Times Square, but across North America and increasingly in countries around the globe. It is now possible for audiences to see American stage musicals that have been translated into local languages and cast with local performers, in cities as diverse as Seoul, Port-of-Spain, Hamburg, and Minsk. It has become newly possible for people across the globe to see or hear countless American stage musicals without ever once having to travel to Times Square. Stage musicals may not be a true mass medium, but the genre has, over decades, adapted to emulate more easily mass-mediated forms for its own purposes and survival.

Nevertheless, the American stage musical remains spiritually—if not always geographically or physically—tied to a minuscule segment of Broadway, the 33-mile avenue that runs up the length of Manhattan, through the Bronx, and into Westchester County. After all, "American stage musical" is hardly a household term; you might even have been wondering what, exactly, I have been talking about in these opening paragraphs. Rather, the expression that instantly connotes the genre is "Broadway musical." To call Broadway just another street in New York would be like calling Paris just another city in Europe or Hollywood just another neighborhood in Los Angeles. Broadway is not only a physical location but also an international brand. And a Broadway musical is now a global commodity (Traub 2005, 239).

Yet well before terms like "international brand" or "global commodity" entered the vernacular, there were myriad reasons that this single avenue—really, just a teeny, tiny segment of it—became so closely associated with the commercial stage in the US. Keep this in mind, though, because we have miles to go, and a lot of practicing to do, before we can make it to Broadway. Before we get there, we will need to trace the earliest influences on the American stage musical, keeping an eye on the birth of the commercial theater industry in the process.

The Colonial Era

Named the Wickquasgeck Trail by the Lenape Indians, a well-trod thoroughfare that initially ran fifteen miles up the length of Manhattan into the Bronx was used for trade with other tribes and, later, with Dutch, French, and British settlers. The Dutch, who arrived in New York in the early seventeenth century under the auspices of the Dutch West India Company, had several names for the path: *Heere Straat* ("High Street"), *Heere Wegh* ("High Way") or *Breedeweg* ("Broadway"). When the British took New Amsterdam from the Dutch in 1664, the name of the street was Anglicized, occasionally as "Broadway Street," but usually just as "Broadway," which was the name that stuck.

The only road traversing the island of Manhattan for some hundred years after the arrival of Europeans, Broadway remained an important locus as New York grew into a colony. Churches, municipal buildings, taverns, stables, slaughterhouses, shops, prisons, and a site for public executions sprang up along the avenue as the city developed northward. Largely absent through the seventeenth century, however, was the one commercial enterprise Broadway would become most famous for: the theater.

There is not a lot of information on theater in the early Colonial Era. Presumably, the earliest colonists were so busy trying to survive that staging popular entertainments was pretty low on their list of priorities. If theatrical events were staged at all, they were probably amateur productions, usually with religious themes. The first physical structure intended for use as a theater was erected around 1716 in Williamsburg, Virginia, which had been settled in 1638. Performances at this venue were typically staged by local amateurs, or by students attending the nearby College of William and Mary, which had been established in 1693 (Stempel 2010, 21).

Initially, the northern colonies were stricter than Virginia when it came to staged entertainments. Dutch Calvinists in New Amsterdam, for example, considered theater to be sacrilegious. Settlers in Massachusetts, Pennsylvania, and Delaware agreed, so all those colonies passed laws prohibiting theatrical performance. Yet as the Colonial Era progressed, anti-theater laws were increasingly ignored by both citizens and officials.[2] Settlers arrived by the boatload on a near-daily basis, and as the colonies grew, a growing population decided that the occasional theatrical production was hardly offensive enough to complain about.

In 1735, advertisements in the *South Carolina Gazette* alerted Charleston residents to performances of the ballad opera *Flora, or, Hob in the Well* at a local makeshift theater. The production proved so popular that the city of Charleston built the Dock Street Theatre, which was the first permanent, professional theater building in the country. The Dock Street was inaugurated with an encore production of *Flora* which, in turn, spurred a national craze for ballad operas. Enormously popular in England, ballad operas—of which John Gay's *The Beggar's Opera* (1728) is perhaps most famous—were satirical operas in English, featuring songs that were either previously composed or newly written in popular styles, and thus recognizable by much of the audience.

As interest in the theater grew across the colonies through the early 1700s, itinerant or "strolling" companies, comprised of actors and musicians, began to travel from town to town on horse-drawn carts in a huge (and probably maddeningly slow) loop. These companies would stop in one town, perform for a few days or weeks, and then move on to another; no American city yet had the funds or population to support permanent performing companies. As strolling companies grew more popular, many chose one city or town to use as a home-base from which they traveled slightly less arduous distances (Preston 2008, 4). Because colonists who disapproved of the theater on religious grounds often tended to be less offended by music, many strolling companies became expert at combining the two, performing, for example, segments from opera, instrumental works, dramatic readings, and excerpts from well-known plays in the course of a single evening (Mates 1962, 6–7).

Because a certain hybridity was established in American theatrical entertainment from the country's infancy, the approach to genre as it developed through the Colonial Era was notably loose. Strolling companies and their audiences showed little concern for rigid definitions, or for keeping various styles of performance distinct from one another. Through much of the eighteenth century, it was not at all unusual for a night at the theater to include both a "play" and an "afterpiece." A "play" could refer to a Shakespeare tragedy, Restoration comedy, opera, ballet, or some combination thereof. An "afterpiece" was usually a short, upbeat sketch with songs accompanied by orchestra, which was performed at the end of the evening. Just about every program in every theater in every colony bridged highbrow and lowbrow tastes, frequently transforming comedy into tragedy and then back again as the evening unfolded (Lewis 2003, 8–9).

Colonial New York was established as a center for trade, so through the late-seventeenth century, the arts initially took a back-seat to the businesses developing on Wall Street, and the city's cultural output lagged far behind that of other east coast cities such as Philadelphia and Boston. Yet a demand in New York for entertainment grew by the turn of the century (Charyn 2003, 26–7). In 1732, a two-story wooden structure known alternately as the New Theatre or the Theatre in Nassau Street opened on Nassau between Maiden Lane and John Street, just west of Broadway. This theater probably also functioned as a brewery, warehouse, or both. When it was used for live entertainment, it could seat about 280 people. At first, the space featured infrequent, and usually amateur, performances. Yet on March 5, 1750, it hosted New York's first documented professional theater production: Shakespeare's *Richard III*, performed by a troupe visiting from England (Frick and LoMonaco 1995, 1165).

By this point, New York was home to approximately 13,000 people—not yet enough to justify a permanent theater company, but certainly enough to keep visiting ones busy and well compensated.[3] The arrival in New York of theater impresario David Douglass in the late 1750s led to the establishment of more theaters in lower Manhattan. Douglass's Theatre in John Street (1767), which could seat 750, became a popular venue until it was demolished in 1798 (ibid., 1167).

In 1774, the Continental Congress resolved to curtail all activities that distracted from the goals of the American Revolution, which commenced the following year. Professional theater activity in the colonies slowed significantly, and strolling companies were banished (Preston 2008, 5). After the war, restrictions against professional theater were lifted; President Washington made a point of attending shows in New York and Philadelphia, thereby encouraging citizens of the newly independent nation to do the same (Kenrick 2008, 51). Strolling companies established before the war came out of exile (Preston 2008, 5), theaters rose across the nation, and for the first time, permanent theater companies and orchestras did, too. The opportunities these new venues provided brought many European musicians and thespians to the new country (Preston 2008, 5).

After the Revolution

The spike in venues across the country was the result of a concerted effort to define the United States as culturally distinct from the European nations that had colonized it and that continued to exert strong influence on its popular arts. More practically, it also reflected a surge in population. Between 1789 and 1840, the population of the country grew from roughly four million to seventeen million, and with this nearly fourfold increase came an equally sharp rise in the demand for diversified entertainment.[4]

New York City's postwar growth was especially remarkable. The city's population, roughly 12,000 at the end of the war, doubled two years later (Burrows and Wallace 1999, 270). Already the most populous city in the US by the time of the first census in 1790, New York had about 300,000 citizens by 1840 (Jackson 1995, 923).[5] Manhattan absorbed newcomers by developing northward, using Broadway as its "commercial and cultural spine" (Kenrick 2008, 51). Yet during the Federalist Era, the hub of the city remained in lower Manhattan, where a number of new theaters—the Park, Chatham Garden, and Bowery—were erected around the turn of the century (Frick and LoMonaco 1995, 1166).

Federalist-Era audiences were larger than Colonial ones, but offerings remained similar, though the performances were more often by resident and not traveling companies. In a single night, early-nineteenth-century-audiences might have been treated to a bill featuring a drama, symphony, dance piece, and opera, followed by a short musical afterpiece over the course of four or five hours. American performance venues had yet to be devoted to specific genres. There were no opera houses, concert venues or recital halls, nor was there sufficient demand to justify their creation (Bordman 2001, 7). As in the Colonial Era, Federalist-Era theater productions might seem, by contemporary standards, numbingly long and disorganized. Spectators at the time did not mind, however; they were, after all, in no rush to get home in time to watch the evening news or late show.

It is perhaps fitting, considering the copious amount of genre mixing, that the early- to mid-nineteenth century saw a rise in popularity of the melodrama. Melodramas blended heightened drama and music to tell "unambiguous tales of right and wrong that appealed directly to the emotions." Usually, a lot of action was involved, though there was not as much attention paid to character development. In melodrama, actors playing two-dimensional characters did not typically sing; rather, the genre relied on "action music" that underscored what the characters were saying as they spoke, as well as to express what they felt or thought when they were not speaking. Like many other theater genres to become popular in the new world, melodrama originated in England, but was quickly adapted for American audiences (Stempel 2010, 39–40). The most popular American melodramas, the music to which has been lost, included William H. Smith's *The Drunkard* (1844), George L. Aiken's stage adaptation of *Uncle Tom's Cabin* (1852), and Dion Boucicault's *The Octoroon* (1859).

Just as genres were mixed on the stages of American theaters, audiences were comparatively well-blended, too. During the Federalist Era, theaters and genres were not as strongly associated with class or race as they would become. For example, because of its size and the fact that it initially had little in the way of competition, the Park Theatre was in some respects an egalitarian place in that it admitted anyone who could purchase a ticket. The egalitarianism, however, only went so far: working-class white men grabbed tickets for the pit at 50 cents a pop, upperclassmen escorted wives and daughters to private boxes that cost twice as much to occupy,[6] and lowerclassmen, prostitutes and black patrons paid 25 cents to sit in the balcony (Erenberg 1981, 15).

Regardless of class or background, late-eighteenth-century-American theater audiences tended to behave more like fans at contemporary sports events than do most present-day theatergoers (Preston 2008, 6). During any show in any American city, prostitutes would conduct business in the balcony, while the men they propositioned shouted at the actors and flung a highly imaginative variety of food items (along with the occasional handful of pebbles) at performers they disliked. The upper-class box-holders, often more interested in seeing and being seen than in what the actors were doing, chatted, flirted, and drank (Lott 1993, 6). When spectators in the pit were not fending off pickpockets, dodging the hot wax dripping from candles in the chandeliers overhead, or sidestepping the food items (and pebbles) that flew toward the stage, they shouted requests at the musicians and actors. Less frequently, they would climb onto the stage to confront the performers (Burrows and Wallace 1999, 404). The copious amounts of alcohol that were available during performances only encouraged crowds to grow rowdier as the evening progressed. By many accounts, the amount of tobacco smoke generated during a typical performance made the air truly "revolting" (Mates 1962, 68). Fistfights and riots broke out among spectators often enough that many theater boxes were designed to lock from the inside, and had extra exit doors that led the wealthiest patrons safely and quickly into the alleyway (ibid., 66).

The Bowery and the growing class divide

In the early nineteenth century, the Bowery in lower Manhattan became New York City's most important entertainment center. A vital commercial neighborhood that had grown around the city's main route to Boston, the Bowery was attractive, if rather smelly because of the many slaughterhouses and tanneries concentrated there. In the 1820s, a group of local businessmen, hoping to rid the Bowery of its alienating stench, convinced Henry Astor, owner of the storied Bull's Head Tavern and several surrounding abattoirs, to relocate his establishments to the rural area east of what is now Gramercy Park. Restaurants, taverns, and theaters were subsequently lured to the newly empty, newly pleasant-smelling Bowery (Burrows and Wallace 1999, 475).

In 1826, the country's largest theater to date was erected on the site where the Bull's Head had stood. Modeled after a Greek temple, the theater had 3,500 seats, faux marble pillars, gold- and red-painted private boxes, and gaslight, which was both a major innovation and the reason for the theater's remarkable flammability. Dubbed the New York Theatre when it opened and renamed the Bowery Theatre in 1828 after the first time it caught fire, the theater was rebuilt after fires in 1836, 1838, and 1845. It finally burned to the ground for good in 1929 (Wilmeth 2007, 123).

With this namesake theater at its heart, the thriving neighborhood catered largely if not exclusively to the working-class New Yorkers populating the adjoining neighborhoods. In its heyday, the Bowery boasted bustling oyster bars, brothels, cockfighting pits, taverns, restaurants, and gambling houses. It also established itself as an important theater center.

Before the mid-nineteenth century, there had been no attempt to centralize the city's theaters, which had traditionally cropped up wherever space allowed and demand justified (Burrows and Wallace 1999, 475–6). But the Bowery's many newly empty slaughterhouses and barns were quickly and easily refurbished as theaters of varying sizes, all of which began offering different kinds of entertainments (Lewis 2003, 13–14).

When it was not on fire, the Bowery Theatre developed a clientele that changed slowly with the neighborhood. At first, it appealed to upper-class patrons with a roster of stars visiting from Europe. These often performed alone or as lead characters in Shakespeare plays, farces, sentimental domestic dramas, operas, classical dances, or a combination thereof. Yet the size of the Bowery worked against it in its failure to draw working-class audiences, and thus to frequently fill to capacity. Within a few years, programming at the Bowery was adjusted to include aquatic displays, equestrian events, novelty acts, and melodramas, which lured a more diversified clientele. Eventually, programming at the theater gave itself over entirely to working-class patrons.

The changing face of the Bowery Theatre and the neighborhood surrounding it relates to profound social changes that occurred in the US between the mid-1820s and late 1840s. At this point, an "unprecedented separation and discrete self-definition of classes" took place among members of the bourgeoisie, middle, and working classes, all of whom began to see themselves as economically and culturally distinct from one another. The solidification of the American class structure had direct impact on, and was reflected in, the development of American popular entertainment (Lott 1993, 69–70). While the country's elite continued to look to and borrow from Europe for its entertainment, there arose a working-class culture that instead began to glorify "American democracy and the average white man," and to self-consciously distance itself from anything hinting at old-world, effete aristocracy (Toll 1974, 3–4). Through the nineteenth century, the country saw the increased segregation not just of audiences, but of actors and theatrical styles (Levine 1988, 56–7). The growing class divide was only exacerbated by the 1849 Astor Place riots, which reflected the extent to which upper-and lower-class taste cultures had diverged by mid-century.

In 1847, a group of wealthy Manhattanites decided to raise money for a new opera house on Lafayette Street between Astor Place and East 8th Street. Designed exclusively for the upper classes, the Astor Opera House made most seats available by subscription only. The venue imposed a dress code demanding that patrons be clean-shaven and very expensively dressed (Burrows and Wallace 1999, 724, 762).

In May 1849, the British actor William Macready headlined at the Astor in *Macbeth*. Macready had a strong upper-class fan base in America, but also a public rivalry with the emotive New York-born actor Edwin Forrest, whose fervent patriotism and outspokenness had made him a working-class hero and one of the Bowery's first celebrities (Levine 1988, 63). On the first night that Macready appeared at the Opera House, his very presence generated such hostility among Forrest's working-class fans that the city's new mayor, Caleb Smith Woodhull, ordered 350 members of the city's militia and 250 policemen to guard the Astor for subsequent performances.

Infuriated by the excessive response, some 10,000 people amassed outside the theater for the next performance (Burrows and Wallace 1999, 763). When the crowd on the street began throwing bricks and stones, the military, for the first time in American history, fired into the crowd (Bernstein 1990, 149). When the ensuing riot ended, eighteen people were dead; four more would succumb to their injuries in the following week. Over 150 people were injured, and 117 people, a vast majority of them working-class men, were arrested (Burrows and Wallace 1999, 764).

Order was quickly restored, but New York City and its theaters were permanently changed. So was the face of the burgeoning entertainment industry, which had long approached the population of the country as one unified mass. After the Astor Place riots, American entertainment and its audiences became increasingly fragmented (Toll 1976, 21–3). The Astor Opera House, now tarnished in the eyes of many New Yorkers, was sold and eventually demolished. The upper classes moved further uptown to the newly affluent Union Square for their theatrical entertainment, while the Bowery continued to cultivate a working-class clientele.

Blackface minstrelsy

It was in the Bowery, New York's own "lower-class world of rough amusement," that the country's first homegrown pop-culture craze developed (Bernstein 1990, 150). Spectacular, complicated, and both overtly and insidiously racist, blackface minstrelsy helped set the tone for much American popular culture to follow. A direct influence on the American stage musical, blackface minstrelsy at its height reflected the nation's growing high- and low-culture divide, as well as white America's anxieties about slavery and the impending Civil War (Lott 1993, 8).

Blackface minstrelsy peaked in popularity between the 1840s and 1890s. The genre was preceded by British characterizations of "negroes," who were typically not depicted with the help of makeup (Lewis 2003, 66), and by solo "Ethiopian delineators" in the US, who often did use makeup. Ethiopian delineators were frequent presences in late-eighteenth-century circuses and traveling shows, where they appeared either as characters in or between the acts of plays (Kenrick 2008, 52). Perhaps the most famous Ethiopian delineator in the US was Thomas Dartmouth "Daddy" Rice, who became all the rage in the early 1830s with his "Jump Jim Crow" act.

Born in lower Manhattan in 1808, young Rice traveled the country as a stagehand and blackface bit-player. At some point during his travels in 1828, he allegedly observed an old, crippled black man singing and dancing while cleaning a stable (Mates 1985, 77). Rice practiced the shuffling dance steps and the little hop and twist he claimed he learned from the man, quickened the pace, and took to the stage in shabby clothing and blackface (Toll 1976, 82). As he traveled from city to city, Rice honed his act and developed an increasingly complex character.

Because his signature song, "Jump Jim Crow," was in simple verse-chorus form, it could easily be extended to accommodate topical and geographically specific references. The song's chorus described the dance Rice performed as he sang:

So I wheel about
I turn about
I do just so
And ebery time I wheel about
I jump Jim Crow

Stanzas, regularly added or switched, often included social or political commentary, local inside jokes, shout-outs and regional references, and frequent boasts about strength, smarts, or sexual prowess (Mates 1985, 77).

Rice appeared at the Bowery Theatre in December 1832 on a bill that featured the actor (and father to John Wilkes) Junius Brutus Booth. The crowd was so taken by Rice's act that they would not let him off the stage, instead demanding he jump Jim Crow some 20 times (Lewis 2003, 10). The Bowery appearance helped catapult Rice to national and then international fame. Between 1832 and the mid-1840s, Rice performed on the best American stages, and made his London debut in 1836. He also contributed to the rise in popularity of white entertainers in blackface, many of whom claimed that their exaggerated performances reflected accurate, authentic portrayals of black people they observed. This went over well with white spectators, a majority of whom lacked the cultural expertise or sensitivity to have even the vaguest notion about whether what they were seeing onstage was accurate or not (Toll 1976, 81–3).

The American craze for solo Ethiopian delineators continued until four such New York-based performers united in frustration over a lack of steady work in the lean years following the Panic of 1837 (ibid., 137). In late 1842 or early 1843, Billy Whitlock, Richard Pelham, Dan Emmett, and Frank Brower devised an evening's worth of entertainment in hopes that by bonding together they could lure more spectators (Toll 1974, 30). As they honed their act of "oddities, peculiarities, eccentricities, and comicalities of that Sable Genus of Humanity," they began calling themselves the Virginia Minstrels (Bordman 2001, 11). The name of the southern state boosted their claims to authenticity; the term "minstrels" capitalized on the contemporaneous popularity of a touring European group called the Tyrolese Minstrel Family (Toll 1976, 84).

The plan worked, and the Virginia Minstrels became a box-office draw. The group's rapid rise to fame resulted in bookings in Boston and New York, and a tour of England in summer 1843. Following their trip abroad, the four men went separate ways (Hamm 1979, 127–8). Yet the brevity of their collaboration belied their cultural impact: the Virginia Minstrels had devised an enormously popular new entertainment form.

Blackface minstrelsy took off across the United States with unprecedented speed and intensity. By autumn 1843, virtually every major city in the country had at least one resident minstrel troupe; itinerant troupes and solo performers toured smaller cities and towns (Hamm 1979, 130). A mere three years after the Virginia Minstrels debuted in the Bowery, New York City alone boasted ten resident blackface minstrel troupes. By the early 1850s, that number had doubled (Kenrick 2008, 53).

There was no one standard format for minstrel shows, but many were organized into a distinctive three-part form that Edwin Pearce Christy (1815–62), founder of the Buffalo-based Christy's Minstrels, took credit for (Knapp 2006, 53). In part one, sometimes called the "concert," the entire troupe sat in a semicircle with the tambourine player ("Tambo") at one end and the bones or percussion player ("Bones") at the other. Often skilled physical comedians as well as musicians, the performers playing Tambo and Bones typically applied heavy dialect, exaggerated gestures, and rapid-fire punning to amuse the audience. Tambo and Bones served as comic foibles for the comparatively pompous Interlocutor, who often sat in the center of the company and served as the MC.

The second section, the "olio," was akin to the modern-day talent show. It offered spectators a lineup of unrelated performances: circus stunts, acrobatic and magic acts, comedy bits, songs, dances, and skits. The olio often took place downstage before a dropped curtain so the stage could be set for the final act: a one-act sketch with songs and dances, which borrowed its name, the "afterpiece," from Colonial-Era entertainments. In pre-Civil War minstrel shows, the afterpiece often featured idealized depictions of plantation life, and portrayed slaves as dimwitted dependents who were cared for by wise and benevolent white masters (Toll 1976, 89).

Virulently racist though it was, minstrelsy allowed white male performers—and, by extension, their audiences—to transgress, often in ways that had less to do with race than with class and gender. The instruments associated with minstrelsy—bones, fiddle, banjo, tambourine—might have been strongly associated with African American culture, but minstrel music was overwhelmingly rooted in European styles. Minstrel shows allowed performers and audiences to reinforce their hard-won position in the nation's cultural hierarchy, if very often by exploiting people occupying the lower hierarchical rungs. The genre also allowed white male performers to behave in ways that were often perceived offstage as effeminate or socially taboo: singing tear-jerking sentimental songs, dancing, cross-dressing. Blackface thus helped cultivate "an environment acceptable to middle-and lower-class white men for music-making and dance that was, if not fully masculine, nevertheless capable of being embodied only by men" (Knapp 2006, 52).

It is no coincidence that minstrelsy was at its most popular in the US before the Civil War, at a time when debates about slavery dominated the national discourse. The emergence of blackface minstrelsy offered many white spectators a means of processing conflicting concerns about slavery on the one hand, and the prospect of absorbing an enormously disadvantaged, newly freed ethnic group on the other (Toll 1976, 84).

Of course, then as now, many spectators probably did not think particularly critically about what any entertainment genre represented along sexual, racial, religious, or cultural lines. Minstrel shows were, for a lot of people, surely little more than innovative, amusing entertainments. But the form helped solidify, for some, the belief that blacks were inferior to whites; still others likely believed that minstrelsy was educational, and its gross caricatures accurate and authentic. Whether for or against slavery, some audience members surely were reassured by pre-war depictions of fantastical plantations, where "dancing darkies" (rarely referred to as "slaves") partied and picnicked, lived like so many "overgrown children," and were "protected by loving masters and mistresses who acted like doting parents" (Toll 1976, 100). Blackface minstrelsy, in short, offered a curious blend of "respect and fear, affection and hate, need and scorn, caring and exploitation" that resulted in a similarly curious blend of guilt, admiration, and curiosity among audiences (Lewis 2003, 70).

The Civil War and the decline of minstrelsy

Months before the outbreak of the Civil War, the newly formed Confederacy severed ties with the North, which plunged into financial crisis. Panic set in through 1860 as debts went unpaid, merchandise intended for southern states sat in warehouses, and the worth of commodities plummeted. By summer 1861, newspapers were estimating northern losses at nearly a half-billion dollars (Burrows and Wallace 1999, 873).

The Confederacy's advantage, of course, did not last long. Once the slave trade collapsed, the southern states were decimated while the Union's redirected economy boomed like never before (Burrows and Wallace 1999, 873–5). Formerly reliant on the Mississippi River, trade instead became dependent on the nation's railroads, which grew and improved everywhere but the South through the 1860s. Wheat, grain, and cattle brought east from the western territories and then shipped to Europe bolstered the Union, as did demand for weapons, ships, uniforms, and medical supplies. The publishing and communications industries grew exponentially as the public demanded news about the war and soldiers craved diversions—printed music, reading material, and photographs (dirty and otherwise)—during lulls at the front (Hamm 1979, 231).

In times of crisis, the demand for entertainment often surges, and the Civil War Era proved no different. Union theaters were sluggish during the first year of conflict (Mates 1985, 31), but the booming economy and desire for distraction from current events led to some of the longest-running, most commercially successful shows the country had yet seen. The shows audiences flocked to see, however, were not especially innovative. Just as the Civil War years "brought no new musical styles to American song," relying instead on the comforting, even mindless familiarity of forms that had long been popular (Hamm 1979, 248), Civil War-era stages were usually home to old favorites: Shakespeare plays, comedies, and melodramas (Bordman 2001, 16). Blackface minstrelsy remained popular, too, though a newly somber tone crept in, reflecting the "unprecedented suffering and anguish" of Americans at war (Toll 1974, 105–7).

After the war, the South lay in ruins while the North continued to enjoy unprecedented prosperity. Railroad lines now spanned the US; it is no coincidence that the ceremonial "Golden Spike" completing the first transcontinental railroad was driven in May 1869, a mere four years after the war had ended. The increased mobility across the country—combined with emancipation, reconstruction, the rapid rise of industry, the continued influx of immigrants, and a postwar spike in migration—resulted in profound changes to American culture and entertainment.

The fragmentation of the entertainment market reflected the country's broader cultural diversity and economic health. Yet it also led to the decline of minstrelsy, which was forced to compete with other, fresher forms of popular entertainment. Established minstrel troupes, too, suddenly had to face competition from within: a rising number of newly freed blacks got their toeholds in entertainment by becoming minstrel performers in the postwar years. As they joined the ranks, black minstrels emphasized their authenticity. Earlier minstrels had merely posed as black, but the new brand of minstrels were, they asserted, the real deal. Their claims worked: white critics wrote enthusiastically about the legitimacy of black minstrel troupes (Toll 1976, 113), and audiences were similarly impressed. By the late nineteenth century, black minstrels were less the exception than the rule.

Blackface minstrelsy permitted black performers a means of entry into the country's entertainment industry in numbers that would have otherwise been unthinkable at the time. Yet the genre forced them to perpetuate—and surely, in many cases, to internalize—highly deprecating portrayals of black American life (Woll 1989, 2). The same went for audiences: the genre grew so popular with black spectators after the Civil War that by the late nineteenth century many theater owners waived their own seating policies, which restricted blacks to the balcony, when minstrel troupes came through town (Toll 1974, 227).

The increase in minstrels, along with the genre's continued popularity, resulted in larger troupes. Early minstrel troupes were typically small: the Virginia Minstrels, after all, featured but four performers. But postwar troupes offered anywhere from fifteen to over 100 players. Troupe managers, eager to compete with newer entertainment forms, also began offering more visual spectacle in their minstrel shows: larger production numbers, more expensive sets, more lavish costuming (Preston 2008, 21). While these new super-sized productions were popular with audiences, they also put added pressures on minstrelsy's industrymen, who had to spend more on their troupes than ever before.

The new scope of minstrelsy accompanied a shift in content. While popular songs written before and during the Civil War reflected current events with remarkable accuracy and a great deal of emotion, postwar songs reflected the nation's collective desire to look ahead and move beyond the emotional exhaustion, sorrow, and anxiety that clouded the war years. A vast majority of American popular songwriters—newly concentrated in the northern, eastern, and western US—thus showed little interest in depicting the lives of southerners, whether black or white. Most songwriters steered clear not just of the South, but of any negative news of the day, in favor of cheerier, more upbeat, more generalized songs (Hamm 1979, 254).

The stereotypes propagated in prewar blackface minstrelsy continued largely unchallenged in the postwar years. Yet after the war, minstrelsy, like popular song, shifted emphasis away from the South and the plantation. Postwar troupes began to focus instead on urban settings. White minstrels, in particular, began to depict ethnic groups other than blacks, if in similarly broad, stereotypical ways: pigtail-wearing, bucktoothed Asians; whiskey-guzzling, belligerent Irishmen; wurst-gobbling, beer-swilling Germans (Toll 1976, 105). In these cases, the use of blackface was less a means for specific imitation as it was a long-familiar stage convention.

In an attempt to avoid competition with newer entertainment forms that became faddish in big cities, minstrel troupes took advantage of the country's new transportation system by touring. Troupes crossed the country by train, playing in small towns and rural areas. While the various approaches that postwar minstrel troupes took to remain viable helped prolong the genre, the entertainment form expanded, changed, and influenced other forms so much that it lost its uniqueness and faded in popularity by the turn of the century (ibid.).

Union Square and Tin Pan Alley

In booming late-nineteenth-century New York City, the sheet music and theater industries grew rapidly and symbiotically, exerting influence on the new entertainment genres that supplanted minstrelsy. By this point, the city's population had grown large enough to support a dizzying assortment of theater styles, and many venues could afford to become newly specific with their programming. Variety theaters, burlesque houses, opera houses, dance venues, and circus arenas cropped up across the city in response to ever-growing demand (Mates 1985, 33). While the Bowery had long been home to a number of important entertainment venues, New York City did not have a truly consolidated theater district—nor did the country have a cohesive entertainment industry—until the mid- to late nineteenth century. Yet as New York grew, the ways that theater was made, produced, and consumed changed significantly, both locally and nationally.

The establishment of a district specifically given over to the theater and its industry is due in part to the development of the city's transit system. Mass transit first commenced in New York in the late 1800s, when elevated lines were constructed along Broadway, which remained a major artery. The elevated lines made points along the long and storied avenue easier to access for the city's increasingly far-flung residents. The aptly named Union Square, where Broadway and Fourth Avenue converged at 14th Street, became one such point. Through the 1870s, Union Square became a thriving retail area, as well as the city's first theater district, or "rialto."

What distinguished Union Square's theater district from the independent cluster of venues still crowding the Bowery was both its new, close connection to the rapidly developing commercial theater industry, and its increasingly tight relationships with other, related entertainment businesses. Union Square became not just the home to a cluster of new theaters, but also to businesses that developed alongside, served, and benefited them: variety houses, talent agencies, printing companies, costume shops, Steinway's piano store, Samuel French's play publishing company, Napoleon Sarony's photography studio, hotels, restaurants, and bars (Traub 2005, 8).

The neighborhood also became home to the first Tin Pan Alley-style sheet-music firm in 1875, when T.B. Harms's company moved to an office at Broadway and 12th Street (Jasen 2003, 171–3). Prior to this point, the music industry, like the theater industry, was unconsolidated. Independent music publishers were spread out all over the country, with the highest concentration in cities such as Boston, Chicago, Philadelphia, Baltimore, and Cincinnati. Yet T.B. Harms managed to distinguish itself by publishing such an enviable string of hit songs through the 1880s that other companies began imitating its business practices—and joining it in Union Square.

By the late 1890s, most of the song publishers in the increasingly crowded Union Square relocated uptown, to 28th Street between Fifth and Sixth Avenues. That block was nicknamed "Tin Pan Alley" shortly thereafter, ostensibly because of the racket the district's many composers and song-pluggers made as they banged away at pianos during business hours in an attempt to compose and sell the newest hit songs to passersby (Hamm 1979, 284–5). The term "Tin Pan Alley" became synonymous with the American sheet-music industry, especially once the many newly consolidated Manhattan-based publishing houses began to corner the market (Stempel 2010, 145).

Uncle Tom's Cabin and *The Black Crook*

During the Civil War era, the rise in popularity of "Tom shows," or dramatized versions of Harriet Beecher Stowe's *Uncle Tom's Cabin*, resulted in the country's first blockbuster stage productions (Frick and LoMonaco 1995, 1167). When, a decade later, *The Black Crook* opened in New York to even more extraordinary commercial success, the theater industry's obsession with long-running productions was born.

Harriet Beecher Stowe's *Uncle Tom's Cabin* first appeared serially in the abolitionist paper *The National Era* in 1851, and was published as a novel the following year. Proof that it "had a profound and polarizing impact" on the country in the lead-up to the war is perhaps reflected in the myriad theatrical adaptations of the story, many with music, which began appearing on American stages following the release of the book (Stempel 2010, 36). One of the earliest and most successful productions was by playwright George Aiken. His adaptation, mentioned earlier in this chapter as an example of popular melodrama, ran for an unprecedented 100 nights in Troy, New York in 1852. It premiered in New York City in July 1853 (Lott 1993, 220–1). There, it surpassed even the most optimistic of expectations by running for over 300 performances at a time when long runs were simply unheard of (Stempel 2010, 37). The show's unusual success hardly went unnoticed: competing versions of *Uncle Tom's Cabin* blanketed the northeast through the remainder of the 1850s (Lott 1993, 222).

Aiken's blockbuster production was so long—30 scenes and eight *tableaux* over six acts—that it required the elimination of an afterpiece, thus influencing the rise of the "one-play entertainment" (Stempel 2010, 39). While a few managers remained certain that the monstrous success of Aiken's *Uncle Tom's Cabin* was a fluke, even the most dogged skeptics were convinced by the power of the long run when, in the following decade, *The Black Crook* arrived in New York for a very long visit (Frick and LoMonaco 1995, 1167).

The Black Crook, which opened at Niblo's Garden on Broadway and Prince Street in 1866, has often, "according to critical consensus and traditional thinking," been designated the first American stage musical as we understand the genre today (Mast 1987, 7). Yet this "first" status has been frequently challenged, since *The Black Crook* was hardly structurally or aesthetically groundbreaking. The show combined a number of forms that had long been popular in the US: dance, melodrama, opera, and extravaganza—the last term a descriptor for shows primarily emphasizing visual spectacle (Preston 2008, 18).

Yet *The Black Crook* distinguished itself by becoming a monstrous commercial hit, which seems the primary reason so many people assume it was the very first musical. It does not hurt that in its passage from page to stage, *The Black Crook* underwent a series of dramatic setbacks and coincidences, which make the show's designation as a happy accident—a hastily concocted stone soup that just happened to result in the birth of a new mass entertainment genre—all the more tantalizing.

The story goes something like this: A little-known (and reputedly lousy) playwright named Charles M. Barras (1826–73) wrote *The Black Crook*, a melodrama, after seeing Carl Maria von Weber's *Der Freischütz* in Cincinnati in 1857 (Knapp 2006, 20). The show was booked into Niblo's by its manager, William Wheatley, less because Wheatley thought it was any good—or even notably different from the Weber original—than because it struck him as just the kind of piece he could break down and rebuild into something more engaging (Stempel 2010, 43).

Meanwhile, two young entrepreneurs, Henry Jarrett and Henry Palmer, had been planning to import "a visual feast of female dancers in a multi-media production with the most modern special effects." The two Henrys scoured Europe for dancers willing to travel to New York to perform in a spectacle called *La Biche au Bois*, which had been a hit in London (Allen 1991, 108). While abroad, they bought 300 costumes and 110 tons of scenery, which they shipped back to the United States, presumably along with the dancers they hired (Lewis 2003, 198). Once back in the states, they booked the Academy of Music on Irving Place to stage their show.

As luck would have it (less for two doomed firemen than for William Wheatley), Niblo's production of *The Black Crook* was still in the planning stages when the Academy of Music, recently outfitted with a sprinkler system, nevertheless burned down in May 1866 ("The Great Fire," 1886, 8).

Stuck with a cast of dancers, costumes, and tons of scenery, the venueless Henrys approached Wheatley in hopes of forming a partnership. About $50,000 worth of alterations needed to be done to Niblo's Garden to accommodate the elaborate set and extra castmembers, but Wheatley agreed anyway—and decided to use the now-enormous cast and cost of production to his advantage.

In the months leading up to the September 1866 premiere, Wheatley took every opportunity to inform the press about how dazzling and expensive *The Black Crook* was going to be. He detailed the "profusion of trapdoors, a deep pit for a water tank, large plate-glass mirrors," and the complicated system of wires required to make the dancers fly. He noted as well that the backstage area had to be entirely rebuilt at no small expense (Lewis 2003, 198). Wheatley's emphasis on the expense and resultant visual pleasures of *The Black Crook* was shrewd and, he likely realized, necessary, since Barras's play itself was "the least original element in the mix" (Stempel 2010, 43).

Set in a seventeenth-century German village, *The Black Crook* focused on the young lovers Rodolphe and Amina. Their devotion to one another enrages the evil Count Wolfenstein, who wants Amina for himself. Wolfenstein causes Rodolphe to fall prey to Hertzog, a crookbacked sorcerer (and the titular character), whose Faustian pact with the devil results in eternal life as long as Hertzog gives Satan a new soul each New Year's eve. As Rodolphe is being led to his horrible fate, he saves a dove from the jaws of a snake. The dove turns out to be the fairy queen, Stalacta, who rewards Rodolphe by taking him to her magic land under the sea. As luck would have it, this land is filled with state-of-the-art scenery and fairies dressed in scanty costumes (Allen, 1991, 109–11). At the conclusion of the five-and-a-half-hour spectacle—which included subplots, comic asides, and scenes depicting "fishes swimming, a sea monster, a boat sinking, child-fairies asleep in shells, [and] gems glittering on the foreshore"—Count Wolfenstein is defeated, Hertzog is condemned to hell, and Rodolphe and Amina are reunited (Lewis 2003, 200). A final sequence with musical underscoring—a melodramatic spectacle to end the melodramatic spectacle—featured the transformation of a "subterranean gallery" into Stalacta's underwater fairyland (Stempel 2010, 47).

After a week-long delay due to technical problems—which Wheatley dutifully and dramatically reported to the press—*The Black Crook* opened on September 12, 1866. Critics were unmoved by Barras's play; one dismissed it as "trashy" and another called it "rubbish." Yet the critic for *The New York Times* acknowledged that *The Black Crook* was a triumph of brilliant spectacle: "No similar exhibition had been made in an American stage that we remember, certainly none where such a combination of youth, grace, beauty and *élan* was found," he wrote, before concluding that *The Black Crook* was *the* singular spectacular event of the time (quoted in Bordman 2001, 20).

The Black Crook ran for 475 performances over the course of sixteen months, taking in over a million dollars at the box office and spawning countless imitations, tours, and revivals in the process. Wheatley continued to fuel the buzz about the show once it opened by "welcoming publicity in any form that might win for the piece not just fame but notoriety" (Stempel 2010, 49). A sermon delivered in November 1866 by the Reverend Charles B. Smyth, which warned against the sexual nature of *The Black Crook*, was hastily printed in the *New York Herald*, thereby helping to sell more tickets (Lewis, 198). When free publicity waned, Wheatley inserted new musical numbers, scenes, and spectacles into the production. The fact that *The Black Crook* so carefully blended the highbrow (ballet, an old-world setting) with the low (stage gimmickry, broad humor, scanty costumes) did not hurt its appeal; rather, it allowed the show to cultivate a "proper" bourgeois audience while simultaneously coming off as just risqué and naughty enough to warrant a visit—or several (Stempel 2010, 49).

While not structurally or stylistically revolutionary, and while earlier historians might have been a bit hasty to claim that it was *the* first musical, *The Black Crook* was nevertheless a landmark production. It helped cement "a convention of visual opulence and inventiveness" that remains an important aspect of stage musicals, and solidified a fascination with long-running productions (Mast 1987, 13). Just as importantly, in combination with the earlier success of *Uncle Tom's Cabin*, *The Black Crook* redirected the burgeoning commercial theater industry from one focused primarily on stock companies to one that favored combination companies.

Stock companies—self-contained groups of actors and artisans who worked together on repertory productions staged at affiliated venues—were the norm from before the Revolution through the Civil War. But the new obsession with long-running shows, combined with the booming economy, the demand for new forms of theatrical entertainment, and the consolidation of the theater industry, led to the breakdown of the stock company system. Following the success of *The Black Crook*, theater owners, managers, and producers began to maximize profits by keeping productions open for as long as spectators would pay to see them. This new approach was additionally appealing because cross-country transportation had improved so rapidly in the nineteenth century. Because of the country's new railways, long-running shows could now be sent out on tour, either after the original production closed or even during its run. This marked shift in the approach to American theater-making coincided with the development of new forms of musical stage entertainments—vaudeville and burlesque—and the continued development of the commercial theater industry, which will be detailed in the next chapter.

CHAPTER 2
THE CIVIL WAR ERA TO THE GILDED AGE

During the late nineteenth century, two popular entertainment styles emerged in the US, both of which surpassed blackface minstrelsy in popularity by absorbing and revamping many aspects of the genre (including its racism). Burlesque and vaudeville were the children of blackface minstrelsy, but they diverged from each other structurally and stylistically. They also appealed to different audiences, which were divided both by sex and class. For their differences, however, burlesque and vaudeville were shaped not only by the minstrel tradition, but by newly powerful businesses operating in or near the country's burgeoning center for commercial theater: Union Square.

Burlesque

At least as it developed in Europe, burlesque was a live entertainment form that combined song, dance, and dialogue to parody other theatrical forms.[1] The practice dates back at least to the sixteenth century in countries including Italy, Spain, and England. In the US, many theatrical forms poked fun at social conventions, parodied other art forms or performance genres, and featured broad, punning humor. But it was not until Lydia Thompson and Her British Blondes arrived in New York in 1868 that a relatively new and distinctly American form of burlesque emerged (Green 1995, 168).

Thompson and her all-female troupe lampooned entertainment forms associated with high culture: drama, opera, and famous works of literature. The brand of burlesque her troupe introduced to America combined visual spectacle—which had only grown in popularity following the success of *The Black Crook* a mere two years prior—with broad physical humor, punning, malapropism, and frequent, sly asides aimed at the audience. Musical numbers often featured traditional or popular melodies that audiences would have recognized, set with new lyrics or newly layered with sly double entendre. Dance numbers, too, poked fun at various folk and classical styles.

Admirers of Thompson were quick to imitate her, but also to bring in material that spoke specifically to American culture. As it developed in the US, then, burlesque borrowed liberally from minstrelsy. The lengthy, involved sketches that Thompson's troupe typically performed in their first act failed to catch on in the US, so the structure of blackface minstrelsy was instead applied to American burlesque.

The first female burlesque troupes, in imitation of minstrel shows, relied on male performers to serve as interlocutors and endmen during the opening act. Eventually, however, those characters were dropped. The traditional semicircle used in the first act of minstrel shows was replaced by a big production number performed by the female cast, punctuated by songs, skits, and the occasional *tableau vivant*, or silent, motionless recreation of a famous painting or historical scene (Allen 1991, 165). An olio section for specialty acts followed, and an afterpiece, in the style of an extravagant production number, rounded out the evening. Sometimes, a short dance or other physical display was tacked on at the very end of a performance (Green 1995, 168).

What distinguished burlesque from competing forms was its emphasis on the bodies of female performers. Such emphasis was remarkably tame by contemporary standards: when not dressed as the men they regularly impersonated onstage, female burlesquers tended to appear in nothing more risqué than knee-length skirts and tights. American burlesque was not, at this point, associated with the striptease, hootchie-cootchie dance, or bump-and-grind; those were added much later, when burlesque was declining in popularity and its industry was scrambling to keep it alive. When it was new to the country and growing in popularity, burlesque featured female performers who went against middle-class conventions of sexuality, gender and class, but who were not truly aberrant while doing so (Friedman 2000, 65). As with *The Black Crook*, then, burlesque's subversiveness proved appealing to bourgeois audiences who were willing to transgress a little bit, but always within appropriate boundaries.

American burlesque did not transform itself on its own, nor was its emulation of minstrelsy purely an artistic choice. Rather, American burlesque was shaped by entrepreneurs such as the producer Michael B. Leavitt (1843–1945), a former minstrel performer with a taste for the extravagant. Leavitt is often mentioned not only as chiefly responsible for Americanizing burlesque, but was also one of the first in the business to send burlesque troupes on national tour by train (Green 1995, 168). Quick to recognize the similarities between minstrelsy and burlesque, Leavitt wasted no time combining the two (Lewis 2003, 68). In 1870, he introduced the all-female Mme. Rentz's Female Minstrels. Later called the Rentz-Santley Novelty and Burlesque Company, this troupe spawned at least eleven other female minstrel companies within the year (Toll 1974, 138).

Tame though it was by contemporary standards, burlesque nevertheless caused concern among religious and anti-vice organizations. Opposition to the form only grew more vociferous through the 1880s and 1890s, as burlesque became increasingly associated with working-class men. Meanwhile, another form that had also long been associated with working-class men, "variety," was rapidly being reshaped as a middle-class, family-friendly, popular entertainment that became known instead as "vaudeville."

Vaudeville (with a side serving of operetta)

As a structure for performance, "variety" simply refers to a bill built of many different acts: singers, dancers, animal trainers, acrobats, comedians, magicians, musicians (Stempel 2010, 56–7). Because they are so easy to throw together, variety shows were and continue to be an integral part of American life. Through the eighteenth and nineteenth centuries—and probably long before—variety shows appeared in summer gardens, dime museums, on riverboats and trains, in circuses, and as parts of minstrel and burlesque shows. At present, they continue to appear on television (*Saturday Night Live* and other sketch shows derive from them), in schools, camps, and at any venue that occasionally hosts a talent show or open mic night (Mates 1985, 154).

During the mid-nineteenth century, variety shows became integral to concert-saloon culture. Concert saloons, also sometimes known as concert halls, cropped up across the country in the 1840s. In their heyday, they boasted free or very low admission. Once inside, audiences were entertained by a succession of highly varied, occasionally crass or "blue" acts. As they watched the show, spectators were encouraged to buy drinks, tobacco, and food by "waiter girls," some of whom doubled as prostitutes. Meanwhile, prostitutes who did not bother to double as waitresses also worked the room.

Concert saloons became associated with rowdy, working-class men, and by association, so too did the variety acts performed in them (Mates 1985, 154). Yet the venues were of little concern to the upper classes until slumming young men started frequenting them in increasing numbers, at which point their moneyed parents began to complain. In New York, newspapers and moral reformers began painting concert saloons as "vile houses" that were suddenly far more dangerous than they had been when they were solely associated with the working class (Stempel 2010, 60–1).

In response to the righteous indignation that erupted over the concert saloon, the New York State legislature passed an act in 1862 stating that alcohol could not be served in venues featuring live entertainment, and that women could not serve refreshments to customers during performances in said venues (Zellers 1968, 583). An even stricter law, passed a decade later, required performance venues to purchase a $500 license from the mayor, who was free to decline the request at his discretion (McNamara 2002, 23).

Most concert saloon owners initially responded to these laws by becoming adept at subterfuge, while most police officers turned a blind eye. But as the laws tightened, concert saloons transformed into venues that emphasized entertainment while deterring drunken or disorderly audience behavior: cabarets, cocktail lounges, and nightclubs. While the more rundown of such venues were still considered disreputable among the upper classes, and while even the finest remained strongly associated with a male clientele, some nevertheless began sponsoring "special cleaned-up ladies' matinees, temporarily banishing the alcohol and cigars for a few hours" (Trav 2005, 67). The attempt to attract women to venues that were typically male-affiliated was nothing new. After all, it was in the best interest of theater managers to constantly appeal to new audience members. Yet the most effective reformer of the time was undoubtedly Tony Pastor (1837–1908), subsequently known as "the father of vaudeville" (Stempel 2010, 62).

As a child, Pastor sang at temperance meetings before joining a minstrel troupe and then apprenticing with John J. Nathan's circus, where he sang, clowned, danced, rode horses, and eventually became ringmaster (Rodger 2010, 42).[2] During the Civil War, Pastor worked as a concert saloon balladeer. In 1865, in partnership with the Philadelphia-based minstrel Sam Sharpley, he secured the Bowery Minstrel Hall at 201 Bowery and renamed it Tony Pastor's Opera House ("'Tony' Pastor Dead" 1908, 7). His first company featured a small orchestra, a few dancers and singers, and a comic who worked in blackface. Pastor, too, often emerged from behind the scenes to take the stage, where he honed a reputation as a warm, jovial "man of a million songs" (Mates 1985, 156–7).

After a decade at the Opera House, Pastor moved uptown to the Metropolitan Theater on Broadway in what is now Soho. He permitted drinking in this establishment, but only in a saloon that was separate from the auditorium (Traub 2005, 9). He began hosting regular "ladies' matinees" at the Metropolitan, and cultivated a loyal female audience by giving away bags of flour or small clocks as souvenirs at performances ("Tony Pastor and His Sixty Years" 1908, SM3). In the many interviews he granted, Pastor repeatedly insisted that his primary goal was to divorce the variety show from the rowdy, crass concert saloon with which it had become so connected (Traub 2005, 9).

Yet Pastor's signature brand of "respectable" variety entertainment was not fully realized until he made his final leap uptown. In 1881, he secured the theater in the Tammany Society Building, just east of Union Square on 14th Street. The theater's location—in the heart of the rialto and at the base of the middle-class shopping district then known as Ladies' Mile—allowed him to cultivate his reputation as a purveyor of quality family entertainment (Stempel 2010, 65), which he accomplished without alienating working-class devotees of variety (Snyder 1989, 22). At the Union Square venue, tickets for non-reserved seats were cheap. Newsboys, Bowery boys, and black patrons were always welcome, so long as the last sat, as per citywide custom, in the balcony.

Pastor's reserved seats, however, were the most expensive of any variety house in town, at $1.50 a pop (Rodger 2010, 235n.6). In exchange for shelling out top dollar, affluent audience members were promised great seats, quality entertainment, and a spotlessly clean, exceptionally well-managed house. A typical show at Pastor's included musicians, minstrels, dancers, singers, magicians, animal acts, comics, and Pastor himself. Arguably more important than the lineup was the atmosphere Pastor cultivated. Even as his evening shows developed a reputation for middle-class respectability, Pastor continued to offer ladies' matinees and, later, ones especially for children. He frequently offered appropriate door prizes and souvenirs to his clients: flowers, dolls, toys, food, sewing patterns, dresses (Traub 2005, 10). He habitually walked around his venue before showtimes, warmly greeting audience members as they arrived. No one who worked for him was allowed to work "blue" or use coarse or suggestive language. Smoking and drinking were prohibited in his theater, though there was a bar within spitting distance of the venue for those who could not get through a show without drinking (or spitting). Beloved by audiences, Pastor also gave a number of theater denizens their big break: the actress and singer Lillian Russell, the "Dutch" comic Lew Fields (later of the comedy duo Weber and Fields), and the song plugger Izzy Baline (later Irving Berlin) all worked for him.

Pastor and his company toured every year, but only briefly, since his duties as theater manager kept him tied to New York. Thus, while his Union Square venue was a smashing success, Pastor never became famous across the country. He also proved inept at what would today be called "branding," since he was careful to set his theater apart in practice, but never in name.

Ironically for one who strove to feminize his clientele, Pastor vehemently rejected the term "vaudeville" as too "sissified" for his tastes (" 'Tony' Pastor Dead" 1908, 7), and refused to apply it to his shows.

On the other hand, Benjamin Franklin (B.F.) Keith (1846–1914) and Edward Franklin (E.F.) Albee II (1857–1930) understood the importance of a new label as a means of distancing their product from variety shows. Pastor polished variety as a performance genre, but Keith and Albee set it in motion as "the basis for a large-scale system of purpose-built theaters, peripatetic performers, and booking agents" (Allen 1991, 180).

The New Hampshire-born Keith and Maine-born Albee both grew up in show business. Unlike Pastor, they cut their teeth not as performers but as animal feeders, tent boys, and shills for cheap trinkets or tickets. In 1883, Keith opened his own dime museum in Boston, which featured attractions including "a baby midget and a mermaid," a very large pig, "a chicken with a human face," and the comedian Lew Fields (who had newly partnered with Joe Weber). Keith referred to his shows not as variety but as "vaudeville," and began offering continuous performances between 10:00 a.m. and 10:00 p.m., the better to pack in as many spectators as possible over the course of each day. Keith eventually partnered with Albee, whom he remembered from their circus days. In a continued quest for respectable audiences to patronize their not-especially-respectable acts, Keith and Albee decided to offer "a pirated version of Gilbert and Sullivan's *The Mikado* five times a day, with vaudeville acts between performances," all for 10 cents a seat (Snyder 1989, 27).

Their offering of operetta amid variety acts was hardly unprecedented. After all, opera segments were regularly included in theatrical productions in early America, and snippets of opera and operetta had long been part of variety acts, burlesque, and minstrel productions. Yet Keith and Albee's choice of this particular operetta was an attempt at capitalizing on a contemporary Gilbert and Sullivan craze, which had begun with the American premiere of *H.M.S. Pinafore* at the Boston Museum on November 25, 1878, a mere two years after the American centennial.

By this point, Americans could appreciate the cultural differences that had developed between the United States and England, but could also feel some degree of communal pride in British entertainments, since so many citizens still traced their roots directly back to the UK (Knapp 2006, 32). This simultaneous sense of distance and familiarity helped make *Pinafore* into an enormous hit, which spread rapidly across the US.

America's embrace of *Pinafore* was immediate and profound. A production opened in San Francisco mere weeks after the Boston premiere;

another opened in Philadelphia in January 1879. By August 1879, Boston alone had hosted some 241 different productions of *Pinafore* (Mates 1985, 71). The show was comparatively late to hit New York City, where it premiered in January 1879. But once there, it refused to leave: by May of that year, different versions of *Pinafore* had played in at least eleven theaters, with anywhere between three and eight productions competing with each other at any given time. Versions of *Pinafore* were offered, as well, for specific audiences: there was "an all-black *Pinafore*, an all-children's company, and German, Yiddish and other foreign language productions in ethnic and immigrant enclaves" across the country (Jones 2003, 6–7).

The many versions of *Pinafore* speak as much to the demands of an increasingly diverse audience as to the fact that there were no copyright agreements between the US and England at the time. *Pinafore*'s success also points to the significance of a light, funny, well-written and composed show featuring "book, lyrics, and music formed to combine an integral whole." Finally, it demonstrates the importance to live entertainment of social commentary that can be easily interpreted—and, as importantly, misinterpreted—by a broad spectatorship (Bordman 2001, 49).

Like many Gilbert and Sullivan operettas, *H.M.S. Pinafore* adhered to "the prevailing standards of respectability" while simultaneously critiquing them, which allowed audiences to read the show in a wide variety of ways (Knapp 2006, 33). Yet regardless of the messages Americans took from *Pinafore*, the operetta's success resulted in swift, widespread imitation. Subsequent Gilbert and Sullivan operettas were (and remain) popular with audiences in the US; the *Pinafore* craze also influenced a new generation of American operettists through the 1890s. These included Reginald De Koven, John Philip Sousa, Victor Herbert, and H.B. Smith (Stempel 2010, 116–17).

Keith and Albee's decision to offer *The Mikado* between variety acts was thus shrewd on several levels. The inclusion of the operetta signaled that theirs was no tawdry, low-class venue, but one eager to appeal to the middle class. This would have been a particularly important message to convey, since in the 1870s most dime museums were associated with lower and working classes. Keith and Albee's sequencing of performances, as well, turned out to be a hugely successful business model. The continuous performance, in which a bill was repeated all day long and the curtain was never lowered (Allen 1991, 181), proved so successful that the partners relocated to a legitimate theater in the nearby Adams House Hotel in 1886 (Snyder 1989, 27). Later that year, they also leased the newly renovated 900-seat Bijou Theater (Allen 1991, 182–3). Keith and Albee's success in Boston allowed them to expand over the next decade (Snyder 1989, 28). Between 1888 and 1893, they opened vaudeville theaters in Providence, Philadelphia, and on Union Square. These venues thrived—even despite the Panic of 1893, which afflicted the country through the late 1890s—largely because their continuous performance model allowed them to keep ticket prices low. No matter what, patrons could grab tickets for anywhere between 15 cents and a dollar (Lewis 2003, 317).

Keith, in particular, took his role as reformer very seriously. Like Pastor, he forbade his acts to work "blue" or use coarse language. But he also actively trained audiences about how to behave properly in his theaters, and in this respect his influence continues today. In all Keith–Albee houses, prominent signs and flyers encouraged "cleanliness and order" on the stage and in the auditorium. Men were told to "kindly avoid the stamping of feet and pounding of canes," to remove their hats, and to refrain from smoking, talking, shouting, whistling, or verbally disrupting performances (Levine 1988, 196–7). Loud snacks were actively discouraged. When Keith observed audiences being unruly, he would lecture them sternly from the stage (Wollman 2006, 68).

By the mid-1890s, vaudeville entrepreneurs had begun to recognize a competitive advantage in "linking their own theaters or small circuits with others," which allowed them to hire particular acts for longer periods (Allen 1991, 190). The Vaudeville Managers Association (VMA), founded in 1900, united 62 of the 67 most successful vaudeville houses in the US. It was headed by Keith and Albee, who had not only shaped the vaudeville industry but had become the most powerful men in it (Snyder 1995, 1226).

Renamed the United Booking Office (UBO) in 1906, the organization mediated between performers and theater managers, and controlled most of the vaudeville houses east of Chicago; the Orpheum Circuit, established by Gustav Walter and later expanded by Martin Beck, controlled most venues between Chicago and the Pacific Ocean. Such was the power of the UBO that any act declining a proffered salary or playing in an unrepresented house seriously jeopardized their careers (Traub 2005, 26–7).

The Gilded Age: The entertainment industry and consolidation

As vaudeville grew—and grew more middlebrow—through the late-nineteenth century, burlesque cemented its position as a purveyor of titillation for the working classes (Allen 1991, 179). Like vaudeville, burlesque's industry consolidated by the turn of the century, but not nearly as successfully. Burlesque had no Albee and Keith equivalent, and thus no dominant force that could quell the internal competition that inevitably arose (ibid., 191).

The burlesque industry developed into two circuits, known as wheels. The central office of each wheel sent traveling companies to burlesque theaters across the country. Entrepreneurs excluded from the wheels learned to compete on the local level with "stock" shows that were often far more risqué than those the wheels provided. As the wheels and stock companies competed, burlesque became so focused on figuring out new and creative ways to exploit female sexuality that it eventually cannibalized itself. External pressure from moral reformers did not help matters; burlesque began a decline that would culminate in the early to mid-twentieth century (Wollman 2013, 16).

The consolidation of the vaudeville and burlesque industries coincided roughly with the rise of the Theatrical Syndicate, a group of theater producers who united in 1896 to control booking in so-called "legitimate" theaters— those that did not specialize in vaudeville or burlesque—across the US. Individually or in partnership, the Syndicate's six members—Charles Frohman, A.L. Erlanger, Marc Klaw, John Frederick Zimmerman, Samuel F. Nixon, and Al Hayman—already owned many venues nationwide. As the Syndicate, they exerted most of their enormous power and influence by controlling the contracts of the country's top performers (Marcosson and Frohman 1916, 186–7). By establishing a monopoly over booking, they forced less powerful producers and managers to go through them to schedule acts for their venues (Snyder 1989, 35).

It is no coincidence that these varying live entertainment forms all came under the control of powerful business consortiums at around the same time. The consolidation of the burlesque, vaudeville, and legitimate theater industries occurred during the Gilded Age, a period that "saw the creation of a modern industrial economy." A number of ingredients contributed to the rise of corporations in many fields. The country now had a national transportation system in the railroad, and the business world also benefited from the invention of several national communication systems: the radio, telegraph, and telephone. The era is well-documented for its rapaciousness, greed, and rampant corruption, all of which certainly applied as much to the burgeoning performance industries as to the manufacturing, food, oil, transportation, and steel industries. During the Gilded Age, the country moved beyond "an agrarian society of small producers" into "an urban society dominated by industrial corporations."[3]

A new theater district in Times Square

As the late nineteenth century slipped into the early twentieth, New York City continued to grow in size, population, and diversity, especially after consolidation on January 1, 1898. Consolidation allowed the five boroughs to behave as one city instead of a fragmented urban sprawl controlled by some forty local governments. Following consolidation, New York's population leapt in a single bound from around 2 million to 3.4 million (Hammack 1995, 277–8). By 1910, it had grown to nearly 5 million (Kantrowitz 1995, 922). After consolidation, Brooklyn, Queens, Staten Island, and the Bronx contributed amply to the life of what became known as the City of Greater New York. Yet because many of the city's commercial, political, social, financial, and cultural institutions had been established (and remain) in Manhattan, that borough continued to serve as the heart of the metropolis. This was especially the case in the early days of the city's transit system. Travel across the metropolitan area became easier through the early twentieth century, but the first subway lines, from which all others radiated, only served Manhattan.

Plans for an underground transportation system had been discussed since the city's elevated train lines began appearing in the second half of the nineteenth century. Yet a lack of financial and technological wherewithal, coupled with bountiful bureaucratic bickering, led to decades of delays. But finally, in 1894, construction on the first subway line, designed to carry passengers from the business districts in lower Manhattan to the northern neighborhoods, was approved.

But where exactly should it go? Running a line from City Hall to East 42nd Street was a given: due to an ordinance barring locomotives south of 42nd Street, a switching yard had long been in operation there anyway, at Park Avenue and 42nd Street. Since 42nd Street was a broad, well-traveled crosstown street that already had trolley lines running across it, city officials eventually agreed that the first subway line would cross the island from east to west there, before heading north to the Upper West Side.

Yet the western stretch of 42nd Street was hardly well developed or appealing. The neighborhood there, which extended north to 59th Street, was something of a no-man's-land known as Longacre Square. Like London's carriage district from which it took its name, Longacre Square housed the city's horse and livery trade; its muddy, filthy streets were thus clogged with "stables, blacksmiths, harness shops, carriage dealers, and the occasional riding ring," and littered with broken vehicles. The area stank of manure and was not yet outfitted with electric streetlamps; the dark, empty streets were well-trod by prostitutes and petty thieves who preyed on affluent strangers with money who traveled to the area in need of repairs (Bianco 2004, 15–17).

Despite its reputation for being smelly, ugly, and filled with criminals, Longacre Square nevertheless piqued entrepreneurial interest. Affordable space has long been a much-desired rarity in New York, and by the 1890s businessmen with investments in theatrical real estate had begun looking beyond cramped, expensive Union Square for cheaper, open land on which to build new venues. In January 1893, producers Charles Frohman and William Harris took a gamble and opened the Empire Theater on Broadway between 40th and 41st streets. That May, T. Henry French opened the American Theatre on Eighth Avenue between 41st and 42nd streets ("The Week at the Theatres," 13). These venues were followed by others, including the enormous Olympia Theater, which opened in 1895. Described by its designer, the impresario (and grandfather of the famous lyricist) Oscar Hammerstein, as "the grandest amusement temple in the world," the Olympia, on Broadway between 44th and 45th streets, was so enormous and poorly designed that it proved difficult to manage effectively.

Though Hammerstein's amusement temple was not so grand after all, it prompted a slow exodus from Union Square. At the turn of the century, commercial theaters began snaking north up Broadway. By the early twentieth century, Union Square was no longer the city's rialto. Longacre Square began to shed its sketchy reputation as it became home to new theaters, as well as plenty of cabarets, bars, restaurants, and hotels. In a holdover from its past, however, the neighborhood never fully shed its well-earned reputation for sexual commerce (Chesluk 2008, 26).

Longacre Square's transformation was not lost on *The New York Times* publisher Adolph S. Ochs, who was growing tired of running his newspaper out of increasingly cramped offices in lower Manhattan and had been scouting around for larger, flashier headquarters. In 1895, one of Ochs's competitors, James G. Bennett, moved the *New York Herald* to a new building between 35th and 36th streets, and between Sixth Avenue and Broadway. *The Herald* had benefited enormously from the publicity, which only increased once the surrounding neighborhood was dubbed Herald Square in its honor. Unwilling to be outdone, Ochs secured property on Broadway between 42nd and 43rd streets, right on top of the site for the new subway line, in 1902.

The Times Tower and the new subway station below it were built simultaneously at no small cost. At midnight on December 31, 1903, *The Times* celebrated its new home by setting fireworks off from its roof for the enjoyment of crowds below. The practice of ringing in each new year stuck; a giant glass ball was added for the 1906 celebration, cementing a tradition that continues to date. The city renamed Longacre Square after *The Times* in 1904, and in that same year, the first subway line opened (Bianco 2004, 23–7).

For all the fanfare, the Times Tower quickly proved too narrow and cramped for the purposes of running a newspaper, and Ochs relocated *The New York Times*'s offices to a more suitable building on West 43rd Street by 1913. Yet by this point, Times Square had become one of the most important gathering places in the city (Traub 2005, 21–2).

The explosion of new theaters also had a significant role in cultivating Times Square's international reputation as a "crossroads of the world." By 1900, less than a decade after the first venues had opened there, some thirty theaters were concentrated near or along Broadway in the neighborhood (Kenrick 2008, 112). Many more would appear in the next two decades, as would electric billboards, luxury hotels, and a number of sumptuous restaurants known collectively as lobster palaces. The fancier theaters and establishments radiated out from 42nd Street and Broadway, while the many side streets offered smaller venues, saloons, cheaper hotels and restaurants, and whorehouses. Collectively, these businesses helped Times Square solidify its reputation as an accessible, varied entertainment mecca for people from all walks of life (Traub, 2005, 27).

The Theatrical Syndicate grows more powerful

The theaters in the young neighborhood might have been new, but the people controlling them were for the most part the same as they were when the industry was concentrated in Union Square. Business trends established in the commercial theater industry in the late nineteenth century only solidified in the early twentieth as demand for live entertainment grew across the country. Increasingly powerful middlemen controlled performers' access to venues, and venues' access to performers. By the early 1900s, the most powerful middlemen of all, the Theatrical Syndicate, controlled nearly 2,000 venues across North America and functioned with all the "megalomania that was rampant in the trust-building frenzy" simultaneously taking place in the industrial world during the Gilded Age (Hirsch 1998, 25–6, 31). Under control of the Syndicate, company managers, who once dealt directly with theater managers to arrange tours, had to answer to Abraham Erlanger and Marc Klaw, the Syndicate's chief booking agents.

In exchange for five percent of gross receipts—and, since there was no real competition, sometimes a little less and sometimes a lot more—the Syndicate arranged tours that left from New York by train. The organization dictated which acts were put into the many theaters they controlled. Since the Syndicate also controlled the contracts of most Broadway headliners, they could not be crossed without fear of serious, even career-ending, consequences. This was especially true of the notoriously vindictive "Napoleon of Broadway," Abe Erlanger, who took great delight in his nickname (Travis 1958, 36). Those producers who dared remain independent from the Syndicate—including Oscar Hammerstein, Harrison Grey Fiske, and David Belasco—endured harassment and even occasional blacklisting for their efforts (Bianco 2004, 30).

While the move toward theater consolidation resulted in plenty of unsavory or even blatantly corrupt business practices, it also resulted in the standardization of a mass entertainment form that had long been completely unregulated. Before the rise of the Syndicate, national theater tours were notoriously disorganized, financially unstable, and wildly unpredictable.

The arguments for and against theater monopolies, which would eventually grow larger than anyone at the turn of the twentieth century could have imagined, have not changed much. The Syndicate was attacked by enemies as a greedy conglomerate that put commerce before art, treated theater and company managers as servants, and smothered the creative freedom of artists. Yet advocates argued that under the control of the Syndicate, theaters across the country were at the very least given what they were promised. Audiences, too, were for the first time guaranteed a night at the theater that was as well-organized and professional in Topeka, Ashtabula, and Ypsilanti as in New York (Travis 1958, 36–7).

Tin Pan Alley and the theater industry join forces

What the industrialization of the commercial theater almost certainly did was unite into one marketplace a group of actors, creative personnel, and producers, all of whom took part in the development of a new genre built from many pre-existing popular entertainments. Part opera, operetta, dance, minstrel show, burlesque, extravaganza, and vaudeville routine, the contemporary American musical took gradual shape on Broadway's stages in the dawn of the twentieth century.

Various scholars have argued that specific productions—including *The Black Crook*, shows by George M. Cohan, and Jerome Kern and Oscar Hammerstein II's 1927 *Show Boat*—constitute the "first" American musical. Yet it is probably more accurate to view the contemporary musical as a genre that evolved from many artistic influences shaped by several mutually beneficial and increasingly powerful entertainment industries. It was only natural, after all, that the vaudeville, legitimate theater, and music publishing industries—the first two concentrated in Times Square, the last a mere half-mile south, and all three catering to the country's growing middle class—would depend on and influence each other as they honed and sold their specific forms of mass entertainment.

At the turn of the twentieth century, vaudeville had become the most popular form of entertainment in the country (Lewis 2003, 315). Because more Americans were exposed to popular song through vaudeville than via any other live entertainment form, vaudeville's top entertainers became highly sought by eager song publishers. After all, then as now, songs performed live by big stars frequently prompted audiences to buy the songs for themselves (Hamm 1979, 287). Tin Pan Alley's publishers thus regularly visited theaters to gauge the pulse of popular culture. Songs were constantly pushed on performers, both by publishers and their song pluggers, whose job it was to publicize new songs. Performers and producers who visited Tin Pan Alley in search of music for their newest acts were regaled with the latest songs, not to mention money, expensive gifts, a cut of the profits, and promises that their names or images would appear on the covers of sheet music. In exchange for such favors, a theater producer or performer would interpolate new songs into their acts (ibid., 288–90).

Vaudeville might have been dominant at the time, but it was hardly the only show in town. Nationwide, vaudeville venues shared clientele with burlesque houses, concert halls, and legitimate theaters, which offered productions that were not vaudeville or burlesque shows. In Times Square, venues served "middle-class and working-class, native and immigrant, male and female audiences—sometimes under one roof" (Snyder 1989, 89). On any given evening, patrons could drop in at one theater to see a vaudeville show, visit another to see burlesque, and stop at yet another for a Shakespeare tragedy, domestic comedy, or extravaganza. Bars and cabarets, too, often featured live music or stage shows. Operettas, whether imported or composed by Americans, remained popular. And minstrel shows, while almost never on the finest stages anymore, still appeared frequently, especially in lower-priced houses (Bordman 2001, 212).

Tricky terminology

Part of what makes the birth of the contemporary stage musical so hard to discuss definitively is the fact that terminology used in describing early-twentieth-century stage entertainments was not standardized, very loosely applied, sometimes directly contradictory, and thus enormously confusing in historic perspective. The term "legitimate theater"—or, as *Variety*, the vaudeville trade magazine founded in 1905 still refers to it, "legit"—described theaters that did not feature burlesque or vaudeville shows. But it was also used to distinguish different audiences: working-class men watching excerpts from a Shakespeare play in a saloon would not have been described in the press as "legit," for example, while middle-class spectators watching the same material in a Union Square theater certainly would have been (Friedman 2000, 96).

Confusing matters further was the fact that most "legit" stages—and there were thousands across the country by this point—offered a variety of performance styles, most of which could also be found on vaudeville or burlesque stages. "Legitimate" venues offered plays into which an ever-changing lineup of songs and dances might be interpolated; operettas which, due to loose copyright laws, were never staged the same way twice; melodramas, extravaganzas, spectacles, and revues; and myriad combinations thereof. Lines were blurred even further, since many stars from burlesque and vaudeville regularly crossed over to the legitimate stage and back again.

The term "musical comedy" existed by the turn of the century, as did the term "farce-comedy," though these were often treated interchangeably, and there seemed to be only vague consensus about what, exactly, either term meant. Both terms were applied inconsistently by critics, producers, and spectators to shows that might be viewed collectively as immediate predecessors to the contemporary stage musical. However they were described, lively productions featuring the scant outline of a plot, into which songs, dances, spectacles, specialty acts, and performers were dropped, moved around, replaced, and revisited during runs in New York or on tour were enormously popular in the late nineteenth century.

A prime example is playwright and producer Charles Hoyt's *A Trip to Chinatown* (1891), which used a zany race through a big city as justification for an ever-changing lineup of ingredients. The biggest commercial hit of its time, *Chinatown* ran a record 659 performances at Madison Square Theater. The production changed with such frequency, both there and on the road, that it is unlikely any spectator ever saw the same show twice (Mates 1985, 169–73).

Both on the stage and behind the scenes, theater folk broadened their specializations as work demanded. Just as many contemporary actors appear in film, television, on stage, and on the web, so too did early-twentieth century performers often appear on burlesque, vaudeville, and legitimate stages. Famous vaudevillians like Lillian Russell, May Irwin, and Fay Templeton, for example, also performed frequently in operettas. Al Jolson performed in burlesque, vaudeville, and minstrel shows before becoming a "legit" Broadway headliner and eventually a huge movie star (Trav 2005, 245–6). Things were no different behind the scenes: composers, lyricists, and directors benefited from working on a variety of projects, and since so many entertainment industries were concentrated in the same neighborhoods in the same city, they often did. Both onstage and off, and whether consciously or not, early-twentieth-century theater personnel had begun to collectively formulate "a single genre that could combine the best of all worlds into a single, unified, coherent whole" (Krasner 2008, 54): the Broadway musical.

Harrigan and Hart, Weber and Fields, and George M. Cohan

Just as minstrel shows had once featured lengthy skits with interpolated songs and dances as afterpieces, vaudeville shows featured comic sketches into which songs and dances were inserted. Some performers built a sizeable enough following to justify developing their signature skits into lengthier pieces that could fill out an entire evening at the theater. George M. Cohan (1878–1942) would achieve fame by doing just this when he became a Broadway headliner, though he was hardly the first to do so.

Before Cohan was born, and before lowly variety had morphed into slickly marketed vaudeville, the comedy duo Edward "Ned" Harrigan (1844–1911) and Tony Hart (born Anthony Cannon, 1855–91) helped "bring narrative continuity to the disparate elements of the variety stage" (Stempel 2010, 68). Harrigan cut his teeth in the 1860s in music halls and variety houses in San Francisco. In 1871, in Chicago, he met Cannon, who had performed in minstrel shows, circuses, and saloons. Eager for a new start, Cannon changed his name to Hart, and the men headed together to New York.

Harrigan and Hart's shows consisted largely of comic sketches about working-class urban life, which usually featured songs by composer David Braham. In 1873, Harrigan wrote the "Mulligan Guard" routine, a ten-minute sketch about neighborhood volunteer militias. Such militias were initially devised to teach local men to shoot and march, but they often served primarily as drunken social clubs. The Mulligan Guard bit, and many of Harrigan and Hart's subsequent sketches, featured a series of characters—initially mostly Irish, German, and black, and later also Italian, Chinese, and Jewish—who represented the diverse working-class neighborhoods of lower Manhattan (Lewis 2003, 95).

The Mulligan series was so warmly embraced by audiences that Harrigan and Hart quickly moved beyond the small stages on which they first honed their act. Initially booked at the Theatre Comique variety house on Broadway between Broom and Spring streets, they became the venue's headliners. Their acts kept growing longer, ultimately displacing other acts on the bill and eventually allowing the partners to secure their own venues (Stempel 2010, 68). From 1875 to 1895, Harrigan and Hart wrote, produced and starred in some 35 plays and 90 sketches, and ran four theaters in New York (Mates 1985, 169).

For their popularity and the diversity of their characters, Harrigan and Hart shows were not especially innovatory for their time, either structurally or in terms of character development. The highly formulaic Mulligan shows featured loose narratives, a lot of broad physical comedy, and songs that usually had little or no relevance to the action taking place onstage (Lewis 2003, 95). Characters were broadly drawn; the black characters, played in blackface by Hart, hewed especially close to stereotype (Stempel 2010, 70). Yet Harrigan infused his characters—especially if not exclusively the Irish-American ones—with a humanity atypical for the late-nineteenth-century stage. Even as his shows grew popular among middle and upper classes, Harrigan remained most interested in connecting with the common folk in the cheap seats (Toll 1976, 189).

Harrigan and Hart's popularity coincided with the end of the surge in Irish immigration that began after 1849. Similarly, the thickly accented, malapropism-heavy "Dutch" act developed by Joe Weber (1867–1942) and Lew Fields (1867–1941) gained traction during the wave of European Jewish immigration that began in the 1880s. Both born of Polish-Jewish immigrants on the Lower East Side, Weber and Fields performed in burlesque houses as children, and established their own company in 1890. They opened the Weber and Fields Broadway Music Hall, on Broadway between 29th and 30th streets, in 1896 (Trav 2005, 96). There, they produced and performed in a series of well-cast, extravagant two-act shows, most of which featured a vaudeville-style olio in the first act and a burlesque parodying other productions in the second (Kenrick 2008, 106).

Like Harrigan and Hart, Weber and Fields demonstrated skillful showmanship onstage, and expert control behind the scenes. Both duos embraced contemporary urban life in general, and the immigrant experience in particular. Perhaps less obviously, both reflected a move away from short bits typical of vaudeville and burlesque, and toward lengthier, more fully integrated productions. For all these men, vaudeville was but a stepping stone—a place to become established and then to leave. In this respect, both teams set a precedent for performers who were lured by the legitimate theater's promise of more status, money, time in the spotlight, and, often, lighter schedules. In vaudeville, after all, even the most popular acts performed at least twice a day. Broadway's schedule, on the other hand, was usually not nearly as grueling (Trav 2005, 243–5).

George M. Cohan's move from vaudeville to Broadway resulted from similar versatility, a tireless work ethic, and brilliant business sense, all of which allowed him to nudge the American musical comedy a few steps along in its development. A proud Irish-American actor, dancer, singer, playwright, composer, producer, theater-owner, manager, and financier, Cohan shared a number of similarities with Harrigan, who wore almost as many hats. Yet Cohan's fast-paced plays, catchy songs, swaggeringly patriotic persona, and up-by-your-bootstraps philosophy helped cement the connection between Broadway musicals and Americanness. A self-described humble song-and-dance man, Cohan was born on July 3, 1878, though he famously insisted that—as one of his most famous songs went—he had been "born on the Fourth of July" (Stempel 2010, 137).

Born in Rhode Island to the vaudevillians Jeremiah and Helen Costigan Cohan, known professionally as Jerry and Nellie, little George took to the road and the stage before he could walk. Often incorporated into skits while still an infant, Cohan began writing songs and sending them to Tin Pan Alley publishers in his teens. The many rejection letters he received only fueled his determination to have a song accepted ("George M. Cohan," 1942, 20).

In 1890, Cohan, his parents, and sister Josephine, billing themselves as The Four Cohans, were contracted at Keith's Union Square. At this point, Cohan also finally began selling and publishing his songs. Through the 1890s, The Four Cohans developed a national reputation, and their act brought in as much as $1,000 a week. By the time he turned 20, George was writing all of his family's material (Hamm 1979, 312–13).

By many accounts arrogant, condescending, and argumentative, Cohan was known to be difficult to work with. Surely, his desire to control all aspects of his own career related in part to the difficulty he had taking orders from others. Yet his varied interests, drive, and obvious intelligence ultimately served him well, his reputation notwithstanding. As he negotiated the various facets of the entertainment industry, he focused with increasing intensity on leaving vaudeville to become a Broadway headliner.

The Four Cohans debuted on Broadway in a show George wrote, directed, and starred in. An expanded version of one of their vaudeville bits, *The Governor's Son* opened in February 1901 at the Savoy on 34th Street. There, it confounded critics and underwhelmed audiences, though it saw more success on the road (Bordman 2001, 201). Cohan's *Running for Office* (1903), at Haverley's 14th Street Theatre, did not fare much better, though both shows had ingredients that would become part of Cohan's winning formula: catchy song-and-dance numbers, an almost manic pace, and a classic "boy meets, loses, and gets girl back" story arc (Jones 2003, 19).

Cohan's musicals were not integrated, and would likely seem very strangely paced by contemporary standards. Some of his shows, for example, bundled all the songs into the first and third acts, and featured highly melodramatic dialogue with underscoring in the second. While some of the jokes, songs, and dances he included in his shows were tangentially related to the scene at hand, most seemed "stitched in" from elsewhere (Mast 1987, 34). Yet his shows offered some important innovations: their breakneck speed, use of colloquial speech and slang, and fervent, unfailing patriotism (Mates 1985, 178–9).

Cohan's third attempt on Broadway, *Little Johnny Jones* (1904), billed alternately as a "play with music" or a "musical play," was his first bona-fide hit in New York (Bordman 2001, 236), though even this show did not catch on with critics or audiences right away. Some critics found *Little Johnny Jones* to be impressively staged and entertaining, but others dismissed it as harshly as they had his previous Broadway shows. The critic for *Life* magazine called it "the apotheosis of stage vulgarity," its patriotism gimmicky, and its score cheap and "mawkish." Only after Cohan took the show on tour, made ample revisions, and reopened two back-to-back Broadway revivals in May and November 1905 did *Johnny Jones* finally connect with audiences.

Yet once *Johnny Jones* found its footing on Broadway, so did Cohan, whose drive and experience helped catapult him to superstardom. By the 1910s, Cohan had become a favorite on Broadway as a director, playwright, composer, manager, theater owner, and headliner. And even his harshest critics acknowledged his importance (Craft 2014, 93–101).

Almost all Cohan's shows were bound up with their author's proud Irish-American identity, but *Little Johnny Jones* was the first to feature the fervid "flag-waving chauvinism" that would become a trademark (Bordman 2001, 236). When Cohan rose to fame, Irish immigration to the US had begun to slow.

Irish immigrants had made significant economic, political, and social strides. The growing population of American-born Irish had gained access to white-collar careers, and thus to middle- and upper-class security. While anti-Irish sentiment had yet to fully dissipate, newer European immigrant populations slowly took the place of the Irish as the newest "undesirable Americans" (Craft 2014, 113–14). Cohan's patriotism arguably encouraged broader acceptance of Irish immigrants at a time when they had "moved up the ladder of respectability" but had yet to be "fully accepted as *Americans*" (Knapp 2006, 105).

Black performers on Broadway

Institutionalized racism prohibited African American performers from asserting the same kinds of claims to Americanness that Cohan could, but black artists nevertheless became increasingly visible on Broadway in the early years of the twentieth century. This was due in part both to the decline of minstrelsy through the late nineteenth century and the growth in population of black New Yorkers through the early twentieth as a result of the Great Migration.[4] Racism remained pervasive, both in New York and across the country, but important strides toward the integration of the commercial theater nevertheless took place at the dawn of the new century.

Blackface minstrelsy had permitted steady if exceedingly narrow entry by black artists into the commercial theater as early as 1855. Yet the legitimate theater remained off-limits to black performers until the end of the nineteenth century. Before 1895, Broadway audiences were regularly entertained by white actors in blackface but few if any black artists. This began to change with the death of minstrelsy and subsequent rise in popularity of new forms influenced by it.

The popularity of the coon song, for example, began while minstrelsy was on its last legs. Stylistically comparable to ragtime,[5] coon songs about black people moved beyond the sheet-music industry to influence vaudeville, burlesque, and Broadway stages through the early twentieth century. The fact that these denigrating songs were written and performed by black and white artists a like should come as no surprise: blacks working on the stage and behind the scenes still had to appeal to predominantly white audiences if they wanted a foothold in American mass entertainment (Woll 1989, 4).

Coon songs depicted blacks much in the way minstrel songs did: as lazy, childish, and ignorant, if occasionally also wily or mystically astute. They reflected, as well, a growing fear of blacks as "devoid of honesty or personal honor, given to drunkenness and gambling, utterly without ambition, sensuous, libidinous, even lascivious," and thus warranting subordination and segregation. The recurring intimation in many coon songs of blacks as dangerous enough to justify suppression coincides with the rise of the post-Reconstructionist Jim Crow South and the subsequent Great Migration.

Far beyond the confines of the American South, the coon song craze likely fed a widespread sense of justification for the country's institutionalized, second-class treatment of African Americans (Dorman 1998, 455 and 465–7). A cruel irony about coon songs lies in the fact that black performers willing to participate in the craze for them could not only thrive commercially, but could also make new inroads both on tour and on Broadway, in all-black productions and eventually in integrated ones.

A pioneering figure in the development of all-black musical productions was John W. Isham. A black man whose fair complexion allowed him to pass as white, and thus to find jobs that would otherwise have been off-limits to him, Isham launched his touring production, *Isham's Octoroons*, in 1895 (Sampson 2014, 50). A year later, his larger, more ambitious *Oriental America* also toured the country, as did *Black Patti's Troubadours* (Johnson 1991, 96). These productions bounced from one second-rate house to the next, where they were usually performed for segregated audiences (Graziano 2008, 93).

In 1898, two landmark productions opened in New York: Robert Cole and Billy Johnson's *A Trip to Coontown*, and Will Marion Cook and Paul Laurence Dunbar's *Clorindy, Or the Origin of the Cake Walk*. *Coontown*'s title referenced the 1891 hit *A Trip to Chinatown*, but with the exception of its focus on contemporary urban life, it had little in common with the earlier show. A comedy with a thin plot about a conman trying to swindle an old man out of his pension, *Coontown* emphasized specialty acts, including contortionists, acrobats, and opera singers. Its story line did little to distinguish it from other black revues of the period; neither did its score, which featured numbers with titles like "All I Wants Is Ma Chickens" and "I Wonder What Is That Coon's Game" (Jones 2013, 32). *Coontown* nevertheless broke ground as the first musical in New York City to be written, directed, produced, and performed by African Americans (Woll 1989, 12–13).

Cook and Dunbar's *Clorindy, Or the Origin of the Cake Walk* is often cited as the first all-black musical to appear on Broadway, and to some extent this is true. The show premiered in July 1898 at the enormous Casino Theatre at 39th Street and Broadway. The house was one of the most celebrated Broadway theatres of its time, not only because it was particularly beautiful but also because it was the first venue in New York to be lit entirely with electricity. Technically, *Clorindy*'s run was not *on* Broadway but *above* it, on the theater's roof garden. This might seem a ridiculous distinction, but at the time, roof gardens were frequent locales for stage shows during the summer, when theaters got too hot and producers instead offered late-night stage entertainments—and often food and drink—under the stars (Miller 2013).

Because *Clorindy* premiered as such an entertainment, it was not performed the way its creators initially conceived it. Written with a full score and libretto, the show was shortened significantly and mounted at the Casino as a brief revue. Despite the fact that the audience demanded ten encores of the Ernest Hogan's rendition of "Who Dat Say Chicken in Dis Crowd?" on opening night, the entire show was over within an hour.

Yet *Clorindy*'s milestone status is well-deserved, as is evidenced by the incredible determination it took Will Marion Cook to get anywhere near Broadway, let alone atop it. Cook shopped *Clorindy* around relentlessly, despite constant rejections by white producers, at least one of whom interrupted Cook mid-audition to tell him that he was a fool to think white audiences would ever "pay money to hear Negroes sing a Negro opera"(Woll, 8). After weeks of being dismissed daily from the offices of the Casino roof garden's manager, Cook finally assembled a cast, rehearsed them, and launched into the show's opening number, "Darktown Is Out Tonight," when the manager arrived at his office one Monday morning (Toll 1976, 121).

A surprise commercial success, *Clorindy* went on tour once it closed at the Casino. Ernest Hogan left the production before the tour began, and was replaced by the up-and-coming vaudeville team of Bert Williams (1874–1922) and George Walker (1872–1911). *Clorindy* did not fare as well on the road as it did at the Casino, but Williams and Walker would become enormously influential by the turn of the century.

The duo met in San Francisco where, at some point between 1893 and 1895, they worked together in the desegregated troupe Martin and Selig's Mastodon Minstrels. Soon tired of the small, dilapidated venues the troupe worked in, Williams and Walker bounced from San Francisco to Los Angeles and Denver to Chicago, where they were cast in a company of John Isham's *The Octoroons*. They were fired a week later, once it was determined that audiences were not warming to them (Toll 1976, 121–4).

Crushed by the dismissal, Williams and Walker re-evaluated their act. During his Martin and Selig days, Williams had renounced the use of blackface after a bad case of stage fright overwhelmed him while he was wearing it. After being fired from *The Octoroons*, he decided to try it again for a show in Detroit. This time, the makeup had a transformative effect: it allowed Williams to devise a buffer between his inner self and his character. The distance with which he could now view and assess his own stage work allowed him to cultivate his sad-sack "Jonah Man" character, and to carefully hone his brilliant comic timing. Walker had always played the comic and Williams the straight man, but at this point, their roles reversed, as did their billing: Walker and Williams rose to national prominence as Williams and Walker (Forbes 2008, 34–5).

They arrived in New York in 1896. After a false start in *The Gold Bug*, a failed operetta by Victor Herbert about miscegenation, they were offered a 36-week run at Koster and Bial's, an enormous vaudeville house on 34th Street between Broadway and Seventh Avenue, where Macy's flagship store now stands. Billing themselves as "Two Real Coons," they were so well received that they soon graduated to even more celebrated vaudeville houses: Tony Pastor's Music Hall, Oscar Hammerstein's Olympia Roof Garden, and B.F. Keith's in Boston. They were the only two black men invited to tour with an otherwise all-white vaudeville troupe, and they steadily built a national reputation as the country's most "celebrated delineators of darky characters" (Toll 1976, 124).

While their invitation to perform at Koster and Bial's was the start of a brilliant career trajectory, it was also a reflection of just how constricted black performing artists were at the time (Ndounou 2013, 62). Vaudeville may have been successfully rebranded as the country's most "democratic entertainment for the masses" in the late nineteenth century, but black audiences were typically not included in said democracy. More often than not, they were ignored by managers and producers, who catered to the white middle classes who made up the majority of audiences, and who were allowed to buy the choicest tickets. Like most performance venues, vaudeville houses usually had strict segregation policies. Those that would admit blacks seated them only in the rear balcony or gallery seats. Complaints about such policies fell on deaf ears; black patrons who could afford better seats were bluntly informed that there were simply none available for them. Black performers were just as carefully curtailed. Whites in blackface continued to perform as the butt of jokes in vaudeville, and houses that hired black performers at all would typically feature just one black act on any given bill (Forbes 2008, 56–7).

As one such act, Williams and Walker did their best to challenge, or at the very least to soften, extant stereotypes as they shot to stardom. Yet while they were beloved by both white and black spectators, they were expected to appeal primarily to whites, a great many of whom surely did not think too deeply about the clownish black men singing coon songs for their amusement. A series of race riots in New York during the summer of 1900—during which white mobs swarmed black neighborhoods, attacked passersby, destroyed property, cried "specifically for the heads of black performers," and dragged George Walker from a passing streetcar—served as a powerful, frightening reminder that even the most loved and respected black celebrities were viewed as threatening Others as soon as they stepped off the stage (Sotiropoulos 2006, 42–3).

Yet Williams and Walker earned such adoration when they were on the stage that they were afforded more power, reach, and influence than most black performers of the time. Their fame coincided with the growth in population of blacks in New York and other urban centers; Williams and Walker took part in the development of a thriving black arts scene in New York, and became associated with a black intelligentsia concerned with upward mobility, fair representation, and equality. Williams was shy and unassuming offstage, but Walker was brash and outspoken, and had a head for business. He eagerly served as the duo's public representative, and both men were happy to serve as role models. "We want our folks, the Negroes, to like us," Walker wrote in 1909. "Over and above the money and the prestige is a love for the race" (quoted in Sotiropoulos 2006, 42).

Under Walker's management, the Williams and Walker Company negotiated for better theaters, recording deals, and song-publishing credits. Walker often spoke out against racism and the unfair treatment of black artists. The duo helped found or support organizations that helped other black performers, including a black entertainment baseball league, a black performers' fraternal organization, and a black-owned music publishing company (Smith 1992, 97, 106–7, 124). After their stint in vaudeville, they teamed with playwright Jesse Shipp on a series of all-black productions to which they contributed dialogue and songs. In New York and on the road, shows like *The Policy Players* (1899) and *Sons of Ham* (1900) allowed them to build a relationship with a national, diverse audience. The duo also secured management by the brothers Benjamin and Jules Hurtig, and their partner, Harry Seamon. Some of the first white theater managers to work with black acts, the Hurtigs and Seamon produced shows under the auspices of Syndicate members Erlanger and Klaw. Their Syndicate ties gave Williams and Walker access to Broadway theaters (Forbes 2008, 100). Their show *In Dahomey* (1903) would become the first all-black full-length musical to play in (not above) a major Broadway house in season.

In Dahomey began in Stamford, Connecticut, in 1902 before playing Boston, Philadelphia, and the midwest through 1903. It was conceived with a more formal structure and developed plot than any of Williams and Walker's previous shows. Billed as a "musical farce," *In Dahomey* touched lightly on the late-nineteenth-century back-to-Africa movement. In the show, two conmen—the conniving Rareback Pinkerton (Walker) and the good-natured, dim Shylock Homestead (Walker)—are hired to find some missing treasure. They soon become embroiled in a second plan "to steal money from a wealthy old man named Mr. Lightfoot and his group of African colonizers." The plot brings many of the characters to Africa, where they win over the Dahomean king with whiskey. Lightfoot returns to the US, but Shylock and Rareback, whom the king has made powerful assistants, choose to stay (Woll 1989, 36–8).

In Dahomey had a score by Will Marion Cook, lyrics by Paul Laurence Dunbar, and a book by Jesse Shipp. The show was so well received in Boston that Hurtig and Seamon more than quadrupled their initial investment of $15,000. The returns allowed them to negotiate successfully with Erlanger and Klaw for an unprecedented move to Broadway, where *In Dahomey* opened on February 18, 1903.

A Broadway milestone, *In Dahomey* nevertheless hardly made a dent in the institutionalized racism pervading the Great White Way. Even before it opened, concerns about the production plagued the theater industry. In its review, *The New York Times* mentioned a "thundercloud" reflected "in the faces of the established Broadway managers," resulting from rampant rumors and deep concern about the possibility that opening night would set off "a race war." The *Times* article conceded that such concerns proved unwarranted, but argued that this was due largely to the fact that the house was kept strictly segregated by employees of Erlanger and Klaw, who stood at the entryway of the theater refusing black patrons—even those offering to "pay more than the dollar price for the orchestra seats"—entry anywhere but the upper tiers of the balcony. Thus the only blacks in the orchestra were music director James Vaughn and the water peddlers. "As the most comfortable chair in the house costs a dollar, such a result is a triumph intact for all concerned. At intervals one heard a shrill kiyi of applause from above or a mellow bass roar that betokened the seventh heaven of delight. All parties were satisfied," the critic concluded ("Dahomey on Broadway" 1903, 9).

Dahomey was a hit, but Broadway's producers and theater owners nevertheless "desired to maintain the status quo fought to keep black performers from having access" to their venues. For the remainder of their partnership, Williams and Walker repeatedly had to "defend their right to Broadway stages" (Forbes 2008, 103–4), while managers and producers just as repeatedly insisted, despite all evidence to the contrary, that black productions were of no interest to white audiences and were simply too risky to back.

Nevertheless, through the first decade of the twentieth century, black productions appeared with more frequency on legitimate stages. Rivalling Williams and Walker's shows were those by brothers James Weldon and J. Rosamond Johnson, along with Robert Cole, whose musicals *The Shoo Fly Regiment* (1907) and *The Red Moon* (1909) appeared at the Bijou and Majestic, respectively (Graziano 2008, 95–6). Broadway saw its first interracial musical even earlier: *The Southerners* (1904) featured whites in blackface *and* a "chorus of real live coons" who joined the white cast for a scene; despite the now-familiar wails of concern among critics, the production was not a hit, but its short run proceeded without incident (Bordman 2001, 233).

In 1908, Williams and Walker appeared in their most critically praised Broadway show, *Bandanna Land*, which would also be their last. *Bandanna Land* featured a book by Jesse Shipp and choral music by Will Marion Cook and Alex Rogers; many songs were interpolated into the show as well. The musical follows Bud Jenkins (Walker) as he tries to cheat a railroad company with a land speculation deal, and to swindle Skunkton Bowser (Williams) out of his inheritance. Jenkins defrauds the railroad company, but Bowser outwits him in the end (Woll 1989, 46). *Bandanna Land* was universally received by critics as joyful and strong, if also condescendingly "natural," "authentic," and "spontaneous" in its southern setting, which was seen as evocative of the plantation and of old-time minstrelsy (Forbes 2008, 158–9).

While touring with *Bandanna Land*, Walker began to lisp, stutter, slur, and forget his lines, all of which are symptoms of late-stage syphilis. He gave his last performance in Kentucky in February 1909. His colleagues initially downplayed his condition as exhaustion, but Walker, who never took the stage again, died in 1911 (Smith 1992, 109–11). Unwittingly, Williams became a solo performer with *Mr. Lode of Koal* at the Majestic in 1909.

Walker's death contributed to a decade-long dearth of black performers and entertainments on Broadway. The historian Robert Toll attributes the exclusion to "the worsening position of blacks in the country," citing among other factors the rise of the Jim Crow South, the introduction of federal segregationist policies by President Wilson, rising anxieties among whites as the Great Migration continued, and a resultant uptick in race riots across the country (Toll 1976, 128). While these factors might well have influenced (white) public opinion about race and the direction of popular culture, more immediate factors also resulted in the period on Broadway that James

Weldon Johnson, in his book *Black Manhattan*, called the "term of exile" (Johnson 1991, 170).

First, a number of innovative black artists who had been active on Broadway during the first decade of the twentieth century either died or turned to new interests during the second. Ernest Hogan died in 1909, and both Robert Cole and George Walker followed him in 1911. Will Marion Cook turned to choral and orchestral music, and J. Rosamond Johnson moved to London before returning to the US to run a music school. These various departures left a vacuum on Broadway that was not quickly filled.

Another reason for the dearth of black artists on Broadway through the 1910s was the *de facto* segregation that continued to plague the commercial theater. Despite laws passed in New York at the turn of the century to end segregation in public spaces, theaters continued the practice well into the 1920s. Complaints by black spectators occasionally spurred attempts at reform by organizations such as the NAACP, or by journalists writing for black newspapers. But the theater industry made little attempt at change, and white critics at papers such as *The New York Times* almost always argued in favor of segregated seating policies. Even with the increased presence of black performers, blacks were not made to feel welcome on stage or in the audience (Woll 1989, 50–53).

Finally, the growing population of black New Yorkers had begun, in the first decades of the twentieth century, to settle in the northern Manhattan neighborhood of Harlem, which had been built rapidly and a bit too optimistically between 1870 and 1910. Overspeculation left realtors with an abundance of vacant if spacious buildings that were ready to absorb the city's new arrivals. Many black performers, writers, editors, artists, and businessmen relocated there before the First World War. Because segregation was rife in most downtown establishments, many clubs, cabarets, and theaters were established in Harlem as its population grew (Sotiropoulos 2006, 200–3).

While there was little in the way of black presence on Broadway in the 1910s, the black performing arts flourished elsewhere in New York. Theater artists in Harlem enjoyed a growing population of black audiences before which to hone their craft; up-and-coming performers who would headline on Broadway during the so-called golden age of black musicals in the 1920s graced Harlem's stages as well. In Chicago, too, and on national tours, black companies performed for black audiences, turning profits despite their lack of presence on Broadway (Woll 1989, 54–5).

One of the few black artists to remain on Broadway during the so-called period of exile was Bert Williams. After *Mr. Lode of Koal*, Williams accepted an offer by Flo Ziegfeld to perform in the *Ziegfeld Follies* of 1910 (Forbes 2008, 193–4). When he accepted, Williams became the first black actor to appear in any of Ziegfeld's illustrious revues. Yet the decision was fraught: many of the performers in Ziegfeld's company threatened to quit upon learning that they would be sharing the stage with a black man. And even by Broadway standards, the *Follies* were selective at best when it came to admitting black spectators.

Ziegfeld easily dealt with his performers' threats to quit the show: he simply told them they were free to leave, since they were expendable and Williams was not. The second issue, however, went unresolved. Black spectators continued to follow Williams's career and celebrate his prominence in a "white show," but were more limited than ever in opportunities to see him perform. Tensions and disappointments resulted: years later, James Weldon Johnson would refer to Williams's work with the *Follies* as a "defection" to "the white stage" (Johnson 1991, 109). The *Ziegfeld Follies* was certainly a major milestone for Williams, who remained with the revue until 1919. But it was never an entirely comfortable place to work, and he endured racism and segregation, onstage and off, in his years there (Forbes 2008, 231).

Williams's decision to work with Ziegfeld was perhaps unsurprising considering Ziegfeld's meteoric rise on Broadway as a producer. In the next chapter, we will examine the impact of Ziegfeld's *Follies*, as well as other musical entertainments produced by him and others during the 1910s, 1920s, and 1930s on Broadway.

CHAPTER 3
THE EARLY TWENTIETH CENTURY

At the dawn of the twentieth century, the continuation of major technological innovations and advances spurred by the Gilded Age resulted in an extraordinary economic boom. The outbreak of the First World War in 1914 was followed by a long period of especially robust economic prosperity. The abrupt onset of the Great Depression, however, brought with it a stretch of crushing economic hardship.

Between the turn of the century and the outbreak of the First World War, the US economy grew significantly in international importance. Steel production fueled the development of the airplane and the high-rise building, a more efficient rail system, and mass production of the automobile (Jones 2003, 13). Across the US, middle-class Americans patronized vaudeville houses and theaters. They also took in comparatively new forms of live entertainment, including organized spectator sports such as baseball, American football, and horse racing. Film, too, gradually became a new item of fascination: nickelodeons cropped up across the country in the early twentieth century, contributing to American leisure time, if not yet seriously competing with live entertainment (Travis 1958, 40).

The early-twentieth-century American stage musical mirrored the country's many ups and downs, both aesthetically and commercially. Until the crash of the stock market in 1929, Broadway boomed. And in darker times, the American stage musical responded to the needs of the nation, and continued to establish itself as an important, meaningful, and lasting live entertainment form.

The *Ziegfeld Follies*

Through the second decade of the twentieth century, as the burlesque industry steadily declined, venues for vaudeville and legitimate productions rose in Times Square to meet the ever-growing demands of a flourishing population. For the first time in its history, Broadway opened over forty new musicals in the 1911–12 season.[1] The quality of these shows was not always as impressive as the quantity; in what has long since become a trend, critics at the time responded to the glut of unmemorable productions by bewailing the sad state of the musical theater and loudly predicting its demise (Bordman 2001, 310–11). Nonetheless, the sheer number of shows staged on Broadway in a single season reflected the growth in size and importance of Times Square as a hub for live entertainment.

There is perhaps no producer whose drive, love of spectacle, and unquenchable passion for beautiful women in skimpy costumes were better suited to early-twentieth-century Times Square than Flo Ziegfeld. Ziegfeld's *Follies* were some of the most influential and emulated productions Broadway had yet seen, and their influence continues to resonate every time contemporary chorines in sequined outfits lock their arms and kick up their shapely legs during a big, flashy, song-and-dance number.

The son of a classically-trained German pianist who owned and operated a successful Chicago music school, Ziegfeld inherited his father's refined demeanor and polished charm. Expected to take over the family business, Flo grew to hate the sound of classical music and to reject his parent's quaint, old-fashioned approach to the world. Instead, he embraced his own "Barnum-like aptitude for promotion and flimflam" (Traub 2005, 31). When his father was tapped to help judge the keyboard awards at the 1893 Columbian Exposition in Chicago, the younger Ziegfeld traveled to New York to help secure talent. There, he met, bought out the contract of, and became manager to the body-builder Eugene Sandow. Sandow has gone down in history not for his ability to play piano, but for his willingness to pose and flex for audiences while clad in little more than a loincloth. Through 1895, Ziegfeld toured Sandow across the US and Europe, where the muscle-man preened for fascinated crowds (Bianco 2004, 67).

On the London leg of the tour, Ziegfeld discovered the singer and actress Anna Held, who became his next client and also his lover (Bianco 2004, 67). Back in New York, where the couple settled at the turn of the century, Ziegfeld made his name by producing Broadway musicals starring Held, whom he promoted with publicity stunts. These included a press release claiming that she took daily milk baths, and a leaked rumor that her waist was as tiny as it was because she had had some of her ribs removed.

In the summer of 1907, Ziegfeld produced the first in a series of rooftop diversions, which he based on popular Parisian revues and dubbed the *Follies* in homage to the well-respected *Folies Bergère*. The first edition, which ran a fast and furious forty minutes, appeared on the roof garden of Erlanger and Klaw's New York Theater, which was renamed the Jardin de Paris in honor of the production. The *Follies*, officially retitled the *Ziegfeld Follies* in

1911, remained at the Jardin until 1913, when it was relocated to Erlanger and Klaw's New Amsterdam Theater (Traub 2005, 31–4).

The *Ziegfeld Follies* benefited from its creator's work ethic, obsession with beautiful women, taste for spectacle, and willingness to pay handsomely for the best designers, directors, choreographers, composers, and performers of the day. Ziegfeld's insistence on quality and his ability to gauge public demand paid off exceptionally well: he began his *Follies* as a side project, but after the first edition, which cost $13,000 and netted almost $100,000, he turned his full attention to developing the series. By 1909, the *Follies* "typified what became standard Ziegfeld fare—fast-paced, lavish productions that focused on beauty, spectacle, and topical humor," and that borrowed liberally from musical comedy, vaudeville, opera, and burlesque. This blend of high- and low-culture entertainment was repackaged and sold to middle-class audiences (Toll 1976, 303).

Because of its enormous size and cost, not to mention its commercial success, the *Ziegfeld Follies* became an industry in and of itself by the second decade of the twentieth century. Ziegfeld oversaw every aspect of each new edition of the *Follies*. Typically, he would open a new edition in New York in spring or summer; this would go on tour in the fall, whereupon he would begin planning the next edition. Beautiful women in elaborate costumes—some of which were enormous, heavy, and incredibly ornate, others of which were feather-light and scandalously sheer—became trademarks. So did rapid-fire pacing, state-of-the-art sets, and some of the best comedians in the business. At the peak of popularity, between 1907 and 1925, the *Ziegfeld Follies* featured comedians like Bert Williams, Fanny Brice, Eddie Cantor, Leon Errol, Ed Wynn, W.C. Fields, and Will Rogers.[2] Other celebrities involved at various points included Bob Hope, Josephine Baker, Irving Berlin, Eva Tanguay, Ray Bolger, Marilyn Miller, and Sophie Tucker.

No hugely successful production on Broadway goes un-imitated, so the *Ziegfeld Follies* had plenty of competition. Between the 1910s and 1920s, rival revues included the Shubert brothers' *The Passing Show* (1912–24), *George White's Scandals* (1919–39), *Earl Carroll's Vanities* (1923–32), Lew Leslie's *Blackbirds* (1926–30 and 1939), and *The Greenwich Village Follies* (1919–28). All of these revues had distinct personalities: some were racy; some focused specifically on dance, comedy, or music; some, like *Blackbirds*, were showcases for black performers. Yet the *Follies*, which essentially consolidated everything that had come before it into one funny, zippy, scantily-clad, highly entertaining package, remained most famous of all (Toll 1976, 305).

While brilliant and innovative in his own right, Ziegfeld benefited in part from a years-long war taking place in the commercial theater industry through the first decades of the twentieth century. The Theatrical Syndicate's monopolistic stranglehold was, for the first time, being challenged on Broadway and on the road by three entrepreneurial brothers who seemed to have emerged from nowhere (actually, they were from Syracuse, New York). As they rose to power, Lee, Sam, and Jacob J. Shubert were frequently locked in heated, nasty, and often astoundingly childish competition with the Syndicate, as both groups scrambled to destroy one another by building and acquiring theaters, competing for audiences, and out-producing each other. As the up-and-coming producer of a hit series that premiered on the roof of a prime Syndicate house, Ziegfeld caught the attention and fueled the hotly competitive spirits of the Shuberts, whose *Passing Show* series was an attempt to unseat him as king of the Broadway revue and, they hoped, hurt the Syndicate in the process.

The demise of the Syndicate: Enter the Shuberts

Lee (1871–1953), Sam (1878–1905), and Jacob J. (1879–1963) Shubert were hardly the first businessmen to challenge the Syndicate. Earlier producers such as David Belasco and Oscar Hammerstein had managed to survive the monopoly with their independent, if never nearly as powerful, careers intact. Yet while the Syndicate had managed to create and sustain a nationally consolidated theater industry, the Shuberts were younger, savvier, and hungrier, if never quite as innovative. Much to the chagrin of their supporters, once they overtook the Syndicate, they merely imitated the very monopoly they had set out to destroy in the first place: "They devised nothing new in the way of circuits, booking offices, theatrical systems. They followed a model; they enlarged its scale; they did not alter its proportions" (Bernheim [1932] 1964, 67). Nevertheless, the Shuberts' legacy remains, as do many of the Broadway theaters they built in their ascent: the Ambassador, Barrymore, Booth, Schoenfeld, Imperial, Shubert, and Winter Garden.[3]

The fact that three unknown young men were, over time, able to beat the large and powerful Syndicate at its own game seems the stuff of folklore. But the Shuberts were quick to take advantage of the larger organization's very significant weaknesses. The Syndicate was a formidable, pioneering organization, but it was never a particularly organized or well-balanced one, and its lack of cohesion contributed to its downfall. Loosely structured as a pool, or informal combination, which tended more toward verbal than written agreements and relied almost entirely on a trust that was usually unfounded, the Syndicate quickly proved dangerously porous, backhanded, and corrupt. Some of its partners were less savvy and more easily bribed than others, and most of its members got into the habit of making secret deals with outside parties or pursuing private ventures that did not represent the group as a whole. The Shubert brothers figured out and took advantage of these weaknesses from early in their careers.

Three of the seven children of Eastern European immigrants who settled in Syracuse, New York, in the late nineteenth century, Sam, Lee, and J.J. had little in the way of formal education due to their family's crushing poverty and their father's alcoholism. At some point in the late 1880s, Sam found work as a program boy at the Grand Opera house; by the age of eleven he was treasurer of a competing venue. At the turn of the century Sam brought his brothers into the business, took control of several road companies, and leased six theaters in upstate New York as well as the Herald Square Theatre in Manhattan (Travis 1958, 39). Some of the venues the Shuberts leased were Syndicate owned, but Sam made a practice of defying Syndicate rules. As often as he could, he bribed middlemen or circumvented Klaw and Erlanger in order to do business with their kinder and conveniently more inept partners, Samuel Nixon and Frederick Zimmerman.

The fact that Abraham Erlanger, by far the most dominant member, was so thoroughly despised hardly helped the Syndicate generate loyalty or retain power. As the Shuberts established a greater foothold in the business, their hatred of Erlanger only grew. Following 26-year-old Sam Shubert's death in a grisly 1905 train wreck outside Harrisburg, Pennsylvania, Lee and J.J. asked Erlanger to honor an agreement he had made with their newly deceased brother. Erlanger dismissed the outstanding contract by snapping back that he never honored contracts made with dead men (Hirsch 1998, 36).

Like the Syndicate, the Shuberts frequently resorted to bribery, lying, double-crossing, and evasion to gain power (Hirsch 1998, 27). But unlike the Syndicate, they had something powerful to focus on toppling and, after Sam's death, personal reasons for doing so. More vigilant, mistrustful, and litigious than the Syndicate, the Shuberts were also a smaller, closer concern; the surviving brothers kept a careful watch over one another and their employees as they grew their empire. While they occasionally made peace with

Syndicate members when a project came along that was mutually beneficial, they typically made it a practice to hire performers or managers who disliked or mistrusted the older, established monopoly. They sent bigger, more spectacular acts to any city where the Syndicate had booked a show. As they grew, they built connections and fostered heated competition, both in New York and on the road (Travis 1958, 40).

The Syndicate's approach was to function on "an economy of shortage"; its members believed that "fewer theaters insured fuller booking and larger audiences." Yet following Sam's death, the surviving Shuberts began building as many theaters across the country as they could manage, frequently appealing to outside patrons and benefactors for money with which to do so. Further, while the members of the Syndicate were never well-respected as producing managers, the Shuberts cultivated themselves as impresarios who had a hand in the shows they put into their theaters (Hirsch 1998, 56). Their approach eventually led to a glut of theaters that neither concern could fill, especially as movies began drawing spectators away from live entertainment. But in the short term, the brothers' tactics managed to strip the Syndicate of much of its power on the road.

At its peak early in the first decade of the twentieth century, the Syndicate began its slow decline around 1907. By 1916 it had shrunk to a third of its original size: Charles Frohman had died, Charles Hayman had retired, and Nixon and Zimmerman had dissolved their partnership. Erlanger and Klaw continued to run the business until Klaw left under bitter circumstances around 1919 (Bernheim 1932, 1964, 67–8). Erlanger continued to produce shows until his death in 1930, but was no longer nearly the powerhouse he had once been. By the time of his death, the Shuberts controlled most venues on Broadway and a great many across the country.

The First World War and ASCAP

Due in part to the US's isolationist, insular stance, American popular entertainment remained fairly lukewarm in its response to the First World War. This was certainly the case on Broadway, where most productions avoided wartime themes—though some revues, including editions of the *Ziegfeld Follies* and the *Passing Show*, featured obligatory grandiose, patriotic production numbers. There was also a small uptick in musical productions with war-related scenes or songs after American involvement in the war began in 1917. Yet the distance most musical productions kept from the war implied that producers usually opted to keep their productions light, and their audiences free from anxiety about international affairs (Jones 2003, 36–42).

And yet the First World War era was hardly a fallow time for the musical, which developed and matured considerably through the 1910s. The country's isolationism fueled the development of new, homegrown genres. Jazz, in particular, proved enormously popular and very quickly found its way onto Broadway's stages. The establishment of ASCAP (the American Society of Composers, Authors and Publishers) in 1914 also had a big impact on the development of the American stage musical: it resulted in a shift away from interpolated scores and toward cohesive ones written entirely by one composer and lyricist.

At the onset of the war, a surge in anti-European, and especially anti-German, sentiment led to the decline in support for "even the most harmless Austro-Hungarian operetta," long a staple of the country's live entertainment diet (Bordman 2001, 343). The rejection of all things operetta coincided with the decline of the road tour and, on Broadway, a growing demand for American-made musicals. The absence of European imports caused a vacuum that was filled by a new generation of American composers, armed with new rights and protections that allowed them to make unprecedented demands of Broadway producers.

ASCAP was founded at the Hotel Claridge in Times Square in February 1914 by a group of composers and music publishers including George Maxwell, Victor Herbert, Rudolf Friml, and Irving Berlin. The performers-rights organization protected intellectual property and demanded regular payments in the form of royalties for its members.[4] Copyright laws existed in the US before ASCAP, but protections extended only to the "purchase and mechanical reproduction of published compositions"—not to live performances. This meant that any published song could be interpolated into any show, anywhere, at any time, and that its composer or lyricist could seek no compensation in exchange. Once ASCAP commenced and, by January 1917, won a series of legal battles, "all hotels, theaters, dance halls, cabarets, and restaurants were required to obtain a license from ASCAP—for a fee—before they could play a piece written by a composer or published by a publishing house belonging to the organization" (Hamm 1979, 338–9).

The impact of ASCAP, both in shaping the popular tastes of the country and on the stage musical, was profound. Much like the commercial theater industry, Tin Pan Alley, and almost all the composers and lyricists contributing to both, ASCAP was based in New York. The concentration of that kind of power in that city resulted in "the urbanization of American popular song." Through the first half of the twentieth century, attitudes about what an American popular song "should be and where it should fit into American culture were . . . . shaped by the climate and taste of New York." Tin Pan Alley style became nationally dominant and "to the extent that Tin Pan Alley songs reflected American culture in a broader sense, they did so because the rest of the country was willing to accept a uniquely urban, New York product, not because New York was absorbing elements of American culture from west of the Hudson River or south of Atlantic City" (ibid., 377–8). On the theater front, ASCAP members now received royalties that permitted more artistic freedom and challenged the power of the producer in controlling what music went into each show. For the first time, interpolations became impractical, expensive and, if done on the sly, illegal. Composers and lyricists could demand to create and to be properly compensated for entire scores.

One result of the birth of ASCAP, then, was the standardization of particular forms: the AABA or 32-bar form became so prevalent that it is still sometimes simply referred to as "Tin Pan Alley form." Another result was the rise in importance to the American musical of ASCAP-supported composers and lyricists, whose output extended across the country, moving beyond theaters and vaudeville houses via sheet music, radios, phonographs, and eventually the talking picture (ibid., 339).

A new generation of composers and lyricists

Many attempts have been made to explain precisely why different periods in American entertainment seem "dominated by one or another of the national or ethnic groups making up the complex web of American society—the English, the Irish, the Italians, the Germans, the Africans"—and, more specifically, why both Tin Pan Alley and the American musical in the first half of the twentieth century seemed so strongly associated with New York-based Jewish Americans (ibid., 327). Theories ranging from the burgeoning industries' relative lack of prejudice against Jews to the cultural importance of music in the Diaspora to the spike in population of Eastern European Jews in New York at the turn of the century have been alternately suggested and refuted as overgeneralized, unsubstantiated, or reductive (Most 2004, 8).

For whatever reason—most likely a complex mix of social, economic, political, and cultural factors—the period between the World Wars saw the "first great contribution to American culture by the New York Jewish community" (Hamm 1979, 327). While they came from backgrounds too diverse to easily quantify—from affluent, assimilated, educated families to newly arrived and desperately poor immigrants—and while there were certainly exceptions, Jewish up-and-comers like Irving Berlin (1888–1989), Jerome Kern (1885–1945), Oscar Hammerstein II (1895–1960), and George (1898–1937) and Ira Gershwin (1896–1983) served as the first generation of composers and lyricists who, thanks to shifting trends in mass entertainment, supplied many of the scores emanating from the country's theaters, and many of the songs disseminated via Tin Pan Alley across the country.

The earliest of this group of composers to establish themselves were Irving Berlin and Jerome Kern. While contemporaries, these men exerted notably different influences on American popular culture. The astoundingly prolific Berlin is known less for his theater scores than for an extraordinary number of hit songs like "God Bless America," "Puttin' on the Ritz," and "White Christmas" (Magee 2012, xi). Kern, who unlike Berlin wore erudition on his sleeve, wrote primarily for book shows, less often for revues, and "never wrote popular songs independent of film and theater scores" (Mast 1987, 57).

Poverty so afflicted Berlin's family that he began working as a small child shortly after they emigrated from Siberia and settled on the Lower East Side in 1893. Sporadically educated at best, Berlin quit school for good at age thirteen after the death of his father. Jobs as a singing waiter and saloon performer led him to Tin Pan Alley, where he found work as a song-plugger and then as a staff lyricist. After collaborating in 1907 with the pianist Mike Nicholson on his first published song, "Marie from Sunny Italy," for which he wrote lyrics, Berlin had his first big hit, "Alexander's Ragtime Band," in 1911.

Less a real ragtime song than a Tin Pan Alley number in march-time with a little syncopation tossed in for good measure, "Alexander" was soon being performed on America's stages by superstars like Al Jolson. In its first year of publication alone, "Alexander" sold some two million copies in sheet music form internationally. The newly in-demand Berlin went on to write hundreds of songs for musicals, vaudeville shows, Hollywood films, and eventually television (Magee 2012, 3–4).

Kern did not mirror Berlin's compositional range or longevity, but his impact on the legitimate theater was more immediate. Most known as the composer of the 1927 landmark musical *Show Boat*, Kern was born in New York into an assimilated, affluent family. After exhibiting a talent for music in early childhood, he was given piano lessons and sent as a young man to the New York College of Music. Following stints studying in Germany and England, he apprenticed as a Tin Pan Alley shipping clerk and song-plugger, and then served as a rehearsal pianist for musicals. He published a few songs that were interpolated into various productions, and eventually became a resident composer at the tiny Princess Theater on West 39th Street. There, he collaborated on a series of shows now collectively known as the Princess musicals (Hamm 1979, 341).

Built in 1913 by producer Ray Comstock, the Shubert brothers, and the actor and director Holbrook Blinn, the 299-seat Princess was designed to be a space for up-and-coming playwrights to stage short plays. But the Princess failed to draw loyal audiences. In 1915, after two years of financial struggle, agent and producer Elisabeth Marbury was brought in to envision a new direction for the theater. Under Marbury's guidance, the theater became home to "small, intimate, clean musical comedy devoid of all vulgarity and coarseness" (Stempel 2010, 159).

When it came to musicals, "small" and "intimate" were really all the Princess could handle, especially on an allotted $7,500 budget, which was minuscule even for the time. The venue had room for very few props, performers, musicians, or set pieces, and thus could not compete with large, moneyed houses built to accommodate enormous sets, complicated stage effects, and dazzling costumes for huge casts. The Princess musicals, then, were borne as much of necessity as they were of any real urge to rid Broadway of perceived vulgarity, which might well have been incorporated had the theater actually been able to afford and accommodate it (Kirle 2005, 17). Nevertheless, Marbury's new program worked: the musicals produced at the Princess connected with audiences, and the theater was soon out of financial trouble.

The first small-scale musical staged at the Princess was a version of Paul Ruben's 1905 London hit, *Mr. Popple of Ippleton*, adapted for American tastes and retitled *Nobody Home* (1915). Marbury hired Kern and playwright Guy Bolton to write the score and refashion the book. Promotional material for *Nobody Home* promised audiences something innovative and intimate: the "[s]martest musical offering of the New York season," featuring "a real plot, which does not get lost during the course of the entertainment." A wacky comedy about complications that arise when "society dancer" Vernon Popple and his girlfriend Violet seek permission to marry from Violet's pretentious aunt, *Nobody Home* was well-received by critics and ran for 135 performances, so Marbury and Comstock eagerly pursued more projects with Bolton and Kern (Bordman 2001, 351–2). The duo, sometimes joined by writer and lyricist Philip Bartholomae and British humorist P.G. Wodehouse, developed four more Princess musicals between 1915 and 1918: *Very Good Eddie* (1915), *Oh, Boy!* (1917), *Leave It to Jane* (1917), and *Oh, Lady! Lady!!* (1918).

Musical theater historians have long debated the groundbreaking nature of the Princess musicals as they relate to the development of the so-called "integrated musical," in which all aspects of a production—dialogue, music, lyrics, and choreography—contribute to a coherent whole. Some scholars feel that the Princess musicals were nothing short of revolutionary, while others argue that they were hardly as cohesive or fluid in their conception or execution as they seem in retrospect. Despite Kern's role as chief composer, for example, many of the shows featured interpolated songs, and in many productions, the dialogue seems stiff, forced or contrived—as if it had been taken from elsewhere and inserted at various points into the script, instead of written specifically to mesh with other aspects of the production (Kirle 2005, 17).

Regardless of just how innovative the Princess musicals were, they certainly took giant steps in the direction of the integrated musical. As they worked together, Kern and Bolton grew increasingly interested in creating shows in which songs had at least something to do with the action at hand, every line of dialogue furthered the plot, and the plots, however silly, were at the very least credible (Jones 2003, 46).

The Actors' Equity strike of 1919

As the First World War waged overseas, composers like Kern and Berlin gained footholds in the entertainment business, and the Shuberts and Syndicate battled over power, money, and control of the commercial theater, stage actors grew frustrated over their lack of agency. Especially since the creation of the Syndicate in 1896, many actors felt unappreciated and abused by managers, directors, and especially producers. As the Shubert brothers rose to power, some performers held out hope that they would be kinder and more magnanimous than the Syndicate had been. But the Shuberts turned out to be just as bad as the old guard in many cases, and in some respects even worse.

Even as the theater industry grew more structured and financially sound, its professional actors were granted a stunning lack of workplace protection. Actors had no standard contracts and were thus at the mercy of managers or producers when it came to jobs they took. Many were called in for weeks of rehearsals, or for extra performances, without compensation. Actors were frequently sent on tours for which no transportation or accommodations were provided, were expected to supply their own costumes, and could be fired or replaced without warning (Bernheim [1932] 1964, 132–3). In response to such mistreatment, a group of 112 actors formed the Actors' Equity Association in 1913.

Yet building membership, let alone becoming an official union, was no small feat. Despite heaps of abuses, many stage performers were unconvinced that such an organization was useful or necessary. Also, the American Federation of Labor, with which Equity aspired to affiliate, would only grant a single charter in each field, and the charter for performers was already held by the vaudevillians' union, the White Rats Actors International, which was not terribly welcoming or encouraging of the new group.

Nonetheless, the association grew in numbers and strength. Within a year, the Shuberts agreed to meet with Equity representatives to hammer out a contract. This was subsequently ignored, not only by the Shuberts but, in an ironic show of solidarity, by all the remaining Syndicate members. As Equity grew, the producers dug in their heels: in April 1919, Lee Shubert formed the Producing Managers' Association, or PMA, to unite producers and theater managers against the actors' union (Hirsch 1998, 112).

Tables were turned three months later when the White Rats surrendered their charter and the American Federation of Labor finally recognized Actors' Equity. The PMA promptly dug in its heels, resolving not only to refuse to recognize Equity, but also to punish its leaders. On August 7, with membership in Equity growing by the day, actors went on strike, refusing to perform in any house represented by the PMA, and swiftly shutting down twelve shows. As the strike continued, a number of established unions, including the United Scenic Artists' Local and the Theatrical Mechanics Union, sided with Equity. When, a week later, Flo Ziegfeld acknowledged that he had secretly become a member of the PMA, the *Follies* dancers, not considered actors and thus not members of Actors' Equity, hastily formed the Chorus Equity Association with support from chorus-girl-turned-star Lillian Russell, and walked off the job in solidarity.

Many of the *Follies* headliners, too, refused to go on, so the *Follies* closed during the strike. So did productions at major venues in eight other American cities, including Washington, DC, Boston, and Chicago. After nearly five weeks, during which many more shows closed, several premieres were canceled, millions of dollars were lost, and Equity's roster ballooned from barely 3,000 members to over 14,000, the producers acquiesced and gave in to most of the union's demands. Following the creation of a five-year contract, the strike was settled on September 6, 1919.[5]

While the strike resulted in progress for Broadway performers, a few of the players who opposed Equity subsequently suffered tarnished reputations. George M. Cohan, in particular, felt that actors were artists, not laborers. His disdain for the very idea of actors unionizing "blinded him to the very real need for such an action." Cohan remained resentful of Equity long after the strike was settled, and his bitterness added to his posthumous reputation as a rigid, difficult man (Kenrick 2008, 154–5).

Less obviously, the strike shed light on some ways the commercial theater had yet to change for its players. Chorus members and dancers, for example, were not invited to join Equity, which implied that work by performers in smaller or more specialized roles was unimportant. The few black performers working on Broadway, too, seem to have been summarily ignored both before and during the strike. One of the more sobering stories centered on *Follies* headliner Bert Williams who, never informed about his cast's decision to walk off the job, reported to work and got into his costume, only to find the "auditorium empty and the strike on." Years later, he recounts returning to his dressing room feeling as if he were trapped in a bad dream. "I knew nothing of it," he remembered. "I had not been told. You see, I just didn't belong" (Forbes 2008, 297). For all the strides made in the theater industry in the early twentieth century, some aspects remained stubbornly unchanged.

The Roaring Twenties

The 1920s are often referred to as "roaring" for very good reasons that have nothing to do with lions. The country, enjoying a postwar boom that helped establish it as a formidable western power, made large and important strides on sociocultural, economic, technological, and artistic fronts. At least until the stock market crash ended the decade with a resolute thud, most Americans, excluding farmers and African Americans, benefited tremendously from the nation's economic upturn. The automobile boom—which was stimulated by new technology and which, in turn, fueled the steel, petroleum, and rubber industries—set off a second industrial revolution. Skyscrapers, apartment buildings, homes, and movie palaces rose across the nation. The sound of jazz, thrilling and new, emanated from nightclubs, theaters, speakeasies, and concert halls. American women, newly granted the right to vote, joined the workforce in record numbers and, along with their male counterparts, often had more money to spend on leisure activities (Jones 2003, 52–3).

The commercial theater industry, not yet as threatened by movies or as financially strapped as it would become during the Great Depression, rose to meet new demands. For the first time in the country's history, more Americans lived in cities than in rural areas. While the theater industry experienced the slow death, beginning around the turn of the century, of touring companies that departed from New York and made various stops across the country, its growing cities saw the rebirth of stock or resident theater companies, which only grew in importance in the postwar years. These companies allowed urban centers nationwide to cultivate live entertainment for local audiences (Bernheim [1932] 1964, 94).

By 1920, New York City's population had grown to nearly eight million and was experiencing truly astonishing economic growth. The city was justified in calling itself a "factory of the new": advertising, fashion, publishing, and design had by this point risen so dramatically in international importance that it was as if "the city were inventing the idea of urbanism, and then retailing it to the rest of the country" (Traub 2005, 55).

Despite the endless in-fighting between some of its key financial players and the decline of touring productions, the commercial theater industry boomed along with its city. Through the 1920s, "Broadway" became synonymous both with Times Square and the live entertainments on offer therein. The illuminated billboards in Times Square were alluring enough to draw some of the estimated 750,000 people who passed through the neighborhood each night. Yet most visitors came to do more than gape at the brightly-lit signs: they sought dinner, drinks, nightlife, sex, and entertainment, all of which were on ample offer.

The wartime boom supported the construction of dozens of theaters, which joined the many already lining the segment of Broadway snaking through Times Square and radiating out among its side streets (Bianco 2004, 82). A dizzying diversity of genres filled the venues: new works by young playwrights like Elmer Rice, George S. Kaufman, Maxwell Anderson, and Eugene O'Neill were produced, as were revivals of older plays. Light comedies (musical and otherwise), vaudeville, cabaret, night-club acts, Shakespeare plays, domestic dramas, and a wide range of *Follies*-inspired revues— sometimes four or five in a season—could be found, too. The number of productions that ran on Broadway in any given season through the 1920s is almost impossible to grasp by contemporary standards: in the 1920–21 season alone, Broadway opened over 150 productions, and it was not uncommon for up to 200 shows to open in a season (Bernheim [1932] 1964, 208), with many musicals among them.

Then as now, theater production was a risky business. A vast majority of shows that opened each season flopped or closed at a loss, and even with the glut of shows on offer, only one or two musicals typically survived for longer than a single season. This was less of a problem, though, since production was not remotely as expensive as it has become. Through the 1920s, production costs remained low enough that shows only needed to run a few months to turn a profit; ticket prices, too, were far lower than they have become (Block 2008, 116). Ticket prices rose so slowly during the 1920s that middle- and working-class audiences could see shows comparatively frequently—if perhaps not in the orchestra on a Saturday night (when tickets cost between $4 and $6), then certainly from the mezzanine on a weeknight or during a matinee at a more affordable 50 cents (Jones 2003, 60). The sheer number of shows, as well as their relative affordability, meant that during the 1920s there was something on offer for everyone.

Shuffle Along

Of course, the term "everyone" needs to be contextualized. From inception, Broadway was primarily interested in appealing to—and thus depicting, or at least reflecting the interests and concerns of—the country's white, mainstream middle class. Nevertheless, at various points in its growth and development, the American musical has reflected more diversification in content and appeal than it has at others. In the 1920s, for example, Broadway showed such renewed interest in all-black musicals that the decade has been referred to as a golden age for the subgenre (Woll 1989, 248).

Cynically speaking, producers would not have been so enthusiastic about all-black productions had one not become a huge, runaway hit at the start of the decade. Yet while the all-black productions staged on Broadway during the 1920s hardly managed to shatter every stereotype or bring true equality to audiences and performers, they helped change the Broadway landscape in significant, lasting ways. *Shuffle Along*, the surprise smash that inspired many all-black musicals to follow it, was a landmark production that simultaneously served as yet another reminder of just how hard it was for black artists to gain a toehold in predominantly white entertainment realms.

Shuffle Along was the result of a lengthy collaboration between four men: the lead performers and book writers Flournoy Miller (1885–1971) and Aubrey Lyles (1884–1932), and the composer-lyricist team James Hubert "Eubie" Blake (1887–1983) and Noble Sissle (1889–1975). Tennessee natives Miller and Lyles began performing together as students at Fisk University, and between 1905 and 1909 were based in Chicago, where they performed at the African American owned and operated Pekin Stock Company. While there, they honed an act that employed rapid-fire malapropisms and intense physical comedy, and that made fun of smalltown Southern life. While with Pekin, they developed the characters Steven Jenkins (Miller) and Sam Peck (Lyles), who eventually became two main characters in *Shuffle Along*.[6]

During his childhood in Indianapolis, Noble Sissle sang in church choirs and his high school glee club. He attended college for a few years, but left to join James Reese Europe's Society Orchestra in 1916. The year prior, he met Blake, a Baltimore native who had been playing piano professionally since adolescence, at a party. The two decided to write songs together.[7] Their partnership was almost immediately successful: their first song, "It's All Your Fault," was quickly incorporated into Sophie Tucker's vaudeville act. After the war, which Sissle spent overseas touring with Europe's orchestra, he and Blake developed their own vaudeville act, whereupon they were approached by Miller and Lyles, who asked them to collaborate on a musical comedy (Woll 1989, 61).

As Blake remembered it, at the time, "there was no money to be had for the production of black shows" (King 1973, 151). Despite the success Williams and Walker had had on Broadway at the turn of the century, contemporary Broadway producers remained stubbornly and erroneously convinced that white audiences would not support shows featuring all-black casts. Nevertheless, Miller and Lyles's agent eventually arranged a meeting with the producer John Cort.

As luck would have it, Cort had recently seen the comedians perform as Jenkins and Peck in *Darkydom*, a revue that had run in Harlem at the Lafayette Theater in 1915. Despite his misgivings, Cort was, by the time he met Miller and Lyles, enough of a fan that he agreed to back their new production, *Shuffle Along*, once it returned to New York after a national tour. Cort booked the show into the 63rd Street Theater, which he had recently secured and had yet to fill (Sotiropoulos 2006, 233).

Shuffle Along's tour probably did not make Cort feel any surer about his investment. The musical's company traveled through Washington, DC, Philadelphia, and New Jersey on a shoestring budget worn so thin that the production quickly fell deep into debt (Bordman 2001, 407). Things did not seem like they would improve much once the musical got back to New York and the *Shuffle Along* company readied itself for its big opening on 63rd Street. Cort was unwilling to invest much in the production, so scenery and props were scant, and costumes were purchased on the cheap from a show that had recently flopped. The venue itself, too, had serious shortcomings. Designed for public lectures, it had a shallow stage that was poorly suited for a big musical (Woll 1989, 62). While technically a Broadway house, it was also so far north of Times Square that it did not benefit from the foot traffic that served the other theaters. These are likely reasons Cort was willing to consider booking an all-black show into the house in the first place.

Shuffle Along opened to an invite-only crowd on May 22, 1921, and to the public on the following night. Some reviews of the musical were, if positive, primarily reflective of the pervasive racism of the time. The critic for *The New York Times*, for example, griped that *Shuffle Along* was disappointing because it was not "conspicuously native" and because it was so "crude—in writing, playing, and direction" as to make the production most comparable to "a fair-to-middling amateur entertainment" ("*Shuffle Along* Premiere" 1921, 20). But other reviews were more effusive, and *Shuffle Along* benefited as well from especially enthusiastic word of mouth.

The book of *Shuffle Along* was hardly a giant step in the direction toward the integrated musical. Like most musical comedies of its time, it was more a mélange that undermined "the already slim divide between musical comedy and vaudeville" (Savran 2009, 73). A razor-thin plot followed two grocers, Jenkins and Peck, who each run for mayor of their small, southern town, Jimtown. They agree that whoever wins the election will appoint the loser his Chief of Police. Jenkins wins dishonestly, but he and Peck disagree on trivial matters that build into one of Miller and Lyles's signature stage fights.

Meanwhile, an honest candidate, Harry Walton, steps in. Walton is eager to put an end to the corrupt ways of Jenkins and Peck; also, his girl, Jessie, has a wealthy father who will not allow the couple to marry unless Harry proves himself worthy. As was typical of the time, the plot of *Shuffle Along* was regularly interrupted so various players could perform pre-existing routines, none of which had anything to do with the through-line. In the second act, for example, the action stopped so Sissle and Blake could perform a short concert derived from their vaudeville act (Woll 1989, 65–9). In both structure and execution, then, *Shuffle Along* owed much to vaudeville and to the pioneering productions of Williams and Walker.

The score, however, was a major departure from what had, to this point, functioned as standard Broadway fare. Heralded as one of the most thrilling and innovative scores of the 1920s, *Shuffle Along* was composed entirely by Blake, with lyrics by Sissle. While they were the sole contributors, their approach to building the score hearkened ironically back to the days when songs were interpolated into pre-existing scripts. When they were approached to score *Shuffle Along*, they went through old songs "that no one had wanted to publish and that we had really originally written for vaudeville," and worked them, one by one, into the show (King 1973, 151–2).

The score might have been derived in a way that was rapidly becoming old fashioned, but there was nothing outdated about the songs, which ran the gamut stylistically from blues, ragtime, barbershop, and jazz to operetta-style ballad. The freshness and variety of the score so impressed audiences that Blake remembers overhearing spectators buzzing about it during the first intermission. "The proudest day of my life was when *Shuffle Along* opened," he would say later. All "those white people kept saying: 'I would like to touch him, the man who wrote the music.' Well, you got to feel that. It made me feel like, well, at last I'm a human being" (Jones 2003, 69).

Shuffle Along became a monster hit that ran for 504 performances at the 63rd Street Theater, which Cort suddenly found the money to renovate in order to better accommodate the large cast. The musical went on a second national tour, raking in almost $8 million and spawning countless imitations through the remainder of the decade. It made such an impact that it is often mistakenly cited as the first all-black musical to run on Broadway. It jumpstarted the careers of Sissle, Blake, Miller, and Lyles, as well as many other members of its original and replacement casts, including such luminaries as Lottie Gee, Gertrude Saunders, Ina Duncan, Florence Mills, Paul Robeson, Adelaide Hall, and Josephine Baker (Woll 1989, 74). *Shuffle Along* was the first Broadway musical to feature a love song, "Love Will Find a Way," that was performed genuinely and tenderly—not just for crude comic effect—by two people of color. Yet perhaps one of the most profound, lasting impacts *Shuffle Along* had on Broadway took place not on the narrow (if eventually widened) stage, but in the house itself.

As it was all over Broadway, the audience for *Shuffle Along* was overwhelmingly white; historians estimate that at most performances, the racial mix was approximately 90 percent white and 10 percent black. This might seem like an enormous discrepancy, but considering the fact that nearly a century later, about 80 percent of all Broadway audiences are white, the breakdown at *Shuffle Along* was more noteworthy than it might initially seem.[8] James Weldon Johnson noted in *Black Manhattan* that many black spectators "flocked to the Sixty-third Street Theatre to hear the most joyous singing and see the most exhilarating dancing to be found on any stage in the city" (Johnson 1991, 186).

While the house at the 63rd Street Theater was far from equally mixed, it was nevertheless the first Broadway venue to desegregate audiences. When *Shuffle Along* opened, a few critics described something that clearly struck them as noteworthy: black patrons sitting in orchestra seats "as far front as the fifth row." Of course, no one production can single-handedly erase a generation of segregation: long after *Shuffle Along*, the balconies of Broadway, known collectively and derisively as "nigger heaven," remained the go-to section for many black spectators, whether due to habit or affordability (Woll 1989, 72). And through the run of *Shuffle Along*, the seats at the 63rd Street Theater were never fully desegregated. Rather, two-thirds of the orchestra seats were always reserved for white patrons. Nevertheless, *Shuffle Along* seems to have been the first Broadway production at which black patrons were seated on the same level and at the same distance from the stage as their white counterparts (Sotiropolous 2006, 234).

The monumental commercial success of *Shuffle Along* resulted in a decade-long surge of all-black musicals on Broadway. Yet while the success of *Shuffle Along* led to a number of important improvements, it was also in some respects seriously constraining. Through the 1920s, *Shuffle Along* became a blueprint of sorts, from which no black production could easily depart. If a show strayed too far from what *Shuffle Along* had inadvertently cemented as a formula for black musicals, white critics would attack it for trying too hard to "aspire" to white productions (Woll 1989, 78). And as all-black shows were increasingly co-opted by white producers and creative teams eager to capitalize on the trend, blacks were denied control of their own images onstage. Producers of all-black shows—such as the vaudevillian-turned impresario Lew Leslie, whose *Blackbirds* revues appeared regularly on Broadway—denied performers their agency, and thus tamped the possibility of a black theater truly by, about, and for black spectators.

As Cort did before *Shuffle Along* became a hit, white producers frequently cried poverty when it came to budgeting black productions, which continued to be booked into the worst theaters and granted comparatively meager budgets and salaries. On some occasions, producers or creative teams even stole promising material from black companies for use in white shows. Producer George White, for example, claimed to hate a new dance number Miller and Lyles featured in *Runnin' Wild* (1923), their follow-up to *Shuffle Along*. White complained vociferously about the number and even brought friends to rehearsals to try to convince the duo that they had to cut the dance from their revue. They refused, White relented, and the number—the Charleston—moved beyond black circles to become a defining dance of the roaring twenties once it hit Broadway. Only much later did Miller and Lyles learn that White was trying to cut the number so he could use it in *Scandals,* his whiter, more established Broadway revue series (ibid., 89–90).

For the continued disparities, the increased popularity of black musicals in the 1920s took Broadway a few steps away from its most overtly racist practices. The all-black musical craze resulted in unprecedented opportunities for black performers, contributed to the desegregation of performing companies and audiences, and added to the diversity of the developing musical genre. It shattered the assumption that white audiences would not embrace black shows and contributed, at the very least, to a gradual move away from some of the vilest of minstrel-derived stereotypes.

Show Boat

Jerome Kern and Oscar Hammerstein II's *Show Boat* was an enormously influential production, the likes of which were unique to Broadway at the time of its premiere on December 27, 1927. With *Show Boat,* Hammerstein and Kern attempted to move the musical comedy beyond its contemporary boundaries by infusing it with more realistic characters and social issues, and by marrying its score and plot more closely to one another than previous musicals had. While certainly deserving of its landmark status, *Show Boat* was also a product of its time and place: it could not have materialized from nowhere, just as its existence did not singlehandedly change the course of the American stage musical.

Show Boat was influenced by many genres and productions, and by cultural and industrial shifts that had taken place long before its run of 572 performances at the Ziegfeld Theater, the glorious new venue that the impresario built with help from William Randolph Hearst on 64th Street at Sixth Avenue. Absent blackface minstrelsy and vaudeville, the rise of ASCAP, the current popularity of all-black musicals, and the philosophies that Kern and Hammerstein brought to the table when they began their collaboration, there would never have been a *Show Boat.*

Based on Edna Ferber's sweeping 1926 novel about three generations of performers traveling up and down the Mississippi river on a riverboat named the *Cotton Blossom*, *Show Boat* is a musical about race relations in the US and about "theater and performance itself" (Hoffman 2014, 32). The plot follows its characters from the 1880s through the 1920s. The owners of the riverboat are Cap'n Andy Hawks and his wife, Parthy Ann; its performers include Steve Baker and his wife, the sultry singer Julie LaVerne; the staff includes Queenie the cook and her husband Joe, a dock worker.

The first act takes place while the *Cotton Blossom* is docked in Natchez, Mississippi. The Hawks's eighteen-year-old daughter, Magnolia, meets and quickly falls in love with Gaylord Ravenal, a local gambler with a heart of gold and an inability to quit his lowdown ways. Later in the act, the town sheriff interrupts the riverboat troupe during rehearsal to inform them that the show cannot go on because two of the company members are guilty of miscegenation. When it is revealed that Julie is biracial and has been passing for white, Steve cuts her finger, drinks her blood and proclaims himself biracial, too. Yet the couple ultimately agree to leave the boat quietly. By the end of the act, Magnolia and Gaylord marry.

The second act opens in 1893 in Chicago, in time for the World's Fair. Gaylord, Magnolia, and their daughter Kim have left the *Cotton Blossom* and are living off Gaylord's winnings. But when Gaylord falls into debt, he abandons his family. Desperate to make ends meet after he leaves, Magnolia auditions at the Trocadero, a music hall whose proprietor is looking to replace his unreliable, alcoholic nightclub singer. This turns out to be Julie, who overhears Magnolia's audition and sneaks away, sacrificing herself to help her old friend. Magnolia becomes a star, as does Kim. At the end of the musical, Julie retires and returns with Kim to the *Cotton Blossom*, where they reconcile with Gaylord. The reunited family joins the rest of the characters, all older and presumably wiser, on the deck of the boat. Only Julie is missing from the reunion.

The stage adaptation of *Show Boat* was somewhat more upbeat than the book: Ferber killed off many of the characters that Hammerstein and Kern kept alive for the finale, and Julie's later life on the streets as a prostitute goes unmentioned in their version. Nevertheless, with its themes of alcoholism, gambling addiction, abandonment, and racism, *Show Boat* hardly fit its original billing as "An All-American Musical Comedy" (Stempel 2010, 195). It was more akin to a musical play: a piece with a relatively serious story about people experiencing real problems, "set to music neither as clipped as typical musical comedy writing nor as fully arioso as operetta" (Bordman 2001, 485).

Like Kern, Hammerstein was interested in developing a musical that might "attain the heights of grand opera and still keep sufficiently human to be entertaining" (quoted in Bordman 2001, 193). The grandson and namesake of the pioneering theater impresario and erstwhile Syndicate foe, Oscar Hammerstein II, was discouraged from pursuing a career in theater by his family. Nevertheless, he dropped out of Columbia Law School in 1917 to pursue work as a lyricist and book-writer. After apprenticing with lyricist and librettist Otto Harbach, who felt strongly that lyrics should relate to the show in question, Hammerstein began working with established theater composers, including Kern, with whom he collaborated on the successful Cinderella musical *Sunny* in 1925 (Stempel 2010, 193).[9]

Kern was reputed to be curmudgeonly and difficult to work with, but he and Hammerstein got along well, perhaps because of their shared desire to create musicals in which song and dialogue contributed seamlessly to plot and character development. With *Show Boat*, the men worked to streamline and simplify Ferber's complex plot, and to infuse their adaptation with music and lyrics that were appropriate for the characters and plot points. Because of this, and to the fact that *Show Boat* spans some four decades, the score is notably varied in its influences. Songs reference distinct periods, and borrow from styles including operetta, spirituals, blues, coon songs, sentimental ballads, parlor songs, and jazz (Savran 2009, 89–90).

The score featured a few interpolations, but these too were justified in terms of plot and character. The song "Bill," sung by Julie in the nightclub, had been written by Kern and Wodehouse for the 1918 Princess musical *Oh, Lady! Lady!!*, from which it was cut. In Act II, which takes place at the end of the nineteenth century, Magnolia appears at the same nightclub and sings "After the Ball," the hit waltz by Charles K. Harris that was written and interpolated into *A Trip to Chinatown* in 1891. Similarly, the performers on the boat each had specialty acts featured at various points during the original production (Kirle 2005, 37–8). This use of specialty acts referenced the waning days of vaudeville, and would likely have appealed to Ziegfeld, the master of the revue and *Show Boat*'s producer (Decker 2013, 49).

Many of *Show Boat*'s characters exhibit behaviors or experience situations that are weightier than was typical of Broadway musicals at the time, but the sociocultural issue the musical brings most consistently to the forefront is contemporary race relations. Even the very name of the titular showboat reflects the separate, unequal lives of American blacks and whites in the late nineteenth and early twentieth centuries, especially in the American south. For affluent whites who patronize it, the *Cotton Blossom* signifies leisure, gentility, entertainment, and the natural beauty of the Southland. For the blacks performing menial jobs on the boat, in the fields, and on docks along the shores of the Mississippi, the boat's name symbolizes a history of enslavement, forced labor, and subjugation.

Musically, Kern's score and Hammerstein's lyrics attempt similarly layered statements about the characters and their situations. The score seems to imply, through its diversity and blending of styles, that racial equality is both possible and positive. In many cases, the musical's songs reveal information about the characters singing them; at times they even anticipate character traits or plot points disclosed later in the show.

A perfect example is "Can't Help Lovin' Dat Man," which blends Tin Pan Alley and the blues, and is written in dialect, much like a coon song would have been a generation prior (Knapp 2006, 192). Yet the number manages to turn the very idea of the coon song on its head. Rather than a song written and performed to demean blacks, "Can't Help Lovin' Dat Man" is sung in Act I by Julie to Magnolia, after Magnolia confesses her blooming love for Gaylord. Queenie, who overhears the number, immediately questions how Julie—whose mixed-race background is at this point still a carefully guarded secret—would have ever heard the song, which, she notes, is only known by blacks. Audiences soon learn of Julie's secret, but with this number, her background is implied. Meanwhile, the song allows Julie, Queenie, and Magnolia to sing happily together, bonding over the complicated love they feel for their respective men.

"Ol' Man River" functions similarly. On its surface a song with lyrics that grossly exaggerate "black speech patterns to ridicule the mentality of the 'coon,'" Joe's number instead launches almost immediately into lyrics describing cruel indifference to the plight of African Americans in the early twentieth century:

Dere's an ol' man called de Mississippi
Dat's the ol' man dat I'd like to be!
What does he care if de world's got troubles?
What does he care if de land ain't free?

He don' plant taters
He don' plant cotton
An' dem dat plants 'em
Is soon forgotten
But ol' man river
He jes keeps rollin' along

In the culminating stanza, Joe's lyrics move beyond the plight of American blacks to neatly encompass the human condition in a few blunt lines:

I gets weary
And sick of tryin'
I'm tired of livin'
And scared of dyin'
But ol' man river
He just keeps rollin' along

Rather than mocking blacks, then, "Ol' Man River" anchors *Show Boat*, and is often hailed as one of the most powerful, effective numbers in the history of the American stage musical. The song works musically and lyrically to remind audiences of "the confinement of the character within his culture," and simultaneously his "almost infinite comprehension" of humanity and the workings of the world (Mast 1987, 59–60).

While its creators' aim was to elevate the musical form by giving its characters new weight and dimension, *Show Boat* has nonetheless been read as demeaning to its black characters. Unlike their white counterparts, such criticism goes, the black characters—Queenie and Joe in particular—"show no character development over the course of the three-hour musical," and serve primarily as "background servants who help the white characters achieve all they can in the decades-spanning work." *Show Boat* was, of course, created by white men who, however well-meaning, nevertheless reflected the sociocultural tenor of the 1920s. In this respect, *Show Boat* remains very much a musical of its time, despite countless revisions and as many revivals, not to mention concert and film versions. Its depictions and unwieldiness in plot and presentation make revivals of the show problematic. Nevertheless, for its time *Show Boat* "raised the bar for what the musical could be and the stories it could tell" through both dialogue and song (Hoffman 2014, 31–2).

Despite its success and impact, *Show Boat* remained something of an anomaly after its run. The musical was revived on Broadway, staged in London, and remade as a film long before it made any lasting impact on the musical theater as a genre. Through the late 1920s, musicals continued largely as they had been before *Show Boat* came along, and there were few attempts to emulate the high-minded, integrated model so successfully demonstrated by Kern and Hammerstein. This points in part to the fact that with *Show Boat*, Kern and Hammerstein had devised a style of entertainment—the integrated musical—that had yet to set any kind of standard for others to emulate. Yet it also points to bigger, more sweeping changes looming on the horizon. Just two years after *Show Boat* triumphed on Broadway, the commercial theater industry and the country nurturing it would be suddenly, unexpectedly transformed.

CHAPTER 4
THE GREAT DEPRESSION TO
THE SECOND WORLD WAR

As you probably know if you paid even the scantest attention in history class, the roaring twenties ended just a tad more resolutely than most decades do. In summer 1929, domestic spending in the US slowed, and with it the production of goods. Despite the minor recession that resulted, stock prices continued to rise precipitously ... until the bubble burst. On October 26, 1929, subsequently known as Black Thursday, investors dumped nearly thirteen million shares of stock that had begun plummeting in value, effectively erasing $10 billion by mid-morning. The banks scrambled to maintain calm, but on October 29—another Black day, this one a Tuesday— an additional sixteen million shares of stock at some $14 billion were dumped (Klein 1992, 575). The comfortable, freewheeling 1920s were very suddenly a memory. The Great Depression had begun.

Despite President Herbert Hoover's initial optimism, and upbeat forecasts by specialists who insisted the country would recover quickly, the Great Depression lasted over a decade. As the 1930s began, Americans remained wary of the stock market and tightened their belts. Industry slowed significantly and unemployment skyrocketed. By 1933, somewhere between 13 and 15 million Americans were out of work, and almost half the country's banks had failed.[1] Franklin Delano Roosevelt assumed the presidency in 1933 and the New Deal, his series of government-supported domestic projects and job-creating programs, helped stimulate the nation's economy. But the Depression colored the 1930s, lifting only once the United States entered the Second World War in December 1941.

Popular imagination looks back on the Great Depression as an era during which all Americans were abruptly plunged into a wretched, hardscrabble subsistence economy: one long, gray breadline peopled by desperate, gray citizens. The statistics were certainly dramatic, and millions suffered mightily through the 1930s in search of food, steady work, and shelter. This was especially the case for people who were already poor and disenfranchised, as well as for Americans who were adversely affected by the Dust Bowl, which hit the American prairie like some sort of cruel joke midway through the decade.

There were, however, also millions of Americans who made it through the era without an overabundance of hardship. Many citizens held onto their jobs (if sometimes at reduced salaries), or benefited from the Works Progress Administration and other New Deal agencies. Even in the worst of times, many remained able to feed their families, meet rent or mortgage payments, and even afford the occasional travel or leisure outing (Jones 2003, 80). After all, if consumer spending had ground to a halt in the US during the Great Depression, mass entertainment would have died along with it.

Instead, as often occurs in times of crisis, American popular entertainment flourished through the darkest days of the Great Depression. Hollywood grew stronger through the 1930s as Americans searched for affordable ways to forget their troubles. And while it took an enormous financial hit from which it had to struggle mightily to recover, the American commercial theater survived, too, growing less financially and artistically frivolous in the process. As its citizenry suffered through the era, America's commercial entertainments not only reflected the times but helped the country through them.

The fact that the Broadway musical entered what is largely considered its golden age in the 1930s is especially noteworthy under the circumstances: the theater industry was forced to constrict significantly at the onset of the Depression and was simultaneously thrown into new competition with a younger, cheaper, more easily replicated entertainment form. After well over a century of being the only option available, live entertainment was given a run for its money, just at a time when money was scarce.

Moving pictures were hardly new in the 1930s. Photographers had been experimenting with ways to capture motion and project images since at least the late nineteenth century. Movie houses had begun to dot the landscape in the early years of the twentieth century, and the first of several movie palaces in Times Square were operational by 1910. By the teens, as the popularity of touring theater companies dropped, many live venues across the country became movie palaces. Long before the Depression, then, the film industry had begun to lure away audiences from live events. In 1910, there were 1,549 venues for legitimate theater nationwide; by 1925, there were just 674 (Traub 2005, 84).

Yet while movies had become more sophisticated and popular through the 1920s, live venues were better able to compete with movie houses before

1927, when the landmark film *The Jazz Singer* ushered in the age of the "talkie." During the vaudeville era, films were simply incorporated into the daily bill. At many vaudeville houses, managers projected movie shorts at various points over the course of each day. Doing so allowed live performers to take breaks during their grueling performance schedules, and also allowed customers to indulge in the new style of entertainment.

Yet once "talkies" were introduced, attendance at the movies nearly doubled, from 60 million a week in 1927 to 110 million a week by 1929. After the stock market crashed, the commercial theater became almost completely unable to compete with the economics of film. Theater was, after all, collectively handcrafted, live, and typically expensive to create and to patronize. By comparison, "hundreds, even thousands, of copies of a movie could be made at incremental cost," which made films easily copied and distributed, and far cheaper to attend (Bianco 2004, 89). Inexpensive, accessible, and easily mass produced as they were, motion pictures quickly became the perfect go-to entertainment during the 1930s.

For all intents and purposes, then, the stock market crash could easily have been a nail in the coffin for commercial theater. Certainly, the Depression forced the theater industry to constrict significantly following its boom through the previous decade. But the newly level playing field—which involved fewer venues, creative teams, performers, and projects—resulted in productions that were often more carefully considered and developed than many of the comparatively frivolous, hastily-drawn productions of the 1920s.

Business on Broadway in troubling times

The Great Depression did not affect the theater as immediately as it did other industries, but in time it steamrolled many of Broadway's most powerful and influential players. Experienced impresarios and producers of some of the most lavish revues and spectacles lost millions when the stock market crashed. Some fell harder, faster, and more obviously than others: Charles Dillingham, a seasoned producer of extravaganzas, melodramas, musical comedies, and elaborate revues staged at the monstrous 5,300-seat Hippodrome on Sixth Avenue between West 43rd and 44th streets was so destitute by the time he died in 1934 that the Shuberts covered his funeral expenses (Hirsch 1998, 163).[2] Others were not totally ruined but still faced significant losses. Lore has it that Flo Ziegfeld was in court fighting over a marquee sign when the market crashed, depleting most of his fortune in minutes. He continued to spend lavishly, nonetheless; after his death from pleurisy in 1932, his second wife, Billie Burke, was left to settle his million-dollar debt (Jones 2003, 82).

Perhaps no industry men put on a better show of moneyed resilience than the Shuberts, who relied a bit too heavily on their sizable pre-crash nest-egg in the earliest years of the Depression. Through 1931, they continued to fill their many theaters with the same kinds of extravagant productions they had offered through the 1920s, even as the rest of the industry scaled back. The Shuberts made a point of bailing out (and in the case of Dillingham, burying) their colleagues, frequently and showily lending money they probably should have safeguarded to theater owners like the Selwyn brothers and producers like the thirty-year veteran Albert H. Woods.

Their grandstanding caught up with them when their company was placed in receivership in 1931. Despite drastic cuts to their staff and attempts to keep their business afloat with personal funds, a court-ordered liquidation of their company was ordered in 1933. Lee Shubert showed up at the bankruptcy sale and bought his own business, which he renamed the Select Theaters Corporation, for $400,000. The bankruptcy diluted the stronghold the Shuberts had wrested from the Syndicate, but it also allowed them to save the family business and to remain in control of many of their theaters, both in New York and across the country (Hirsch 1998, 163–7).

The theater industry's money problems caused the number of shows typically produced on Broadway to drop off considerably, and permanently. As noted, it was not uncommon through the 1920s to see well over 100 shows open in a single season. The present standard is more to the tune of around forty productions, with the number of musicals each season usually somewhere in the high teens. This precipitous decline began during the Great Depression.[3]

None of this happened overnight. The 1929–30 season was hardly abysmal. More than 100 productions opened through the summer of 1930, and the decline in musicals from the season prior—34, down from 42—was hardly worth panicking over, especially considering the financial struggles many other industries were experiencing at the time. At least in terms of statistics, Broadway was still thriving when the Great Depression first took hold.[4]

Yet soon, both the numbers and kinds of entertainments on offer in Times Square began to reflect the times. Commercial productions remained plentiful on Broadway through the decade, but as the Depression set in, they shrank in budget and size. Musicals took an especially significant hit. Book musicals dropped dramatically, hitting an all-time low of just thirteen by the 1933–34 season. Revivals, not included in this number, did not fare terribly well either: there were only about a dozen in that season (Bordman 2001, 534). In general, the offerings on Broadway through the early 1930s tended to be smaller, less extravagant, and weightier thematically, in keeping with the tenor of the times.

Of course, producers were not offering smaller, darker shows to a bruised populace by choice. Times Square has always relied on cash flow to survive. As audiences declined, producers had to pull back accordingly, and the theater industry was forced to downsize. In turn, many of the neighborhood's live entertainment venues—which no one could afford to maintain, raze, or redevelop—were sold or leased to entrepreneurs eager to capitalize on the economic downturn by providing cheaper forms of entertainment.

The small, narrow theater venues lining 42nd Street were poorly suited as movie houses, so many were converted into other kinds of cheap attractions: dance halls, penny arcades, freak shows, flea circuses (Traub 2005, 86–7). Vaudeville, already on the decline due to Ziegfeld, film, and radio, met its end in the Depression. In 1930, Keith and Albee's flagship vaudeville house, the beloved Palace Theatre, was wired for sound and repurposed as a movie house. The Palace joined a number of other large, new movie theaters in Times Square—the Paramount, the Roxy, the Strand, and the Rivoli— most of which incorporated the kinds of elaborate live shows before and after movie screenings that the legitimate Broadway houses once had the money and space to mount. Stars contracted by increasingly powerful Hollywood studios played in these new movie palaces through the decade. While their presence—along with chorus girls, dancers, comedians, and orchestras—preserved the live component of Times Square, it did little to benefit the remaining legitimate theaters, or the industry in general (ibid., 104).

Like vaudeville, burlesque had been on the decline prior to the onset of the Depression. Increasingly viewed by the middle classes as a crass, lowbrow form of entertainment, burlesque had long been relegated to sleazier joints well beyond the bright lights of Broadway. But the stock market crash allowed the burlesque industry to take a last stab at middle-class respectability, by securing spaces in Times Square that the legitimate theater had been forced to abandon.

At this point, in an effort to stay viable amid an increasing number of competing entertainment forms, burlesque had introduced the "hoochie-coochie" dance, the runway, and the striptease. The Minsky brothers—Abe (1880–1949), Billy (1887–1932), Herbert (1881–1959), and Morton (1902–87)—who ran some of the best-known burlesque houses in the city (none of which were renowned for their class or good taste), took control of Oscar Hammerstein's gorgeous old Republic Theater in 1931 once they learned that its owner, Hammerstein's son Arthur, was struggling financially. Other burlesque outfits followed suit, quickly filling Times Square venues that Broadway producers could no longer afford. The burlesque industry thus enjoyed one last attempt at the mainstream—if not at mainstream respectability—before social reformers, Times Square property owners, and the city government drove it out of town in the early 1940s (Wollman 2013, 16).

In general, Times Square responded to the Great Depression by giving more of the city's people a wider variety of cheaper entertainments. This kept the neighborhood alive and thriving through the Depression, but also caused it to grow distanced from the middle- and upper-class audiences the commercial theater industry had actively cultivated and catered to in the first place. The legitimate theater, however diminished, survived the times. Yet the neighborhood surrounding it continued to decline in mainstream appeal and reputation through much of the rest of the twentieth century.

Broadway musicals: Boom and bust

Through the Depression years, the Broadway musical experienced what seems at first glance to be a number of contradictions. First, while the theater industry struggled to survive, the musical as a genre flourished. Second, while many of the stage musical's most talented and dedicated creators hightailed it to Hollywood following the drop-off of regular work in New York, Broadway still managed to offer some of the most meaningful, lasting musicals to date. Additional contradictions seemed to affect the neighborhood that housed the theater industry: Times Square began its decline at the same time that Hollywood films began to represent it as a magnificent, magical place where even the lowliest Broadway baby could rise to stardom with drive, talent, pep, and gumption.

Yet the state of the Broadway musical through the 1930s was not as paradoxical as it first seems. With limited finances and fewer projects to back, producers were compelled to more carefully consider the shows they *did* choose to nurture and mount. Rushing multiple frivolous productions to the stage made good business sense when shows could run for only a few months and still recoup, but those days were over.

Further, once many spectators began looking to films for entertainment in the 1930s, Broadway was left largely to its own devices. This loss of status as a "proving ground for national culture" resulted in smaller audiences, but also ones who were dedicated and necessarily moneyed. In a class divide that remains persistent to date, film became the country's most accessible mass entertainment form, while theater was, if newly financially hindered, also newly free to look far and wide for engaging, penetrating, relevant subject matter—at higher ticket prices (Traub 2005, 92).

It did not hurt the aesthetic growth of the musical that the early 1930s saw a perceived strengthening of critical standards among theater journalists, after which stage musicals "were suddenly deprived of the easygoing, favored treatment they had so long received." Whether the newly stringent criticism was the result of journalists' concerns about their readership's tightened entertainment budgets, or borne of a shared conviction that they had to be more critical to keep their jobs, is anyone's guess. But for whatever reason, theater critics' tolerance for light, mildly entertaining fluff seemed to vanish along with a healthy, secure stock market (Bordman 2001, 511).

The theater critics, of course, were not alone. During the Great Depression, the mood in the US darkened considerably. A looming sense of frugality and collective struggle had a hand in influencing the kinds of shows produced on Broadway. Gone were the casts of thousands, the sequined costumes, elaborate scenery, and endless set changes. No one on Broadway had the money anymore, and anyway, Hollywood was suddenly capable of creating the kinds of enormous, elaborate spectacles—filmed at myriad angles and enhanced with all sorts of camera tricks, no less—that Broadway had had on offer through the 1920s. It is no accident, for example, that Busby Berkeley (1895–1976), the film director and choreographer known for kaleidoscopic dance extravaganzas with huge casts of dancing girls, left Broadway for Hollywood in 1930. Once there, he directed and choreographed many film musicals about the magic and appeal of Broadway, most of which featured elaborate numbers performed by enormous casts that Broadway directors could suddenly only dream about.

Berkeley was not alone in ceding to Hollywood's charms. Many people in show business went west out of necessity. By 1931, an estimated two-thirds of Manhattan's playhouses had ceased to function as theater venues. By 1932, about 2,200 New York actors had registered with various Hollywood casting agencies. Broadway composers and lyricists including Jerome Kern, Buddy DeSylva, Richard Rodgers and Lorenz Hart, George and Ira Gershwin, Irving Berlin, Vincent Youmans, and Cole Porter looked to Hollywood for bigger audiences and better pay (Jones 2003, 83). But ultimately, very few Broadway people permanently abandoned the stage for the screen. As they had in the vaudeville days and still do at present, performers and behind-the-scenes practitioners took whatever work they could find in whatever medium came calling. While less powerful than it had been even in very recent memory, Broadway lured its artists home when it could afford to. And many of its artists came back, having never planned to stay away for too long in the first place.

The show must go on: Depression-Era revues

The Depression precipitated the demise of a number of popular, serialized revues, most of which were known for spectacle and glamour: *Earl Carroll's Vanities*, *George White's Scandals*, and Ziegfeld's *Follies* were, through the early 1930s, scaled down, mounted less frequently, or discontinued. Yet the revue format remained viable through the era. Revues have a loose, endlessly variable structure: simply decide upon a connective theme and fill the evening out with related songs, sketches, and dance numbers, any of which can be reworked, replaced, recast, or reordered, even on short notice. With a new eye toward moderation, 1930s producers found that while the glitzy costumes, enormous casts, and elaborate sets had to go, revues themselves could be produced on a shoestring and still appeal to crowds.

Because they were received with enormous inconsistency by audiences and theater critics through the 1920s, and because of persistent racism, all-black Broadway revues had an unshakable reputation among producers for being uncertain investments in economic boom times. Yet during the bust, all-black musicals and revues surged: there were six in the 1930–31 season and five in 1931–32. The number of all-black offerings had not been so high on Broadway since the post-*Shuffle Along* craze in the early 1920s (Woll 1989, 135–6).

The resurgence of shows with all-black casts was due both to economic reasoning and the social imbalance that had long existed on Broadway. With the exception of the biggest and most established stars, most black artists active in the 1930s received less pay than their white counterparts. Whether cast with black or white performers, revues did not require as much rehearsal as plotted shows. Instead, producers could open their scaled-down revues quickly and, in some cases, even before they had been sufficiently rehearsed. Or they could try them out in nearby lounges, nightclubs, or restaurants to determine whether it was financially prudent to move them to Broadway. Although short runs were less preferable than steady, long-term work for performers, the preponderance of all-black productions did allow for black talent to remain active on Broadway at a time when employement was especially tenuous (Jones 2003, 84).

Notable for their quantity, the all-black offerings that cropped up on Broadway in the 1930s have not been remembered for their quality. This is not for lack of talent, which was newly emphasized in lieu of expensive stagecraft and spectacular costumes. But revues such as Lew Leslie's *Blackbirds of 1930, Rhapsody in Black* (1931), *Fast and Furious* (1931), *Blackberries of 1932*, and *Yeah Man* (1932) remained most strongly influenced by *Shuffle Along*, both in terms of subject matter and presentation. As such, they did not offer audiences anything especially innovative. Easy and cheap to mount though they were, most were not big commercial successes.[5]

Broadway saw its fair share of all-white and mixed-cast revues in the early 1930s, as well. As with the all-black revues, these tended to be smaller and more focused on talent than spectacle. The ones that resonated most with audiences struck a careful balance between topicality and escapism. Many spectators, it seemed, were newly turned off by the lavishness and excess that had been the style during the 1920s. At the same time, however, audiences still craved light diversions that did not constantly remind them of the economy.

A noteworthy flop on this front was the 1932 revue *Americana*. Produced by Lee Shubert and staged in the theater that still bears his name, *Americana* featured music by composers including Jay Gorney (1894–1990), Harold Arlen (1905–86), and Herman Hupfield (1894–1951), with lyrics by E.Y. "Yip" Harburg (1896–1981), later the lyricist for the classic film *The Wizard of Oz*. Among other topical issues, sketches in *Americana* referenced breadlines, the Dust Bowl, and the corruption hearings of former New York City Mayor Jimmy Walker. Noted by critics for its ambitious dance numbers, choreographed by modern dance denizens like Doris Humphry (1895–1958) and Charles Weidman (1901–75), *Americana* is perhaps most noteworthy for introducing Gorney and Harburg's iconic Depression-era song "Brother, Can You Spare a Dime?" This number was originally performed with disarming seriousness by comedian Rex Weber:

Once I built a railroad, I made it run
Made it race against time
Once I built a railroad, now it's done
Brother, can you spare a dime?

Once I built a tower up to the sun
Brick and rivet and lime
Once I built a tower, now it's done
Brother, can you spare a dime?

While "Brother" quickly became an anthem for the era, *Americana* failed to connect with audiences, due in large part to its pervasive solemnity. In his review for *The New York Times*, critic Brooks Atkinson quipped, "'Americana' has kept its sense of humor under remarkable control." Its sketches, he added, made constant, heavy-handed reference to "a vast and dismal subject, merely reminding us of the suffering we are powerless to relieve." The result, at least for him, was a "disgruntled mood" that settled in during the show and was tough to shake after the curtain call (Atkinson 1932, 19).

A more successful topical revue was *As Thousands Cheer* (1933), a collaboration between Irving Berlin, who wrote the score and lyrics, and playwright Moss Hart (1904–61), who wrote the sketches. Warmly greeted by critics and audiences, *As Thousands Cheer* starred Marilyn Miller, Helen Broderick, Clifton Webb, and Ethel Waters. Waters (1896–1977), a black vaudevillian who had appeared on Broadway in the 1930 edition of Lew Leslie's *Blackbirds* and in his *Rhapsody in Black* a year later, was recruited for *As Thousands Cheer* by Berlin himself, once he saw her perform at the Cotton Club (Woll 1989, 149).

Loosely connecting the songs and sketches of *As Thousands Cheer* was an overarching "ripped from the headlines" structure. Each new song or scene began with a news headline: "HEATWAVE HITS NEW YORK; JOAN CRAWFORD TO DIVORCE DOUGLAS FAIRBANKS, JR.; WORLD'S WEALTHIEST MAN CELEBRATES 94TH BIRTHDAY" (Stempel 2010, 220). Sketches depicted Herbert Hoover leaving the White House and aiming a Bronx cheer at his former cabinet in the process, John D. Rockefeller reacting with dismay when his children give him Rockefeller Center as a birthday gift, and a radio broadcast from the Metropolitan Opera during which commercials constantly interrupt the performance (Bordman 2001, 535). Songs from *As Thousands Cheer* that became hits include "Heat Wave" and "Easter Parade."

Berlin's lyrics rarely reflected the social consciousness more typical of lyricists like Yip Harburg or Oscar Hammerstein II, and yet *As Thousands Cheer* did occasionally touch on issues that were a tad weightier than Noël Coward's trip abroad or the heatwave that had recently hit New York. The revue steered clear of the Depression and kept a respectful distance from FDR's recently-implemented New Deal programs, but took a dark turn early in Act II when, following the headline UNKNOWN NEGRO LYNCHED BY FRENZIED MOB, Ethel Waters performed the number "Supper Time."

"Supper Time" depicts a wife struggling with how to tell her children that their father "ain't comin' home no more." So forcefully did Waters perform "Supper Time" that Berlin and his co-producer, Sam Harris, were pressured to cut it from the otherwise lighthearted revue for fear it would upset audiences (Jones 2003, 100–1), but the men insisted it remain. Nightly, Waters stunned audiences who, while not constantly reminded of every sociopolitical ill plaguing the US in the 1930s, were confronted with one of the bigger ones.

Book musicals gain weight

The book musical grew more artistically sophisticated in the 1930s, which again relates to the economic landscape. Producers, newly concerned about the bottom line and the number of productions they could afford to mount in a season, grew more selective with the projects they agreed to back. With fewer representative productions, artistic teams, too, were newly exacting with the shows they devised. This was especially the case since a show with a solid score, or even just a couple of catchy songs, could now reach wider audiences. The radio, a comparatively new mass medium that had gained traction in the 1920s, had become an important (and cheap) source for news, information, and entertainment.

What with the Great Depression, subsequent labor unrest and union growth, the Dust Bowl, the repeal of Prohibition, and Hitler's slow rise to power overseas, the 1930s was a period during which the book musical grappled with new, creative ways to simultaneously entertain audiences and reflect the contemporary world. As theater critic and Pulitzer Prize jurist

John Mason Brown wrote in 1938, "There are now a great many things to be thought about in our musicals. They no longer permit us to be pleasantly relaxed. They demand us to be jubilantly alert. Our laughter at them is the surest proof that we are thinking" (quoted in Green 1971, 12). Plenty of frivolous, escapist book musicals were mounted in the 1930s, but those making the most lasting impact blended the escapist with the provocative. Many such productions picked up where *Show Boat* left off, whether aesthetically, structurally, or in an attempt at greater cultural commentary than was typical of book musicals in the past.

It did not hurt that during the 1930s, a number of new developments aided in the increased perception of the Broadway musical as a multifaceted art form. Broadway's stages benefited, for example, from a major technical innovation: the mechanized revolving stage, which allowed for greater fluidity of action during and between scenes. Also in the 1930s, classical ballet and modern dance became more intrinsic to the stage musical, since established choreographers including George Balanchine (1904–83), Agnes de Mille (1905–93), José Limón (1908–72), and Helen Tamiris (1905–66) began collaborating on Broadway (Leve 2016, 86).

Dance had long been an aspect of Broadway musicals, as its presence in shows ranging from *The Black Crook* to Ziegfeld's *Follies* implies. But the use of classical and modern dance forms on Broadway in the 1930s was newly reflective of influence from Hollywood musicals, a surge in popularity of dance as an entertainment form, and an uptick in collaborations among artists working under the auspices of the New Deal.[6] As the book musical became more sophisticated in the 1930s, so too did its choreography.

George and Ira Gershwin

The composer George Gershwin's embrace of all music genres, from classical to popular, resulted in a unique compositional style that was intelligent, democratic, and accessible. Born in Brooklyn to Russian-Jewish immigrants, George began studying classical piano as a child. He also immersed himself in jazz and the popular songs emanating from Tin Pan Alley, all of which he took just as seriously. Never much of a student, he dropped out of high school in 1914 to become a Tin Pan Alley song-plugger; he soon became known within the sheet music industry for his remarkable rhythmic and melodic dexterity. His first song, "When You Want 'Em, You Can't Get 'Em;

When You've Got 'Em, You Don't Want 'Em," was published in 1916, but his first really big pop hit was "Swanee" (1919), which Al Jolson interpolated into his long-running show *Sinbad*, and subsequently kept as a signature song (Mast 1987, 67–8).

By the early 1920s, George began collaborating with his brother Ira, who wrote lyrics. Their first Broadway hit, *Lady, Be Good* (1924), starred the real-life siblings Fred (1899–1987) and Adele Astaire (1896–1981) as down-and-out sibling vaudevillians who become entangled in (and eventually gain entry into) high society. The highly polished, consistently uproarious musical ran successfully on Broadway and in the West End, marking the start of a close collaboration between the brothers that would last until George's death at thirty-eight from a brain tumor (Stempel 2010, 252–3).

Through the early 1930s, the Gershwins helped set a satirical tone on Broadway with a trilogy of musicals lampooning contemporary American politics, all of which were written in collaboration with George S. Kaufman. The first of the three, *Strike Up the Band*, was written in 1927, but bombed with Philadelphia audiences during the out-of-town tryout. *Strike Up the Band* was revised and mounted on Broadway in 1930, by which point audiences were arguably more willing to entertain a biting if ultimately optimistic musical about American aggressiveness, big business, "self-serving patriots," "phony heroes," and "bungling politicians" (Green 1971, 17–18).

The original version of *Strike Up the Band* featured a plot in which the US declares war on Switzerland after that country complains about an American tariff on cheese. The war is financed by, and thus named for, American cheese manufacturer Horace J. Fletcher, whose patriotism is called into question when he is spotted wearing a Swiss watch. The revised version, for which the dramatist and then-Socialist activist Morrie Ryskind (1895–1985) was enlisted for rewrites, changed cheese to chocolate, had the war turn out to be a dream from which the hawkish Fletcher awakens a changed man, and featured a score more influenced by jazz than the original Gilbert and Sullivan-inspired one. *Strike Up the Band*'s "pertinence and impertinence" and tongue-in-cheek political commentary inspired a slew of muckraking musicals, which mixed shrewd social observations in with the song and dance (Bordman 2001, 507–8).

Strike Up the Band ran for a perfectly respectable 191 performances, but its successor struck gold. *Of Thee I Sing* (1931), again with a score by the Gershwin brothers and a book by Kaufman and Ryskind, was by far the most critically and commercially successful of the three satirical musicals the men created together. It became the first Broadway musical to be published and released for popular readership, and the first to win the Pulitzer Prize for Drama (Jones 2003, 92). A spoof targeting the American electoral process, *Of Thee I Sing* was optimistic, but also took plenty of digs at American politics. The musical was unsparing when it came to politicians with money and power, which went over well at a time when many Americans lacked both.

Of Thee I Sing follows the candidacy of John P. Wintergreen, who wants to be president of the US, and has come up with a catchy campaign song:

Of thee I sing, baby
You have got that certain thing, baby
Shining star and inspiration
Worthy of a mighty nation

Stirring though the song may be, Wintergreen nevertheless lacks a platform and a spouse, both of which are hindrances to a successful election. His campaign managers meet in a hotel room where they ask a passing chambermaid what she thinks is most important in life. When she responds that money and love are more important than anything else, the managers decide that Wintergreen's platform will simply be "love." When they subsequently realize that such a platform makes no sense as long as Wintergreen is single, a Miss White House pageant is hastily arranged. The winner will get Wintergreen as a prize and, should he win the election, the role of First Lady to boot. Meanwhile, the vice presidential candidate, Alexander Throttlebottom, is a melancholy schlub whom no one can remember, and who is embarrassed to tell anyone, even his mother, that he is the Vice Presidential candidate.

Wintergreen wins the election, and one Diana Devereaux wins the pageant. Yet by this point Wintergreen has fallen in love with his secretary, Mary Turner. He marries her instead of Devereaux, who proves less than understanding about the situation. When it is discovered that the jilted, angry Devereaux is descended from Napoleon, France becomes infuriated and national support for the president plummets. Yet Mary turns out to be pregnant with twins, and due to Wintergreen's resultant "delicate condition," Throttlebottom is constitutionally obliged to save Diana's honor. He marries her, she and France are appeased, Wintergreen is again embraced by the populace, and everyone lives happily ever after (Stempel 2010, 255–7).

The plot of *Of Thee I Sing* was such a skillful mix of jollity and biting satire that the advances the show made in terms of musical trajectory are often overlooked. But the Gershwins' score was almost constant throughout the production, rather than built from a more typical sequence of individual songs that stop during lengthy sections of dialogue. Throughout *Of Thee I Sing*, songs regularly segued into lengths of underscoring and vice-versa. Many of the musical numbers pushed the plot along, either by describing characters' motivations or their actions. Some scenes featured such a sophisticated series of solos, choruses, and underscoring that the music became just as important as the staging and dialogue (Green 1971, 59).

The final effort by the Gershwins, Kaufman, and Ryskind was not as successful as *Of Thee I Sing* or even *Strike Up the Band*. *Let 'Em Eat Cake* (1933), a sequel to *Of Thee I Sing*, featured many of the same characters but this time placed them in situations that came off to critics and audiences as too bitter for comfort. In *Let 'Em Eat Cake*, Wintergreen has failed in his bid for re-election. Out of work and stuck with a surplus of blue shirts that his wife Mary has gone into business to produce, Wintergreen decides to supply the blue shirts to citizens and, with their support, overthrow the government and resume power. His plan is thwarted and the electoral process survives, but *Let 'Em Eat Cake* did not land well. It is possible that spectators, already weighed down by the Depression and increasingly concerned by Adolf Hitler's appointment to Chancellor of Germany six months prior, were repelled by a show about a blue-shirted populace overthrowing the government (Kirle 2005, 90). *Let 'Em Eat Cake* lasted a mere eighty-nine performances. Once it closed, its creative team parted ways.

George Gershwin's presence on Broadway and Tin Pan Alley in the 1920s and 1930s did not preclude his work in other styles and venues. He composed a number of works, including *Rhapsody in Blue* (1924), *Concerto in F* (1925), *Three Preludes* (1926), and *Cuban Overture* (1932), which became perennial favorites in classical music venues. Through his short life, he also exhibited a continued fascination with jazz and other black popular and folk music styles. Due to the ease with which he crossed boundaries and blended seemingly disparate musical genres, it should come as no surprise that Gershwin frequently voiced a desire to compose an "American folk opera" steeped in both classical and American vernacular styles.

One of his earliest attempts at such a piece, the 25-minute opera *Blue Monday*, was written with the lyricist Buddy DeSylva for the second act of

George White's Scandals of 1922. A variation on the Frankie and Johnny legend set in a Harlem bar, *Blue Monday* was performed by whites in blackface, and was so vehemently panned by critics who found it long and boring that it was cut from the production after opening night.[7] A 1925 remounting of the piece at Carnegie Hall was more respectfully received, though it never caught on in classical circles, either (Woll 1989, 160–62).

In 1925, the writer DuBose Heyward, a white South Carolinian with an interest in local black (Gullah) culture, published a novel titled *Porgy.* Set in a fictional, poor, black enclave called Catfish Row, *Porgy* told of its title character's attempts to save a local woman, Bess, from her abusive lover, Crown, and her cocaine dealer, Sportin' Life. After *Porgy* was released, Heyward and his wife Dorothy wrote a stage version produced in 1927 by the Theatre Guild (Knapp 2006, 195). Performed at the playwrights' insistence by an all-black cast, *Porgy* was well-received by white critics, though black critics were cooler about yet another white depiction of poor, superstitious, drug-addled black characters. *Porgy* ran for a year at the Guild (now August Wilson) Theater on Broadway.[8]

Shortly after *Porgy* was published, George Gershwin approached the Heywards in hopes of adapting it as an opera, but the couple, busy with their own adaptation process, declined. Gershwin contacted them again in 1932, only to learn that Kern and Hammerstein had optioned the property as a possible Al Jolson vehicle. In his response, Gershwin expressed surprise and concern that the characters would be played by whites, and promised the Heywards that he had "a much more serious thing" in mind (Woll 1989, 164). When Kern and Hammerstein dropped their option shortly thereafter, the Heywards and Gershwins began negotiations.

In the summer of 1934, George moved to Folly Island, a Sea Island off the coast of Charleston, South Carolina, to immerse himself in Gullah language, culture, and music. He spent nearly two years composing, orchestrating, and writing vocal arrangements for the opera, which placed new emphasis on Bess and was thus eventually titled *Porgy and Bess.* The Gershwins considered the Metropolitan Opera as a potential producer, but chose to work instead with the Theatre Guild, the same organization that had produced the original production of *Porgy.* Tickets, the Gershwins reasoned, would be more affordable on Broadway than at the Met; also, the Met claimed that it could not promise a full cast of black opera singers, and the Guild voiced no such limitations. Once the venue had been determined, the creative team retained the original *Porgy* director, Rouben Mamoulian, to direct the opera as well.

The Russian-Armenian director, who had made his name in Hollywood as a director of film musicals, had proven particularly democratic when working with black actors (ibid., 164–5).

Boasting a typically sophisticated blend of American folk and blues idioms, jazz, Broadway show-stoppers, and operatic arias, *Porgy and Bess* opened on October 10, 1935 at the Alvin (now Neil Simon) Theatre. Because it was so atypical for Broadway, most newspapers sent both their drama and music critics to review the show. This ended up harming the show's reception, since at the time, many "drama critics, who normally covered musicals, tended to view opera as a debased form of drama'" while "music critics, who normally covered operas, tended to view musicals as a debased form of opera" (Stempel 2010, 387–8). Thus criticized for being on the one hand too lightweight to be a "real" opera and on the other too heavy to be an effective musical, *Porgy and Bess* confounded spectators as it had critics. Further, its unsparing depictions of desperately poor, disenfranchised southern blacks were hard on Depression-era audiences. Whether *Porgy and Bess* was more an opera or a musical became the least of its problems. The show ran for 124 performances, and though the Guild sponsored a tour after it closed, *Porgy and Bess* did not earn back its $50,000 investment (Bordman 2001, 546–7). Disappointed, George Gershwin quit Broadway for Hollywood, where he remained until his death two years later.

Appreciation for the artistry of *Porgy and Bess* has grown significantly since its premiere, and the piece is frequently revived both in opera halls and theater venues. But *Porgy and Bess* has never been free of controversy. While the Heywards and Gershwins "made a conscientious effort to depict Negro life as realistically as possible," the opera, like the novel on which it was based, was filled with black characters who were drawn by whites, with the intention of reaching predominantly white audiences (Green 1971, 116).

The premiere of *Porgy and Bess* in 1935 inadvertently reflected "the white usurpation of what had initially been a black cultural form." By this point, a "black musical" referred more to the color of its cast and less to its almost always all-white creative teams (Woll 1989, 154). While the cherished score of *Porgy and Bess* is filled with songs that have become American standards—including "Summertime," "It Ain't Necessarily So," "I Got Plenty o' Nuttin'" and "Bess, You Is My Woman Now"—the piece has been accused both of cultural appropriation and of perpetuating stereotypical depictions of black American life. When the piece is revised or reimagined for contemporary audiences, as it was for the 2012 Broadway revival, the hackles of purists who believe musicals should remain as their creators left them are inevitably raised.[9] *Porgy and Bess* has arguably appreciated somewhat less comfortably on social grounds than it has on artistic ones.

The Cradle Will Rock

During the Great Depression, the Theatre Guild, producer of both *Porgy* and *Porgy and Bess,* was not unique in supporting theatrical productions deemed artistically worthwhile if not necessarily commercially viable. The 1930s was a significant period for political—and often politically radical—theater, due to the development of several left-leaning actors' collectives and the rise, especially after 1935, of public funding for the arts under the auspices of the Works Progress Administration. One of the more noteworthy performers' collectives, the Group Theatre, was founded by Theatre Guild members Harold Clurman, Cheryl Crawford, and Lee Strasberg.

The Group Theatre promoted a disciplined, collective approach to forceful, naturalistic theater that de-emphasized individual stars. It produced plays by Americans such as Irwin Shaw and Clifford Odets, and supported the careers of, among others, the actor Harry Morgan, writer and director Elia Kazan, acting teachers Stella Adler and Sanford Meisner, and composer Marc Blitzstein (1905–64). Blitzstein would become a key figure in the WPA's Federal Theatre Project, or FTP (Klein 2001, 595).

Run by producer and playwright Hallie Flanagan (1890–1969), the FTP was founded in 1935 to employ some of the nearly 30,000 people with careers in the theater who lost their jobs when the Depression struck. In its four years of existence, the FTP hired over 12,000 people at around $24 weekly and staged a number of diverse projects: avant-garde and children's theater, Shakespeare plays and other classics, theatrical documentaries, and musicals. Frequently attacked by various congressional committees as financially wasteful and a hotbed for Communist influence, the FTP was a locus for controversy practically from inception (Green 1971, 144). Not all shows affiliated with the FTP were especially left-leaning, or even politically minded. But Marc Blitzstein's *The Cradle Will Rock* (1937) added fuel to many an anti-FTP fire.

Blitzstein was born in Philadelphia to affluent parents, and educated in music composition, first at the Curtis Institute and then in Europe with Arnold Schoenberg and Nadia Boulanger. Convinced of the arts' potential to unite the masses, he took the advice of his idol, Bertolt Brecht, and wrote the book, words, and music of a jazz-infused "proletarian opera" that he titled *The Cradle Will Rock* (Jones 2003, 104).

The Cradle Will Rock is a morality musical that expounds upon the importance of labor unions. Without unions, the musical argues, people would fall prey to autocrats and be "forced into a kind of prostitution, forced to do whatever they do—teach, preach, edit newspapers, paint, make music, practice medicine, work in factories, etc.—not out of love but according to the dictates of whoever is paying" (Knapp 2006, 112). The musical's symbolically-named characters live in Steeltown, USA, which is controlled by the Mister family: the wealthy and powerful Mister Mister, his greedy and vacuous wife, Mrs. Mister, and his selfish, spoiled children, Junior and Sister Mister.

At the start of the musical, the prostitute Moll is arrested for solicitation. In jail, Moll meets several members of the anti-union Liberty Committee, whom Mister Mister's police force have mistaken for union organizers and arrested. Moll also meets Harry Druggist, who has lost his business to Mister Mister and been arrested for vagrancy. Through a series of flashbacks, Harry fills Moll in on Mister Mister's rise to power and crusade against union organizer Larry Foreman. When Foreman is beaten and arrested, he tells Moll about the importance of unions and promises that they will grow in power, thereby rocking the capitalist cradle and creating positive change. At the end of the musical, Mister Mister arrives to bail out the Liberty Committee, and tries to bribe Foreman to stop organizing. Foreman refuses, vowing instead to overthrow the wealthy and powerful, thereby restoring equality for all.[10]

Written in a straightforward, stirring style that borrowed liberally from folk and mass song, standard Broadway fare, and musical modernism, *The Cradle Will Rock* proved unappealing to Broadway producers, who felt its plot was too heavy-handed, its characters too one-dimensional, and its score too eclectic for Broadway audiences. Of course, the stringent anti-capitalism of *Cradle* did not exactly help warm Broadway's money-men to the project, either (Green 1971, 144).

Broadway was no stranger to political theater, but the ardently pro-union *Cradle* might have raised the hackles of many a bottom-line-minded producer, especially at the time in question. The mid-1930s saw a major uptick in the presence and power of unions. President Roosevelt took a notably pro-union stance, and Congress had recently passed legislation permitting collective bargaining and granting new protections for both employers and their employees.[11] But with the new power of unions came considerable growing pains: work stoppages, strikes, dissent from both the sympathetic left and the anti-union right, and plenty of clashing ideologies within the ranks of unionizers and union members themselves (Klein 2001, 586).

An important industrial center, New York City was a hotbed for union activity in the 1930s. "[B]readlines and eviction protests spurred class consciousness" in the city, and work provided by the Temporary Emergency Relief Administration and the Works Progress Administration "shrank the potential number of strikebreakers among the vast numbers of un-employed" (Klein 2001, 586). Whether due to concern about the rise of unions or just a sense that *The Cradle Will Rock* would not work commercially, Broadway producers all passed on the musical when Blitzstein first shopped it around.

The musical did, however, win the admiration of director Orson Welles (1915–85) and producer John Houseman (1902–88), who had worked together on the FTP Negro Theater Unit's acclaimed *Macbeth,* commonly nicknamed the "Voodoo Macbeth," in 1936. With Flanagan's approval, Houseman and Welles agreed to stage *Cradle.* Welles conceived the musical as a morality play, and commenced rehearsals nine weeks prior to the planned opening in June 1937 (Vacha 1981, 136).

Anxiety over the production grew in Washington, DC, during the rehearsal period, especially following the deadly Memorial Day Massacre that occurred during the Little Steel Strike in Chicago.[12] That incident, combined with growing dissent among anti-New Dealers in Congress, led to rumors about massive FTP cutbacks once the act that had led to the creation of arts relief projects expired in June (ibid., 138). The timing, it was believed, was no accident: many people involved with the FTP and the production of *Cradle* felt the musical "was the specific target of these cuts" (Knapp 2006, 113).

On June 10, a week before *The Cradle Will Rock* was scheduled to enter its preview period, the WPA cut the New York branch of the FTP by 30 percent, resulting in the immediate dismissal of some 1,700 workers. Pleading assurances by Flanagan, who had gone so far as to bring assistant director Lawrence Morris from the WPA's Washington office to New York to watch a rehearsal of *Cradle,* made no difference. Nor did Morris's report that what he saw was "magnificent." On June 12, the FTP directors were told to prohibit the opening of any new play, performance, or gallery exhibit before July 1 because of impending cuts and plans for reorganization. The fact that several less politically-minded, federally-funded shows opened undisturbed in New

York and New Jersey during the period in question fueled further suspicion that the June 12 memo was specifically aimed at *The Cradle Will Rock* (Jones 2003, 105–6).

Welles and Houseman refused to comply with the order. They invited guests to a dress rehearsal at the Maxine Elliot Theater on the evening of June 14. This would turn out to be the only performance of *Cradle* before audiences in the Elliot. The next morning, company members arrived to find the theater padlocked and surrounded by uniformed WPA guards (ibid.). Furious, and determined to find a new place to stage the production on short notice, Welles and Houseman rushed to their office and shut themselves in, fearful that if they left it, they would be unable to access it again.

During the mad scramble to secure a new theater for the fervently pro-union musical, an ironic conflict arose in the form of clashes with Actors' Equity and the musicians' union. The president of Equity would not approve "the appearance by the cast on any stage not under WPA auspices," while the musicians' union announced that any appearances by musicians in non-WPA theaters "would require full Broadway salaries and an augmented orchestra." As crowds gathered in front of the padlocked theater on the night of June 15, Houseman frantically sent a production assistant to rent a piano, which Blitzstein himself agreed to play. When spectators grew impatient, actors mingled with them, frequently breaking into bits from the show or singing rousing ballads to deter them from leaving. By around 8:15 p.m., as word spread that the Venice Theater on 59th Street had been secured for the performance, the company and many spectators began the walk uptown (Vacha 1981, 141–4).

The actors were prohibited by Equity from performing on the stage of the Venice, so they delivered their lines and songs from the orchestra seats. Blitzstein played the score at center stage while Welles, sitting a few feet away, narrated some of the action. The left-leaning crowd's enthusiasm built, and by the end of the evening, which was close to midnight, the company reprised several songs so the audience could sing along.

The extraordinary circumstances surrounding the performance of *The Cradle Will Rock* resulted in enough press attention for Houseman to secure private backers, who kept this necessarily minimalist—or, as it became known, "oratorio style"—version of *Cradle* running at the Venice for two weeks, with actors now seated on chairs on the stage and Equity bond posted. Shortly thereafter, Houseman and Welles resigned from the FTP to form the Mercury Theater, where they remounted *The Cradle Will Rock* on Sunday evenings through 1937 (Jones 2003, 110–11). In January 1938, *Cradle*, still in oratorio style, ran on Broadway at the Windsor Theater for 108 performances. When it closed, the revue *Pins and Needles* moved there from the aptly titled Labor Theater—formerly the Princess, where Jerome Kern had once honed his intimate musicals.

Another ardently pro-labor show, *Pins and Needles* had music and lyrics by the young, leftist composer Harold Rome (1908–93), sponsorship by the International Ladies' Garment Workers' Union (ILGWU), a revolving cast drawn from that union's locals, and sketches contributed by none other than Marc Blitzstein. Yet *Pins and Needles* was not nearly as polemic as *Cradle* was. It was heavy on humor, light in tone, and as quick to poke fun of unions as capitalists. Regularly updated and recast with willing ILGWU members, *Pins and Needles* remained fresh for over a thousand performances. By the time it closed, the Great Depression had lifted, Welles and Houseman had moved to Hollywood, the FTP had been terminated, and *The Cradle Will Rock* had become the stuff of Broadway legend.

Cole Porter and *Anything Goes*

Not all 1930s musicals made a point of commenting directly on social, political, or cultural issues of the time. Just as Depression-era Hollywood churned out plenty of musicals that peddled in escapism—think of Fred Astaire and Ginger Rogers, expensively dressed and gliding through any number of well-appointed settings—so too did Depression-era Broadway. One of the most quintessential of well-made if breezily diverting 1930s productions is Cole Porter's *Anything Goes*, which premiered on November 21, 1934, at the Alvin (now Neil Simon) Theater. The musical ran for 420 performances, became the fourth-longest-running musical of the decade and remains a frequently-revived favorite.

Unlike many of his contemporaries, the Broadway composer and lyricist Cole Porter (1892–1964) was born gentile, midwestern, and ridiculously wealthy. Raised in Peru, Indiana, Porter went to Yale and then Harvard, where his domineering grandfather expected him to earn a law degree. Porter quickly realized that he would rather make music than take the bar, so in his second year, he dropped out of Harvard Law and enrolled in the music school. Eventually, he quit Cambridge entirely and moved to New York, where his first Broadway musical, *See America First*, opened in March 1916, only to close after 15 performances.[13]

Stung by the disappointment, Porter left New York for Paris and then Venice, where he hobnobbed, galavanted, and enjoyed a well-connected social life. Though gay, he entered into a marriage of convenience with a close friend, the divorced socialite Linda Lee Thomas, which lasted until her death in 1954. Before returning to New York in 1928 with his first hit musical, *Paris*, Porter kept his distance from Broadway, contributing only a handful of songs for interpolation into a few productions.

Paris, which introduced the number "Let's Do It" and was made into a movie a year after debuting on Broadway, helped establish Porter as a household name in theater and film circles. He became only more well-known through the Depression years, with a string of successful productions including *Fifty Million Frenchmen* (1929), *The New Yorkers* (1930), and Fred Astaire's last stage show, *Gay Divorce* (1932).

As both composer and lyricist, Porter specialized in songs evocative of the cheerful, extravagant 1920s at a time when most American popular entertainment was busily distancing itself from excess. Porter made no attempt in his songs to hide his affluence, downplay his erudition, or deny his cultivation. Yet he managed to strike a careful balance with his audiences, to whom he never seemed to condescend. Rather than expecting them to marvel at his wealth and style, Porter seemed eager to invite them to laugh along with him over how drolly absurd the world could be.

Porter's extensive travels exposed him to all kinds of music, elements of which he frequently incorporated into his own songs. In this respect, he was vaguely similar to Gershwin in his eclectic compositional style. Lyrically, Porter had a gift for wordplay and double entendre. He often made long lists from his lyrics, into which he inserted sly social commentary or a dizzying blend of high- and lowbrow cultural references (Greher, 159–60). Every person who heard Porter's songs might not catch every turn of phrase, French expression, or reference to high culture, but broader jokes, double meanings, and puns—which were often about sex and just as often hilarious—would inevitably follow the denser references. Everyone likes to be in on a joke, and Porter reflected no qualms about that certainty in his lyrics.

The gleefully silly *Anything Goes* was rooted aesthetically to the "snappy and joyous" Princess Theater musicals of the 1910s. It was "light, fast, flip, hip, with good jokes, comic specialty acts, shrewd cultural observations, and terrific songs," not all of which necessarily hang together. For its throwback elements, however, *Anything Goes* reflected a change of the guard and an era during which musical and lyric sophistication were increasingly valued on Broadway (Mast 1987, 195).

Anything Goes was the brainchild of producer Vinton Freedley (1891–1969), longtime champion of the Gershwins, whose January 1933 musical *Pardon My English* went so over budget and flopped so quickly that Freedley fled the country to escape his creditors. He spent most of 1933 and 1934 fishing, surely morosely, from his yacht off the Pearl Islands, paying off his debts and planning a comeback. His stars, he decided, would include the comedy team of William Gaxton and Victor Moore, as well as Ethel Merman (1908–84). Merman, the Queens-born former stenographer with a voice like a bulldozer, had made her Broadway debut in the Freedley-produced 1930 Gershwin hit *Girl Crazy*.

At first, Freedley wanted Jerome Kern to score his comeback show, *Anything Goes*. Guy Bolton and P.G. Wodehouse were enlisted to write the book and lyrics. When Kern's involvement fell through, Freedley tapped the Gershwin brothers, but they were too busy with *Porgy and Bess* to consider the offer. The score of *Anything Goes* finally went to Porter, whose star by this point was still very much on the rise (Knapp 2006, 88).

Newly debt-free, Freedley sailed to France to confer with Wodehouse, who had moved there, and Bolton, who traveled from London to meet them. Relieved of the lyrics, which Porter himself would provide, Wodehouse and Bolton sent Freedley the draft script, in August 1934, about an eccentric crowd of characters who get shipwrecked while on a pleasure cruise (Green 1971, 105). Although not especially impressed with the script, Freedley began rehearsals by the end of that month.

Mere weeks later, the *SS Morro Castle*, an ocean liner headed from Havana to New York, spent a final and very possibly cursed journey being pummeled by a nor'easter, losing its captain to an apparent heart attack, and finally bursting into flames off the coast of Asbury Park, New Jersey. Of the 549 people aboard, 137 died in the fire or the scramble to escape it, and the company of *Anything Goes* realized that a wacky musical about a shipwreck was suddenly an absolutely terrible idea. The book was thus hastily revised by director Howard Lindsay, whom Freedley paired with press agent Russel Crouse. This marked the beginning of what would become a long and fruitful partnership, but Lindsay and Crouse were for the moment both green and terrified enough to come up only with the famously haphazard semblance of a plot that made it to the stage when *Anything Goes* opened in November (Block 2009, 43). In their hasty rewrite, a loopy assortment of characters—all of whom are either in love with one another, running from the law, preaching the gospel or some combination thereof—embark on a cruise. This time, the ship never crashes, but chaos and wackiness nevertheless ensue.

Despite its last-minute overhaul and flimsy plot, *Anything Goes* was warmly received by critics, who took its loose book in stride and focused instead on its instantly memorable songs, among them "You're the Top," "It's Delovely," "I Get a Kick Out of You," and the title number. *Anything Goes* was the big hit of the 1934–35 season, made a Broadway legend of Ethel Merman, and cemented Cole Porter's legacy.

Rodgers and Hart and *Pal Joey*

Cole Porter was not alone in taking up the reins from Kern and the Gershwins as the 1930s progressed. Irving Berlin remained very much on the scene, as he would for decades to come. Oscar Hammerstein II's career had slowed since the success of *Show Boat*, but he would soon dominate the Second World War era in a new partnership with the composer Richard Rodgers (1902–79). Rodgers himself was very active during the 1920s and 1930s, in collaboration with the brilliant if tortured lyricist Lorenz Hart (1895–1943). Rodgers' partnership with Hammerstein was so extraordinarily successful and influential that his partnership with Hart, long and fruitful though it was, is often given comparatively short shrift.

Lorenz Hart and Richard Rodgers met as students at Columbia University in 1919, and worked together until Hart's death of exposure-borne pneumonia in 1943 (Kirle 2005, 19). For their close partnership, they were remarkably different men: Rodgers was polished and professional, if by most accounts also cold, impenetrable, and distant. Hart, a depressive alcoholic and closeted homosexual, was widely considered the more personable, emotionally transparent, and endearing of the two.

Both men were, however, strongly influenced by the many kinds of music and theater that had surrounded them through their upbringings in culturally rich New York City. In his childhood, Hart regularly saw Yiddish- and German-language productions, vaudeville shows, and early Broadway confections. From an early age, he found himself striving to emulate the many different kinds of lyrics he heard. Rodgers, on the other hand, gravitated more to concert music. His extended family frequently gathered around a piano or attended concerts of classical music, as well as operas, operettas, and shows on Broadway. Both Hart and Rodgers were particularly passionate about the small, cohesive Princess musicals by Kern, Wodehouse, and Bolton (Symonds 2015, 8–10). And both men were convinced that musicals could achieve "a far greater degree of artistic merit in every area than was apparent at the time" (quoted in Stempel 2010, 275–6).

One of their earliest songs, "Any Old Place with You," was interpolated into the musical *A Lonely Romeo* (1919). The following year, seven of their songs were interpolated into Sigmund Romberg's *Poor Little Ritz Girl*. But while many benefits, gala events, and amateur productions followed, it was not until 1925, when they scored the revue *The Garrick Gaieties* and the Revolutionary-era musical *Dearest Enemy*, that the duo found lasting success on Broadway (Block 2009, 83).

Rodgers and Hart had an established rhythm to their collaboration: Rodgers composed music for a number, after which Hart would pen "nimble" and "penetrating" lyrics, many of which demonstrated his knack for "polysyllabic and internal rhymes" (Hischak 2008, 327–8). It has been noted that one of the pleasures of listening to a Rodgers and Hart song is the frequent juxtaposition between Rodgers' sweet, lyrical, memorable tunes and Hart's "biting, cynical, brutal, and intellectual lyrics" (Mast 1987, 169).

Before heading to Hollywood in the the earliest, leanest years of the Depression, they collaborated on twelve musicals, three of which—*The Girl Friend* (1926), *Peggy-Ann* (1926), and *A Connecticut Yankee* (1927)—were especially successful. In Hollywood, Rodgers and Hart scored several feature films including the Al Jolson vehicle *Hallelujah, I'm a Bum!* (1933). But the duo quickly tired of Hollywood's approach, in which composers and lyricists were paid well but granted no creative control during the filming and editing of a movie (Stempel 2010, 279). Once the initial shock of the Depression wore off, Rodgers and Hart were only too happy to return to Broadway, and the collaborative process to which they were accustomed.

In keeping with the aesthetics of the period, Rodgers and Hart's 1920s musicals tended toward the broad, madcap, and carefree. Yet even during this period, the men regularly grappled with "different elements of performance like design, atmosphere, lighting, and especially dance" in a quest to aid "the dynamics of performance" overall (Symonds 2015, 264). After their return from Hollywood in 1935, Rodgers and Hart put out a string of successful Broadway musicals that remain more squarely in collective memory than most of their 1920s productions: *On Your Toes* (1936), *Babes in Arms* (1937), *The Boys from Syracuse* (1938), and *Pal Joey* (1940). These shows reflect significant strides toward the integrated musicals Rodgers and Hammerstein would soon be lauded for.

On Your Toes is considered a landmark musical because dance—long a Broadway staple, if one that typically stopped rather than advanced a musical's plot—was so integral to its storyline. Initially devised in Hollywood, *On Your Toes* was to star Fred Astaire as a vaudeville dancer who gets involved with a Russian ballet troupe. But Astaire, busily dancing up a storm with Ginger Rogers, passed on the project. Rodgers and Hart decided instead to develop *On Your Toes* for Broadway, and commenced collaborations with the producer, director, and playwright George Abbott (1887–1995). Ray Bolger (1904–87), later the Scarecrow in *The Wizard of Oz* and an already seasoned vaudevillian, was cast in the lead role (Block 2003, 85–6).

A noteworthy member of the creative team was the Russian ballet dancer and choreographer George Balanchine (1904–83). Balanchine's interest in commercial stage musicals stemmed both from a desire to build American audiences for dance and to keep his own dancers steadily employed. A relative newcomer to Broadway (and to the US, where he emigrated in 1933), Balanchine had a history of reaching beyond classical dance venues. In both London and Paris, he had choreographed dances for use in revues, operettas, and variety shows. In New York, his agent, who also represented Lorenz Hart, recommended him for his first Broadway show, the 1936 edition of Ziegfeld's *Follies*. Hart, in turn, introduced him to Rodgers and Abbott (Hardy 2006, 16).

The plot of *On Your Toes* centers on Phil "Junior" Dolan, a vaudeville hoofer teaching at a WPA-sponsored college extension program. One of his students, Frankie Frayne, has eyes for him and a talent for composing pop tunes. Another, Sydney Cohn, composes the jazz ballet "Slaughter on Tenth Avenue," which Junior brings to the attention of Sergei Alexandrovitch's flagging Russian ballet company. The ballet company agrees to perform the work. Alexandrovitch's prima ballerina, Vera Barnova, develops an aggressive crush on Junior, much to the dismay of both Frankie and Vera's lover, the dancer Konstantine Morrosine. When a pre-show scuffle between Alexandrovitch and Morrosine leaves Morrosine unconscious, Junior steps in to dance opposite Vera. Once revived, the jealous Morrosine sets some gangsters on Junior who, thanks to a tipoff by Frankie, is spared the fate implied in the ballet's title by dancing until the police can arrive to make arrests. Afterward, an exhausted Junior embraces Frankie and the musical, like the ballet within it, ends (Hischak 2008, 551).

On Your Toes has not aged well. Its first Broadway revival, eighteen years after the original production, was poorly received because the book was newly deemed "labored, mechanical, and verbose" by what were at that point contemporary standards (Block 2009, 87). Yet the strides *On Your Toes* took in uniting various dance styles and presenting them as part of a broader but increasingly accessible art form were unparalleled at the time.

Dance infused the entire musical, but three numbers in particular are representative of Balanchine's approach to popularizing dance, and to breaking down class assumptions and stylistic boundaries. The "Princess Zenobia" ballet closing Act I parodied Michel Fokine's 1910 choreography for Rimsky-Korsakov's *Scheherazade*, and featured a hilariously rubber-legged and confused Bolger in the lead. The title number, in Act II, featured tap and ballet dancers performing together using choreography that "presented the two styles as a single American art form," rather than two competing ones. And the lengthy finale, "Slaughter on Tenth Avenue," blended classical ballet, modern and jazz dance, and was so integral to *On Your Toes* that the musical can only end once the dance within it has. Dance was so intrinsic to *On Your Toes*, which opened to accolades at the Imperial and ran for 315 performances, that Balanchine became the first person to be listed in a program as the choreographer for a Broadway musical (Hardy 2006, 17). Ballanchine continued to work on Broadway, collaborating with Rodgers and Hart on *Babes in Arms*, *I Married an Angel*, and *The Boys from Syracuse* before heading to Hollywood in 1938.

One of Rodgers and Hart's last musicals, *Pal Joey*, was also their favorite and most celebrated (Block 2009, 101). *Pal Joey*'s book was cohesive enough that it can be successfully revived for contemporary audiences without requiring extensive modifications. One of their most truly integrated shows, *Pal Joey* was also their darkest and most controversial. Its characters were morally questionable at best and often downright unlikable, its settings and situations were seamy, its sexual themes blunt and base. Yet its grit was also its strength: its characters were fleshed-out enough, its plot coherent and believable enough, and its songs and dances integrated enough that many critics quickly recognized it as a landmark that advanced the Broadway musical genre. By the time *Pal Joey* was first revived on Broadway in 1952, most critics and historians considered it the most important musical of Rodgers and Hart's output (Sears 2008, 147).

Pal Joey was based on a series of thirteen epistolary stories by John O'Hara that were published serially in *The New Yorker* through 1939. Always signed "Your Pal Joey," the letters were written by the character Joey Evans to his "Pal Ted" in New York. Joey, an amoral, uneducated, street-smart nightclub singer who drifts from Ohio to Chicago, is not a particularly mean or vengeful person, but he is also not especially self-aware, generous, or capable of personal growth. Joey blames the world for denying him the success he feels entitled to, and views other people as a means (or barrier) to his sexual or material ends. O'Hara's stories, like the musical based on them, end more or less the way they begin: Joey parts ways with people he seemed close to, and begins his search anew for someone on whom to harness his dreams of success and fame (Mast 1987, 174–5).

O'Hara approached Rodgers and Hart about adapting the stories, and subsequently wrote the script, which was revised by Rodgers, Hart, and George Abbott. The stage version of Joey, often considered musical theater's first anti-hero, is a "self-serving, two-timing little twerp" working at a sleazy nightclub on the South Side of Chicago and dreaming of owning a classier joint. Early in Act I, he woos the sweet, comparatively naïve Linda English with the now-standard song "I Could Write a Book." After Joey and Linda begin dating, Joey also starts seeing the slumming socialite Vera Simpson, who is older, harsher, and more self-serving than Linda.

In exchange for sexual favors, Vera buys Joey expensive clothing, rents him a fancy apartment, and bankrolls his dream nightclub, Chez Joey. She also expresses, with a frankness remarkable for the late 1930s, the pleasure she derives from sex with him in the song "Bewitched, Bothered, and Bewildered":

When he talks he is seeking
Words to get off his chest
Horizontally speaking
He's at his very best

Vera adds later that while she is "vexed again" and "perplexed again" as she enters into the affair, she is nevertheless grateful to be "over-sexed again." Vera may not have fit comfortably into the contemporary conception of a "proper" American woman, but she, like the rest of *Pal Joey*, was bluntly, refreshingly honest.

Eventually, both women dump Joey: Linda loses interest in him and Vera, fearing that her husband will find out about him, abruptly removes him from her life. Newly broke and single, Joey is unfazed: clearly, this sort of thing has happened to him before and will probably happen again. *Pal Joey* thus ends as it begins—with Joey blithely picking up a new woman by singing a reprise of "I Could Write a Book" (Bordman 2001, 576).

The book and lyrics to *Pal Joey* were filled with double entendre and suggestive language, spouted by characters who were notably tough to cozy up to. Many of the show's musical numbers emanated naturally from either the sleazy nightclub Joey and Vera first meet in, or in Chez Joey. These aspects of the show only added to its gritty, natural feel. In a stroke of genius, the creative team countered the transgressive production with conservative casting: the "charming" soprano Vivienne Segal played Vera against type, infusing the hardened, self-absorbed character with more grace and charm than she might otherwise have had. And the young Gene Kelly, in the title role, apparently "achieved the impossible by making Joey not only sexually attractive but also irresistibly lovable" despite his many flaws (Kirle 2005, 100).

Pal Joey connected with audiences, who seemed generally unperturbed by Brooks Atkinson's famously barbed review of the musical in *The New York Times*. Quick to acknowledge that *Pal Joey* was expertly written, staged, and performed, Atkinson still called the story "joyless" and "odious," its characters not worth the audience's time or attention, and the sexually loaded lyrics to "Bewitched, Bothered and Bewildered" "scabrous." He concluded his review by questioning whether one could "draw sweet water from a foul well" (Stempel 2010, 286).

Yet other critics lauded *Pal Joey* for refusing to sugarcoat its themes or characters. Especially with Kelly in the lead, audiences found *Pal Joey* appealing enough to support for 374 performances. Atkinson revisited the musical when it was revived in 1952 and admitted finding it newly palatable, especially given the "changed moral climate and more relaxed theatre standards" (Bordman 2001, 577).

By the early 1940s, Rodgers and Hart's relationship was strained. In 1941, Rodgers was approached by the Theatre Guild about musicalizing the 1930 Lynn Riggs play *Green Grow the Lilacs*, a Broadway flop that had developed new life in the regional theater. Hart, whose chronic alcoholism had begun to affect his ability to stick to deadlines or show up for meetings or rehearsals, did not like the idea. He refused to work with Rodgers on it, even after Rodgers threatened to accept the project and find another lyricist (Sears 2008, 148). Hart held firm; his last work with Rodgers was on a November 1943 revival of their 1927 hit *A Connecticut Yankee*. After being ejected from a performance of that production for drunken disorderliness at Rodgers' request, Hart disappeared. He was found five days later in a Times Square gutter with a raging case of pneumonia, to which he succumbed on November 22, at the age of 48.[14]

About eight months prior, Rodgers' adaptation of *Green Grow the Lilacs*, with lyrics by his new partner Oscar Hammerstein II, opened at the St. James Theater to the kinds of ecstatic accolades Rodgers and Hart had never seen. Virtually every critic raved about the production, which ran for an unprecedented 2,212 performances over the course of five years. Hart was in the audience on opening night, dutifully applauding, laughing, and hooting approval from his orchestra seat. But his decades-long partnership with Rodgers was truly over (Stempel 2010, 287). As the Depression gave way to the Second World War, Broadway's players, output, and cultural resonance would shift again to meet the needs of a changing nation.

CHAPTER 5
THE SECOND WORLD WAR TO 1960

Oklahoma! has long been regarded as so monumentally important to the history of the American stage musical that in some surveys it is treated as the very linchpin of the genre: both the culmination of everything that came before it and an indelible influence on everything that followed. The partnership of Richard Rodgers and Oscar Hammerstein II enjoys similar treatment. No history of the Broadway musical would be complete without discussion of their many contributions to the genre.

Without question, *Oklahoma!* was a watershed musical created by and marking the debut of an extraordinarily important partnership. Both *Oklahoma!* and the seemingly charmed partnership that created it emerged at a time when the commercial theater industry had not only solidified but weathered seemingly impossible challenges, and the country was uniting under the kind of intense patriotism that only external conflict can engender. *Oklahoma!* was a musical that was important not only for its stylistic contributions, but also because it was so well-shaped by and so sharply reflective of its era. Something similar can be said about Rodgers and Hammerstein themselves.

The Second World War and popular culture

Wars are sometimes given weirdly positive nicknames. The First World War was known as the "Great War," for example, and the Second World War the "Good" one; current global conflicts have been officially, collectively labeled "Operation Enduring Freedom" by the US government. While such monikers reinforce the historical importance of a given war or international dispute, they also gloss over the messiness, contradictions, violence, and heartache such events cause, emphasizing instead their positive impact on the nation. There was, after all, nothing "good" about the Second World War for those whose homes or cities were destroyed, those who were grievously injured or killed in battle, or those who lost their brothers, fathers, or sons. Yet the Second World War has earned a hallowed place in American history in part because it seemed to pit a clear good against a clear evil, as well as because it was fought at a distance that put the US at a safe advantage over the swaths of Europe and Asia that were decimated in combat. It was also "good" because it unified the populace and rebooted the economy more quickly and successfully than any number of WPA projects could possibly have managed.

Due to the lingering impact of the Depression, nearly eight million Americans remained unemployed in the early 1940s prior to the country's entry into the war. Wartime demand, however, saw the rapid creation of tens of millions of jobs. By 1944, unemployment had plummeted to a low of around 800,000. Many of the new jobs were filled by women, who went to work in unprecedented numbers in the absence of men sent to fight overseas. Despite continued inequality, millions of African Americans, too, enlisted in the war effort; those who remained at home had increased access to jobs in manufacturing, as skilled craftsmen, and with unions. Due to the Great Migration, which continued through the 1940s, the growing concentration of blacks in northern urban centers allowed as well for easier participation in civil rights activities, greater access to cultural and political organizations, and less difficulty registering to vote (Brinkley 2007, 19).

The American media fostered both enthusiasm and unity among American citizens well before the US entered the war. Prior to the attack on Pearl Harbor, newspapers, magazines, and radio programs regularly covered news from Europe and Asia. Once the US responded to the Pearl Harbor attacks, its new Office of War Information generated its own propaganda in the form of newsreels, radio broadcasts, pamphlets, and advertisements. These encouraged American citizens to unify in support of the country's war effort by buying bonds, donating goods, and participating in food or supply drives. The result was a remarkably strong, sustained sense of national unity, borne primarily of wartime but also of the newly robust economy (Jones 2003, 123–4).

Such economic abundance, especially after over a decade of restraint, stimulated "a striking buoyancy in American life in the early 1940s that the war itself only partially counterbalanced. Suddenly, people had money to spend again and—despite the many shortages of consumer goods—at least some things to spend it on." As often happens during dark times, the film, music, and theater industries did record business in the war years. Hotels, resorts, sporting events, and casinos, too, prospered anew as Americans sought to forget their concerns (Brinkley 2007, 17–18).

Most mass entertainment forms incorporated wartime themes of democracy, unity, patriotism, and support. During the war years, the government depended to some degree on the self-regulation of various entertainment markets to, for example, record patriotic music or depict upbeat, positive scenes of men serving the country. But government committees, too, were formed to encourage "nearly every segment of the American public to unite in the wartime effort, including agencies whose specific charge was to make sure Hollywood, radio broadcasters, and the sound-recording industry kept the war before the public," albeit never in graphic or upsetting ways.[1]

An exception was Broadway, which was deemed too small to function effectively in the spread of wartime propaganda and was thus largely left to its own devices (Jones 2003, 129). This does not mean that the commercial theater industry ignored the war. Swept up in patriotic sentiment with much of the rest of the country, many Times Square venues began performances with the national anthem, and Broadway proudly sponsored wartime fundraisers and bond drives. And, of course, many stage musicals to open at the time reflected aspects of the country and its people at war.

The war and Broadway

In the Second World War era, Broadway embraced many of the same contradictions inherent in American culture at large. As the Broadway musical reached maturity and entered what many historians consider a golden age, it reflected both "delight in the apparently limitless opportunities America afforded for self-invention" and, simultaneously, the country's international status, power, prestige, diversity, national culture, and wartime anxieties (Most 2004, 1–2). By the early 1940s, the commercial theater industry was far smaller than it had been before the Depression. The Broadway musical nevertheless reached important heights in its artistic output, critical and commercial reception, and influence on later productions.

The prosperity of the Second World War-era New York—a state that surpassed all others in war production and thus anchored the country's "arsenal of democracy"—resonated in the theater industry. Broadway responded with productions that were, on the whole, weighty, sentimental, innovative, and preoccupied with what America represented culturally (Klein 2001, 600–1). The Second World War-era Broadway is often lauded for its cultivation of the integrated musical—a goal that by this point had been sought for decades and that was seen to have been realized by the partnership of Rodgers and Hammerstein. Yet beyond this oft-celebrated accomplishment, it is perhaps the "escapist turnback to real or exaggerated joys of a bygone Americana" that became wartime Broadway's most "impressive and lasting contribution to the lyric stage" (Bordman 2001, 583).

Between the 1940s and early 1960s, the Broadway musical was dominated by a small, concentrated number of enormously talented artists whose output benefited from time and place, the cohesiveness of its industry, the consolidation of its audiences and critical corps, and a growing reliance on formulas that simultaneously embraced old European and contemporary American artistic ideals. While the output on Broadway remained typically heterogeneous—not all productions were, after all, integrated works by Rodgers and Hammerstein—the war- and postwar years set the stage for contemporary Broadway, and exerted numerous influences that continue to resonate.

Rodgers and Hammerstein and the "birth" of the integrated musical

As noted through these pages, creators of the American stage musical have long aspired to an integrated art form in which plot, character, song, dance, and setting would serve a unified whole, perceived as artistically superior for its cohesion. Stylistic integration became even more desirous through the 1930s once realism in the movies became more popular and theater artists scrambled to "re-position self-conscious theatricality in the cultural marketplace" (Most 2004, 30). In striving to create commercial productions blending dance, music, and theater into a populist whole, musical theater creators sought a distinctive, American take on the Wagenerian concept of *Gesamtkunswerk* ("total art work"). This, it was reasoned, would allow the Broadway musical to incorporate weightier subject matter and more "classical aesthetic principals" while exposing audiences to a wider variety of performing arts, all of which would benefit commercially and artistically in the process (Kirle 2005, 21–2). The idealization of arts integration is thus in part culturally derived: integrated musicals were seen as "elevated" in importance due to film and critical trends, and the increased involvement on Broadway of artists from the dance and classical music worlds.

Both the timing and reception of *Oklahoma!*, which opened at the St. James Theater on March 31, 1943, were of great importance in setting commercial and critical standards on Broadway. No entertainment industry is wise to ignore a big hit, after all, and *Oklahoma!* was no mere success—it was "an indisputable blockbuster of remarkable coherence," a blindingly white-hot ticket that was almost immediately emulated (Riis and Sears 2008, 164).

It takes several ingredients to create a blockbuster, among them good timing, skill, innovation, and keen business sense. With regards to the last, it is worth noting that Rodgers and Hammerstein, talented as they were with crafting musicals, also had plenty of business experience between them. Their partnership might have been brand new, but well before it began, each man had built a solid reputation for being as hard-driving on the business end as he was brilliantly creative on the artistic front (Hirsch 1998, 224). Together, they were fiercely protective when producing their own shows, and soon proved similarly formidable when it came to producing others' works. They produced the 1946 hit *Annie Get Your Gun*, for example, and helped shape it by bringing Irving Berlin out of semi-retirement to write it when its first composer, Hammerstein's former partner Jerome Kern, died unexpectedly in 1945 (Knapp 2006, 209).

When it came to *Oklahoma!*, timing and theme could not have been better. Rodgers and Hammerstein's premiere musical, which opened just over a year after the US entered the Second World War, was steeped in Americana. Many of its innovations were couched in nationalistic sentiment and themes of strength in unity. Set in Oklahoma territory in the early twentieth century, *Oklahoma!* never directly references the Second World War, but its unwavering love of country comes through with crystal clarity. As the oft-referenced lyric from the titular song goes, "we know we belong to the land / and the land we belong to is grand."

Oklahoma! balances its innovations with tradition. Like many subsequent musicals, it features a dual plot structure that Hammerstein borrowed from classic operetta. Dual plot structures tend to balance a serious or even tragic romance with one that is comparatively light or comedic (Mast 1987, 208–9). *Oklahoma!* also has a classic boy meets, loses, and wins girl back trajectory. Yet while modeled on structures typical of older entertainment forms, *Oklahoma!* departs from tradition in important ways, eschewing ingredients long assumed critical for the commercial success of a stage musical.

For example, *Oklahoma!* bluntly dispenses with the notion that a large group of leggy chorines had to be present, smiling, and kicking up a sequined storm at the opening curtain. Instead, following the overture, *Oklahoma!* emulates the opening of the Riggs play on which it is based by featuring Aunt Eller alone on stage churning butter, and Curly wandering in while singing the opening strains of "Oh, What a Beautiful Mornin'." Further, *Oklahoma!* demonstrated that mixed choruses—"usually reserved for shows with serious operatic pretensions"—could be employed to dance and sing in any number of scenes (Riis and Sears 2008, 165). In general, *Oklahoma!* proved that a logical, well-executed plot, carefully threaded with well-crafted, memorable songs, could justify any innovation. More "flexibility in the creation of scenarios and even occasional violence resulting in an on-stage killing could be included," especially if some of the characters were exonerated or saved in the end. Dance, too, could further the plot or add dimension to the motivations or emotional states of characters; choreographer Agnes de Mille was lauded for staging *Oklahoma*'s dream ballet, which wordlessly depicted Laurie's courtship-related, and thus romantic and sexual, anxieties (ibid.).

Hammerstein's lyrics, too, were carefully crafted to mirror the way characters talk and behave through the use of dialect, accent, and "verbal imagery" (Mast 1987, 217). All of these allowed characters' actions and motivations to be plumbed to new depths. Rodgers and Hammerstein were adept at using songs to tip off audiences about the subconscious desires of characters, hence the frequent use in their musicals of what are often called conditional or hypothetical love songs, performed in early scenes. These songs—like *Oklahoma*'s "People Will Say We're in Love" and, later, *Carousel*'s "If I Loved You"—helped transmit to spectators two characters' romantic interest in one another, long before the characters themselves realize or act on their feelings.

The plot of *Oklahoma!* traces two love triangles that are resolved before a backdrop drenched in patriotic sentimentality. The primary love triangle involves Aunt Eller's niece Laurie, the amiable cowboy Curly, and the gruff, vaguely threatening farmhand Jud Fry. Laurie is drawn to Curly and fears Jud, who lives on Aunt Eller's farm in a smokehouse that he has covered with pictures of naked women. When Jud invites Laurie to a boxed lunch social, she accepts his invitation to spite Curly. The prospect of going with Jud causes Laurie great anxiety, and puts the tension borne of love triangles into action, fueling the plot.

The second, more comic love triangle involves cowboy Will Parker, farm girl Annie (nicknamed "Ado Annie" because of her healthy interest in men), and the Persian peddler Ali Hakim, with whom Annie flirts while Will is away. As these love stories play out, progress in Oklahoma territory is disrupted by tensions between the cowboys and farmhands, which is outlined in the number "The Farmer and the Cowman."

All conflicts are neatly resolved by the end of the musical. The farmers and cowmen eventually, if grudgingly, accept one another. Ali leaves the territory, and Annie and Will marry. Tensions simmer between Curly, Jud, and Laurie until a drunken Jud picks a fight with Curly, during which he accidentally falls on his knife and dies. Curly and Laurie marry, Oklahoma becomes a state, and the people in it collectively rejoice. Without mentioning the contemporary US once, *Oklahoma!* frequently marvels over Americans' innovations, industriousness, ability to tackle and resolve conflicts through hard work, morality, and belief in the common good.

A darker, moodier musical than *Oklahoma!*, Rodgers and Hammerstein's highly-anticipated follow-up, *Carousel* (1945), nevertheless similarly impresses the importance of community support, hard work, and a collective desire for "a future where no one walks alone" (Mast 1987, 210). For its differences and bleaker tone, *Carousel* again featured a blend of innovation and tradition that was by this point rapidly becoming a Rodgers and Hammerstein trademark.

Like *Oklahoma!*, *Carousel* was adapted from a literary work. It featured long musical scenes with frequent reprises and extended ballet sequences, again choreographed by Agnes de Mille, which provided deeper insight into the lives of its characters. Its plot, like *Oklahoma*'s, featured two sets of lovers, one less fraught than the other. And while set in America's past, *Carousel* allowed audiences to reflect on the American present.

Adapted from Ferenc Molnár's 1909 play *Liliom*, *Carousel* relocates the action from late-nineteenth-century Hungary to late-nineteenth-century Maine, and renames the original title character Billy Bigelow. Bigelow is a smart if gruff and frustrated man with a quick temper and a widely swaying moral compass. He works as a carousel barker at a local parade grounds, where he meets Julie Jordan, a millworker whose naïveté and quiet, dreamy personality belies her iron-clad strength and survivor instinct. In the secondary, lighter plotline, Julie's friend and fellow millworker Carrie Pipperidge is courted by and eventually marries a local fisherman named Enoch Snow.

Julie and Billy establish an interest in one another early in Act I with the conditional love song "If I Loved You"; their growing affection for one another costs them both their jobs. They marry after a brief courtship, but their life together proves difficult. Both are preoccupied with money and finding work, and they struggle to communicate their love for and devotion to one another. Julie soon admits to Carrie that Billy hits her; Carrie, in turn, tells Julie that she and Enoch have become engaged to be married.

Late in Act I, Julie tells Billy that she's pregnant. "Soliloquy," the number Billy sings in response to the news, tracks his mixed feelings about impending fatherhood: anxiety, elation, doubt, and finally stolid determination to support his child. Yet Billy's inability to make wise choices proves his undoing. Desperate for money, he agrees to help his morally bankrupt friend Jigger Craigin rob Julie's former boss, the mill owner. The robbery goes wrong when the intended victim pulls a gun on Billy and Jigger. Jigger runs away, but when Billy realizes that he will be shot if he tries, he instead falls on his own knife. As he dies, Julie arrives to finally profess her love for him; in a show of community support, Julie's cousin Nettie sings the ballad "You'll Never Walk Alone."

Billy goes to purgatory, where time passes more slowly than on Earth. He sees his daughter, Louise, now fifteen years old; a lengthy dance sequence, "Billy Makes a Journey," depicts her as a sad, lonely teen who feels shunned by her community because of her dead father's bad reputation. Hoping to redeem himself and gain entry into heaven, Billy returns to visit Louise and tell her not to isolate herself. He also finally tells Julie, who cannot see him but detects his presence, that he truly loved her. *Carousel* ends with a reprise of the number "You'll Never Walk Alone"; it is suggested that Billy has been redeemed, and that Julie and Louise will find strength in their community. Like *Oklahoma!*, *Carousel* reinforces the power of American solidarity in times of hardship.

Many musical theater scholars, including Raymond Knapp, Bruce Kirle, Andrea Most, and Warren Hoffman note that for Rodgers and Hammerstein's frequent emphasis on inclusiveness and community, their musicals nevertheless focus overwhelmingly on white, middle-class values and concerns, while eliding deeper, more realistic conversations about race, ethnicity, and difference. In many respects, this is a reflection of the time and culture in which Rodgers and Hammerstein worked, and of Broadway's typically white, middle- to upper-class audience base. Recent revivals of their musicals have incorporated color-blind casting and subtle directorial and dramaturgical adjustments "in an effort to make them relevant to a different cultural moment" (Kirle 2005, 39). A much-loved 1994 Broadway revival, for example, featured the white actor Eddie Korbich as Enoch, introduced the African American Broadway superstar Audra McDonald to audiences as Carrie, and joked about its own casting choices by featuring eight children of diverse ethnic and racial backgrounds as their offspring.

Such contemporary casting choices would, of course, not have translated well to Broadway audiences in Rodgers and Hammerstein's time. Yet while musicals during the Second World War era primarily emphasized white middle and upper classes, the 1940s was nevertheless a period during which new steps toward racial integration, both on and off the stage, were slowly taking place.

Social integration through the war years

During the Harlem Renaissance, W.E.B. Du Bois wrote of the need for an African American theater movement that would create productions about, by, for, and near black audiences. His call to action "fit within the larger push toward self-expression and self-determination that burgeoned within African American communities of the 1920s," and which resulted in the establishment such black theater companies across the country. In New York, several such companies operated out of the basement of the Harlem Library, which first became a performance space when Du Bois himself founded the Krigwa Players in 1926. Following the demise of that company in 1929, other like-minded groups used the same space: the Harlem Experimental Theater (1929–33), the Harlem Players (1931), and the American Negro Theater (1940–9). This last company was co-founded by Frederick O'Neal (1905–92), who would in 1964 become the first African American president of Actors' Equity (Shandell 2013, 108–9). The growth of the so-called Negro Little Theatre Movement through the mid-twentieth century created new opportunities for black artists, and options for spectators who "sought meaningful alternatives to the racist tendencies of American culture" (ibid., 104).

The Negro Little Theatre Movement was deemed necessary in large part because mainstream commercial theater continued to provide little for black entertainers and audiences. On Broadway in the 1940s, there remained the occasional musical with an all-black cast, but these were increasingly rare. The Vernon Duke and John Latouche musical *Cabin in the Sky* was a hit in 1940, and later "a beneficiary of the wartime emphasis on racial harmony in motion pictures" when it became the first musical with an all-black cast to become a Hollywood film (Woll 1989, 195). In 1946, *St. Louis Woman*, featuring Pearl Bailey in her Broadway debut, ran at the Beck for 113 performances. This was the rare musical to feature a mixed-race creative team: its book, based on the 1931 novel *God Sends Sunday* by Arna Bontemps, was adapted by Bontemps with the poet Countee Cullen; its score was by Harold Arlen and Johnny Mercer.

But in general, "black musicals" on Broadway rarely reflected the "by, about, for and near" tenet outlined by Du Bois. Rather, as vehicles for white composers, lyricists, and book writers to explore black American culture for overwhelmingly white audiences, most followed the *Porgy and Bess* model: black casts performed work by white creative teams that was backed by white producers. Through the mid-twentieth century, black book writers, composers, choreographers, and lyricists—not to mention directors and producers—were rare, if not nonexistent on Broadway, though the poet Langston Hughes collaborated with composer Kurt Weill on *Street Scene* (1947), and Katherine Dunham was a regular presence as both performer and choreographer through the 1940s. In terms of power and economics, race relations on Broadway "remained deeply unequal, with whites largely controlling the narrative of the shows, as well as their production and business practices" (Oja 2014, 155).

Nevertheless in subtle, gradual ways, the cultural shifts taking place in the US during the mid-twentieth century were reflected on Broadway. On its stages, in its orchestra pits, and in its long-desegregated seating areas, white and black people mingled. And while racism was still rife, glimmers of increased understanding occurred. Stories of grossly imbalanced business practices and unequal pay-scales faded, and anecdotal evidence emerged that implied more empowerment among artists of color who appeared on Broadway's stages. On several occasions during rehearsals for *St. Louis Woman*, for example, cast members openly questioned or challenged the white director Rouben Mamoulian about what they perceived as offensive representations of black characters in the production (Woll 1989, 200). A number of musicals, too, showed glimmers of what would become the American Civil Rights Movement.

During and just after the Second World War, a number of American institutions took sure steps toward desegregation. In 1941, FDR issued Executive Order 8802 prohibiting discrimination in American defense industries, and establishing the Fair Employment Practices Commission. In 1946, the US Supreme Court ruled that segregation in interstate travel was unconstitutional. In 1947, Jackie Robinson broke major league baseball's color line when he was signed to the Brooklyn Dodgers. And in 1948, President Truman signed an executive order desegregating the armed forces.[2]

On Broadway, integrated casts became more typical, as did shows promoting social progress and racial equality. Harold Arlen and Yip Harburg's 1944 production *Bloomer Girl*, for example, was marketed as another *Oklahoma!* due to its integrated structure, de Mille choreography, historic American setting, and involvement of *Oklahoma!* original cast members Celeste Holm and Joan McCracken. *Bloomer Girl* was not as artistically resonant or serious as *Oklahoma!*, but its cast featured black performers, and the musical used its historic setting to comment on contemporary concerns, including women's rights and racial equality. The Civil War ballet de Mille choreographed for *Bloomer Girl* was perhaps less relevant to the musical than it was to wartime audiences: the dance "poignantly depicted the grief of wives and mothers whose loved ones will never return," and thus "had a certain thinly disguised timeliness." *Bloomer Girl* was not the enormous hit *Oklahoma!* was, but it resonated with audiences nonetheless. It ran for 657 performances before closing in 1946 (Bordman 2001, 597).

Of course, on Broadway as elsewhere, there remained stubborn structural and representational throwbacks. While one of the more important wartime productions, Irving Berlin's now oft-forgotten 1942 revue *This Is the Army*, featured a mixed-race cast,[3] Berlin initially conceived of an opening number featuring the entire cast in full military uniform … and blackface. Already fifty-three when the US entered the Second World War, Berlin had been active on Broadway for over thirty years, and was drawing on forms, however offensive, with which he was familiar and comfortable.

This Is the Army was Berlin's second wartime revue. He wrote his first, *Yip Yip Yaphank* (1918), while he was stationed at Camp Upton, Long Island, and initially intended *This Is the Army* as a revival of *Yaphank*. *Yaphank* had run on Broadway in August and September of 1918, grossing over $50,000 and closing only because the members of its military cast were "required to become soldiers again." *Yaphank*—for which Berlin composed "God Bless America," though the song was cut from the show—had a big opening sequence modeled after the first act of a traditional minstrel show: the huge, all-male cast stood on risers with a sergeant serving as the interlocutor. The sequence featured sentimental ballads and coon songs, and cast members frequently donned drag, blackface, or both for the comic bits (Magee 2012, 69–72).

When the US entered the Second World War, Berlin jumped at the chance to help with morale by updating *Yip Yip Yaphank*. After receiving permission from General George Marshall to embark on the project, proceedings from which would be donated to Army Emergency Relief, Berlin hired Ezra Stone, an actor, producer, and director serving with the Army's Special Services, to direct (Grimes 1994, 12). Younger than Berlin by nearly three decades, Stone convinced Berlin not to use blackface in *This Is the Army*. Arguments about the practice being outdated and offensive fell on deaf ears, so Stone instead noted that there would be no time to get the cast out of blackface once the opening number ended. Berlin conceded, and when *This Is the Army* opened at the Broadway Theater on Independence Day 1942, it featured a mixed-race cast that was, at the time, "the only integrated company in uniform." Its huge opening number remained rooted in minstrelsy, but no one wore blackface.[4] *This Is the Army* ran for 113 performances and then, with regular changes to the cast and material, went on a tour that lasted as long as the war did. The revue was made into a movie in 1943; coupled with the sale of the film rights, the show earned $10 million for the Army (Jones 2003, 135).

The 1944 dance musical *On the Town* shared *This Is the Army*'s light touch, mixed-race cast, embrace of American idealism, and rooting in the traditional musical revue, but was more innovative for its time. Its ambitious choreographer, Jerome Robbins (1918–98), like Rodgers and Hammerstein, ascribed to the idea of "totally integrated," accessible stage entertainments that blended ballet, social dance, and contemporary music (Kirle 2005, 21–2).

On the Town was inspired by and based on *Fancy Free*, a short ballet Robbins choreographed to a score by Leonard Bernstein (1918–90), which premiered in April 1944 at the old Metropolitan Opera House on Broadway between West 39th and 40th streets. *On the Town* opened on Broadway a mere eight months later, in December of the same year. Like *Fancy Free*, *On the Town* depicted three Navy men sightseeing and looking for women during a 24-hour shore leave in New York City. The musical's book and lyrics were contributed by the comedy duo Betty Comden (1917–2006) and Adolph Green (1914–2002), who drew material from their nightclub act.

The resultant musical was as dense a mix of high-, middle-, and lowbrow elements as its disparate influences imply. In some numbers, moody, classical dance sequences were accompanied by Bernstein's symphonic scoring; in others, hips rotated suggestively to jazz or blues accompaniment. The plot featured erudite and elitist characters mixing with crass ones, ridiculous situations and deeply moving ones. Plenty of jokes, whether subtle, corny, recurring, cheap, or dirty, kept the energy high.

When they were developing *On the Town*, the left-leaning, politically active creative team responded to an effort by various civil rights organizations to encourage mixed-race casting and "nonstereotypical racial representation." The original Broadway cast featured four black dance chorus members and two black singers. One of its female leads, Miss Ivy Smith, was originated by Sono Osato, a dancer of Japanese and European heritage whose father was interned during the war as a result of the Japanese American Internment Policy. White performers outnumbered those of color, but *On the Town*'s racially mixed casting was quietly remarkable for its time. Cast members acted and danced together instead of in segregated groups, and all the characters were considered part of a typical urban landscape. Black and white men appeared together as sailors, dockworkers and citizens, and one black chorus member played the recurring role of a police officer. These choices were daring enough that Robbins recalled having trouble in some of the cities the touring production visited (Oja 2014, 154–5).

While more subtle than overt, and certainly not without plenty of contradictions, wartime musicals reflected a new interest in artistic integration and, more cautiously, in racial integration. Both types of integration would be reflected through the postwar era on Broadway, which continued to promote, if not always successfully, unity, harmony, and goodwill for all citizens of a country that was on its way to becoming a global superpower.

The postwar era

Just after 7 p.m. on August 14, 1945, the Times Tower's street-level news ticker announced the official surrender of the Japanese to the Allied forces. As news spread through the neighborhood, there erupted a thunderous roar of exultation that some news sources reported lasted almost twenty minutes. People in office buildings showered the growing throngs below with paper and confetti, and by 10 p.m., two million people had amassed between 40th and 52nd streets from Sixth to Eighth avenues, where they became "one solid mass of joyful humanity, kissing, hugging, sobbing, or simply gazing in wordless relief and delight" (Traub 2005, 100). The war was over and the US was victorious.

There was certainly good reason to dance in the streets. While countries in Europe and Asia needed to heal, restructure, and rebuild, the US emerged comparatively unscathed, economically strong, and newly powerful. Yet as the country eased into the postwar era, its fabric nevertheless remained pocked with cultural anxieties and contradictions.

Politically, the US moved slowly to the right while socially, it edged to the left. Many Americans, newly aware that it was impossible to "reconcile a commitment to freedom and democracy with the effort to deny one group of citizens a set of basic rights guaranteed to everyone else," grew newly willing to confront the country's race problem. Yet still others "considered the war not a challenge to but a confirmation of their commitment to preserving the old racial order" (Brinkley 2007, 21).

The American workforce's wartime reliance on women had brought new opportunities and freedoms that were not easy to rescind. Many women returned to the domestic front once they lost the jobs they had taken in the absence of American men, but a significant number simply sought new employment. The number of women in the workforce never receded to pre-war numbers, and continued to climb in the postwar era.

At the same time, the new freedoms enjoyed by many American women proved threatening enough that obstacles to equality not only persisted but grew. The postwar years saw significant growth in the influence of images and nationalized sentiments idealizing "traditional" American women and their roles as dutiful, passive wives, homemakers and mothers (ibid., 22–4). Mixed messages abounded: women were free to work, but why would they want to if they could marry a man and have children? Especially among the white middle classes, postwar American women were expected to desire a quiet life on the domestic front, while men were expected to venture into the public sphere to earn the household salary (Wolf 2011, 27).

Mixed messages extended well beyond gender roles. After decades of uncertainty, the country's economic prosperity and increased international power were thrilling, but also cause for anxieties about new issues and conflicts, including the Korean War, the Cold War, the rise of McCarthyism, nuclear power, and "the growing bureaucratization and impersonality of mass society." Concern increased as well over the possibility that the country's triumph in the Second World War could somehow soften the nation, that war-torn or broken families were contributing to a perceived spike in juvenile delinquency, and that as the US rose in global status, there would be that much further to fall. And, of course, for all the new prosperity, many Americans—among them women, people of color, gay men and lesbians, and the poor—continued to live in ways that did not reflect the country's strength, wealth, solidarity, freedoms, and power (Griffith and Baker 2007, 81).

This swirl of concerns and cultural contradictions was endlessly reflected in postwar popular culture. This grew more sophisticated and influential through the 1950s, especially with the exponential growth in American ownership of television sets, and the recognition among various entertainment industries of a burgeoning, economically viable youth culture.

In a holdover from the war years, American popular culture continued to promote themes of democracy, unity, and patriotism—as well as traditional gender roles and the assumed universality of the white middle class.

As the Cold War reinforced the idea of consolidation against a lurking enemy, mass entertainment, especially in its cultural themes and messages, became "more homogenous than Americans had previously known." Homogeneity was compounded by the newly centralized and effective dissemination of popular entertainment, as well as by a decline in immigration, resulting in the drop-off of ethnic or foreign-language periodicals, theater companies, social groups, and music organizations (Marchand 2007, 98).

Postwar Times Square

The advent of new mass media, coupled with the postwar suburbanization boom, slowed business in Times Square, which once again adjusted its offerings for maximum profit. The neighborhood's dime museums, arcades and 24-hour second- and third-run movie houses—known as "grinders"—grew shabbier. Once the Port Authority bus terminal opened in the far southwest corner of the neighborhood in 1950, such establishments were joined by "rip-off retailers" peddling "overstock, seconds, and other dubious merchandise." Many of these places paid noisy hawkers to stand on the street and attempt to lure pedestrians (Bianco 2004, 126–7).

Times Square's bizarre blend of high- and lowbrow offerings was alternately celebrated and decried by the businesspeople, theatergoers, film-buffs, artists, poets, transients, junkies, winos, and runaways who spent their time there. When he was elected in 1954, Mayor Robert Wagner attempted to rid the neighborhood of its seedier establishments by making drastic changes to local zoning codes. This helped close plenty of arcades, dime museums and cheap restaurants, but inadvertently paved the way for a slew of adult bookstores and peepshows.

The city's middle and upper classes began to associate the "clamor and vulgarity of 42nd Street" with the "rising rates of assault, rape, and murder in the city" through the era. Yet at the same time, the neighborhood remained a mecca for creative outsiders. It birthed the Beat movement; its remaining dime museums were favorites of the photographer Diane Arbus and the comedian Lenny Bruce; it functioned as a thriving gay enclave; its grinders were frequented by future filmmakers like Stanley Kubrick, Martin Scorsese, and Woody Allen (ibid., 130–3).

Times Square would become even seedier and more alienating to the city's middle classes, visitors, and political leaders through the 1960s and 1970s. But just after the war, it struck a delicate enough balance between classy and squalid, welcoming and sinister, that the Beat writer Jack Kerouac described it in his 1950 novel *The Town and the City* as welcoming to all: the "Broadway weisenheimer-gambler ... The mellow gentleman in the De Pinna suit headed for the Ritz bar, and the mellow gentleman staggering by and sitting down in the gutter, to spit and groan and be hauled off by cops ... The robust young rosy-cheeked priest from Fordham with some of his jayvee basketballers on a 'night of good clean fun,' and the cadaverous morphine-addict stumbling full of shuddering misery in search of a fix" (quoted in Traub 2005, 102).

Meanwhile, the theater industry faced concerns that were not far removed from those of the surrounding neighborhood. Through the 1950s, the number of venues, and of live entertainments to put in them, contracted as audiences moved to the suburbs, went to the movies, turned on radios or record players, or switched on new television sets.

Unable to compete with the growing and vastly more powerful mass media, the commercial theater instead experimented with new ways to harness itself to it. Broadway personnel continued moonlighting in Hollywood. And as television took off, the theater industry began working with studios interested in broadcasting musicals or featuring Broadway stars on television shows.

Even as its musicals trailed behind more easily mediated entertainments in terms of power, reach, and influence, Broadway continued to serve as the country's live entertainment mecca, and thus to retain some of its prestige. Recording artists, movie stars, and television personalities still chose to assert their connections with fans by appearing in Broadway shows; cast recordings, too, could now be played on turntables, broadcast across the country on the radio, or performed on televised variety shows (Traub 2005, 103).

As the theater industry adapted for the postwar era, the Shubert empire, still the most powerful in the business, saw new troubles. In 1950, the US Attorney General hit the organization with an anti-trust suit, accusing it of monopolizing the industry and "stifling fair trade by controlling 'practically all of the theatrical booking in the United States"'—in short, of behaving exactly like the monopoly the Shubert brothers toppled during their initial climb to power (Hirsch 1998, 213–15). Members of the theater industry sided with or against the Shuberts, who mourned Lee's death in 1953 and restructured their business several times in his absence while the lawsuit dragged on. In 1956, the Shuberts surrendered twelve of their theaters in six different cities, including four in New York. They closed their more suspect booking agencies and severed ties with "any ticket agency in any city with a Shubert house." The concessions hardly destroyed them; in fact, the forced downsizing ended up stimulating profits. But the Shuberts bore the embarrassment of becoming "the first theatre entrepreneurs ever to be challenged and rebuked by federal authorities" (ibid., 229).

As if suburban flight, new developments in mass media, and increased scrutiny by the government were not stressors enough, the theater industry was also forced to compensate for inflation and the nation's rising cost of living. During the first fifteen years of the postwar era, the cost of production on Broadway increased sharply, especially for musicals, which often demand more than straight plays in terms of casting, costuming, scenery, technology, orchestral accompaniment, and crew. The number of original musicals to open on Broadway through the 1950s dwindled more than at any point since the Depression, and the pressure to keep musicals running for longer stretches to recoup intensified. Between 1944 and 1960, ticket prices on Broadway doubled. Costs were not yet steep enough to make Broadway prohibitively expensive, but they marked the beginning of a climb that escalated through the end of the century (Jones 2003, 162–3).

And yet the show not only went on, but was celebrated for its increased sophistication, sociocultural relevance, and artistic depth. In fact, during the postwar era, the American musical "witnessed a sustained seriousness of approach unknown before on the lyric stage." This was even more impressive considering "the remarkably small number of inspired creators" contributing scores, scripts, and lyrics (Bordman 2001, 583). While theater industry economics were in constant flux, the Broadway musical itself was being celebrated like never before for its innovations and artistry (Mast 1987, 291).

Rodgers and Hammerstein after the war

Rodgers and Hammerstein continued to exert influence on Broadway in the postwar era, though a notable interruption in their string of hits was *Allegro* (1947). *Allegro* was something of a departure for Hammerstein, who conceived of and wrote the book and lyrics to the musical himself, instead of adapting previous source material. *Allegro* was not an outright flop: it ran for a respectable 315 performances and, due to a huge advance in ticket sales, even made a small profit. But it was not remotely as glowingly received by critics or audiences as *Oklahoma!* or *Carousel* were.

The plot of *Allegro* traces the life of Joseph Taylor, Jr., a small-town doctor who leaves home to become a prominent if unsatisfied physician in Chicago. Choreographed and directed by Agnes de Mille, *Allegro* pushed ahead—for some, a bit too far—with Rodgers and Hammerstein's innovations. Its enormous cast featured over forty principal actors and nearly 100 chorus members, some of whom served as a Greek chorus. The complicated set made use of two tiers, state-of-the-art lighting, and many projections, and the score was so closely knitted to the plot that songs often extended through entire scenes, making them and the show itself hard to grasp for many spectators.

Critics were mixed about *Allegro*. Some heralded it as brilliant and ahead of its time, while others called it a confusing, pretentious bore. Stung by the failure, Hammerstein tinkered with *Allegro* long after it closed. He was apparently rewriting it for television at the time of his death (Sears 2008, 156–7).

Yet he was hardly so devastated that he could not focus on new projects. Rodgers and Hammerstein's next two musicals, *South Pacific* (1949) and *The King and I* (1951), were both more typical of their creative process. The former was adapted from James Michener's 1946 Pulitzer Prize-winning book *Tales of the South Pacific*, the latter from Margaret Landon's *Anna and the King of Siam* (1944). Both musicals were more accessible than *Allegro* and more directly linked to American postwar culture and politics. *South Pacific,* which opened just four years after the war ended, played simultaneously on American's collective healing from and nostalgia for the Good War. It also touched on a number of contemporary issues and concerns, including shifting gender roles and the country's new status as a global power. Finally, it reflected Hammerstein's interest in social justice and civil rights causes.

Plotwise, *South Pacific* mirrors the structure of Rodgers and Hammerstein's first two musicals in its use of parallel romantic couples. Early in *South Pacific*, Ensign Nellie Forbush, a self-described optimistic hick from Kansas, meets and falls for the French plantation owner and widower Emile de Becque. Meanwhile, American Lieutenant Joseph Cable meets and falls for Liat, daughter of the Tonkinese merchant Bloody Mary. What links these love affairs, beyond setting and situation, are Nellie and Cable's reactions to cultural or racial difference. Midway through the musical, Nellie learns with horror that de Becque's first wife was Polynesian, and abruptly ends the relationship. Similarly, Cable realizes with great shame that despite his love for Liat, he lacks the courage it would take to bring her home to his white, affluent, prejudiced American family.

South Pacific features a veritable jukebox of songs that have become American standards: "Bali Ha'i," "I'm Gonna Wash That Man Right Outta My Hair," "Younger Than Springtime," and "Some Enchanted Evening." Yet it is Cable's scorching "You've Got to Be Carefully Taught" that drives home Hammerstein's philosophy about prejudice as learned and cultivated, if also potentially overcome:

> You've got to be taught to be afraid
> Of people whose eyes are oddly made,
> And people whose skin is a diff'rent shade,
> You've got to be carefully taught.
>
> You've got to be taught before it's too late,
> Before you are six or seven or eight,
> To hate all the people your relatives hate,
> You've got to be carefully taught.

After finishing this number, Cable vows that if he survives the war, he will remain with Liat no matter what. But he never has the chance: he is killed in a spy mission. De Becque, who is on the same mission, survives, and Nellie, "the embodiment of American youth, optimism, energy, and power," realizes that love can overpower prejudice (Most 2004, 165). When de Becque returns from the mission, Nellie and his children are waiting for him at his plantation, and the four sing lovingly together as the musical ends.

Like Rodgers and Hammerstein's previous musicals, *The King and I* features plenty of headstrong, well-developed characters, humor, and dance. It also emphasizes Hammerstein's passion for universal understanding and acceptance. The plot of *The King and I* centers almost entirely on people from different places and with different worldviews who work to overcome culture clashes. At the same time, however, it reflects both the sociopolitical influence and political dominance of the western world.

Set in the 1860s, *The King and I* traces the experiences of the widowed schoolteacher Anna Leonowens, who travels to Siam (now Thailand) to tutor the king's children. Once there, Anna, who is British but often read as symbolically American, and the king "butt heads on every conceivable subject, from whether the children should be taught Western rather than

Siamese geography to proper modes of etiquette and paying respect to royalty" (Jones 2003, 153–4). While not overt in the script, a romantic interest between these two strong, stubborn characters is implied. More explicit is the emphasis on changing gender roles: throughout the musical, "both East and West profess consternation at the place of women within the other's culture" (Knapp 2005, 263).

While Rodgers and Hammerstein regularly attempted to educate audiences about racial, ethnic, and cultural acceptance, they have since been criticized for only going so far in promoting social harmony. It has been noted, for example, that for *South Pacific*'s stance against prejudice, the Asian characters, and especially Bloody Mary, are drawn broadly and stereotypically, and that Cable's death allows the musical to conveniently skirt any real possibility of interracial marriage. Similarly, *The King and I* has been criticized for Eurocentrism and "treating as childlike a culture and people eminently worthy of respect in adult terms," even as it unironically purports "to teach us the importance of respecting cross-cultural difference" (ibid., 264–5).

Of course, Rodgers and Hammerstein had to temper their social commentary lest they alienate theatergoers. During the out-of-town tryout of *South Pacific*, several advisers to the creative team advocated cutting "You've Got to Be Carefully Taught," because even this fairly straightforward declaration was widely considered too risky for Broadway. A permanent union between Liat and Cable, or an overt romance between Anna and the King, would certainly have alienated or offended many spectators at the time of the musicals' premieres (Lovensheimer 2010, 85–6). Rodgers and Hammerstein may have been well-intentioned, but were ultimately creatures of their time and place.

After *The King and I* came a string of Rodgers and Hammerstein musicals that are less well-known, either because they were not as commercially and critically successful or because they are less frequently revived, or both. These include *Me and Juliet* (1953), *Pipe Dream* (1955), and *Flower Drum Song* (1958). The team's final big hit was also their swan song. *The Sound of Music* (1959) lives on in the collective consciousness as a beloved film classic and oft-revived stage musical. A year after it premiered on Broadway, Hammerstein died of stomach cancer. His death ended one of the most powerful and influential collaborations in the history of the American musical.

Postwar musicals not by Rodgers and Hammerstein

Musical theater audiences had, by the early 1950s, grown attuned to "exactly what a book musical was supposed to be: a romantic drama of conflicting characters, alternately comic and dramatic, based on a literary source, ancient or modern, with at least eighteen musical slots, some sung, some danced" (Mast 1987, 290). Most audiences by this point knew, as well, to expect a medley of songs played by the pit orchestra as an overture; early scenes that would introduce characters, plot, and setting; and a blend of songs performed as solos, duets, small ensemble numbers, and a few featuring the entire cast. The most sophisticated of audience members might even have recognized recurring musical or thematic devices: the intersection of main and secondary plots; the use of the conditional or hypothetical love song; and perhaps an "I Want" song or two. These last are usually featured very early in the first act to establish the desires of specific characters and to set the plot in action (Wolf 2011, 25).

Through the 1950s, a curious pattern emerged in which strong seasons for Broadway musicals were followed by notably lousy ones (Bordman 2001, 637), but in general, the decade was strong for the genre. In keeping with the steady decline in demand for stage musicals as the twentieth century elapsed, fewer musicals were produced in the 1950s than in decades prior. But a large number of the shows to premiere during the decade made particularly huge profits, and many continue to be regularly revived, and performed in schools, regional, and community theaters (Wolf 2011, 30).

While most new forms of mass media worked more to hinder than help the commercial stage musical, one innovation actively helped the genre, especially through the 1950s and early 1960s. Broadway benefited enormously from the advent of the LP, or long-playing record, which was introduced in the US in 1948. After an incomplete original cast recording of *Oklahoma!* (released by Decca on several 78s in 1943) sold a million copies, record companies grew eager to release original Broadway cast recordings (OBCRs), which were typically made available on LP. By the 1950s, OBCRs were no longer an exception but the rule. OBCRs allowed Americans to bring a slice of Broadway into their homes. In this way, the advent of new entertainment technology allowed the Broadway musical to cultivate new devotees—even among people who, unable or unwilling to see shows on Broadway, were nonetheless interested in American cultural products that were both "entertaining and meaningful" (Leve 2016, 133–5).

One of the most successful musicals of the 1950s was also one of the decade's first. *Guys and Dolls*, a "sassy, irreverent love poem of lowlife in New York," featured a book by Jo Swerling and Abe Burrows that drew from journalist Damon Runyon's short stories about prohibition-era gangsters, hustlers, and gamblers. Its score was by Frank Loesser (1910–69), a Tin Pan Alley composer whose number "Baby, It's Cold Outside" had won the 1949 Academy Award for Best Original Song. *Guys and Dolls* opened on Broadway at the 46th Street Theatre on November 24, 1950, where it remained for over three years; it has been revived on Broadway five times since then (Bordman 2001, 629).

Neither of the two love stories in *Guys and Dolls* is tragic, or even very serious, but one is more broadly comic than the other. The two romantic leads are the gambling-, drinking- and fun-averse Salvation Army Sergeant Sarah Brown and the gambler Sky Masterson (who is also perfectly comfortable with fun and booze). The second couple consists of the marriage-averse gambler Nathan Detroit and the long-suffering nightclub performer Miss Adelaide, to whom he has been engaged for fourteen years.

Guys and Dolls' action begins when the perpetually broke Nathan learns that following a police crackdown, the only place he can host his "permanent floating crap game" is in a garage whose owner wants a $1,000 retainer. Nathan bets Sky that amount that Sky cannot convince Sarah to fly to Havana with him for dinner. Sky promises Sarah "one-dozen genuine sinners" in exchange for the date. She initially rebuffs him, but changes her mind when she learns that her mission may close for lack of souls to save. While she is gone, Nathan moves his crap game into her mission.

Meanwhile, Adelaide and Nathan squabble over their long engagement and Nathan's refusal to stop gambling. Adelaide learns that her chronic cold is a psychosomatic condition caused by frustration with her fiance. The song she sings about this realization, "Adelaide's Lament," is one of the highpoints of the musical and has become a classic of the genre.

Sarah falls in love with Sky in Havana, but when she discovers the crap game Nathan is hosting in her mission she blames Sky and ends their relationship. Nathan again moves the game, this time to a sewer below Times Square. Genuinely in love with Sarah, Sky bets the crap players a thousand dollars each against their souls. If he loses, he will pay them all; if he wins, they all have to attend a meeting at Sarah's mission. Sky wins, thereby not only saving the mission but proving his love to Sarah. In the end, both guys give up gambling for their dolls, and presumably live happily ever after—though Nathan begins to sneeze on the way to the altar.

Without trying too hard or digging too deeply, *Guys and Dolls* captures a number of contradictions inherent in 1950s American culture. It drives home the notion of Times Square as simultaneously grungy and gorgeous, sleazy and romantic. It touches on the postwar myth of America as a melting pot—"a society that tolerated ethnic and cultural differences and that had learned to recognize the similarities that existed beneath strongly differentiated exteriors." In its portrait of big-hearted gamblers with strict honor codes, religious folk who always find the goodness in sinners, and couples who resolve even the most contentious of fourteen-year engagements, *Guys and Dolls* is ultimately an American fairytale that depicts New York as a place "where opposites of whatever kind rub against each other freely, creating inevitable frictions but leaving no real trace on the capacity of each differentiated group to muddle through without undue interference from the other" (Knapp 2005, 138–9).

Guys and Dolls also demonstrates a contradiction typical of many stage musicals of the time in its depiction of characters, especially female ones, who simultaneously adhere to traditional gender roles and move beyond them. Both Adelaide and Sarah desperately crave lives of traditional domesticity; this desire allows them to bond despite their obvious differences in class, education, personality, and vocal style (Adelaide is an alto, Sarah a soprano). It also justifies the last number of the musical, "Marry the Man Today," in which the two women scheme to coerce their men into marriage and "train them subsequently." At the same time, they are both independent working women with strong opinions and firm beliefs. They both exhibit clear intelligence—and in Adelaide's case, some of the funniest, most memorable numbers in the musical (Wolf 2011, 39–40).

When it comes to shifting gender roles, perhaps no 1950s musical is as telling or as enormously popular for its time as *My Fair Lady*, a smash hit based on George Bernard Shaw's 1913 play *Pygmalion*, with a new book and lyrics by Alan Jay Lerner (1918–86) and a score by Frederick Loewe (1901–88). *My Fair Lady* premiered at the Hellinger Theater in March 1956 and ran for 2,717 performances over six years, toppling *Oklahoma!* as the longest-running musical in Broadway history in the process.

Like *Guys and Dolls*, *My Fair Lady* seems rooted in traditional gender tropes that assume men are smarter and more powerful than women. But again, the characters and plot ultimately imply otherwise: just as Nathan and Sky prove no match for the women who love them, *My Fair Lady*'s Eliza Doolittle is hardly the sort of passive, agreeable little twit of a woman that was so often idealized in the 1950s. Instead, she is headstrong, driven, and intelligent, and her accomplishments are ultimately her own.

Set in London in the early twentieth century, *My Fair Lady* is a Cinderella story about the transformation of a cockney flower saleswoman who becomes the subject of a bet between the snobbish, misogynist phonetics professor Henry Higgins and the linguist Colonel Pickering. Upon first encountering Eliza in a London square, Higgins bets Pickering that in six months he can transform her into an upper-class lady by teaching her to speak accordingly. Eliza, whose early "I Want" song "Wouldn't It Be Loverly?" makes clear the fact that she dreams of more comfort and leisure than her lot in life allows, takes Higgins up on his offer of elocution assistance.

Pickering and Higgins commence lessons with the aim of presenting her at a fancy society ball. After much work and great frustration, Eliza has a breakthrough with the celebratory number "The Rain in Spain," after which she can speak with grace and erudition. More lessons help her behave like a member of the upper class. Higgins brings her to social gatherings, where she wins the affection of the aristocrat Freddy Eynsford-Hill; while neither Eliza nor Henry will admit it, Freddy is an irritant to them both because he disrupts their growing affection for one another.

Eliza is a success at the Embassy Ball, where even the most highborn members of European society believe her to be of royal blood. But when Higgins claims all the credit for her transformation, she explodes in fury and leaves him. After realizing that she cannot go back to her old life, she contemplates marrying Freddy, though she does not love him.

While ambiguous for a Broadway musical of its time, the ending of *My Fair Lady* is nevertheless more positive and hopeful than that of *Pygmalion*, which implies that Higgins and Doolittle are ultimately incompatible as lovers. In *My Fair Lady*, Higgins realizes that Eliza has vastly improved his life and admits to himself that he has come to rely on her as much as she has on him. He is listening to old recordings of their lessons when she walks back in; the curtain falls on a scene that is, while still uncertain, open to the possibility that this odd couple will live happily ever after. In softening the ending, Lerner and Loewe not only "reverse the musical roles of their protagonists," but also challenge traditional 1950s gender roles (Block 2009, 270).

As products of their culture, musicals frequently invite gendered interpretations. As with film and television shows, a vast majority are, after all, built on the assumption that a happy ending requires love to bloom between two heterosexual characters. Yet this is hardly the only way to "read" a musical: the genre can also be interpreted as commentary on broader collective hopes, desires, or concerns. For example, *The Music Man* and *West*

Side Story—two very different musicals that premiered on Broadway in 1957—are primarily love stories about seemingly mismatched individuals who nevertheless fall in love. But as Carol Oja points out, they also touch on concerns typical of the middle class in 1950s America.

West Side Story was developed by a team of highly accomplished Broadway players. Conceived, directed, and choreographed by Jerome Robbins with a score by Leonard Bernstein and a book by screenwriter and playwright Arthur Laurents (1917–2011), *West Side Story* was highly innovative and dedicated to the philosophy of arts integration. The musical's "tense, vibrant" dances and score blended classical and popular music elements, both of which were carefully integrated into the plot to help set the scene and illuminate the musical's young, intense characters (Bordman 2001, 661). The one newcomer on *West Side Story*'s creative team was its lyricist, Stephen Sondheim (1930–), who had been mentored through childhood by Oscar Hammerstein II, and who would soon become a highly accomplished Broadway composer in his own right.

In its earliest drafts, which Robbins, Bernstein, and Laurents sketched in the late 1940s, *West Side Story*'s working title was *East Side Story*. The team intended to develop a version of *Romeo and Juliet* set among Jews and Catholics on the Lower East Side during the Easter and Passover holidays. But the project was shelved after the team decided that the oft-revived and cinematized 1922 comedy *Abie's Irish Rose* would keep audiences from taking any love story about a Jew and a Catholic seriously.

In 1954, Bernstein and Laurents, chatting poolside at the Beverly Hills Hotel, noticed a headline on a nearby copy of the *Los Angeles Times* about gang warfare between white and Mexican youths. The headline inspired a new direction for the musical, which the creative team relocated from the lower *East Side* to the upper *West*. Instead of Jews and Catholics, the characters became recent Puerto Rican immigrants and more settled, if still poor and disenfranchised, white kids of Polish and Irish descent, all of whom were vying for turf in the same densely populated urban ghetto. *West Side Story* thus instantly became more topical than it would have been had it remained set among more established if similarly adversarial religious populations.

One way postwar anxiety was reflected in America was through middle-class concern about the rise of "juvenile delinquents," especially among black and working-class populations. This anxiety persisted throughout the 1950s, even in areas where youth-related violence and crime had been steadily decreasing since the war years (Graebner 1986, 81). There are many explanations for this preoccupation, among them generalized fear about uncontrollable elements capable of contaminating or infecting American culture, whether from abroad or within. The cultural obsession with juvenile delinquency, after all, occurred in the mid-1950s, concurrent with feverish concerns about communism that stimulated the McCarthy hearings. Fear about violent young ruffians was likely due as well to the newly "socializing force of the mass media"—especially comic books, movies and, increasingly, rock 'n' roll—which resulted in the media's growing reputation among distrusting adults as a frightening outside influence capable of corrupting young people (Fass 1987, 153). The introduction of new media frequently causes such concern—think, for example, about similar fears associated with video games, hip-hop, and the Internet. In the 1950s as now, there was an awful lot of new media to contend with . . . and thus to worry about.

West Side Story might have touched on topical concerns, but its creative team was careful not to play into the fears of potential spectators. The musical was sympathetic to its characters, who were portrayed as complex, tragic victims of time and circumstance. The youths depicted tended not to be vilified; the only truly unlikable characters in *West Side Story* are its few adult authority figures: the pathetically inept social director, Mr. Glad Hand; the bigoted, threatening policemen, Lt. Schrank and Officer Krupke. Only Doc, owner of the drug store where the Jets hang out, approximates a positive role model, though he too is incapable of soothing gang-related tensions.

Like the Shakespeare play on which it is based, and like many musicals to open before it, *West Side Story* follows two pairs of lovers. Tony, a reformed Jet now working for Doc, falls in love with Maria, a Puerto Rican girl promised to Chino, a member of the rival gang, the Sharks. Maria's brother, Bernardo, is leader of the Sharks; he and his girl, Anita, form the second couple. Yet *West Side Story* is atypical in that neither couple gets to live happily ever after. With the exception of the Act I number "America"—in which the Shark girls debate whether life is better in Manhattan or Puerto Rico—and the Act II number "Gee, Officer Krupke!"—in which the Jets lament the ineptitude of adults who are supposed to help them—there is little in the way of comic relief in *West Side Story*. The musical's weight is one of its chief innovations.

After falling in love at first sight at a dance in the school gym, Tony and Maria dream of running away together to a place where they will be understood and accepted. Before they can, Maria begs Tony to stop a rumble planned by the warring gangs. Tony goes, but when Bernardo stabs and kills

Tony's best friend, Riff, during the scuffle, Tony stabs and kills Bernardo in a fit of rage.

When she learns of Bernardo's fate, Maria is furious but realizes that her love for Tony is unshaken. They plan to rendezvous and run away together; "Somewhere," an extended dance sequence depicting the violence around them and their escape to the countryside, is performed as they dream together of their future. Anita initially berates Maria for forgiving Tony, but eventually accepts their love as true and strong. She agrees to warn the Jets that Chino is armed and looking to exact revenge on Tony. Yet when she appears at Doc's with the message, the Jets attack her verbally and physically before Doc stops them. Blinded by anger, Anita tells the Jets that Chino has killed Maria.

When Doc tells Tony of Maria's death, Tony comes out of hiding to search for Chino, whom he hopes will kill him too. He is momentarily calmed when Maria steps from the shadows, but as they run to one another, Chino appears and shoots Tony. He dies in her arms as she sings a reprise of "Somewhere," and the Jets and Sharks gather around. *West Side Story* diverges from *Romeo and Juliet* in its final moments. Whereas both Romeo and Juliet die, Maria not only lives, but blames both gangs for contributing to the deaths of Riff, Bernardo, and Tony. The musical ends with a shred of hope as the Jets and Sharks come together to carry Tony's body offstage.

West Side Story ran for 732 performances and made an impact on Broadway due to its cohesiveness, intensity, eclectic score, and atypically downbeat conclusion. But its success at the time of its premiere paled in comparison with that of *The Music Man*, which opened in December of the same season, ran for for 1,375 performances, and took most of that year's biggest Tony Awards. With a book, music, and lyrics by Meredith Willson (1902–84), *The Music Man* was more upbeat and less obviously socially relevant than *West Side Story*, if nevertheless innovative and culturally reflective in its own right.

Set in Iowa in 1912, *The Music Man*'s score is evocative of early-twentieth-century America. The opening patter song, "Rock Island," emulates both the rhythm of train travel and the excited banter of the traveling salesmen on board; "Ya Got Trouble" is a musicalized sales pitch by the central character, the conman Harold Hill. Other numbers, like "Iowa Stubborn" and the concurrent "Pickalittle" and "Good Night Ladies" reflect aspects of small-town life. Still others, like "Sincere" and "Lida Rose" are performed by a barbershop quartet, while "Seventy-Six Trombones," perhaps the show's most famous number, is reminiscent of Sousa marches and thus exudes American patriotism.

The quirky characters in *The Music Man* almost all find redemption in music. Some also find love in the process, not to mention satisfaction with the innocence and simplicity of small-town American life (Knapp 2005, 144–7). "Professor" Harold Hill, a phony traveling salesman, regularly cons townspeople into purchasing instruments and uniforms for a boys' band that he promises to establish, only to sneak off with the money before any materials arrive. But when he gets to River City, Iowa, he meets his match in Marian Paroo, the town's prim, self-protective librarian and piano teacher.

Like the female characters in *Guys and Dolls* and *My Fair Lady*, Marian is in many respects shrewder than her shrewd leading man, so she quickly realizes that Hill is a fraud. But she keeps the information to herself when she notices that her much younger brother, Winthrop, who is painfully self-conscious about his lisp, has overcome his shyness at the prospect of learning an instrument and joining a band. Over time, Marian and Winthrop's growing love for Harold is returned, and the bond transforms all three characters. Just as Marian and Winthrop protect Harold from being exposed, he chooses to remain with them, return their love, and refrain from taking advantage of their fellow townspeople. None of the boys can play their instruments at the end of *The Music Man*, but the townspeople are so overcome with pride upon hearing the horrible sounds their children make that they overlook Hill's failure to teach them to play, and everyone presumably lives happily ever after (Bordman 2001, 662).

A musical set in small-town Iowa in the early twentieth century might not seem to have much to do with postwar America, but *The Music Man*'s emphasis on a patriotic, overwhelmingly white town in the heartland—one that embodies "an artificial and imaginary homogenous America"—evokes a specific sort of escapism that was reflected in concurrent television shows like *Father Knows Best* (1954) and *Leave It to Beaver* (Hoffman 2014, 93). For their seemingly vast differences, *West Side Story* and *The Music Man* can be seen as two sides of the same coin. *West Side Story* "dealt with a troubled time by placing a near-agitprop focus on race and immigration, teen violence, and urban decay" while *The Music Man* "sought to calm jitters through rhapsodic constructions of a simpler America" (Oja 2009, 17). Both musicals ran together on Broadway for a while, perhaps inadvertently reassuring some of Broadway's overwhelmingly white, middle-class audiences that their recent move from city to suburb was a wise decision indeed.

As the so-called Golden Age of the American musical came to fruition, Broadway became "a simultaneous site of fertility and contraction, artistic health and commercial decay, creative confidence and progressive cultural withdrawal" (Mast 1987, 293). While this tangle of artistic growth and industry constriction inevitably served the development of the American stage musical well through the onset of the postwar era, the 1960s was a different story. This is the case not only in terms of Broadway's output, but also in terms of new challenges and even greater changes to American culture and society, popular entertainment, and the mass media. In the early 1960s, as Tin Pan Alley began to wheeze its last dying breaths, Broadway again found itself at a precipice.

CHAPTER 6
WE'VE SURELY GOT TROUBLE:
THE 1960s AND 1970s

Few decades in America's history are as emotionally wrought or as nostalgically recalled as the 1960s. The decade was so fraught that "The Sixties" often refers not merely to the years 1960 to 1969, but to a more general, less decade-bound period in American history marked by civil unrest and seismic social, political, and cultural change (Jones 2003, 235). As the decade itself began, the US continued to wrestle with its postwar status and robust economic health; its growing tensions with other newly powerful nations; its new technologies, entertainment forms, and media outlets; and the shifting needs and demands of its changing, growing population. As if these issues were not enough for a single decade, the US also saw the intensification of the Civil Rights Movement; escalated involvement in and growing opposition to the Vietnam War; widening class, generation, and gender gaps; and the unprecedented development of a youth culture and accompanying youth market, all of which worked to cause disturbances in the country's cultural, social, and political order.

While national in scope, the "troubles" of the 1960s affected various groups and communities in dramatically different ways. Some Americans greeted the country's cultural shifts, political conflicts, and societal growing pains by organizing to hasten reform and encourage permanent change. Others resisted in fear, anger, and frustration (Farber 1994, 1). The period was marked by conflict, anxiety, and euphoria, strides toward peace and justice, and setbacks filled with violence and disappointment. Beloved leaders were gunned down, men flew to the moon, and millions marched for civil rights at home and to end an unpopular war abroad. Drug culture and the sexual revolution blossomed. Rock 'n' roll, the dancy teen music faddish in the 1950s, took hold, morphing as it did into a more musically varied and sociopolitically aware genre known simply as "rock."

By the early 1960s, Broadway had long been competing with film, radio, and television, contending with shrinking audiences, and compensating for rising ticket and production costs. But the new decade brought with it a mess of interrelated technological and sociocultural hurdles to negotiate. The Broadway musical, once at the center of American commercial entertainment culture and through the 1950s still lauded as an important American art form, again grew anemic as new entertainment forms gained speed, Tin Pan Alley died away, and the rising youth culture began to dismiss the Broadway musical as a corny, old-fashioned, and out of touch. At a time when one popular slogan was "Don't trust anyone over thirty," Broadway was dismissed as positively ancient in the eyes of a newly powerful and influential swatch of the population.

The rise of youth culture and the decline of Tin Pan Alley

Before the postwar era, the word "teenager" was exceedingly rare. The *Oxford English Dictionary* suggests that the variation "teen-ager" was first used in the early 1940s, appeared more frequently through the 1950s, and lost its hyphen by the early 1960s.[1] There is good reason that the word became more familiar as the postwar era elapsed: before then, "teenagers," at least as we understand the term today, did not exist.

Of course, long before the term "teenager" entered common parlance, millions of people between the ages of thirteen and nineteen roamed the Earth at any given time. Quite a lot of them even lived in the US. But the very *concept* of the modern-day teenager—a person whose age and socioeconomic status make them part of a group that is differentiated from children on the one hand and adults on the other—is comparatively new. In a culture where people were, for generations, either "children" (culturally viewed as wholly dependent) or "adults" (culturally expected to be wholly responsible), "teenagers" surfaced in the mid-twentieth century as "the products of an emerging advanced industrial society for which a long period of formal education became a necessity." The postwar booms, both economic and baby, led to the development of a group now viewed as a unique segment of the population. This group is differentiated primarily by age, but also by taste and social behavior. While not yet fully independent, teenagers are, as anyone who has ever met or been one knows, fully capable of forming opinions, voicing preferences, and seeking out social and entertainment outlets.

The affluence of the 1950s allowed a growing number of adolescents to remain in school for longer periods of time, instead of having to leave after (or in some cases well before) high school to help support their families. Increased affluence also allowed adolescents to have more in the way of discretionary income, which they earned through part-time jobs or allowance, and which they could spend on things they desired, rather than on things they or their family needed (Weinstein 2015, 37–8).

In growing numbers, then, adolescent Americans began making enough money and enjoying enough leisure time to influence the country's economy in the 1950s and 1960s. The burgeoning youth culture exerted pressure on all aspects of the commercial market, which duly responded with movies, television shows, clothing, print matter, and personal items that were developed for and marketed to teens. One of the most influential ways this emerging group swayed the market was through their tastes in, and the manner by which they consumed, popular music.

Since the nineteenth century, Tin Pan Alley was the chief purveyor of popular music sold to middle- and upper-class urban, literate, white Americans. The industry had long been less interested in or adept at serving the tastes of lower classes, people of color, and populations in comparatively rural areas. These very significant populations had cultivated their own preferred music styles—blues, country music, and other folk-derived forms—which were largely perpetuated via the oral tradition. Beginning in the 1920s and 1930s, these styles benefited enormously from new technologies, including the commercial radio and the phonograph record (Hamm 1979, 379).

Through the first half of the twentieth century, Tin Pan Alley composers profited from inclusion in ASCAP, which boasted a selective, urban, overwhelmingly white, musically literate membership. Rural country and blues composers, who often played and wrote from memory, were typically not welcome to join (Covach and Flory 2015, 106). When the contract between ASCAP and the largest radio networks expired in 1940, ASCAP asked the networks to double their $4.5 million-a-year fees. The networks refused, ASCAP went on strike, and the radio stations, unable to play music by ASCAP composers, began playing a lot of recorded music by pre-ASCAP composers such as Stephen Foster. That got boring fast, so many stations turned to music by contemporary, non-ASCAP musicians, who were hurriedly invited to join Broadcast Music Incorporated (BMI), a new organization formed to represent them. ASCAP settled with the networks in 1941, but the organization had done itself great damage: during their holdout, radio stations had introduced national audiences to rural genres like country and blues—the foundations of rock 'n' roll (Hamm 1979, 389).

The radio strike contributed to the decline of the sheet-music industry that was only exacerbated by technological advances and the developing generation gap. In the early 1950s, marketing polls revealed little in the way of varied tastes among age groups. Parents and children tended to listen to the same music, which was typically chosen by the heads of any given household. Until the later 1950s, producers did not consider age as a factor when they promoted music. Yet as the decade elapsed, the average age of Americans who purchased music fell steadily. This was especially the case after the introduction of the transistor radio and 45 rpm record, both of which were inexpensive, durable, and easy to transport (Marchand 2007, 106). A number of factors, then—from technological advances to radio's newly beneficial relationship with music that came from beyond the confines of the Manhattan-based music industry—resulted in the demise of Tin Pan Alley in the middle of the twentieth century.

Broadway courts the new youth culture

Because Broadway and Tin Pan Alley had enjoyed a long, lucrative, mutually beneficial relationship, the decline of the latter was initially met with stunned denial by the former. Convinced that rock 'n' roll was a silly, noisy fad that would fade once teenagers grew up and embraced "real" music, the theater industry preoccupied itself through much of the 1960s with other concerns. There were, as usual, plenty. Times Square was growing into an ever-lurid breeding ground for petty crime, prostitution, and pornography. Inflation, fueled by the war in Vietnam, caused hikes to the cost of production and the price of tickets. Many producers attempted to compensate by cutting back on cast size and scenery budgets, thereby attempting to offer audiences less for more. Broadway's audiences continued to shrink (Bordman 2001, 699). And as young people's tastes diverged from those of their parents, Broadway's audiences were aging precipitously, to boot.

At least initially, the interest in adapting rock music for use on Broadway was thus borne of necessity. Yet the composers attempting to emulate rock music's sounds and structures clearly did not much like or understand what they were hearing. Some of the earliest examples of rock 'n' roll on the Broadway stage, in short-lived revues like the fiftieth-anniversary edition of Ziegfeld's *Follies* (1957) and the Bert Lahr-Nancy Walker vehicle *The Girls Against the Boys* (1959), only served to further alienate young people. These shows' respective "rock 'n' roll" numbers, "I Don't Wanna Rock" and "Too Young to Live," were performed by much older actors: Lahr, in his sixties in 1957, failed to appeal to teenagers by donning a leather jacket and a youthful sneer. Both of these shows, and others that featured songs influenced by contemporary popular music, ended up merely mocking the new youth culture with songs that were repetitive, loud, and condescending.

One musical, however, managed to depict the generation gap with affectionate humor, and to offer songs approximating rock 'n' roll without seeming nasty. *Bye Bye Birdie* premiered in spring 1960, with a book by Michael Stewart (1924–87), and music and lyrics by Charles Strouse (1928–) and Lee Adams (1924–). Inspired by Elvis Presley's induction into the Army in 1958, the plot of *Bye Bye Birdie* is set in motion when rock 'n' roll heartthrob Conrad Birdie is drafted. This causes his agent and songwriter Albert Peterson great distress, but Albert's secretary and girlfriend Rosie Alvarez devises a brilliant publicity stunt that promises to result in a healthy stream of royalties while Conrad serves: Conrad will sing a new song, "One Last Kiss," to a member of his fan club live on *The Ed Sullivan Show*. Meanwhile, Rosie hopes that once Conrad enlists, Albert will quit the music business, marry her, and become an English teacher.

When young Kim McAfee is selected as the fan club winner, Albert, Rosie, and Conrad travel to her town, Sweet Apple, Ohio, to prepare for the big show. Conrad is greeted ecstatically by Sweet Apple's teenagers, with the exception of Kim's jealous boyfriend, Hugo Peabody. Kim's Ed Sullivan-worshiping father, Harry, also dislikes Conrad, who strikes him as rude, entitled, and dumb. Albert's racist, overbearing mother Mae also shows up, with the aim of sabotaging her son's relationship with Rosie.

All hell breaks loose during *The Ed Sullivan Show*: the starstruck Harry gets in the way of the cameras, and Hugo rushes the stage to punch Conrad. Rosie, convinced that Albert will never stand up to his mother, breaks up with him, and Kim with Hugo. Yet after an evening of wild revelry ("wild" being a relative term; this is, after all, a 1960 Broadway musical depicting a tiny Midwestern town), everyone reconciles: Kim and Hugo make up, Conrad reports for duty, and Albert stands up to his mother, proposes to Rose, and informs her of a Midwestern town in need of an English teacher— preferably, in keeping with the weird, constrictive tenor of the times, a married one.

A structural throwback featuring parallel romances and good-natured humor, *Birdie* made fun of contemporary teenagers and their new culture, but it also gently mocked their parents' generation for being so resistant to change. The approach worked: *Bye Bye Birdie* ran for over 600 performances, appealing to both adults and younger spectators with a blend of age-appropriate numbers. The songs performed by the teens and Conrad are all influenced by rock 'n' roll, while the adults' numbers are standard Broadway fare. Little in the musical functioned as "real" rock 'n' roll, but *Birdie* was as close as Broadway came to emulating the new style for most of the rest of the decade.

New competition from beyond Broadway

While Broadway has long served as the country's commercial theater center, New York City has also served as home to many smaller, independent theaters that did not follow the commercial industry in its slow move uptown from the Bowery to Times Square.[2] In 1909, the playwright Percy McKaye wrote of a theater movement that was "wholly divorced from commercialism," and came up with the term "civic theatre" to collectivize the many small, diverse theaters and troupes scattered across the city. The term never stuck; within a few years, small theaters and troupes unaffiliated with Broadway had become more typically known as "Little Theatres." The expression "Off Broadway," sometimes used to describe the many Little Theatres in Manhattan, has been in use since at least the mid-1930s, but it did not become the predominant phrase until the early 1950s (Hischak 2011, 1–2).

Through the 1950s, the Off Broadway movement grew increasingly popular with audiences, critics, and benefactors, and became more moneyed. By the early 1960s, a looser, less organized collective of theaters and troupes arose in response to what was perceived as Off Broadway's increased commercialism. The resultant Off Off Broadway movement, concentrated in the East Village and Greenwich Village neighborhoods in lower Manhattan, explored ways theater might stimulate sociocultural or political change in a tumultuous era. To varying degrees, troupes and theaters like the Caffe Cino, Judson Poets' Theater, Play-House of the Ridiculous, Theatre Genesis, La MaMa, Bread and Puppet Theater, and Open Theater blended political and aesthetic radicalism, pushed the boundaries of what was considered theatrically appropriate, and encouraged audiences to engage directly with and thus become part of performances.

Because many of these theaters and collectives drew from the philosophies of the broader youth culture—whether the politically engaged New Left, the socially engaged counterculture, or some combination of both—and because they relied on people willing to work hard for little or no money, Off Off Broadway appealed to younger, less established artists and drew audiences that tended to be more adventurous than Broadway's was.

Adding to Broadway's troubles during the 1960s, then, was a freewheeling collective of ragtag theater groups who were suddenly winning the respect of young, engaged theatergoers and the city's more open-minded theater critics.

The concept musical

The 1960s was hardly the easiest era in Broadway's history, but it was not all gloom, doom, and despair. Stark claims by historians of Broadway's precipitous decline into bland, forced frivolity are overstated. Yes, Broadway musicals had even more to contend with in the 1960s than in previous decades. Then again, at this point, Broadway's industry members and creative personnel were hardly unaware of what they were up against in advocating for a genre that could not be mass mediated and that was aging precipitously. While there were plenty of forgettable musicals that came and went on Broadway's stages in the 1960s, there were also important innovations that took place there during this most tumultuous of decades. Several 1960s musicals—among them *Fiddler on the Roof*, *Cabaret*, and *Hair*—rank among the most beloved, inventive, and commercially successful productions in Broadway's history.

The 1960s was the era of what is often referred to as the "concept musical," in which all elements, both "thematic and presentational, are integrated to suggest a central theatrical image or idea" (Block 2009, 346). The term "concept musical" has been criticized alternately as too vague to be of much use, or as descriptive of shows that are ultimately not terribly different from either the integrated musicals that inspired them or the megamusicals that followed them.

Adding to the problems people have with the term is that it is often used in blanket descriptions of musicals helmed by powerful stage directors, many of whom cut their teeth as performers, choreographers, stage managers, or producers. While some of these men, for example Jerome Robbins, were established on Broadway well before the 1960s, others rose to prominence during that decade, becoming increasingly sought-after through the 1970s and 1980s. Among them are Michael Bennett (1943–87), Bob Fosse (1927–87), Gower Champion (1919–80) and Harold "Hal" Prince (1928–). These directors became central to the notion of the concept musical, since it was the director's overarching concept that was honed, developed, and nurtured to fruition.

"If musical comedy was typified by the star as cocreator and if the integrated musical, throughout the 1950s, increasingly repositioned the author as seemingly autonomous," Bruce Kirle wrote, "the concept musical turned the integrated musical into a vehicle for the auteur-director," a figure who became so powerful that his name—and it was always a he—was "often as bankable as their over-the-title performers." The creative vision of the director was at least as important in a concept musical as its book, stars, dance numbers, or score (Kirle 2005, 109).

Whether due to the tenor of the times, the continued influence of integrated musicals, newer influences from the innovative Off Off Broadway movement or all of the above, concept musicals pushed at the stage musical's stylistic boundaries with themes that were often sober and complex. While scholars continue to ponder the meaning and applicability of the term, Kirle might have put it best when he suggested that in the end, a concept musical is simply one "that confronts the audience with ideas it usually goes to musicals to escape" (ibid., 111).

One of the biggest hits of the 1960s, *Fiddler on the Roof*, is often described as a pioneering concept musical. The production, directed and choreographed by Jerome Robbins, featured music by Jerry Bock (1928–2010), lyrics by Sheldon Harnick (1924–) and a book by Joseph Stein (1912–2010). Stein based his script on the Yiddish writer and playwright Sholem Aleichem's stories about Tevye, a dairyman in the fictional Jewish village of Anatevka, in turn-of-the-century Russia. Now a classic, *Fiddler* was structurally unconventional for its time, in that it was less a tightly cohesive narrative than a series of loosely developed subplots that all related to the musical's unifying themes.

The three subplots in *Fiddler* focused on the three oldest of Tevye's five daughters. Each focused on the challenges Tevye's daughters "poses to her father's authority and to her community's customs and beliefs by how she marries." Tevye's oldest, Tzeitel, chooses her own mate instead of acquiescing to the desires of the village matchmaker and her parents. The second oldest, Hodel, seeks her family's blessing but not their permission to marry a man she falls in love with and gets engaged to on her own. The third oldest, Chava, falls in love with a gentile from a nearby village and eventually elopes with him (Stempel 2010, 260).

While clinging to his beliefs and customs, Tevye simultaneously realizes that if he does not bend some rules and adjust to the changing times, he will alienate his children. With the exception of Chava, whose intermarriage he only eventually, grudgingly acknowledges, Tevye comes to accept and even to respect his daughters' choices. The constant seesawing between tradition and innovation throughout *Fiddler* culminates in the biggest change of all: the village of Anatevka is liquidated by the Russians, and its inhabitants must leave in search of new homes and communities.

Fiddler's opening number, "Tradition," sets the scene and introduces the characters. It also establishes the musical's unifying thread by introducing the titular character. If absent tradition, Tevye explains, "life is as fragile as a fiddler on the roof." As Tevye reconciles his beliefs with the changing times and demands of his children, he interacts with the fiddler, who appears through the production as a silent and yet vitally important character. As Anatevka empties at *Fiddler's* end, Tevye beckons to the fiddler, who jumps down from his perch to follow Tevye and his family to America (Kirle 2005, 110).

Fiddler opened on September 22, 1964, and became a huge hit, running 3,242 performances over eight years and assuming the title of longest-running Broadway musical. Initial concerns that it would not appeal to non-Jews proved unwarranted. *Fiddler*, after all, opened at a time when older generations were being challenged by an outspoken youth culture, social mores were shifting, and the links between tradition and change seemed stretched to the limit. On the surface, *Fiddler* might have been about early-twentieth-century Russian Jews, but its themes resonated with broader audiences.

Two years after *Fiddler* opened, the producer Hal Prince, who had backed musicals including *The Pajama Game* (1954), *Damn Yankees* (1955), *West Side Story*, and *Fiddler*, chose as a directorial project a musical version of John Van Druten's play *I Am a Camera*, itself an adaptation of Christopher Isherwood's *The Berlin Stories*. *Cabaret* established Prince as an innovative director of dark, challenging material. *Cabaret's* score was written by two relative newcomers to Broadway: John Kander (1927–) wrote the music and Fred Ebb (1928–2004) the lyrics. Also considered a concept musical, *Cabaret* had a fragmented plot about several interconnected characters in Berlin in the 1930s, just prior to the rise of the Third Reich.

The plot structure of *Cabaret*, which follows two couples, hearkens back to the Rodgers and Hammerstein model. The primary coupling consists of Clifford Bradshaw, an American writer who has come to Berlin to write a novel, and Sally Bowles, a British nightclub singer who works at the Kit Kat Klub, a gritty cabaret. An amoral party girl, Sally initially resists Cliff's advances, only to appear on his doorstep in hopes that he will let her share the boarding-house room he rents from Fraulein Schneider. Meanwhile, the widowed Schneider is courted by Herr Schultz, a Jewish grocer who also rents one of her rooms. As the couples fall in love, Berlin's political climate grows darker.

Cabaret departs from tradition by alternating scenes about the two couples with non-narrative ones set in the dim, seedy Kit Kat Klub. Overseen by a spectral, androgynous character known only as the Emcee, the scenes in the Klub provide musical commentary about the action taking place beyond its strange interior. Both the Klub and its Emcee symbolize Berlin's gradual descent into Nazism.

To say that *Cabaret* does not end well is like saying that the Titanic's maiden voyage was a little rocky. *Cabaret* is one of the darkest, most unsettling musicals in the canon and no one gets out of it happily. Cliff realizes the gravity of the situation and begs Sally, now pregnant, to return to America with him, but she refuses. More committed to herself and her own good time than she is concerned about politics, she sells her coat to afford an abortion and insists on remaining willfully ignorant in Berlin. Herr Schultz is blasé about the rise of anti-Semitism, arguing that he is, after all, a German *and* a Jew, but Fraulein Schneider, under pressure from friends and acquaintances, breaks off her engagement to him in a fit of fear and cowardice.

Both couplings, then, are doomed. Driving this home is the final sequence, in which the Emcee bids the newly Nazi-dominated audience of the Kit Kat Klub a detached, robotic "auf wiedersehen/A bientot/Good night." This last scene has been staged in myriad ways, but the message is always the same: even within the once-bohemian confines of the Kit Kat Klub, the Nazis have won.

Cabaret was not meant to be uplifting; its pervasive, creeping darkness was part of Prince's overall concept. Rattled by the often violent resistance to the Civil Rights Movement in the American south as he planned the production, Prince intended the not-so-distant past explored in *Cabaret* to serve as a cautionary tale for contemporary Americans. The comparisons were ultimately subtle: his initial plan to end the show with footage depicting the Selma march and riots in Little Rock, Arkansas, were scrapped in favor of a huge, tilted mirror that hung over the stage. Before and after the performance and during intermission, spectators faced an exaggerated, funhouse version of themselves that reflected back at them from the stage. While not as obvious as clips of protests and riots, the mirror implied that, "as Cliff says in the show, 'if you're not against all this, you're for it—or you might as well be'" (Jones 2003, 241–2).

Hair: Enter the rock musical

Many scholars have described *Hair: The American Tribal Love-Rock Musical* as another concept musical, but its real claims to fame were its Off Off Broadway pedigree, innovative staging, much-talked-about (if brief and very dimly lit) nudity, and especially its amplified rock score.[3] It is this last feature that caused *Hair*, which opened on Broadway at the Biltmore Theater in April 1968, to be hailed by some critics as a revolutionary production that would transform Broadway's sound, relevance, and audience.

Of course, still other critics dismissed *Hair* as a loud, confusing show about stoned, shaggy, unwashed hippies. But its supporters praised the musical's ability to harness the theatrical mainstream to the energy and experimentalism taking place Off Off Broadway, as well as its affectionate depictions of contemporary young people. Clive Barnes, drama critic for *The New York Times*, lauded *Hair* for doing what had long been thought impossible: it blended rock music with traditional Broadway fare in a way that did not condescend to young audiences or alienate older ones (Barnes 1968).

Hair's book was by Gerome Ragni (1935–91) and James Rado (1932–), two actors active in the Off Off Broadway movement. In 1966, they worked together on *Viet Rock*, a collaborative anti-war piece staged at the Open Theater. Between rehearsals, Ragni and Rado hung around the West Village with a group of hippies who inspired them to develop a musical about the counterculture. They based the two central characters on themselves: Claude, a quiet dreamer from Flushing, Queens, was inspired and originated by Rado; Berger, a charismatic high-school dropout and leader of the tribe of hippies with whom Claude socializes, was inspired and originated by Ragni. Presented as a series of loosely interconnected vignettes, *Hair* follows Claude as he debates whether he should go to Vietnam to please his parents, or burn his draft card and stay with his hippie friends. He ultimately chooses to go to Vietnam, where he is killed; *Hair* ends as the hippies mourn his death and celebrate his life.

Ragni and Rado developed *Hair* for Broadway, but after endless rejections, they approached Joseph Papp (1921–91), producer and founder of the Public Theater. Papp chose *Hair* as the inaugural production of the Public's then-new space on Lafayette Street in the East Village, with two conditions: Ragni and Rado had to cut their long, rambling script, and find someone to compose an acceptable score. A mutual friend introduced them to composer Galt MacDermot, who had recently arrived in New York from Montreal, and plans for a limited run at the Public in October 1967 commenced.

At the Public, *Hair* caught the attention of Michael Butler, a Chicago businessman who secured the rights to the musical after Papp—who, at the time, took a staunch anti-Broadway stance—let them expire. The experimental director Tom O'Horgan was brought in for the transition. Under O'Horgan, *Hair* retained a distinct Off Off Broadway sensibility. O'Horgan employed non-traditional casting, bringing in both seasoned experimental actors and talented amateurs. The cast and creative team worked collectively to build trust, rework the script, and stage the musical numbers. Among the show's many innovations, aside from the live rock band on the stage in lieu of a traditional orchestra in the pit, were its disjunct structure, frequent disregard of the imaginary fourth wall that traditionally divides spectators from performers, and its use of stage nudity during the recreation of a human be-in at the Act I finale.

Hair was additionally noteworthy for its liberal approach to contemporary social and political issues. While ultimately as traditional in its treatment of women as the counterculture and New Left could be, *Hair* tackled race, class, colonialism, the environment, the generation gap, Vietnam, and the sexual revolution. Its contemporary themes and setting, and its catchy, bouncy, innovative score appealed to many traditional Broadway spectators, as well as to more young people and people of color than was typical of Broadway at the time (Horn 1991, 133–4).

Hair's success resulted in the kind of pop-culture success Broadway had not seen in a very long time. Seven months after it premiered on Broadway, the original cast recording hit number one on the *Billboard* album chart. Through the turn of the decade, radio stations across the country blared covers of songs from the show, including The 5th Dimension's medley of "Aquarius" and "Let the Sun Shine In" (The Flesh Failures), Three Dog Night's version of "Easy to Be Hard," the Cowsills's "Hair" and Oliver's rendition of "Good Morning Starshine," the last of which also showed up on the children's television show "Sesame Street" (Wollman 2006, 53).

Of course, the critics who thought *Hair* would somehow revolutionize the American musical were wrong. The many rock musicals that were rushed to Broadway in the years immediately following *Hair* worked instead to convince producers that the successful rock musical was less a paradigm shift than a lucky fluke. *Jesus Christ Superstar*, the 1970 platinum-selling double album by composer Andrew Lloyd Webber (1948–) and lyricist Tim Rice (1944–), did well enough on Broadway when it was adapted for the stage by *Hair* director Tom O'Horgan in 1971, but the production was not nearly as commercially successful as the album that had inspired it. Fates were even less kind to several other rock musicals to open (and close) on Broadway at the turn of the decade: *Soon* (1971), *Dude* (1972), and *Via Galactica* (1972), all of which suffered savage reviews and lasted a mere handful of performances. *Hair* would eventually prove influential for late-twentieth-century musicals like *Rent*, but for the time being, the term "rock musical" was soon verboten on Broadway.

The 1970s

Rarely revered as a glorious or even especially memorable era in contemporary American history, the 1970s are often dismissed as a protest-weary, economically strapped, drug-addled, self-centered stepchild to the revolutionary decade that came before it.[4] Even as it progressed, the decade was painted as one of failure, disappointment, and national exhaustion. Perhaps this is no wonder: during the 1970s, the US saw defeat in Vietnam, watched the first president in its history resign in scandal, and experienced staggering economic problems, disenchantment, and disenfranchisement. It did not help the decade's street cred that it was host to so many ridiculous fads, like the pet rock, mood rings, high-heeled sneakers, and streaking.

Yet to dismiss the 1970s as a deflated, burned-out waste of a decade is to ignore the immense strides Americans made toward racial, sexual, and gender equality during the decade. Through the 1970s, the Civil Rights Movement continued to resonate, while gay men and lesbians began in growing numbers to step from the closet and demand equal rights. American women, too, began in growing numbers to demand equal treatment in the home and the workplace. Subsequent generations frequently assume that these social movements arose in the 1960s, but they belong solidly in the 1970s.

There are several reasons for this confusion. First, mass movements were so important to the 1960s that subsequent ones are often automatically associated with that era. Second, many of the people involved in the women's and gay liberation movements cut their teeth as Civil Rights and anti-Vietnam War activists in the 1960s. Finally, while the women's and gay liberation movements gained most momentum through the 1970s, they both had origins in earlier decades.

The women's movement is often referred to as the "second wave" in a nod to the first, which took place during the nineteenth and early twentieth centuries and focused primarily on suffrage. The second wave took root in the US between the early 1950s and late 1960s; the publication in English of Simone de Beauvoir's *The Second Sex* (1953) and Betty Friedan's *The Feminine Mystique* (1963), are often cited as milestones in the burgeoning movement. Similarly, the gay liberation movement, sparked by riots at the Stonewall Inn in Greenwich Village in late June 1969, was the more vocal offshoot of a quieter, less nationally organized movement that had taken root in earlier decades. The pioneering gay rights organizations the Mattachine Society and Daughters of Bilitis were both founded in the 1950s; through the 1960s, gay and lesbian activists shifted away from prioritizing personal identity and toward a more politically organized struggle against institutional and cultural discrimination.

The 1970s was thus a decade during which different approaches to equality and acceptance "filtered into broader consciousness." Increased awareness of gender and race issues trickled into all forms of American mass entertainment: groundbreaking television shows like "All in the Family," "Good Times," and "One Day at a Time"; popular songs like Helen Reddy's "I Am Woman," and the Village People's "YMCA" and "Macho Man"; movies like *Alice Doesn't Live Here Anymore*, *Sweet Sweetback's Baadasssss Song*, and *An Unmarried Woman*. They could also be detected in countless Broadway musicals. The 1970s was not the cheeriest decade, but to dismiss it is to ignore the identity politics and breadth of related artistic expression that infused it (Wolf 2011, 92–4).

The Broadway musical in the "Me" Decade

In a decade remembered for the cultivation of personal identity, it is perhaps fitting that several powerful individuals would helm the development of Broadway's most innovative concept musicals. Hal Prince remained an influential director and producer; his power on Broadway was matched by a handful of other director/choreographers such as Bob Fosse and Michael Bennett. Through the 1970s, Prince mounted a string of Stephen Sondheim musicals, among them *Company* (1970), *Follies* (1971), *A Little Night Music* (1973), *Pacific Overtures* (1976), and *Sweeney Todd* (1979).

While most did well enough at the box office, many of the Prince–Sondheim collaborations were more critically acclaimed than commercially successful. They were repeatedly lauded for their innovations, layered artistry, and depth. Sondheim's material, like Prince's approach, often proved ideal for an era bound up in personal cultivation and identity politics. After all, many Sondheim works, whether written during the 1970s or not, are about outsiders: complex, alienated, neurotic loners in search of direction and meaning in a difficult world (Lundskaer-Nielsen 2014, 97).

Take for example *Company*, with music and lyrics by Sondheim, book by George Furth, musical staging by choreographer Michael Bennett, and direction by Prince.[5] *Company* opened at the Alvin Theater on April 26, 1970. Its disjunct narrative, disorienting approach to time, and emotionally frozen, sexually ambiguous central character touched a nerve with audiences and critics, many of whom acknowledged that *Company* was both deeply unsettling and an artistic triumph.

Company focuses on Robert, an upper-middle-class, 35-year-old Manhattan bachelor. In scene after scene, which might or might not be happening chronologically if at all, Bobby visits his many friends, all of whom are married and unhappy. When not with friends, he dates three different women, none of whom he can commit to. While it is never clear whether Bobby's friends know one another, they all exhibit an almost desperate urge to see him find a mate, despite or perhaps because of their own marital woes. At the end of the musical, Bobby is still unsure if he wants commitment, but decides—maybe—that marriage might be better than being alone. The disjointedness of *Company*'s plot and neuroses of its characters relate to the pessimism and uncertainty of the era during which it premiered. The musical manifested "the bitterness, rejection, and uncertainty displayed in affluent, educated, upper-middle-class New York society" in its questioning of traditional values like marriage, and the legitimacy of American social mores (Bristow and Butler 1987, 253).

Yet while *Company* caused discomfort for some spectators, it was empowering for others. Many gay men interpreted the musical as a coming-out parable and read Robert as a coded gay or bisexual character. There are a few reasons for this interpretation, even though Robert's sexual ambiguity was referenced just once, disparagingly, in the original production: during the number "You Could Drive a Person Crazy," Robert's girlfriends, Kathy, April, and Marta vent their frustrations over his commitment issues, at one point questioning his sexual preferences:

I could understand a person
If it's not a person's bag
I could understand a person
If a person was a fag.[6]

Yet the interpretation of Robert as a queer character does not rest solely on this snippet of song. Some of it relates to Sondheim's tendency to gravitate toward disenfranchised characters, as well as to his own oft-discussed outsider status as a gay, Jewish man. One does not have to make much of a leap, after all, to envision Sondheim himself in Bobby's shoes: a New York bachelor who feels disconnected from his straight friends and who abides endless pressure, as many gay men did at the time, to remain closeted and embrace heteronormativity.

Sondheim and Furth both insisted that Bobby was never intended to be read as gay, but the interpretation persists. Spectators often connect emotionally with mass entertainment, drawing from it whatever helps them negotiate their own lives. For countless gay men coming of age in the 1970s, Bobby's discomfort at the idea of settling into a traditional marriage was proof enough he had been created in their image.

Like Hal Prince, Bob Fosse was an active presence on Broadway for decades before becoming a director. He made his stage debut as a dancer in the late 1940s and became well-known as a choreographer in the 1950s. Through the 1960s and 1970s he combined choreography with direction, both on Broadway and in Hollywood. Unlike many classically trained choreographers, Fosse danced during his Chicago youth at decidedly lowbrow venues: burlesque houses, nightclubs, late-generation vaudeville theaters, and strip clubs (Hischak 2008, 261). His exposure to the seedier side of entertainment fueled his work on Broadway, where he became known for highly distinctive, often exaggeratedly playful and erotically charged choreography. Among his trademarks were stooped shoulders and the frequent use of top-hats (Fosse saw himself as somewhat hunched, and often used hats to hide his premature baldness when he danced), splayed fingers held in "jazz-hands" style, turned-in knees and other bodily contortions, swiveling hips, and bobbling pelvises (Stempel 2010, 580–1). His style was adapted by performers with whom he often worked, among them his wife Gwen Verdon (1925–2000), Ann Reinking (1949–), Ben Vereen (1946–), and Chita Rivera (1933–).

Many of Fosse's musicals reflected contemporary issues: the sexual revolution, the hell of war, the drive for self-actualization. His musicals *Pippin* (1972) and *Chicago* (1975), both of which are set in the distant past, thus resonated with 1970s audiences. *Pippin*, with music and lyrics by Stephen Schwartz (1948–) and a book by Roger O. Hirson (and an uncredited Fosse), took place in the Middle Ages but focused on its restless title character's search for happiness in a war-torn, sexually excessive world. The more cynical *Chicago* featured music by *Cabaret* team Kander and Ebb, with a book by Ebb and Fosse, who also choreographed and directed. A musical version of the satirical 1926 play with the same name by Maurine Dallas Watkins, *Chicago* was inspired by two unrelated women accused and acquitted of murder in that city in 1924.

Chicago follows the amoral, celebrity-starved Roxie Hart (originated by Verdon), who "has an affair and murders her lover; manipulates her husband, the law, and the press to get herself acquitted; then trades on her newfound notoriety" to develop an act with vaudevillian Velma Kelly (Chita Rivera). Kelly, too, had been accused and acquitted of murdering her husband and sister after catching them in bed together. Fosse conceived *Chicago* as an extended vaudeville show, with song-and-dance numbers evocative of popular styles made famous by old vaudeville giants like Sophie Tucker ("When You're Good to Mama"), Bert Williams ("Mister Cellophane"), and Eddie Cantor ("Me and My Baby"). But *Chicago* also drew connections between its characters' deceitfulness and "the corruption of national life that the Watergate scandal had recently disclosed," ultimately finding moral decay in every system from the press to the law to the entertainment world (Stempel 2010, 581–3).

Unlike its 1996 revival, which currently holds the record for longest-running musical revival in Broadway history, the original production of *Chicago* received mixed reviews and ran for just over two years. While hardly a flop, this was also not an especially lengthy run by contemporary standards. *Chicago* was criticized for being too dark even for the cynical time in which it premiered. Further, *Chicago*'s premiere in June 1975 was eclipsed weeks later by an almost universally celebrated new musical that would become the hottest ticket in town, and win most of the major Tony Awards and the 1976 Pulitzer Prize for Drama. *Chicago* did not stand a chance against *A Chorus Line*.

A musical about dancers auditioning to win a part in the chorus line of a fictional Broadway musical, *A Chorus Line* takes place in real time. As it proceeds, audiences observe characters fretting over their chances, simultaneously bonding and competing as they go through several rounds of tryouts before learning whether or not they have been cast (Wolf 2011, 119). Developed and staged at the Public before moving to Broadway, *A Chorus Line*, like *Hair* a few years prior, reflects Off Off Broadway innovation and collective creation. Its move to Broadway also worked to correct business mistakes that Joe Papp had made with *Hair*.

In allowing the rights to *Hair* to lapse after its inaugural production at the Public ended, Papp and the Public lost out on the millions of dollars *Hair* generated on Broadway, just when the Public was trying to find its footing and properly fund its enormous new space. Furious at himself for failing to reap the financial windfall, Papp resolved not to make the same mistake again. When *A Chorus Line* sold out its limited run at the Public in April 1975, Papp rushed the show to the Shubert Theater, where it reopened in July. *A Chorus Line* ran on Broadway for 6,137 performances, closing in 1990 after an unprecedented fifteen-year run. Some $30 million of its earning was put into a trust that continues to support new projects at the Public to date (Turan and Papp 2010, 392).

The concept for *A Chorus Line* is usually credited to Michael Bennett, who approached Papp with recordings of some all-night rap sessions held among a group of Broadway dancers in 1974. Intrigued, Papp gave Bennett rehearsal space, all the time he needed, and a weekly stipend to hone the tapes into a musical (Hoffman 2014, 146). A creative team was assembled: Marvin Hamlisch (1944–2012) composed the score and Edward Kleban (1939–87) wrote the lyrics. *A Chorus Line* was workshopped at the Public over the course of the year until the creative team decided it was ready.

Bruce Kirle has pointed out that not since *Oklahoma!* "has a musical so reflected the profound changes in middle-class ideology," not all of which are for the better. *A Chorus Line* can be seen to celebrate "the cog in the American wheel" in its examination of chorus dancers who must "compromise individual autonomy with the corporate establishment." The people depicted in the musical are not stars, nor are they vying for the choicest roles. Rather, *A Chorus Line* traces the lives of "gypsies" (dancers so named because they bounce from show to show), who are rewarded for their hard work with "anonymity and negation of self" (Kirle 2005, 151–2). The audience listens, through *A Chorus Line*, to characters' "detailed, moving stories about their lives," thereby getting to know them as individuals. But in the final scene, the characters dance onto the stage with precision choreography and identical outfits, singing "One"—a song devoted entirely to the unseen star of the show they have been cast in. The audience is thus left with the image of a chorus line of performers whose "personalities are essentially vaporized, made meaningless by the anonymity that the line imposes on them" (Hoffman 2014, 145).

The cynicism of the ending went blithely unnoticed by countless spectators who flocked to see *A Chorus Line* in the years during which it was the hottest show on Broadway. Misinterpreting the show was easy to do, since the final scenes seem to celebrate Broadway performers who are typically taken for granted. Yet *A Chorus Line* ultimately makes sly commentary about the relationship between the individual and the collective at a time during which "the desire for individual autonomy and alternate lifestyles was challenged by an increasingly corporate society" that seemed to reward conformity at every turn (Kirle 2005, 151).

New directions and new diversity on Broadway

In summer 1967, the formidably shrewd producer David Merrick (1911–2000) began pondering ways he might keep his Gower Champion-directed production of *Hello, Dolly!* running despite declining sales. Notorious for creative publicity stunts that could stimulate interest in even the most poorly reviewed of shows, Merrick was not willing to close his cash cow withouth a fight. *Dolly*, with a book by Michael Stewart based on Thornton Wilder's play *The Matchmaker*, and music and lyrics by Jerry Herman (1931–), had been a big hit when it opened in January 1964 with Carol Channing in the title role. After Channing left the Broadway production to join the national tour, Merrick replaced her with a succession of actresses including Ginger Rogers, Phyllis Diller, Betty Grable, Ethel Merman, and Martha Raye, all of whom had continued to draw crowds. But by 1967, interest in the show had cooled. A typically mercenary idea occurred to Merrick: Why not capitalize on the Civil Rights-related news of the time by recasting the entire production with black actors?

A producer's acquisitive ploy to squeeze every last dime out of a Broadway show by casting black performers in roles typically played by white ones was hardly a giant leap forward for civil rights. Yet Merrick offered the role to Pearl Bailey, a brilliantly engaging actress who, despite her own wariness, nevertheless grew intrigued by the idea of breaking down barriers. She took the role, and Merrick took out a full-page ad in *The New York Times*, where he characteristically overstated the casting choice as "the event of the century." His plan worked: ticket sales spiked and the production, which also featured Cab Calloway, Clifton Davis, and a very young Morgan Freeman, ran another three years before closing in 1970 (Kissel 1993, 365–6).

Mercenary or not, the Pearl Bailey-helmed *Dolly* spurred a new interest in all-black or majority-black Broadway musicals, which arrived on Broadway through the 1970s with more regularity than they had since the 1920s. Some, like *Dolly*, were all-black versions of musicals traditionally performed by white actors (and, as usual, steered by all-white creative and producing teams). Among these was a 1976 revival of *Guys and Dolls* starring Robert Guillaume as Nathan Detroit. Several musical revues celebrated black entertainers from the past; these included the Harlem Renaissance homage *Bubbling Brown Sugar* (1976) and the Fats Waller tribute *Ain't Misbehavin'* (1978). There were also a number of original musicals featuring all-black or black-majority casts. In 1970, Ossie Davis's 1961 plantation comedy *Purlie Victorious* was musicalized as *Purlie* by the white creative team Peter Udell and Gary Geld; *Raisin*, a musical version of Lorraine Hansberry's 1959 play *A Raisin in the Sun*, adapted by a team including Hansberry's widowed husband Robert Nemiroff, ran on Broadway in 1975. *Don't Bother Me, I Can't Cope* (1972), with book, music, and lyrics by Micki Grant, focused on the contemporary black experience and became the first Broadway production to be directed by a black woman, Vinnette Carol (1922–2002). *The Wiz* (1975), an all-black version of *The Wizard of Oz* with a book by William F. Brown, music and lyrics by Charlie Smalls (1943–87), and direction (and costumes) by Geoffrey Holder reaped numerous Tonys and ran on Broadway for four years.

One of the edgier original all-black productions to open on Broadway in the 1970s, or really ever, was *Ain't Supposed to Die a Natural Death* (1971). This show was written and composed by Melvin Van Peebles (1932–), a novelist and filmmaker who made the seminal film *Sweet Sweetback's Baadasssss Song* in 1971. Directed by Gilbert Moses (1942–95), *Ain't Supposed to Die* was set in a contemporary urban ghetto. Over a through-composed funk-, blues-, and soul-steeped score, monologues and songs were performed in a fluid, stylized manner by an ensemble portraying drug dealers, pimps, prostitutes, junkies, hustlers, corrupt cops, alcoholics, and beggars, as well as upright citizens whose hard work did nothing to ease the poverty and discrimination keeping them from easier, upwardly mobile lives. An unapologetically dark piece, *Ain't Supposed to Die* ended with a lengthy monologue titled "Put a Curse on You," delivered by a homeless woman who had until this point silently observed the action around her. Delivered to the audience while the rest of the cast stood staring into the house behind her, the monologue cursed anyone who "sits by and watches the degradation extant in our country without becoming outraged and moved to action."

The city's predominantly white critical corps was palpably uncomfortable reviewing *Ain't Supposed to Die*. Some attacked it as frightening and angry, while others admitted that they did not feel qualified to discuss it intelligently. After the reviews came out and attendance by white patrons plummeted, Van Peebles dismissed the critics as products of an establishment that had long prioritized sanitized, white-controlled depictions of blacks. He threw his energies into marketing the show to black patrons. He contacted churches, schools, clubs, fraternal organizations, and community centers all over the tri-state area to sell tickets. He invited black actors, politicians, and activists to host talkbacks after the matinees, and pursued television talk shows that often featured Broadway casts but had not invited his production. Van Peebles' efforts paid off. Initially rumored to close at the end of the same week it had opened, *Ain't Supposed to Die* ran for 325 performances and garnered several Tony nominations. More importantly, the show proved that with ingenuity and effort, Broadway could reach new, diverse audiences.

Broadway and the financial crisis

Many of the musicals that ran on Broadway through the 1970s were inventive, creative, and newly reflective of the country's diversity, but the decade was overshadowed by the state of the nation, and more immediately by the continued decline of Times Square. The neighborhood's demise was related to New York City's fiscal woes, which began in the late 1960s and culminated in the 1975 financial crisis.[7]

Through the early 1970s, New York City suffered with the rest of the country from stagflation, a punishing blend of inflation and stalled economic growth that few had previously believed actually existed, but that proved itself a reality when it settled in to make America miserable. In New York City, stagflation, along with the rising costs of city services through the late 1960s and a declining stock market in the early 1970s, resulted in serious financial problems. The city came close to declaring bankruptcy in 1975, when its main source of capital, the municipal bond market, dried up. During the height of the financial crisis, 20,000 civil servants from over 60 city agencies, the transportation authority, 19 municipal hospitals, 17 colleges, and the public school system were furloughed, laid off, or fired. The quality of life for the city's millions of residents sagged accordingly.

To the rest of the nation, 1970s images of New York City in crisis depicted an urban hellscape overrun by filth and crime. Even before the height of the financial crisis, tourism had been dropping precipitously, and since visitors made up almost a third of audiences at the time, Broadway suffered mightily. Producers slashed budgets, audiences shrank, and venues sat empty or were rented out by concert promoters or traveling productions. By the mid-1970s, most of the Broadway theaters not controlled by the Shuberts were up for sale. Many craft and construction companies, costume shops, and scenic painters who rented space in the theater district departed for larger, cheaper, safer spaces in the suburbs or other American cities.[8]

Amid concerns that all the space abandoned by theater personnel would be taken over by the commercial sex industry already swamping Times Square, the Shuberts tried to buy up some of the empty theaters. In doing so, they entered into competition with the Nederlanders, a family of theater owners from Detroit active since 1912 and present in Times Square since the late 1960s (Schumach 1975, 32). Still under scrutiny after their 1950s antitrust suit, the Shuberts were not given permission to acquire new venues in the area until 1981, by which point the Nederlanders had purchased or become managers of ten of the empty theaters (Holland 1981, 12). Another new competitor, the Jujamcyn Organization, had acquired five. These companies, now the largest theater owners on Broadway, displayed amazing foresight by acting when they did: Times Square had become such a problem during the 1970s that the typical shrieks about the imminent death of Broadway theater had reached a near-hysteric pitch.

Broadway was hardly about to die, but its surrounding neighborhood was crowded, dingy, dirty, and filled with petty crime. Due to a series of mid-century Supreme Court rulings that relaxed the definition of what could be legally considered obscene, it had also become overrun with sex stores, peepshows, XXX movie theaters, and massage parlors. What Times Square was seen to lack, then, was the kind of middle-class respectability the theater industry had once enjoyed and never stopped hoping to reclaim. The industry found itself walking a fine line through the 1970s: How, exactly, to lure audiences back to a troublesome neighborhood during a severe economic decline?

Suggested remedies that were eventually enacted, many of which remain in practice, included the elimination of Monday night performances in favor of a Wednesday matinee, which would counter some theatergoers' concerns about being in Times Square at night. Student-rush tickets were introduced and all box offices were converted to accept major credit cards. Curtain times for evening performances were moved from 8:30 p.m. to 7:30, which allowed audiences to get home (or back to their hotels) an hour earlier. And in 1973, TKTS, the ticket booth that distributed same-day half-price tickets, and which still operates just north of the old *New York Times* building, opened to great fanfare and instant success.

New York State pulled itself out of crisis with Herculean effort: there were generous tax breaks for new businesses and the linking of social welfare programs with private-sector growth. A new commerce commissioner, economic affairs cabinet, and economic development board were instituted, and investments in the state's infrastructure were encouraged (Klein 1992, 705). There were also new appeals to tourists.

The rebranding of New York as a tourist destination began in 1976, during which the Democratic National Convention and several well-publicized celebrations to honor the country's Bicentennial took place in the city. The result was encouraging: New York City had its biggest tourist boom since the late 1960s, and generated around $4.5 billion in revenue. The famous "I Love New York" campaign, still used today, was created by the State Department of Commerce in 1977; it was no coincidence that many advertisements featured Broadway casts singing the "I Love New York" jingle as voice-over actors described affordable theater packages to interested viewers. By 1979, New York City was setting records for tourism and resultant revenue.

While the increase in tourism proved wonderful for Broadway, it put new pressure on the Off and Off Off Broadway realms, which had exerted strong influence on Broadway in the 1960s and early 1970s. This trend began to reverse itself by the end of the decade. Successful Off and Off Off Broadway productions continued to transfer to Broadway, but the rising costs of real estate and production, and the new emphasis on courting tourists, forced many of the city's smaller theaters to turn away from an emphasis on innovation and toward an interest in financial stability, larger audiences, and higher ticket prices. Off and Off Off Broadway remain less expensive than Broadway, but the distinctions between the realms began to blur as the decade unfolded.

As the city rebounded in the 1980s, long-debated plans for the renovation of Times Square grew more heated. Tourism would reach new heights, and the Broadway musical, having weathered yet another storm, would reinvent itself anew, reach an increasingly global market, cultivate bigger and younger audiences, and continue to remain fresh, appealing, and relevant. Yet as a result of the overhaul, the comparative freedom during the 1970s to produce risky theatrical pieces was compromised, and theatrical production became radically different from what it had been only a few years prior. In the 1980s, as New York rebounded from crisis, audiences were plentiful, business boomed . . . and risks on and beyond Broadway would become harder to take.

CHAPTER 7
THE MEGAMUSICAL TO *HAMILTON*

In November 1980, Ronald Reagan beat incumbent President Jimmy Carter in a landslide election that was a culmination of the country's slow political swing to the right through the 1970s. Reagan's two-term presidency saw the "continued decomposition of the old New Deal Democratic coalition forged by Roosevelt," a newly galvanized Republican party stimulated by a shift in allegiance among white southerners and conservative Christians, and a huge increase in military spending.

Reagan continued a wave of deregulation, begun in the late 1970s, that resulted in the intensified concentration of media ownership by fewer corporations (Griffith and Baker 2007, 350–1). Deregulation influenced American commercial entertainment in profound ways, since media companies that had long been prohibited from uniting suddenly could. The impact of deregulation was initially more evident in the worlds of commercial film, television and music, but it also eventually influenced Broadway.

As the new president took office and the new decade began, New York continued to recover from near-bankruptcy. California remained the top American state for tourism in the early 1980s, but the new efforts by New York yielded remarkable results. New York City alone attracted millions of tourists from hundreds of countries and saw an increase in business travel at a time when travel to other American cities was slowing (LeMoyne 1984, D11). The boom in tourism had a swift and lasting impact on the city's commercial marketplace, and thus on its theater industry.[1] By 1983, the "I Love New York" campaign had resulted in a 43 percent increase in tourist spending (Klein 1992, 706–9).

Broadway in the 1980s

The early 1980s saw increases in the costs of production, steeper city and state taxes, significant changes in the ways shows were produced, and a growing demand for new and expensive stage technologies, all of which caused the demands of the commercial theater to soar well above typical rates of inflation. Between 1980 and 1982, production costs on Broadway increased by a whopping 62 percent, while operation costs rose by 45 percent. The skyrocketing inflation had a particular impact on Broadway musicals, which are generally more expensive to produce than dramas.

All the factors contributing to the rising cost of production, combined with trends that placed the director in God mode, resulted in the development of a new division of labor in the theater industry. In the past, costs were managed solely by a producer. Flo Ziegfeld, for example, was chiefly responsible for securing and apportioning funds during his reign. But by the early 1980s, company managers, as well as powerful directors like Bennett, Fosse, and Prince, had become so central to productions that they began to have a say in controlling costs. This approach to production was not especially cost-effective, but it was newly decentralized: more people with artistic control became involved in the development and staging of shows (Rosenberg and Harburg 1993, 7–18).

Depictions of difference in the 1980s

While there were important individual achievements in politics, society, science, and the arts, the 1980s was not a very progressive one for minorities or women. Social policies eroded as federal funding was cut, an "individualistic, pick-yourself-up-by-your-bootstraps" mentality replaced political centrism, and social and political agendas moved to the right in an embrace of "traditional values" over the left-leaning social movements popular in previous decades. The nation's conservatism was reflected in many Reagan-era musicals. Some of Broadway's biggest, most popular, lucrative productions resorted to traditional gender norms in depicting men as active, brave, and daring, and women as passive, adoring muses or supporters (Wolf 2011, 129–31). Nevertheless, a few Broadway musicals that premiered in the 1980s depicted people who were not white, middle class, and heterosexual.

Dreamgirls, which opened at the Imperial Theater on December 20, 1981, was composed by Henry Krieger (1945–), with book and lyrics by Tom Eyen (1940–91). *Dreamgirls* was directed, co-produced, and co-choreographed by Michael Bennett; the production would be his last on Broadway before his death from AIDS in 1987. While *The New York Times* critic Frank Rich, by this point the most influential theater critic in New York City, raved about the show, other critics were more tepid. It did not matter: *Dreamgirls* ran for 1,521 performances before closing in August 1985.

Loosely based on the Supremes' ascent from struggling girl group to Motown superstars, *Dreamgirls* follows the rise of a black female singing trio from a Chicago ghetto in 1962 to the early 1970s. At the start of the show, the Dreamettes compete in a talent show at Harlem's Apollo Theater. They lose but gain a manager in the ruthless Curtis Taylor, Jr. Determined to cross the music industry's color barrier, Taylor renames the group the Dreams, alters their sound from R&B to pop, and replaces the group's heavyset founder and lead singer, Effie, with a slimmer, softer-sounding singer who he feels will be more appealing to white audiences. As the Dreams "blunt the raw anger of their music to meet the homogenizing demands of the marketplace," Rich wrote in his review, "we see the high toll of guilt and self-hatred that is inflicted on those who sell their artistic souls to the highest bidder. If 'dreams' is the most recurrent word in the show, then 'freedom' is the second, for the Dreams escape their ghetto roots only to discover that they are far from free" (Rich 1998, 124).

For the strengths of its depictions, both of black people's struggles in a white-dominated entertainment world and, in the case of Effie, of women who do not conform to Western beauty standards, *Dreamgirls* was a throwback to pre-1970s black musicals in that its black cast contrasted with an all-white creative and production team. Critics were quick to point out this irony; *Dreamgirls'* plot, after all, revolves around black entertainers who compromise to succeed in a white-driven world. "The white structure that demands so much soul drain is never really seen; it exists as an abstract ghost off-stage," Stanley Crouch wrote in *The Village Voice*. "A harsher examination would have symbolically questioned the way in which the show itself reached Broadway—white generals mapping out the strategy for singing, dreaming, and suffering black troops to take the bright hill of the musical smash" (quoted in Wollman 2006, 135). *Dreamgirls'* feel-good ending, in which the backstabbing Curtis is driven away, the Dreams reconcile with Effie, and the group looks toward successful solo careers after their farewell concert, allowed the musical to evade condemnation of structural racism in America and its entertainment systems.

A similarly contradictory Broadway musical, which simultaneously broke down barriers and clung to old-fashioned cultural modes, was *La Cage aux Folles*. *La Cage* featured music and lyrics by *Mame* and *Hello, Dolly!* composer Jerry Herman (1931–) and a book by Harvey Fierstein (1954–), whose play *Torch Song Trilogy* premiered Off Broadway at La MaMa in 1978 and ran on Broadway in 1982. *La Cage* opened in August 1983 and ran for 1,761 performances through the height of the AIDS crisis.

La Cage aux Folles was not the first Broadway musical to focus on a gay male relationship; the musical *Sextet*, which flopped in 1974, was about three couples, two straight and one gay. And just two months prior to *La Cage's* premiere, *Dance a Little Closer* (May 11, 1983), which closed on opening night, featured a subplot about two gay flight attendants who at one point sing the duet "Why Can't the World Go and Leave Us Alone?" Yet *La Cage* was the first commercially successful Broadway musical about gay life and romance for its time.

Based on Jean Poiret's 1973 play of the same name, *La Cage* is set in Saint-Tropez, France, where Georges, owner of the drag bar La Cage aux Folles, lives above the club with his partner, Albin. Albin, who goes by the drag name Zaza, is La Cage's star performer and the leader of Les Cagelles, the troupe of performers. The action of the musical is propelled when Georges' son Jean Michel, the result of a brief heterosexual liaison with a woman named Sybil some two decades prior, announces that he has become engaged to a woman named Anne Dindon. There is one catch: Anne's ultraconservative, homophobic politician of a father plans to close down the local drag clubs. Jean-Michel begs his father to ask Albin, who has raised Jean-Michel from infancy, to stay away when the time comes to meet the new in-laws. He also asks Georges to pretend that he is married to Sybil. Devastated by Jean-Michel's requests, Albin dismisses Les Cagelles from the stage during his nightclub performance and sings the musical's fervent, anthemic number, "I Am What I Am," before throwing his wig at Georges, storming off the stage, and resolutely ending Act I.

Georges and Albin quickly reconcile, and Albin reluctantly agrees to meet the Dindons while posing as Jean-Michel's heterosexual Uncle Al. Yet when news arrives that Sybil will not make it to the elaborate charade, Albin hurriedly dons drag and introduces himself to Anne's family as Jean-Michel's mother. All goes smoothly until after dinner, when Albin agrees to perform a song. Caught up in a climactic moment, he rips off his wig, thereby revealing his identity to Anne's horrified parents.

The Dindons beg Anne to break off the engagement but she refuses. Jean-Michel apologizes to Albin. The Dindons prepare to leave, but find that the press has arrived in hopes of catching the anti-gay politician at La Cage with Zaza. Georges and Albin agree to help the Dindons escape, provided they give Anne and Jean-Michel their blessings. Les Cagelles disguise the Dindons, who escape in full drag. Georges and Albin reaffirm their love with a tender song and kiss.

La Cage Aux Folles can be seen as groundbreaking merely because it was the first successful Broadway musical to depict a strong, loving gay partnership. Yet some of its appeal was due to its underlying conservatism, both in structure and its reliance on unsophisticated humor and gay stereotypes. These have been frequently criticized by critics and historians as tactics used to evade any real political or cultural statements about tolerance or understanding.

The scholar John Clum argued that while *La Cage* was "hyped as a great leap forward for gay men in musical theater," it functioned more as "a fantasy version of gay life for tourists" that appeased straight audiences rather than attempt to educate, inform, or challenge stereotypes. *La Cage*, he argued, depicted a highly heteronormative gay couple who came off as sanitized, sexless, and thus neatly universalized instead of specifically, culturally gay (Clum 1999, 182–4). And John Bush Jones argued that the ample use of drag in the musical actually reinforced ignorance. Many of the characters, he noted, "aren't just drag performers in the club but drag queens offstage, whose dialogue and mannerisms consistently portray them as homosexual stereotypes," thereby allowing audience members to leave a performance entertained, but "with their prejudices largely intact" (Jones 2003, 340–1). Despite the criticisms, *La Cage* remains a frequently revived chestnut. This is largely due to the strengths of its central characters, who reflect a love and mutual respect that was rare on Broadway for same-sex characters—even despite the many gay men who, for generations, have toiled behind the scenes to bring musicals to the stage in the first place.

Enter the megamusical

La Cage and *Dreamgirls* both relied heavily on human bodies in motion and eye-catching costumes for their spectacle. Yet by the early 1980s, many Broadway musicals were moving beyond these tried-and-true means of wowing audiences. The approach to spectacle began to change with the rise of new technologies that allowed the theater to emulate film, both visually and in terms of newly sophisticated sound design. The early 1980s brought with it trends that favored the latest in mechanically-produced stage effects. New musicals emphasizing the technologically spectacular would eventually help uproot theatrical production from its local confines on Broadway, and transform it into international big business.

As noted in the last chapter, Andrew Lloyd Webber and Tim Rice's Broadway production of *Jesus Christ Superstar* was not as successful as they had anticipated. But their later productions, both in collaboration and apart, became enormously popular with audiences on Broadway, in the West End, and eventually across the globe.

Lloyd Webber's catchy tunes, Rice's clever and frequently humorous lyrics, and their productions' emphasis on the visually spectacular helped spur their popularity. They also had particularly good business sense. Lloyd Webber, in particular, spent ample time "working with productions all over the world, learning how to solve problems of translation, casting, and staging in any given city," while also investigating ways to best handle his newfound wealth (Sternfeld, 68).

After *Jesus Christ Superstar*, Lloyd Webber vowed to maintain "iron control over all aspects of his productions" (Walsh 2000, AR1), and thus founded the Really Useful Company in 1977. An entertainment and production company meant to oversee his theatrical productions, the organization went public in 1985 and was renamed the Really Useful Group. It has ventured into film, television, sound recording, publishing and merchandising, theater ownership, and management (Sternfeld 2006, 70). Beginning with *Evita*, which opened in the West End in 1978 and on Broadway in 1979, Lloyd Webber has had the final say when it comes to how his shows look and sound, no matter where they open or who directs them.

Evita, Lloyd Webber's last Broadway production with Rice, was loosely based on the meteoric rise and untimely death of Eva Perón (1919–52), wife of the Argentine dictator Juan Perón. The composer–lyricist team took wild liberties with their subject matter: the actions of the title character, depicted as a power-hungry opportunist who sleeps her way into Argentine society, were commented upon by *Evita*'s narrator, who is not necessarily supposed to be the Marxist revolutionary Che Guevara, but who is a revolutionary named Che nonetheless. *Evita*, which catapulted its leads, Patti LuPone and Mandy Patinkin, to stardom, was the first of many Lloyd Webber productions to get mixed-to-negative reviews and nevertheless become hugely popular with audiences.

Evita ran on Broadway for four years, a run that paled in comparison with Lloyd Webber's next project. *Cats* would become the first in a wave of big, technologically dazzling musicals that have since become known as "megamusicals," many of which were imported from Europe by the Really Useful Group. Megamusicals dominated Broadway through the 1980s and early 1990s. Considered a modern approach to nineteenth-century grand opera due to their dazzling stage effects, sung-through scores, lavish orchestrations, large casts, and emphasis on universality, social justice themes, and sentimentality, megamusicals were frequently savaged by critics and yet so beloved by audiences that they popularized the phrase "critic proof" (Prece and Everett 2008, 250–1).

Cats was the first musical for which Lloyd Webber teamed with the British theater impresario Cameron Mackintosh (1946–), a formidable theater producer with a knack for marketing and an eye toward the potential stage musicals had in the global marketplace. Mackintosh and Lloyd Webber recruited an impressive team to bring the new musical to the stage. *Cats* was helmed by the esteemed Royal Shakespeare Company director Trevor Nunn (1940), who would later direct the megamusicals *Les Misérables* and *Sunset Boulevard*. *Cats* opened at the New London Theatre in the West End on May 11, 1981, and arrived, following enormous hype and a huge advance in ticket sales, at Broadway's Winter Garden Theatre on October 7, 1982.

Essentially a revue, *Cats* borrows from T.S. Eliot's poetry collection *Old Possum's Book of Practical Cats*, and is held together with the thinnest of plots. At the beginning of the show, the godlike Old Deuteronomy cat announces that by the evening's end, one cat will go to cat heaven (called the heaviside layer). *Cats* concludes as down-and-out Grizabella sings the show's best-known song, "Memory," before being granted the dubious honor of ascending heavenward on a giant, mechanized car tire that serves as the show's most elaborate stage effect. What falls between the introduction and conclusion are songs and dances in styles ranging from swing to dancehall to operetta to rock, all performed by actors costumed and made up to look like cats.

Many musicals fail to win audiences due to a weak plot or over-reliance on spectacle, and critics found *Cats* to be guilty of both. But the revue-like form and stunning visuals turned out to be assets. The impressive costumes, makeup design, and imaginative set—a huge (if notably sanitary and fresh-smelling) garbage dump filled with oversized candy wrappers, soda cans, and worn-out shoes—arguably helped sell as many tickets as the music itself. *Cats* arrived in New York in the early stages of the contemporary tourist boom, and tapped into an international audience that did not need to understand English to follow *Cats* or marvel at its visual attributes.

By the time it closed on Broadway in September 2000 after an eighteen-year run, *Cats* had become the most internationally profitable theatrical venture in history. It spawned productions in hundreds of cities worldwide and countless international touring companies, which have been seen by many millions of people (Rosenberg and Harburg 1993, 59). *Cats* is thus remarkable less for its artistry than its commercial impact.

Cats' success made Mackintosh and Lloyd Webber remarkably powerful on both sides of the Atlantic. Working individually or in tandem, the two would be responsible for a number of megamusicals to open through the 1980s and 1990s in New York, London and, via franchise, around the world. Among them are Schönberg and Boublil's *Les Misérables* (1987) and *Miss Saigon* (1991), and Lloyd Webber's *The Phantom of the Opera* (1988) and *Sunset Boulevard* (1994), all of which were produced either by Mackintosh, Lloyd Webber's Really Useful Group, or both in partnership.

Megamusicals were frequently criticized for placing technical spectacle over content, which of course would have been impossible in decades prior. *Cats'* giant ascending tire and outsized garbage dump set were just the beginning in this respect. *The Phantom of the Opera* arguably drew crowds as much for its crashing chandelier and watery underground lair as for its plot and score. *Les Misérables* boasted a huge cast on a revolving stage; in the scene depicting the fall of Saigon, *Miss Saigon* had a helicopter that landed onstage and took off again.

Lloyd Webber and Mackintosh were two of the first to figure out how to transcend specific locations to make musical theater a global business with the potential for unprecedented profit-making (Sternfeld 2006, 79). *Cats* opened a worldwide market for musicals, allowing the commercial theater industry to mine the benefits of regional, touring, and international productions. Lloyd Webber's musicals might not all be remembered hundreds of years from now, but his business model stands a chance.

As the cost of production skyrocketed in the 1980s, Broadway producers became more reliant on the idea of spending money to make money, which resulted in higher ticket prices for ever-larger technology-driven spectacles. Meanwhile, smaller, less expensively produced shows became tougher to sell, and less spectacular productions were, on the whole, not as successful on Broadway during the decade.

The megamusical craze began to wane by the end of the 1980s, at which point both Andrew Lloyd Webber and Tim Rice experienced major disappointments. In 1987, Lloyd Webber's *Starlight Express* opened in New York after hit productions in the West End and Bochum, Germany. A musical about toy trains that come to life and race against one another, *Starlight* featured a cast on roller-skates scooting at high speed around an enormous track. It closed after 761 performances, which would have been ample time to recoup in years past, but not by the late 1980s; *Starlight Express* became the first Lloyd Webber venture on Broadway not to recoup its investment. His *Aspects of Love*, which opened in 1990, fared even worse, closing after 377 performances and losing its entire $8 million investment. *Chess*, Tim Rice's 1988 collaboration with former ABBA members Benny Andersson and Björn Ulvaeus, also closed at a loss. While *Miss Saigon* would do far better in the early 1990s, this relatively late arrival to the megamusical canon did not premiere in New York City without its share of controversy.

Miss Saigon has been called a "quintessential megamusical" because it boasts every feature the subgenre had to offer: a lush, sung-through score by Schönberg and Boublil, a lead producer in Cameron Mackintosh, a plot that plays on strong emotions and elaborate, expensive, spectacular sets (and the aforementioned helicopter). Loosely based on Puccini's *Madama Butterfly* and set just prior to the fall of Saigon in 1975, *Miss Saigon* was larger in scope than the original opera (Sternfeld 2006, 293).

Miss Saigon tells the tragic tale of Kim, a seventeen-year-old Vietnamese girl whose family is killed in the war. In desperation, she goes to Saigon to work as a bargirl at a sleazy club owned by a mercenary half-Vietnamese, half-French hustler known as the Engineer. During her first night on the job, Kim meets and falls in love with Chris, a traumatized American marine about to leave for home. Chris promises to take Kim back to the US with him, but they are separated in the chaos when Saigon falls. Three years later, Kim continues to hope that Chris will return for her and, now, for their son, Tam. Chris, however, has searched extensively for Kim and has presumed her dead. He has married Ellen, an American, though he suffers from post-traumatic stress disorder and still longs for Kim, about whom he has recurring nightmares.

When Chris and Ellen learn that Kim is alive, they travel to Bangkok and find her dancing at a bar also owned by the Engineer. Kim assumes she and Chris will be reunited, but when she meets Ellen, she realizes her hopes have been dashed. In the final scene, the Engineer leads Chris and Ellen to Kim's room, where she steps behind a curtain and shoots herself. She dies in Chris's arms, leaving Tam to him and Ellen (Hischak 2008, 498).

Miss Saigon opened in the West End in September, 1989. Mackintosh announced plans to bring it to Broadway in 1991 with members of the original cast: Lea Salonga as Kim and Jonathan Pryce as the Engineer. The show became a hot ticket well before it opened in New York, breaking the record for largest advance in ticket sales—$24 million—before rehearsals began. But in July 1990, complaints were filed by members of the Actors' Equity's ethnic minorities committee, alleging that the casting of Pryce, a white Welshman, was offensive, especially since Pryce used "yellowface" makeup and eye prostheses in the West End production to suggest a darker skin-tone and Asian eyes.

Equity initially sided with the complainants, announced that it could not "appear to condone the casting of a Caucasian in the role of a Eurasian," and attempted to bar Pryce from performing the role in New York. The controversy grew as the many Equity members took sides, critics began to weigh in, and petitions were circulated both for and against the practice of Caucasian actors playing characters of color. Mackintosh responded by simply canceling the production, thereby denying roles to some fifty actors, a majority of which were to be Asian. The union hurriedly reversed its decision, welcomed Pryce and wished the production a successful run (Rothstein 1990).

The controversy eventually subsided. *Miss Saigon* opened as expected, earning typically mixed reviews and enormous commercial interest. Pryce performed on Broadway without yellowface or prosthetics, and won a Tony for his performance. After his departure and for the duration of *Miss Saigon*'s ten-year run on Broadway, the Engineer was portrayed by actors of Asian descent. And at the very least, the controversy helped raise awareness of the fact that many minorities were, even at the end of the twentieth century, still woefully under-represented and often reduced to caricature on American theatrical stages (Sternfeld 2006, 303–4).

The megamusical craze ended in New York with the closing of *Miss Saigon*, though one might argue that the subgenre was merely supplanted by something even bigger, slicker, and more spectacular. Disney's arrival on Broadway in the mid-1990s resulted in changes to both Times Square and the commercial theater industry that made the megamusical seem quaint and old-fashioned by comparison.

The 1990s

The final decade of the twentieth century saw the definitive end of the Cold War and a political shift to the left with the election of Bill Clinton in 1992. Advances in technology hastened the availability of computers and cell phones. These helped stimulate rapid increases in globalization, and reshaped the nature of American business, commerce, culture, and leisure time. The American economy moved away from manufacturing and toward service, and experienced "heightened competition, rapid innovation, increased organizational flexibility, and more fluid capital and labor markets." This transition to what some titled the "new economy" allowed the US, following a recession in 1991, to enter the longest period of economic growth it had experienced since the Second World War. Not everyone benefited from the newfound prosperity, which was "distributed with startling inequality, reversing the trend toward greater equality that had prevailed from the Second World War through the 1960s." The rich got richer and the poor got poorer as the millennium approached, while those in the middle found themselves newly in need of more than one household income and, in many cases, saddled with debt (Griffith and Baker 2007, 394–5).

The country's economic growth benefited New York City, if, again, more its professional classes than its lower and working ones. During the tech boom, the city transitioned into an important center for post-industrial capital. Between 1995 and 2000, some 300,000 new jobs were added to New York's workforce of 3.6 million. Factory work, on the other hand, reached a new low of 7 percent of the total. By the turn of the twenty first century, New York City "was adding private-sector jobs at a pace ahead of the country's for the first time in fifty years." Immigration picked up as well: by 2000, the city was in full melting-pot mode, with a third of its residents born outside the US (Klein 1992, 728–9). Crime across the five boroughs plummeted, neighborhoods gentrified, and tourism continued to boom. Ironically, the one neighborhood that continued to resist a viable gentrification plan was Times Square, the very crossroads the city was trying to sell as an important part of any tourist package.

The renovation of Times Square

In the mid-1990s, city officials announced that the Walt Disney Company would become active in Times Square as an investor, real estate owner, and theater producer. Disney's new presence in the area heralded a significant increase in business activity by other entertainment conglomerates, the arrival of which exerted immediate influence on Broadway's commercial theaters in particular and American theater in general. For better and worse, the involvement of entertainment conglomerates on Broadway at the turn of the century allowed Broadway to extend its reach globally, and thus to work its way back into the web of American popular culture from which it had been severed during the rise of rock 'n' roll and the death of Tin Pan Alley in the mid-1950s.

Heavy construction in Times Square did not begin until the late 1990s, but plans to overhaul Times Square had been made, scuttled, and made again over some thirty years, outliving "three mayors, four governors, two real estate booms and two recessions" (Bagli 2010, A17). During the lengthy debate over how to improve the area, proposals had ranged from the boring to the bizarre—from extending midtown's business district into Times Square on the one hand, to enclosing the neighborhood in a giant glass bubble and making it an indoor amusement park and shopping mall on the other (Traub 2005, 134–5).

Curiously, Broadway theaters were not central to most of these plans; international tourism, after all, was not the windfall it would become late in the century. Under the Dinkins administration (1990–93), however, an idea took shape that envisioned Times Square as a cleaner, brighter, less porny, more tourist-friendly version of itself. The city and state of New York, sensing profits from an increase in tourism that international media companies might lure to the area, began courting Disney.

City officials had tried to get Disney executives interested in Broadway theaters before. Since the late 1980s, high-ranking politicians had approached the company at various points, only to be put off or ignored. But in the early 1990s, Disney was having its own identity crisis. Still reeling from the disastrous 1987 opening of Euro Disney (later renamed Disneyland Paris), the company was also combating new competition borne of the tech explosion, as well as a slew of international bad press that painted it as more interested in the bottom line than in quality entertainment. Suddenly, restoring a historic theater and developing family-friendly musicals to put in it did not seem like such a terrible idea (Bianco 2004, 277–8).

This was especially the case after the 1991 release of *Beauty and the Beast*, Disney's first blockbuster film in a long time, and one that several film critics wrote was more inventive and entertaining than anything Broadway had on offer at the time (Traub 2005, 231). After so much bad press, Disney finally had something positive to promote. Why not adapt their successful film for Broadway, just to test the waters? By late 1992, Disney CEO Michael Eisner had approved the development of a new branch of Disney Studios named Walt Disney Theatrical Productions. In spring 1993, he toured the New Amsterdam Theater, once the celebrated home of Ziegfeld's *Follies* and now host to a variety of urban flora and fauna, which had access to water dripping steadily from holes in the roof and creating huge, stagnating puddles on the once-lushly carpeted floor (Bianco 2004, 279).

Negotiations regarding Disney's renovation of the New Amsterdam took over a year and a half, and extended into a new mayoral administration. When Rudy Giuliani took office, he pushed through zoning restrictions on sex shops and peepshows, which were dying out with the rise of the Internet anyway (Klein 2001, 729). Meanwhile, the Broadway version of *Beauty and the Beast* opened in April 1994, at the Palace.

A record $12 million production, *Beauty* offered prodigious technological spectacle, lots of smoke and lights, and cinema-style sound design (Prece and Everett, 268). The look of the show was akin to a megamusical on steroids, and *Beauty and the Beast* was similarly received. Most critics were tepid to negative about the show, but it did not matter: the Disney musical broke box office records previously held by *Phantom of the Opera* when it sold over $1 million in tickets in a single day. *Beauty and the Beast* ran on Broadway for thirteen years, only closing in 2007 when Disney chose to replace it with a stage adaptation of their 1989 film *The Little Mermaid*.

While *Beauty and the Beast* was just starting to draw crowds on Broadway in 1994, Disney finalized a deal with New York City. The corporation agreed to renovate the New Amsterdam Theater at the cost of many millions of dollars. In exchange, it would enjoy exclusive use of the theater, which it currently occupies under a 49-year lease. The city and state agreed to lend Disney an additional $28 million in low-interest loans in return for 2 percent of all ticket receipts from shows staged at the theater. Because old theaters are costly to maintain, Disney was further encouraged to expand its presence in Times Square through the development of other properties and productions, including a street-level studio for Disney's ABC television, now at the corner of 44th Street and Broadway.

Other entertainment conglomerates followed Disney into the area, establishing new headquarters, theme stores, and restaurants, or venturing into theatrical production. The city continued to fund the rehabilitation of the area, not only by courting prominent companies, but by condemning old buildings, restoring theaters, and erecting new offices, hotels, rehearsal studios, and retail complexes (Kennedy 1995, B2).

By the end of the 1990s, an area considered a problem for decades had been transformed into a slicker, more tourist-friendly version of itself. Critics argued that the redevelopment would result in a loss of local flavor, while advocates cited a more attractive neighborhood, less porn and petty crime, and hundreds of new jobs. Both sides turned out to be right: while some still miss the days when Times Square was home to B-movies and local businesses, the neighborhood has become one of the city's top tourist destinations, and the continued home of commercial theaters that now annually pump billions of dollars into the city's economy.

The musical in the 1990s

The presence of Disney on Broadway was met by many theater aficionados, critics, and historians with skepticism and concern about the "Disneyfication" of the commercial theater. Worries that entertainment conglomerates would somehow manage to transform the whole of Times Square into another theme park or some generic, flavorless version of itself have, however, proven unwarranted. Broadway offers the same kinds of entertainments—musicals, revues, comedy acts, specialty shows, and "straight" or nonmusical plays— that it always has.

Yet the presence of corporations in Times Square has certainly resulted in changes in the industry, and thus in the ways American commercial theater is conceived, produced, and staged. What has changed most is the scope: shows cost more than they ever have, but also have the potential for a much broader reach, longer runs, and longer lives on tour or in productions around the world. Corporations are almost always wealthier than even the most financially successful individual. Whereas even powerful individuals like Cameron Mackintosh began having difficulty single-handedly producing musicals on Broadway once corporations became active as theater producers, companies like Disney can easily spend millions adapting commercial properties for the stage, or developing new ones. Most entertainment companies take losses, after all, that are far larger when one of their films or television shows flops.

Unlike individual theater producers, entertainment corporations can also more easily afford to advertise and market their properties internationally and for extended periods of time. Disney owns film production studios from which to borrow material, recording studios in which to record original cast albums, and media outlets, theme parks, and stores from which to advertise themselves. Such access to the mass media extends far beyond the reach of independent producers, who have since formed extensive partnerships in order to stage productions. Look at any *Playbill* next time you go to see a show on Broadway (or visit the Broadway League's Internet Broadway Database, at ibdb.com), and check out the lengthy lists of producers under any recent production.

Disney is large and lucrative enough not to need help from other companies to produce their shows (though they did join forces with Cameron Mackintosh for the 2006 Broadway production of *Mary Poppins*). They can afford to spend more to develop productions and to cross-market their shows, reaching more people than Mackintosh ever could. The stage version of Disney's 1994 animated movie *The Lion King*, which was the inaugural production of the newly refurbished New Amsterdam in 1997 and which remains a hot ticket on Broadway to date, is a case in point.

Eager to prove itself after *Beauty and the Beast*'s tepid critical reception, Disney hired esteemed Off Broadway director Julie Taymor (1953–) to direct *The Lion King*. Their choice was a significant departure from *Beauty and the Beast*, which had been directed to look as much like the animated film as possible. By the time Taymor came aboard for *The Lion King*, she was an experienced, award-winning director with her own approach and style, which Disney encouraged her to apply in adapting their film.

In doing so, Taymor drew on African music and culture, and borrowed from theatrical forms she had studied in her youth, including Indonesian *wayang kulit*, or shadow puppetry (Stempel 2010, 632). She also designed the production's costumes, puppets, and masks, some of which she stitched or beaded by hand. Most of the actors wear masks and headdresses in the production, but these are used less to obscure the performer than to highlight the intimate relationship between character, actor, and audience.

The Lion King was not just a commercial smash, but a critical darling as well. It was also, and continues to be, marketed exceptionally well in myriad ways, all over the world. *The Lion King* film helps sell the Broadway musical and vice-versa; tie-ins like books, stuffed animals, clothing, and related merchandise sell both. Under Taymor, *The Lion King* was developed into a beautiful, moving Broadway musical, but the power of the corporation behind it helped it become the "top box office title in any medium" as of 2014, when global sales rose above $6.2 billion (Cox 2014).

Yet for all the power of entertainment conglomerates, Broadway has not become an artless tourist trap filled with nothing but staged versions of movies. Commercial theatrical production has become more global, more expensive, and more intertwined with mass mediated commercial entertainment. But in many respects, things have remained on Broadway as they were before Times Square was renovated: new and revived musicals, as well as new and revived plays, are still performed for audiences eight times a week. Some shows go straight to Broadway; others are workshopped and staged before audiences in regional theaters to test their popularity and marketability. Still others originate Off Broadway and move uptown by popular demand.

In January 1996, just as Disney was finishing renovations on the New Amsterdam, the nonprofit Off Broadway venue New York Theatre Workshop was preparing its spring musical. *Rent,* with music and lyrics by Jonathan

Larson (1960–96), was well on its way to becoming a hot ticket even before Larson died unexpectedly of undiagnosed Marfan Syndrome on the morning of the first preview. A rock musical based on the Puccini opera *La Bohème* and set among young artists, addicts, bohemians, and squatters in New York's East Village, *Rent* was moved in April 1996 to the Nederlander Theater on Broadway, where it ran until 2008.

By the time *Rent* opened, many musical theater composers, like Larson himself, had been raised with a love for both Broadway fare and contemporary popular music, and were more capable than earlier generations of mixing these influences into their scores. Out of fashion since the 1970s, rock- and pop-inspired musicals continue to succeed on Broadway to date; one might argue, in fact, that there are now fewer musicals that are *not* influenced by contemporary popular music than there are shows with no pop music influence at all.

Rent was no anomaly. The nonprofit world continues to have a strong presence on Broadway, where it operates alongside enormous corporations. Since the death of founder Joe Papp in 1991, the Public Theater has continued to transfer productions to Broadway when demand justifies the move; so have other Off Broadway and nonprofit theaters, including Second Stage, Manhattan Theater Club, MCC, and Playwrights Horizons. While globalization and corporatization have influenced the ways that the commercial theater is selected, produced, staged, and sold, Broadway has not died on the one hand, or become dominated by entertainment conglomerates on the other.

A new century: From the aughts to the teens

At the turn of the century, the US continued to adjust to the impact of globalization and the shift from an industrial to a service economy, which was not easy since global "communication, trade, and capital flow all grew more rapidly than either national or international political systems could fully comprehend or control." Worldwide income disparities rose into sharper focus, and the influence of Western culture on all corners of the world intensified. Questions arose as to American foreign policy following the Cold War era: should the country act as an "imperial police officer"? Was increased globalization "a threat to American living standards and national sovereignty" on the one hand, or "an irreparable threat to the global environment" on the other? Such concerns only intensified after the attacks on the World Trade Center and Pentagon on September 11, 2001 (Griffith and Baker 2007, 509–10).

So have questions about American identity, difference, and acceptance. At the turn of the century, terms like "multiculturalism," "diversity," and "race" became hotly debated buzzwords (Wolf 2011, 163–4). Whether gays and lesbians should be granted the right to marry became the subject of intense debate on the state and federal levels. So too did the civil rights of transgender citizens. The rise of technology has helped reveal continued civil rights injustices. For example, videos of black Americans being treated unfairly and often more violently than their white counterparts by police officers resulted in increased scrutiny, debates about racial injustice, and the rise of the Black Lives Matter movement. These debates, legal actions, and social movements continue to shed light on the continued need for social, cultural, and political reforms in the US.

Broadway in and after crisis

In the sad, frightening weeks following September 11, 2001, tourism in New York took a major hit, and thus so too did Broadway. Ticket sales following the attacks plummeted. Many shows closed immediately, while others posted closing notices.

The first week following the attacks was one of the worst in Broadway's history. Ticket sales dropped by as much as 80 percent industry-wide. Shows that could afford to stay open were kept temporarily dark, or were performed before nearly empty houses. Even the hottest musicals, like *The Phantom of the Opera, Rent, Chicago, The Lion King,* and *The Producers,* lost millions through the autumn.

Shortly after the attacks, Broadway's trade organization, the League of American Theaters and Producers (now the Broadway League), began meeting to manage the financial strain until sales could improve. Many producers agreed to take significant financial hits to keep shows running. The Shuberts, Jujamcyns, and Nederlanders agreed to waive theater rents until sales could improve (McKinley 2001, E1).

A month after the attacks, sales began to stabilize, though international tourism remained sluggish. Due largely to marketing campaigns aimed at luring local and national audiences back to Broadway, and encouraged by city officials' frequent public suggestions that the best way to help New York was to visit and spend money in it, Broadway sales improved by the second week of October (Bohlen 2011, E1).

By late October, critics were writing about audiences attending Broadway comedies and musicals in a near-desperate quest for "the palliative effects of the theater ... the restorative powers of a night in a darkened hall—particularly one in which comedy is promised." Actors reported hearing laughter from audiences that was "stunning in its explosiveness." At *Mamma Mia!*, the first musical to open after the attacks, actress Judy Kaye observed among spectators "faces that hadn't smiled in weeks" (Marks 2001, AR5).

While the 2001–02 season was weaker financially than the previous year, with grosses of $643 million down from $666 million, Broadway bounced back in full the following season, with a gross of $721 million. Some subsequent years have been stronger than others, but in general, grosses continue to climb. Broadway typically earns well over a billion dollars in ticket sales in any given year.[2]

Broadway today: Reflections of contemporary media, culture, and society

Broadway musicals have long been considered middle-of-the-road entertainments, both aesthetically and politically. As a recycler of other art forms, and as a mass entertainment often created with one eye on art and the other on commerce, most musicals shy away from sentiment that might be perceived as too far to the political left or right, since such extremes are likely to alienate potential spectators. At the millennium, the Broadway musical, newly bound with entertainment conglomerates, newly expensive, and newly eager to appeal to as many tourists as possible, was arguably more middle-of-the-road than ever (Wolf 2011, 164–5).

While slow to reflect contemporary concerns about inclusiveness, some Broadway shows nevertheless began to depict a broader diversity of characters. Shows like the aforementioned *Rent,* William Finn's *Falsettos* (1992), Nicholas Hytner's revival of Rodgers and Hammerstein's *Carousel* (1994), Paul Simon and Derek Walcott's *The Capeman* (1998), A.R. Rahman and Don Black's *Bombay Dreams* (2004), and Tony Kushner and Jeanine Tesori's *Caroline, or Change* (2004) together reflect Broadway's increasing pluralism. The fact that many of these musicals were honed in the nonprofit realm, either Off Broadway or in the regional theater, is hardly coincidental. In the new millennium, the influence of nonprofits on the commercial musical has continued to grow.

At the same time, the American musical continues to reflect the influence of entertainment conglomerates, which have exerted influence on the costs of production and the types of shows developed for Broadway. At the turn of the century, adapted films and so-called "jukebox musicals" have become standard Broadway fare. The influence of Hollywood on Broadway remains palpable.

Broadway has played host to musicalized versions of popular films like *Footloose* (1998), *Saturday Night Fever* (1999), *The Full Monty* (2000), and the mega-hit *The Producers* (2001), all of which were adapted or produced by people or companies responsible for the original films. Often the biggest tourist draws, these musicals appeal to global audiences due to their familiar titles, characters, plots and, usually, songs from film soundtracks.

In some cases, as with *Hairspray* (2002), *Shrek The Musical* (2008), and *School of Rock* (2015), creative teams involving experienced musical theater people—the composers Marc Shaiman (1959–), Jeanine Tesori (1961–), and Andrew Lloyd Webber, respectively—were involved in reconceiving the films for the stage. In other cases, relative newcomers to Broadway teamed with more seasoned personnel to adapt a show, as pop star Cyndi Lauper did with Harvey Fierstein for *Kinky Boots* in 2013. Critics are quick to point out that musicalized films can seem like mercenary ploys on the part of risk-averse producers to make money from recycled material. But the companies or individuals who adapt films into successful musicals benefit from name recognition, renewed interest in beloved films, and audiences eager to see their favorite movies in a new light.

A newer subgenre known as the jukebox musical works in much the same way. Jukebox musicals use previously-released, well-known popular songs to make up most or all of the score. In some respects, jukebox musicals hearken back to the days when Broadway was in its infancy, and Tin Pan Alley songs were regularly interpolated into musical productions. Today, jukebox musicals have become so popular that there are many different kinds, ranging from old-fashioned revues to dance musicals to elaborately plotted full-length comedies.

Some jukebox musicals highlight the work of specific performers or songwriters, like the long-running revue *Smokey Joe's Cafe* (1995), which featured songs by Jerry Leiber and Mike Stoller. Others include the ABBA musical *Mamma Mia!* (2001), the Frankie Valli and the Four Seasons musical *Jersey Boys* (2005), and *Beautiful*, which traces the life and career of Carole King (2013). Other jukebox musicals focus primarily on dance. *Movin' Out*, the 2002 hit choreographed by Twyla Tharp, featured a score built of Billy

Joel songs. Still others are filled with songs that evoke entire eras or subgenres, as in the 1980s heavy metal musical *Rock of Ages* (2006) and *Motown: The Musical* (2013).

Another more recent subgenre is the self-referential musical, which uses inside jokes and broad humor to mock the very canon it represents. The self-referential musical reflects a postmodern aesthetic and appeals to spectators who are not entirely comfortable with the more stolid conceits of the musical theater, such as characters bursting suddenly into song or otherwise displaying high levels of emotional sentiment. Self-referential musicals do not shy from such conceits; instead, they point them out and make fun of them. Self-referential musicals can at times overlap with the form's other subgenres. For example, there have been many adapted film musicals that are also self-referential musicals, and many jukebox musicals, like *Rock of Ages*, that rely heavily on self-referential humor.

A successful self-referential film adaptation was the hit of the 2000–1 season, *The Producers*, adapted by the comedian Mel Brooks from his 1968 film of the same name. *The Producers* made constant, winking reference to the film on which it was based, and to Broadway's past depictions of gays, blacks, and Jews. It featured a much-talked-about, decidedly postmodern montage at the start of Act II, during which the actor playing Max Bialystock re-enacts the first half of the show, including the intermission, at breakneck speed. *The Producers'* show-within-a-show, *Springtime for Hitler*, featured elaborate, Busby Berkeley-style choreography, and chorines in sparkly, elaborate (and Nazi-themed) costumes in a joking reference to Ziegfeld's *Follies*.

Similarly, *Monty Python's Spamalot* (2005), Eric Idle's adaptation of the film *Monty Python and the Holy Grail*, featured several musical numbers that mocked Broadway conventions. One, "The Song That Goes Like This," is a sendup of romantic Broadway ballads ("Once in every show / There comes a song like this / It starts off soft and low / And ends up with a kiss"). Self-referential humor has been used successfully as well in original musicals like *[title of show]*, with music and lyrics by Jeff Bowen and book by Hunter Bell, who also starred as versions of themselves. An ever-evolving musical, *[title of show]* chronicled its own development as an entry in the New York Musical Festival (2004), an Off Broadway production at the Vineyard Theater (2006), and a Broadway production at the Lyceum (2008).

Musicals that rely on familiarity, nostalgia, and self-referential humor have proven popular with local audiences and tourists alike. The appeal to tourists has become especially important, since the ratio of locals to tourists visiting Broadway has flipped from what it was in the mid-twentieth century.

Tourists once made up about a third of the market, but they now make up roughly 70 percent of ticket buyers (Paulson 2015).

Yet it is incorrect to assume that all American musicals are developed for and sold primarily to tourists looking for the biggest, most extravagant Broadway experience. Especially since the renovation of Times Square and new influence from media companies, the commercial theater industry has become more sophisticated with advertising and marketing strategies, and has improved its reach to increasingly diverse audiences. Minority groups remain under-represented on Broadway, both on the stage and behind the scenes, but the twenty-first century has seen the emergence of productions more reflective of the country's diversity in terms of race, sexual orientation, and ethnicity. The small but growing presence of women and minorities as directors, choreographers, composers, lyricists, and producers has helped contribute to a Broadway that is, at the very least, less segregated and more self-aware than it once was.

Contemporary Broadway has also become more appealing to younger audiences than it was through the end of twentieth century. The reputation of Broadway as corny and out of touch, especially pronounced during the 1960s and 1970s, persisted through the end of the millennium. Disney's presence on Broadway helped attract young audiences, but so too did the initiatives of producers who, by the late 1990s, grew increasingly concerned about the future of Broadway and the need to cultivate young audiences. *Rent* and the tap revue of African American history *Bring in 'da Noise, Bring in 'da Funk*, both of which moved from Off Broadway in 1996, were the first productions to court young audiences with the promise of cheap tickets for some of the best seats in the house. The producers of both shows initially reserved a few rows of seats each day for $20 to students on a first-come, first-served basis (Baldinger 1996, H5). When the demand for these tickets became overwhelming, the productions shifted to a day-of lottery system, which continues to be emulated by many Broadway shows to date.

Appreciation for Broadway musicals among young people has grown significantly, especially with new emphases on youth cultures and their concerns. The corps of mostly male (and entirely adult) New York theater critics were overwhelmingly tepid about *Wicked* (2003), an alternate retelling of *The Wizard of Oz* with music and lyrics by Stephen Schwartz (1948–) and book by Winnie Holzman. But they failed take into consideration the musical's feminist themes, which resonated deeply with young women and girls. Despite poor reviews, *Wicked* caught on with audiences through word of mouth, and became an enormous hit, which continues to play to sold-out houses filled with tourists and locals alike.[3]

Big, spectacular shows like *Wicked*, *The Lion King*, *Aladdin*, and *The Phantom of the Opera* reflect the presence of for-profit, commercial producers. Yet they do not dominate Broadway, but instead compete with nonprofit companies that remain important forces on Broadway and beyond. Most Off Broadway, regional, and subscription houses now develop and produce new musicals, the strongest of which move to Broadway. No longer unique in its development of innovative new musicals that are nurtured Off Broadway and moved uptown, the Public Theater continues sending successful shows to Broadway when audience demand dictates. Some of the Public's musicals, for example *Passing Strange* (2008) and *Bloody Bloody Andrew Jackson* (2010), were big hits at the Public but failed to connect with Broadway audiences when they reopened in larger theaters. Yet others have met with critical accolades and enormous commercial success, whether Off or on Broadway.

Fun Home and *Hamilton*, both of which premiered at the Public and subsequently moved to Broadway, are recent, important cases in point. The former was adapted from cartoonist Alison Bechdel's 2006 graphic novel of the same name by playwright Lisa Kron (1961–) and composer Jeanine Tesori. Widely heralded for its artistry, emotional depth, and realistic characters, *Fun Home* is a memory musical about Bechdel's relationship with her father, a closeted gay man who committed suicide four months after Bechdel came out to her family as a lesbian.

Fun Home focuses on Alison's coming of age, with songs that draw from traditional Broadway influences, but also disco, Motown, and the singer-songwriter tradition. Songs explore Alison's sexual and gender identity, first in childhood, then in college and as an adult ("Ring of Keys," "I'm Changing My Major to Joan," and "Telephone Wire," respectively). *Fun Home* resonated deeply with queer spectators, many of whom lauded the unflinchingly honest, sensitive depictions of a butch lesbian and closeted gay man. The musical won the admiration of broader audiences, many of whom identified with a highly realistic portrait of a contemporary American family that was deeply flawed, yet ceaselessly loving.

Fun Home's successful transfer to Broadway was followed by one of the most widely praised and enthusiastically received musicals in decades. *Hamilton*, a biographical musical about the life of Alexander Hamilton, was written by composer and actor Lin-Manuel Miranda (1980–). Set in Colonial America, the musical features a score that melds hip-hop and R&B with more traditional Broadway fare, and casts actors of color as members of the founding generation. *Hamilton* sold out its run at the Public in spring 2015 and moved to Broadway in July of the same year. Over the course of the 2015–16 season, the musical won a trove of awards, from the Pulitzer Prize for Drama to several Tony Awards to the Grammy for best Musical Theater Album. One of the hottest shows Broadway has ever seen, tickets for *Hamilton* sell out months in advance. The show has proven popular with people of all ages, backgrounds, and political affiliations. At least until it became associated with the Democrats during the bruising 2016 presidential campaign, it was embraced by both the political left and right. Barack Obama, who hosted Miranda and the original cast at the White House on several occasions, once quipped that *Hamilton* was just about "the only thing Dick Cheney and I can agree on."[4]

Unquestionably an excellent, well-constructed musical that appeals to a wide range of spectators due to its artistry, *Hamilton* is nevertheless, like all musicals, very much the product of its place and time. The musical resonates as thrilling mass entertainment, and also works on a number of sociocultural levels. At a time when the US is experiencing growing racial and class tensions, political fractiousness, and a sense that the American dream is untenable, *Hamilton* serves as sociopolitical wish fulfillment. It has come to symbolize a rapidly diversifying if not yet fully integrated Broadway.

Hamilton has driven the form forward with its innovative score, which is regularly called revolutionary, just as *Hair* was decades prior. It has been embraced by people of different races and cultural backgrounds and, for the first time in a long time, different ages: the Broadway cast recording of *Hamilton* debuted at number twelve on the Billboard 200 (Caulfield 2015), brought families together to listen to selections or the entire album together and managed to make colonial American history cool among the adolescent set. Running on Broadway at a time when Hollywood has been lambasted for its lack of diversity, *Hamilton* is not only popular in its own right, but is helping Broadway enjoy the kind of mass popularity usually reserved for films, pop songs, and television shows.

The availability of the album on various streaming sites is reinforced by Miranda's embrace of social media, which he used to build interest in his first Broadway show, *In the Heights* (2008). *Hamilton*, and Miranda himself, have reached audiences far and wide, generating interest among people who might never get the chance to see the production itself, through tweets, uploaded clips, promotional material, interviews, and articles posted on social media sites like Facebook, Instagram, and Snapchat. Along with television, radio, film, and the print media, these tools have all been incorporated by the commercial theater industry for use in advertising and promotion.

For its immense popularity and breathless critical reception, *Hamilton* is hardly unique in driving home the fact that the American musical remains an enormously viable and important entertainment form, both in the US and now across the world. Through wars, economic downturns, the Great Depression, terrorist attacks, and political and social turmoil; through the advent of radio, film, television, and the Internet; through the tenures of the Syndicate, the Shuberts, and the Walt Disney Company, Broadway is not only not going anywhere but has grown well beyond its borders. No longer just a muddy patch of ugly land known for its prostitutes and stench of horse manure, "Broadway" has become an international symbol for live productions that charm, thrill, delight, and inspire the millions of people who, night after night and year after year, eagerly "come and meet / those dancing feet." Whether said feet belong to George M. Cohan, Ethel Merman, Mary Martin, Audra McDonald, Nathan Lane, Lin-Manuel Miranda, or some future entertainer who is currently being spoonfed while her parents stream the original Broadway cast recording of *Kinky Boots* from a speaker in the kitchen does not matter. There will always be something for everyone on old Broadway.

CHAPTER 8
CRITICAL PERSPECTIVES

**PUTTING IT TOGETHER: A STEP-BY-STEP LOOK AT
MUSICALS FROM THE PAGE TO THE STAGE**
Robert Meffe

Robert Meffe lived and worked in New York City as a professional music director, conductor, arranger, keyboardist, pianist, and orchestrator for twenty-two years. On Broadway, he was associate conductor for *Little Women* and for the last six years of *Les Misérables*, and played keyboards for *Evita* (2012 revival), *Newsies*, *The Phantom of the Opera*, *Avenue Q*, *The 25th Annual Putnam County Spelling Bee*, *Grey Gardens*, and *Bombay Dreams*. He was music director for national tours of *Evita* and *The Phantom of the Opera*, and associate conductor of *Les Misérables* and *Sunday in the Park with George*. Off Broadway, he worked on the productions *Myths & Hymns*, *Violet*, *The Prince and the Pauper*, and *Gutenberg! The Musical!* Television shows he has worked on include *Earth to America* (TBS) and *Renee Fleming—Live at Lincoln Center* (PBS). He is currently the head of the MFA Musical Theatre Program at San Diego State University. In addition to playing for San Diego musical events, including touring companies of *Wicked* and *Priscilla, Queen of the Desert*, he has established a professional/academic partnership between SDSU, the Old Globe, and La Jolla Playhouse to develop new musical theater.

It all begins with an idea.

Every musical that makes it on Broadway takes a unique path from idea to fully-realized production. In the process from page to stage, there are often enormous triumphs and dangerous pitfalls. There is frightening drama and remarkable collaboration. There are hundreds of people with greatly disparate skill sets who come together to push the idea to completion. Looking back on the history of how musicals come to fruition, it is amazing that any of them make it at all. Even though many aspects of theater-making in the US have changed in the past hundred years, musicals are still made because people believe in and love them—and can make money producing them.

In the beginning, there are two things that matter: who has the idea, and where does the idea come from? Most musicals are based on pre-existing stories, whether fairy tales (*Into the Woods*), movies (*Hairspray*), plays (*My Fair Lady*), biographies (*Jersey Boys*), or television shows (*The Addams Family*). And many different types of people have ideas about what might make a good stage musical. For instance, the composer Stephen Schwartz first thought to adapt Gregory Maguire's novel *Wicked* into a musical that shares the same title. Many years prior, the producer David Merrick thought Thorton Wilder's play *The Matchmaker* would make a great show, so he lined up a creative team that included composer Jerry Herman to write what became *Hello, Dolly!*

Every idea requires two ingredients to proceed: creativity and money. Because most musicals are based on pre-existing material, the creative team that wants to write a musical has to get permission to use someone else's idea. It is not enough to think that *The Princess Bride* would make a great musical—you have to get the rights to do it from the person who wrote the original book or screenplay.

Many writers avoid this step by using ideas drawn from the public domain. Andrew Lloyd Webber and Tim Rice, for example, did not have to pay royalties to the authors of the Bible when they decided to write *Jesus Christ Superstar*. Some people create musicals that are completely original, as Rodgers and Hammerstein did with *Allegro* and Lin-Manuel Miranda did with *In the Heights,* but this is relatively uncommon, especially now: the current trend is to develop and promote musicals that already have a built-in audience. Even an original musical like *Avenue Q* trades on an audience's familiarity with both *Sesame Street* and the Muppets.

Lots of ideas for musicals get stuck right here: someone wants to write a show, or has sketched out an idea for one based on someone's movie, novel, life-story, or play. But then, the original rights-holder decides they do not want their property to be made into a musical. In this case, the project ends before it begins.

Then again, many rights holders are looking for ways their property can create new revenue streams. In this case, there is very little in the way of downside to granting an option to someone who wants to make a musical out of their work. Granting permission does not cost anything; in fact, the writers of the proposed musical have to pay the original writer for an option. This is completely negotiable, so one could write in financial terms regarding gross income of proceeds from the musical. Usually, options have time limits, so if a musical is not completed by a certain deadline, the option automatically goes back to the original writer. But once the legal right to musicalize a story is established, the writing can begin.

Getting it written

Creating a musical is a collaborative effort. When someone decides to write a book, he or she can hide away in a study, an office, or a remote lighthouse for a month or two and come out with a great American novel. But with a musical, the three ingredients are the score, the lyrics, and the book, all of which are often written by different people.

The score comprises all the music for the show: the songs, overtures, entr'actes, scene-change music, and underscoring. The writer of the music is the composer; often, the composer does not work alone on the score. It is one thing to be able to come up with a melody; it is another skill-set entirely to be able to write the music down so that other musicians can play it exactly as you want it to be played. While some composers are trained musicians who have no trouble notating their ideas in complete, specific ways, other composers, especially those working today, have less formal training, and thus rely on other musicians for help with notation. Still other musical theater composers have the training, but not the time or patience for the laborious task of transcribing their ideas, so they assemble a staff of assistants to help.

For example, contemporary writer Ryan Scott Oliver is a classically trained musician and professional music copyist. His scores are notated so well that they come to the music director ready to be published. On the other hand, when I worked with country music legend Larry Gatlin, he told me on the first day we met that he was "not a lines and staves kind of guy." Because he could not notate music, Larry played guitar and sang his songs into his iPhone, and then sent me the recordings, which I transcribed onto paper. This way, our cast and musicians could play and sing his songs. On yet another hand, the contemporary composer Adam Guettel is a tremendous musician, but he feels that the notation process interrupts his creative flow. He thus plays his ideas into a computer software program and hires assistants to convert the data into musical scores.

The lyricist is responsible for all the words sung in a musical. Some composers, such as Stephen Sondheim and Cole Porter, write both music and lyrics. Most lyricists, however, specialize in lyric writing and form a close collaboration with a composer. Some of these collaborative partnerships are legendary: Rodgers and Hammerstein, Lerner and Loewe, and Kander and Ebb. Other lyricists have worked with a number of different composers throughout their career. Jule Styne wrote successful Broadway shows with Comden and Green (*Bells Are Ringing*), Sammy Cahn (*High Button Shoes*), Bob Merrill (*Funny Girl*), and Stephen Sondheim (*Gypsy*).

The lyricist–composer collaboration has many different forms, depending on the habits of the parties involved. When he worked with lyricist Lorenz Hart, for example, Richard Rodgers always wrote the music first, because Hart liked to fit his clever words to a specific tune. But Rodgers always waited for Hammerstein to write the lyrics first, because Hammerstein was more concerned with fitting specific songs into the story (to this end, Hammerstein also wrote the script for many of their musicals). Hammerstein's painstaking approach became the source of friendly frustration between the two men; he would sometimes spend weeks getting the words to a song exactly to his liking, only to deliver the lyrics to Rodgers, who would pound out the tune in a single afternoon.

The book writer is the least understood yet perhaps most crucial part of the collaborative process. The book comprises the unsung words—the dialogue—of a musical. Book writers come from all walks of life. Many are playwrights (Terrence McNally), though some are also directors (James Lapine), or screenwriters (Arthur Laurents). Sometimes, a book writer is involved from the initial idea for a show, but in other cases, a book writer is brought to a project after the score is completed. In this case, the book writer's job is to string together the songs, and fashion a plot around them. Regardless of their backgrounds, the best book writers understand the economy of words in a show. Lyrics fit to music take time to unfold before an audience, so a libretto for a musical typically cannot have as much dialogue as a play might.

Some composers have a long, continuous relationship with specific book writers. Stephen Sondheim worked with James Lapine for several shows in the late 1980s and early 1990s; together, they created *Sunday in the Park with George*, *Into the Woods*, and *Passion*. Sondheim is so indebted to his book-writing collaborators—who also include George Furth, Arthur Laurents,

James Goldman, Burt Shevelove, Larry Gelbart, Hugh Wheeler, and John Weidman—that he dedicated his first compilation of lyrics, *Finishing the Hat: Collected Lyrics (1954–1981) with Attendant Comments, Principles, Heresies, Grudges, Whines and Anecdotes,* to them all.

Hearing it out loud

Once a team—a composer, lyricist, and book writer—has completed the initial work on a musical, the next step is hearing it. For many shows, this is the longest and most frustrating part of the journey from page to stage. Initially, a team needs to hear their work spoken and sung aloud. It is one thing to create dialogue and music at home on paper or a computer. It is another thing entirely to hear your work performed by actors.

These initial hearings are often performed by friends of the writing team. When producers come from large, multi-media conglomerates, executives set schedules and deadlines for official readings of a team's work. But for most projects, this initial work is very informal: the composer teaches the music to a group of actors, and the book writer or lyricist helps them understand the intention of the words.

These informal gatherings are essential to the development of a show. Writers need to have a keen, critical ear with which to listen to their own work. It helps to have opinionated, intelligent, honest friends who will tell writers what is working, what is not, and why. The value of the writing and rewriting process cannot be underestimated. The vast differences between an original first draft and the finished product are often astounding. In many ways, the success of a show depends on the writers' ability to think critically, accept feedback, and produce many versions of the work to fine-tune the property into a musical that will succeed on both artistic and commercial fronts.

Like many forms of popular entertainment, the stage musical walks a fine line between art and commerce. There are as many ways to achieve the delicate balance between the two as there are stories to be musicalized. Every show walks this tightrope; every creative team has different priorities. One might assume that producers are only focused on the bottom line, while creative teams are more interested in creating groundbreaking art. While it would be easy to understand the dynamic this way, such black-and-white descriptions fall short of the reality of producing musicals, whether on Broadway, Off Broadway, or beyond New York City. Few writers enter into the lengthy, endlessly frustrating process of developing a musical without the hope that there will eventually be some compensation for the effort. Similarly, it is a very poor producer who takes on a show they do not believe has some artistic merit.

Here's where the money comes in

The next step in the development process involves getting the show heard by potential investors. This requires money. At this stage, the creative staff expands from the initial composer–lyricist–book writer trio; a financial backer or group of backers also becomes attached to the project. On the writers' side, the most important addition is the director. Sometimes, a director is involved from the beginning, but most of the time a director is brought in when it becomes time to stage a reading of a new musical. The director has to work with the writers to create a vision for what the final production might look like. The relationship between the director and writers helps determine the success of a show. Many shows try out different directors in a number of different readings, while others stick with the same director for the entire production.

Other additions to the creative team are the music director and the music staff. The music director becomes the "ear" of the composer. In the same way a director has a vision for the production, a music director works with the composer to realize the final version of the score. Other musical staff may be added at this point, for example an arranger to create piano arrangements of songs, dances, scene changes, and underscores.

On the financial side, the most important new member of a production is the producer or producers. Producers wear many hats. They are responsible for raising the money needed to produce a show. Many producers also push, pull, and prod writers into shaping and reshaping a show to realize its maximum artistic and commercial value.

To get a show seen by potential backers, a reading is planned. Readings of new musicals started in the late 1960s, but today have developed into a small cottage industry in New York. Readings range in complexity. Sometimes, they consist of a number of actors sitting around a table in a rehearsal studio, but others are done in small theaters, complete with props, suggested costume pieces, and dance routines. Readings before potential investors are important, because at this point money needs to be raised so the people involved with the project can begin to get paid.

Oddly, the first people to get paid are not the writers, even though they have already put an enormous amount of time and energy into the work.

Instead, funds initially go to directors, music directors, choreographers, arrangers, and other essential people who work for hire. These creative forces have a vested interest in a show's success: if it moves to a commercial venue, they stand to gain a more lucrative position with the production. Nevertheless, they typically do not share any royalties that come from a successful show.

The biggest hope for the writers is that a show will break even on Broadway. If this is the case, they will all share a certain pre-negotiated percentage of the box office gross. This percentage is called "points." Thus, if your royalty agreement gave you 2 percent of the gross, you would have two points in the show. For the writers, then, the substantial investment of time up front is a risk that can eventually pay off in the form of royalties. Such a payout can be substantial. Lin-Manuel Miranda, the writer, composer, and lyricist of *Hamilton*, retains five points in the box office gross of that hit musical. At the time of this writing, *Hamilton*'s box office pulls in around $1.5 million a week, so Lin-Manuel pockets approximately $75,000 every Sunday night.

There are two primary goals to a reading. The first is to allow a director and creative team to hear their show performed by professional actors in front of a small audience, so they can see how it works and get feedback to improve it. The second goal is to attract investors willing to put up money required to move the show to the next level of development. Even the most experienced composers have trotted their work out to wealthy businesspeople in hope that some will be willing to contribute money. In the early 1940s, when their partnership was new, Rodgers and Hammerstein organized readings of their work so the Theatre Guild, their financially struggling producer, could raise the money to get *Oklahoma!* into the St. James Theatre. In those days, money was raised by producers from independent investors for out-of-town tryouts before a commercial run on Broadway.

The difference between then and now is that the amount of money needed to bring a musical to Broadway (called the capitalization cost) has increased by a staggering amount, even adjusting for inflation. In his 1974 book *Contradictions*, Hal Prince mentions that he had to raise $300,000 to produce *West Side Story* at the Winter Garden Theatre in 1957. In 2010, *Billy Elliot* opened at the Imperial at a cost of $18 million. Between 1957 and 2010, inflation rose 771 percent, but the percentage change in capitalization cost was over eight times that increase, at 6,000 percent.

In today's market, a more likely route is to get a nonprofit organization involved. Many nonprofit theaters are interested in developing new musicals for both artistic and commercial reasons. An early indicator of this trend was when the Public Theater in New York produced *Hair* at their new Off Broadway venue in 1967. The resulting production became a hit Broadway show, but because the Public had not negotiated points in the Broadway version, they lost out on enormous revenue. The Public was thus very careful when it moved *A Chorus Line* from its Off Broadway venue to Broadway in 1975. The Broadway production made so much money for the Public that it continues to help fund new works there. Similarly, proceeds from *Jersey Boys*, which moved to Broadway in 2005, continue to help keep the lights on at La Jolla Playhouse in San Diego, which helped develop the show.

In the 1980s, Andrew Bishop and Ira Weitzman, through Playwrights Horizons and later the Lincoln Center Theater, mentored many new creative teams and ushered in many musicals that otherwise would not have been picked up by traditional Broadway producers. Because they had the security of a subscription audience and a strong donor base, they could afford to take chances. The results were palpable: artists like Stephen Sondheim could try out shows like *Sunday in the Park with George* at Playwrights Horizons before opening it for a commercial run at the Booth Theater on Broadway. Other writers, including Lynn Ahrens and Stephen Flaherty (*Once on This Island*), William Finn (*Falsettos*), Jeanine Tesori (*Violet*), and Adam Guettel (*The Light in the Piazza*) were mentored and produced by Bishop and Weitzman over the years.

In our story of how a musical gets from page to stage, the path starts to diverge here. Some shows attract the attention of commercial Broadway producers who option them. This gives a producer or production team the exclusive right to produce a musical in a determined window of time. Most large-scale productions go this route. *Wicked*, for example, attracted the attention of producer David Stone, who commandeered it through many readings and workshops, and produced the out-of-town tryout for the show in San Francisco (which was reportedly disastrous). Despite the disappointing run out of town, Stone persevered and raised the money for the Broadway run at the Gershwin Theatre. It was a bet that paid off: despite poor reviews when it opened in 2003, *Wicked*, at the time of this writing, is still regularly grossing over $1 million per week and remains one of the most popular musicals on Broadway.

Other musicals attract powerful Broadway producers who, in turn, form partnerships with non-profit organizations to spread out the cost (and risk) for their investment. This is the path that producer Jeffrey Seller took with

Lin-Manuel Miranda's *Hamilton*. *Hamilton* had a workshop at Vassar College, then headed to the Public Theater for a short collaborative run in February 2015 before opening on Broadway in August 2015 and becoming the hottest ticket in town.

Getting commercial producers involved is perhaps the most difficult and frustrating part of an already difficult journey. Fortunately, there are many ways for creative teams to get their work seen and heard. The NAMT (National Alliance for Musical Theatre) holds an annual New Works Festival that brings short, excerpted readings of new shows to regional theaters. The New York Musical Festival (NYMF) has produced over 350 new shows with limited runs and budgets since its inception in 2004. And the BMI Lehman Engel Musical Theatre Workshop has been training musical theater writers since 1961. Artists who have graduated from the BMI program include Maury Yeston, Alan Menken, and Robert Lopez. Increasingly, other creative teams are turning to universities for readings and workshops. Solid programs that support new musical theater exist at Pace University, Penn State, Northwestern, and many other schools across the country.

Once the money is in place, a limited liability partnership is created, a managing agency comes aboard, and a hiring spree commences. The director and producers have to round out the design team. They hire designers for the lighting, set, costumes, sound, orchestrations, and projections (if required). A stage management team is put in place. Advertising and press agents and marketing experts need to be hired. Sets need to be constructed, loaded into the theater, and safely installed. Casting decisions are made, and actors are hired. Often, actors who participate in readings of the show are offered parts in the commercial run, but this is no guarantee. For example, Stephanie Block did countless readings of *Wicked* before being replaced by Idina Menzel for the starring role of Elphaba. On the other hand, Kristin Chenoweth, who was also in almost every reading, was offered the role of Glinda in the Broadway production.

As a show is fine-tuned, it might undergo a 29 Hour Reading, a Staged Reading, a Workshop, or a Lab. These terms are often used interchangeably, but they each have different meanings, which relate to very specific contracts with the Actors' Equity Association. Such contracts either provide or deny the protection of an actor's creative contribution to a show. A "reading" typically refers to the Equity 29 Hour Reading contract, which limits the rehearsal and performance for a reading to no more than twenty-nine hours. There are a lot of other restrictions—for example, no admission, no advertising, no sets, props, wigs, or costumes—and performances are typically capped at three. In return, actors receive a stipend of $100 plus basic transportation costs. Most importantly, participating actors are not guaranteed to continue with the show, and they agree to share no subsequent earnings that the show accrues.

If producers want to rehearse for more than twenty-nine hours, they must step up to a Staged Reading Contract, which stipulates that producers have to hold required Equity Principal Auditions. Minimum compensation levels are $500 a week for actors. Actors receive health and pension benefit contributions. In return, producers can rehearse for longer periods, add choreography and other elements, and retain the option to capture footage for promotional purposes. There are no "conversion rights" (see next paragraph) for actors, who are given no guarantee that they will go on with the show. There is also no profit sharing.

The next step up is the Workshop Agreement, which may be used for up to four weeks and four presentations. Actors are paid between $631 and $757 a week, depending on how many days of rehearsal there are. There are health and pension contributions and, most importantly, contributing actors retain what are called "conversion rights." Normally, this means that each actor has the right of first refusal for their role. Thus, if the show goes on, the actor *must* be offered the role before any other actor is. Also, the cast shares a percentage of the gross for the show—usually a "point" in the production.

The idea for the Workshop Agreement began with Michael Bennett, who asked many of his colleagues and friends to contribute their stories for a new musical based on the lives of Broadway dancers. This eventually became the mega-hit *A Chorus Line*. Actors in the original cast shared one point of the weekly gross income from the show, which turned out to be quite lucrative. This agreement with Equity was refined later in the 1970s with Bennett's production of *Ballroom*; it eventually became part of the standard contract. This Workshop Contract has become a great source of revenue for many actors, who have put in a lot of work on many different shows in hopes that one would succeed. Unfortunately for current actors, Equity has revised this agreement with the League of Producers, and created a Lab Contract. This contract takes the essence of a workshop: it can be used for any purpose for up to four weeks with four performances. It pays the actors more money—at present, about $1,000/week— but it eliminates conversion rights. With this new Lab Contract in place, it is highly unlikely that official Workshop Contracts will ever be used again. This is an enormous loss of protection and potential revenue for professional actors.

Once casting is completed, every set piece is built, every prop found, light hung, wig blown dry, and rehearsal completed, a musical moves out of a rehearsal space and into the theater for technical rehearsals, or "tech." During tech, changes are made around the clock. This is perhaps the tensest time in a production. Tech rehearsals are long—often up to twelve hours at a stretch. They are dark and messy, and often excruciatingly boring for everyone except the people who are on the spot at any given time. And because time is money, the stakes could not be higher.

During tech, the orchestra rehearses new music, and the sound designer makes sure that every note from the band and every word spoken by the cast can be heard from every seat in the house. Once tech is complete, the show is ready for its first preview. Often, a producer will invite a special audience of friends and people in the theater community for what is called a "gypsy run-through" of the show. This is essentially an invited audience that comes to the final dress rehearsal before the box office starts to sell tickets to paid previews. I attended the gypsy run-through of *Ragtime* at the brand-new Ford Center for the Performing Arts in 1996. The cast came on stage before the show, and the lead actor, Brian Stokes Mitchell, led the cast and audience in an invocation for the theater. It was a moving moment in a venue that had recently been rebuilt from the ruins of two old theaters.

After the gypsy run-through, ticketed customers pass through the doors. The writers, director, and designers watch each performance, refining and revising the show throughout previews. Many times, major changes happen during the preview period. In my experience with *Little Women*, a new song was inserted into the show, replacing another number, during the preview period. There was no time to orchestrate the song, so I played the accompaniment on the piano for one performance before the writers decided to go back to the original song. As some point during the preview period, something magical happens: the director and creative team decide to "freeze" the show, meaning there will be no more changes in the musical. It is smart for a team to freeze a show long enough in advance of the opening; it allows the cast and crew to adjust to one version of the show before the press and other opinion makers see it just prior to the official opening.

By the time previews start, the running crew of a theater is in place. Many people do not realize just how many people are working behind the scenes of a musical. The website newyork.com did some research on how many people it takes to run *Wicked*; they came up with thirty-six actors, ninety-four front-of-house employees, and eighty-one backstage workers. Backstage, there are fourteen people in wardrobe, two company managers, thirteen carpenters, twenty-four musicians, three sound techs, four stage managers, six in props, five spotlight operators, five electricians, and five hair and makeup artists. In the front of the house there are three ticket-takers, three bag checkers, four doormen, twenty-four ushers, one lottery manager, eight treasurers, two house managers, two directresses, one chief, twelve bartenders or concession workers, twelve porters, cleaners, and matrons, and twelve merchandise sellers, for a total of 211 employees.

A new musical starts with an idea, and now hundreds of professionals have a vested stake in its success. When opening night arrives, it is celebrated with an early curtain, many gifts, congratulatory hugs, and a blowout party. Reviews from critics are read and discussed, marketing plans are established, and everyone hopes the show will have a long, healthy run. Yet the chances are not good. It is a long-shot to get this far; hundreds of new musicals vie for the opportunity to move into an empty theater. Once they do, seven of ten Broadway musicals fail to turn a profit.

Then again, when it works, it really works. Building a musical from written page to Broadway stage is a long, arduous process, but magic can happen. Hundreds of professionals work together and become a close-knit family, while giving audiences the joy and unparalleled emotion only a Broadway musical can provide. The odds are slim, the work is hard, but when the result is a hit, everyone benefits from the effort.

MAKING MUSICALS FOR SERIOUS PLEASURE
Stacy Wolf

Stacy Wolf is Professor in the Program in Theater and Director of the Program in Music Theater at Princeton University. She is the author of *A Problem Like Maria: Gender and Sexuality in the American Musical* and *Changed for Good: A Feminist History of the Broadway Musical* and co-editor with Raymond Knapp and Mitchell Morris of the *Oxford Companion to the American Musical*.

Introduction: Junior Theatre Festival and BroadwayCon

On Martin Luther King weekend in January 2016, two events took place in different parts of the US that signaled the importance of Broadway musicals in contemporary American culture. The first was the Junior Theatre

Festival, a gathering of 4,000 middle school-aged kids.[1] In its thirteenth year, the Atlanta-based event was the biggest ever, and included fifteen-minute segments from musicals performed by ninety groups from schools, community theaters, and afterschool programs across the country. The weekend was filled out with presentations from Broadway artists, appearances by special guests, and workshops for the participants. Though a majority of the groups came from the southeastern part of the US—that is, driving distance from Atlanta—others arrived by airplane, rented a van, or car-pooled. Some groups or schools asked parents to fund the trip, others used profits from within their organizations, and many held numerous bake sales to raise money. Registration for the weekend cost $675 plus hotel rooms and food for each group, whose sizes ranged from twenty to forty children.[2]

In midtown Manhattan during that same weekend, during one of the biggest blizzards on record, the first BroadwayCon conference welcomed 5,000 people, 80 percent of them female and 50 percent under the age of thirty.[3] The event consisted of panels with actors, directors, and writers from Broadway shows including *Fiddler on the Roof*, *The King and I*, and *Fun Home*, and the session BroadwayCon-goers stood in line over an hour for: *Hamilton*. Other panels focused on topics like diversity on Broadway and the jobs of lighting designers, set designers, and stage managers. There was a merchandise hall filled with t-shirts, tote bags, scripts, and cast albums, plus photo booth and autograph sessions for access to Broadway stars. There were singalongs and mainstage events.

Though one of the above events promoted itself as being about performance (the adjudicated mini-musicals are the center of the Junior Theatre Festival) and the other celebrated fandom, they both revealed the contiguity between fandom and participation in amateur musical theater in the US. Many fans are also amateur artists who perform in, direct, choreograph, design, stage manage, work backstage for, or produce musicals.

BroadwayCon, modeled on Comic-Con International, would have been unimaginable before the existence of sites such as Twitter, Facebook, and YouTube. It was the brainchild of Mischief Management's Melissa Anelli and Stephanie Dornhelm, self-designated RentHeads, who teamed with *Rent* actor Anthony Rapp. Either because Rapp is a powerful enough figure in the Broadway community that he could persuade everyone in town to show up and speak on a panel, or because Broadway artists know their bread and butter is ticket-sales by adoring fans—many who have seen shows numerous times—the performers were there en masse: Celia Keenan-Bolger (*The Glass*

Menagerie, Peter and the Starcatcher), Michael Cerveris (*Sweeney Todd, Fun Home*), Jessica Hecht (*Fiddler on the Roof*), Lin-Manuel Miranda and other cast members of *Hamilton*, to name a few. The event signaled a mass national presence for Broadway fans, many of whom traveled from far away and paid $250 plus hotel and food to attend.

As they chatted between sessions and sang at the Disney Singalong, BroadwayCon attendees showed themselves to be amateur musical theater performers as well as fans. Some dressed as their favorite characters were actually costumed in what they wore when they played the roles themselves. Many attendees could rattle off the parts they played in high school or community theater as quickly as they could name their favorite performer, show, or number from *Hamilton*. It did not take much of a leap to the see the tweens at the Junior Theater Festival gathered at BroadwayCon in a few years.[4]

Why amateur musical theater?

Both the Junior Theater Festival and BroadwayCon foster and rely on the presence of the amateur. The word derives from the Latin *amator* ("lover") from the verb *amare* ("to love"),[5] but also carries negative connotations: "a person considered contemptibly inept at a particular activity."[6] Nonetheless, hundreds of thousands of people in the US participate in musical theater for pleasure—children and adults of every race, ethnicity, and socioeconomic background, in every city and town from Maine to Hawaii, Alaska to Puerto Rico. Amateur musical theater is a national performance practice.

Amateur musical theater sustains the Broadway musical, which feeds touring shows and regional theaters all over the US. Were it not for amateur musical theater, there would be no Broadway musical. Why? First, there would be no artists, as virtually every professional actor, director, choreographer, and designer began in a high school musical, a summer camp show, or a community theater production. Second, there would be no Broadway audiences, because a vast number of spectators see musicals on Broadway that they already know from seeing or performing in them at home. Third, there would be no Broadway repertoire, because licensing companies gain considerable profit through amateur musicals—50 percent of their gross. Even a musical that flops on Broadway—and 80 percent do—can earn back its investment through amateur productions.

But amateur musical theater is also an activity to be valued for its contribution to the community, and to individuals' lives. As Tim MacDonald,

President of iTheatrics, says, "I estimate that 99% of Americans will never see a show on Broadway. Their Broadway experience takes place in school theaters, community theaters and regional theaters. . . . [W]e've experienced musical theater programs in inner city schools, suburban schools and rural schools. These folks don't know who Stephen Sondheim or Christen [sic] Chenoweth are (nor do they care) but they do have a great time putting on a musical for their community."[7] As a low-tech, live, intimate, hands-on collaborative practice, amateur musical theater is more akin to other direct, unmediated events like amateur sports teams, orchestras, and choirs than to other entertainment forms like movies, television, or video games. In this way, amateur musical theater counters the anti-communitarian trends of contemporary culture noted by sociologists such as Robert Putnam, who observes that "the bonds of our communities have withered" over the twentieth century.[8] To the contrary, musical theater brings people together in the same room, often across generations, to make something new together. It adds art and culture to the life of the community. For the individual, it invites imaginative creative expression; for children in particular, it develops intellectual skills of reading and interpretation, and emotional skills of patience, perseverance, and cooperation.[9]

Amateur musical theater in the US exhibits unique traits that differ from other leisure activities and from professional theater. In most amateur contexts, the actors and artistic team know the audience, and vice-versa. In some situations, people move back and forth over the course of a season, at times onstage or backstage, and at times into the audience, blurring the distinction between those who produce and those who consume. This community component intensifies investment and connection on and offstage. Also, with a repertoire of Broadway musicals such as *In the Heights*, *Les Misérables*, and *The Sound of Music*, amateur artists must navigate what theater scholar Marvin Carlson calls the production's "ghosts." Theater "is the repository of cultural memory," writes Carlson. "The present experience is always ghosted by previous experiences and associations."[10] Well known, popular, or iconic performances, which abound in musical theater, leave a trace. We are "haunted by the memory of that interpretation, and all actors performing the role must contend with the cultural ghost of the great originator."[11] A production team almost always knows the show they are doing through the cast album, Broadway production or film version, or YouTube clips, so they must decide whether to work against the original, ignore it, or emulate it. On the other hand, the canon of musicals forms a national repertoire to which amateur productions contribute.

Every amateur production of a musical takes on the flavor, accent, and racial, ethnic, and socioeconomic demographics of the local setting. Within one place, a range and variety of theaters might be found at schools, afterschool programs, and community theaters, each saturated with that region's idiosyncrasies. People move across these venues. For example, kids perform in school shows and also participate in afterschool programs; summer camp counselors are high school drama teachers during the school year; a director of one community theater show produces another and acts in another and designs another. Over time, cycles continue: a child performer in community theater plays a lead role in her high school musical, and then opens her own studio. Her child learns to stage manage in her studio, then oversees musicals at a summer camp, and so it goes. Each type of theater feeds into the local culture, and they all sustain each other.

The repertoire and licensing

Even though most of the participants in amateur musical theater are unpaid, the scripts, scores, and musical arrangements of every show must be licensed from the company that owns the property and distributes shares to the composers, lyricists, and librettists. The publishing company Samuel French was founded in 1830. The Tams-Witmark Music Library Inc., which licensed the first high school musical (an operetta of *Robin Hood*), was established in 1925, and Dramatists Play Service was founded in 1936. The Rodgers and Hammerstein Organization, the first licensing company owned by the musicals' own creators, began in 1944.[12] As the musical theater repertoire grew through the middle of the twentieth century, so did the licensing companies' properties. The Rodgers and Hammerstein Organization, which owned *Carousel* (1945), *South Pacific* (1949), *The King and I* (1950), and later *The Sound of Music* (1959), profited handsomely. The pair's repertoire was filled with valuable cultural products that amateur artists, including schools and community theaters, wanted to perform.

Tams-Witmark and R & H controlled most amateur musical theater licensing until 1952, when composer and lyricist Frank Loesser (*Guys and Dolls*) opened a new licensing and publishing company, Frank Music Corporation, to control and profit from his titles.[13] Two years later, Loesser joined with orchestrator Don Walker to found Music Theater International (MTI) to deal with Loesser's properties and compete with R & H and Tams.[14] In 1988, former entertainment lawyer and music producer Freddie Gershon bought the company. In 1990, he teamed up with the producer Cameron Mackintosh, who backed *Les Misérables* and most of Andrew Lloyd Webber's musicals. MTI eventually became the largest musical theater licensing company in the world. As of 2015, it owned 300 titles, R & H owned 100, and Tams-Witmark owned 150.[15] Amateur rights account for 50 percent of MTI's gross income,[16] and almost anyone who directs a musical deals with a licensors' amateur division.

What follows is an overview of some of the most common venues for amateur musical theater production in the US.

High school musicals

A group of 15-, 16-, and 17-year-olds stands in a clump center stage. Two boys are dressed as peasants with loose pants and suspenders and one in a tweed hat. Two more boys are decked out as fairytale princes in velvet frontispieces, leather boots, and swords. The girls' characters are easier to identify: Cinderella in her ball gown, Rapunzel with ridiculously long blond hair, and a witch in a green mask with a hooked nose and all-askance hair dyed purple in places. At this final dress rehearsal for *Into the Woods*, the teens are attentive, arms crossed or on hips, slouched in their teenage stance, listening to the director who stands on the floor in front of the stage. Off to the side is a small ensemble also made up of students: piano, clarinet, flute, violin, cello. Their leader, a teacher in the school, perches on a stool, baton in hand, waiting for the director's instructions. "Okay, guys," the director says. "We open tomorrow night. I know everyone will be nervous and excited, and I know the energy will be there—I've seen it before. But I need to see it today, too. You've got the notes and lines down. And you've worked hard to create these characters. But let me feel your energy out here, even in the back!" She backs up the aisle, the students' eyes following her. This moment took place in February 2016 at the Garrison Forest School in Baltimore, Maryland, but it could have been at any of the many schools that did *Into the Woods* in recent years.

Virtually every high school in the US, whether public, private, parochial, urban, suburban, or rural, produces a musical each year, whether in an auditorium, multipurpose room, or well-equipped theater, accompanied by a single piano or a full student orchestra, wearing costumes poached from home closets or professional, rented ones.[17] Depending on the school, the musical might be an activity kept afloat by a few enthusiastic students and a volunteer teacher, or it might be a schoolwide extracurricular activity. It might be rehearsed during the school day as an elective taught by a teacher, or it might be solely an afterschool activity. It might attract young people who are not interested in athletics, or the students involved might be equally at home on stage and the sports field. Either way, the school musical brings the community together and often provides a counterbalance to a school's investment in athletics.

Teenagers learn the basics of music, theater, dance and how a show is produced by participating in a high school musical. Most professional actors get their start in high school musicals, though few high school stars go on professionally. And yet, as many teachers of all age groups attest, musical theater teaches innumerable intellectual, social, and emotional skills. Teacher-directors welcome students with backstage interests to stage manage, build sets, hang lights, organize costumes, help with advertising and selling program ads. Schools in socioecomically affluent towns frequently see parents and guardians get involved as boosters and fundraisers.

Regional awards recognize the achievements of high school musicals, and the stakes are high in areas with large public high schools and sufficient resources for specialty teachers. The National High School Musical Theatre Awards, sponsored by the Broadway League and the Shubert Organization, gathers hundreds of high schoolers whose performances have been vetted by thirty-one local contests of 1,000 schools to compete for the Jimmy Award.[18] Students' choice of songs to perform and each school's representative musical number reveal the popular shows of that year. A National Public Radio analysis of *Dramatics* magazine, which has published a survey of the most frequently produced plays and musicals since 1938, found that *Beauty and the Beast, Into the Woods*, and *Grease* were the top musicals in the 2010s.[19] In some conservative or religious schools or communities, parents and administrators regulate the appropriateness of certain musicals, not infrequently censoring productions of, for example, *Rent, Sweeney Todd*, and *Spamalot*.[20] That fact that high school musicals frequently come under attack underlines their importance in the life of a community.

Middle school and afterschool programs

While most high schools produce a musical of some sort, middle school productions are less consistent. Adolescents with interest in musical theater typically participate in one of thousands of afterschool programs across the country, some of which are free and sponsored by the YMCA, a community center, or a church. Others are pay-to-play programs. In many ways, these musical theater programs imitate sports programs like soccer leagues, Little League baseball, or swim teams; similarly, they support the development of a hobby and encourage lifelong interest. For some, they offer the potential for a professional career.

Some of these ventures grew out of dance studios. Most are led by women who earn their living teaching classes and directing shows. Like high school musicals, virtually every town in the US has at least one afterschool program of some sort.

Marilyn Izdebski's vibrant operation in affluent Mill Valley, north of San Francisco, is a good example. Trained as a dancer, she opened a studio and then started directing musicals in 1979. She has directed 146 shows, including *Evita* four times, *Annie* six times, and *Guys and Dolls* seven times.[21] She usually casts 80 or 100 kids of all ages in a show, always in elaborate costumes. Even the chorus members have several costume changes and sometimes wear tap shoes. Izdebski produces at least six shows a year, one each semester for different age groups, and two in the summer. During the school year, the children rehearse in her studio once a week over a period of ten weeks, and then move to a different space for tech and dress rehearsals. Most of "Marilyn's kids," as they call themselves, go on to do high school musicals and community shows, and a few become professional actors, most typically in the Bay Area.

Marilyn is a fixture in the community, though not the only youth musical theater game in town, and her influence over children's lives is significant. Children often do their first "Marilyn show" when they are six or seven and continue through middle school, performing in twenty or more. Some return from college or as adults to help out in the theater. Marilyn treats the children with love and respect, and she is strict and demanding. Even a seven-year-old knows how to audition by walking onto the stage, saying their name and which song they are singing, and ending with a "thank you." For her part, Marilyn nods, says "thank you," and writes two scores on her worksheet: one for singing, one for "expressiveness." Once the show is cast, she never stops pushing, coaxing the display of emotion and passion at every turn. One girl said, "She wants the show to get done but she's so kind to people and so loving underneath this rough, go-getting exterior. She's such a sweetheart underneath it all."[22] Her assistant, a twenty-something former performer said, "She's like a second mom. I've learned so much about how to be in the world, if that makes sense."[23]

Broadway JR. licensing and materials

In 1995, MTI, under the leadership of president Freddie Gershon, launched the Broadway JR. series of scripts and scores. According to Gershon, Stephen Sondheim and Arthur Laurents came to his office fretting about the legacy of classic musicals because young people were no longer performing them in schools. Gershon had an idea: "Let's adapt your shows for kids. Let's make them shorter and re-do the score to be in the range of young voices."[24] Gershon decided to start with *Into the Woods* because its first act would be playable on its own and appropriate for kids.[25] He quickly realized that kid-friendly scripts and scores ready for use by teachers and community theater directors would sell. If MTI could provide a "musical in a box," schools would benefit by having readymade, professionally edited scripts and scores, and MTI and the artists whose work they licensed would profit for years to come.[26] At the same time, MTI was busy digitizing its materials and developing ancillary products, such as "Rehearse Score," a proprietary application in which a score has been converted into Musical Information Digital Interface (MIDI) files, which teachers or directors can rent and use in rehearsal or share with kids to learn their parts.[27]

Into the Woods took two years to make it to production, so the less musically complicated *Annie JR.* was the first show MTI piloted, in a tiny town in upstate New York. The adaptation process that was later regularized began with *Annie*: a writer on MTI's staff (for *Annie JR.* it was playwright and lyricist Jim Luigs) drafted a sixty-minute script and crafted the lyrics for shorter musical numbers. The digitized music files simplified transposition to kid-friendly keys, melodies, and easier harmonies. All changes were approved by *Annie*'s composer Charles Strouse, lyricist Martin Charnin, and librettist Thomas Meehan, who made revisions as necessary. The ready-to-try version was sent to a school, community theater, or summer camp to see if the script was easy to understand and follow, and the music appropriate for kids' voices. Included was an "Accompaniment CD" that could replace a rehearsal pianist, and later, demo cd's with children singing to help kids learn their parts. (For *Annie JR.*, a full orchestra recorded the score, but for *Fiddler on the Roof JR.*, their second show, they opted for less expensive synthesized music.)[28] Then-teacher Cindy Ripley (now iTheatrics's Lead Educational Consultant) directed the first production and wrote the first Director's Guide—a model for the how-to book that now accompanies every licensed Broadway JR. title.[29]

Over the next few years, MTI reached out to other composers and lyricists who agreed that trimming their shows for youth was worth it to keep the properties selling, and the Broadway JR. catalogue grew.[30] Other new titles ranged from *The Pirates of Penzance JR.*and *The Music Man JR.* to *Seussical JR.* and *Willy Wonka JR.*[31] In 2004, the Disney Theatrical Group (DTG) began adapting their animated musicals into JR. and thirty-minute KIDS' versions, expanding the catalogue even more with musicals that kids already knew and loved, including *The Jungle Book JR.* and *KIDS, The Little Mermaid JR., Aladdin JR.* and *KIDS* (both English and bilingual English/Spanish editions) and *The Lion King JR.* and *The Lion King KIDS.*[32] From 1997 to 2005, MTI licensed 20,000 productions of JR. and KIDS' shows.[33]

In 2006, Tim McDonald, who oversaw MTI's JR. division, left MTI (with Gershon's encouragement and blessing) to found iTheatrics, the company that creates all of the Broadway JR. scripts, scores, and supplementary materials (except for the Disney shows, which Disney Theatrical Group constructs in-house), and organizes and produces the Junior Theater Festival.[34] Other licensors followed suit: in 2010, Tams-Witmark Library, Inc. hired iTheatrics to develop their Young Performers' Editions, including adaptations of *The Wizard of Oz* and *Bye Bye Birdie.* The Rodgers and Hammerstein Organization launched the Getting to Know Collections, whose titles include *The Sound of Music, Oklahoma!, Once Upon a Mattress,* and *The King and I.* Both Tams and R & H also distribute supplementary materials similar to MTI's.[35]

The Broadway JR. scripts and scores differ from full-length versions in ways that are attuned to the needs of young people's performances.[36] First, teachers and directors who work with kids need a show that is shorter in duration.[37] The sixty-minute format (or thirty minutes for KIDS' shows) is designed to fit into a school day's schedule. Dialogue is reduced, songs are transposed to keys that are comfortable for kids' voices, harmonies are simplified, and the songs are shorter. Because most children cannot sustain a song for two or three minutes, lyrics are edited to capture the essence and meaning of the song in a minute or so.[38] For *The Music Man JR.*, for example, six songs were cut, including Harold Hill's song of seduction, "Marian the Librarian," and several love songs.[39] In addition, shows for young people need larger casts to accommodate as many kids as possible. Characters with names and lines are at a premium, so minor parts are divided into multiple roles in a JR. script. Ensembles are given as much as possible to do.

Schools and afterschool programs and community theaters that produce musical theater with children interact with MTI and its subsidiaries across a continuum of intensity. At one end are groups that eschew licensing and knowingly or not perform musicals illegally without permission. To be sure, it is easy enough to find a script, download some sheet music, and look for choreographic and staging inspiration on YouTube. But MTI aggressively warns prospective theater makers that doing a show without a license is stealing. Many of its branding and outreach efforts are meant to make doing musical theater as easy and inexpensive as possible, and to encourage directors to purchase a license and do a show legitimately. Most groups buy the license, rent the scripts, and do the show on their own without further engagement with the company. Other directors take advantage of the supplementary materials, especially when the group is young and new. MTI strives to make amateur musical theater production possible for any situation, even as they make money hand over fist in the process.

Elementary schools and Disney's influence

In 2004, Disney Theatrical Group began adapting their animated films into thirty- and sixty-minute KIDS and JR. versions appropriate for elementary and middle schools.[40] MTI licenses their shows—eleven JR. and eight KIDS titles as of 2016—and the package includes elaborate ShowKits with detailed instructions on how to produce a musical from auditions through the final performance with few resources and little or no experience. It also includes a fully-orchestrated accompaniment cd that eliminates the need for a pianist (or teacher with musical expertise). Though elementary school teachers have always gathered their crew to do little plays and sing songs from musicals, especially for holiday assemblies, Disney and MTI have upped the ante, effectively enabling a new generation of musical theater artists. This product was a major shift in Disney's philosophy, as the company began to see young people as producers of musicals, not only as consumers.

Musical theater production in elementary schools often involves the whole grade. At E.K. Powe Elementary School in Durham, NC, for example, music teacher Jessica Tanner and newly-hired theater teacher Sara Bader joined forces in spring 2016 to present *The Lion King KIDS*.[41] The entire fifth grade class took part, and each child could choose to perform or contribute backstage. Auditions were intentionally low-key, and everyone who auditioned was cast. Other kids were involved making papier maché masks, painting the jungle backdrop, applying makeup or moving set pieces, which consisted of brown fabric draped over chairs and tables to represent rocks. The cast was racially diverse and at the rehearsal I watched, the children were fully engaged. After the show, eleven-year-old Lia Pachino told me, "I learned responsibility when I was making the hyena's mask because I knew it was a performance for the whole school. I had to talk to my model, and I had to run around and get all of the materials because I wanted it to be good." She said of her classmates, "We put a lot of effort into it and it paid off. We were relieved that it went so well." She is eager to do another show, either in the chorus or behind the scenes.[42]

Disney Theatrical Group's outreach

In 2009, the Disney Theatrical Group launched Disney Musicals in Schools (DMIS), a program to support musical theater production in ten underserved New York City (NYC) public schools. By 2016 the program had expanded to ten additional cities, where it was administered by local performing arts centers.[43] DMIS' gift to participating schools consists of three parts: free licensing rights to one of the thirty-minute Disney KIDS titles, including scripts and scores for the whole cast; the ShowKit with Director's Guide and the other bells and whistles; and the semester-long presence of Disney teaching artists to work with teachers to produce the show. The Disney Theatrical Group education team prioritized all three components, which they deemed necessary for a school to produce its first musical. But DMIS aims to seed self-sustaining musical theater programs—that is, "to develop a culture of theater production within high-need urban elementary schools."[44] Disney's model is to slowly decrease support in subsequent years, forcing each school to harness local resources and find ways to sustain its production of musicals. Remarkably, almost every school initially funded by DMIS has continued to produce shows. "Disney is the gateway art," said Kristin Horsley of the Tennessee Performing Arts Center, the site of the first out-of-NYC program.[45]

While a production is taken on with the utmost seriousness and highest expectations, every adult with whom I spoke stressed the importance of "process over product," and the fun of the children's experience above all. To be sure, every child's answer to, "What did you think about doing the Disney show?" was, "It was fun!" "We got to learn new dances, we got to sing fun stuff," said a fourth-grade Nashville girl.[46]

Here lies a contradiction in Disney's engagement with musical theater and kids: on the one hand, every aspect of the Disney Musicals in Schools program is designed to allow Disney to control its product. On the other, the home office knows that theater is messy and each production unique. Moreover, for many children, there is a steep learning curve for both performance skills and theatrical culture. The teachers at Buena Vista Elementary School in Nashville explained that their students knew the story and songs from the movie of *The Jungle Book*, which was their first play in 2014, but that none had ever been to the theater or knew what a live play was.[47] They did not know what it meant to learn lines or blocking, portray a character, or wear a costume especially made for them in front of an audience. Team leader and teacher Joe Ashby found another school's production on YouTube, which the teachers watched with the children before starting rehearsals, and each student followed along in his or her script. By the second year's auditions for *Aladdin KIDS*, the whole school had experienced *The Jungle Book KIDS* and had seen their first play.[48] This is how cultural capital is acquired.

By loosening its famously tight grip on its product and allowing schools to produce the shows legally, Disney has increased revenue and become an instigator of social change and youth empowerment through musical theater. At the same time, DTG oversees its product with a sharp eye. In this way, Disney shifted its vision to accommodate a new populist agenda. Disney Musicals in Schools balances profit and corporate interests with philanthropy and grassroots artistic activism.

Summer camps

Amateur musical theater production for youth continues in the summer at sleepaway camps like the pre-professional Stagedoor Manor (attended by Lea Michele and Natalie Portman, among others) and French Woods; at all-around camps; and at religiously-affiliated camps, such as Jewish Ramah camps, where they perform musicals in Hebrew, or Christian camps that include bible study and stress social justice activities. Private schools and community centers supplement the year-round pay-to-play programs (like Marilyn's), and operate short-term day camps that specialize in theater and culminate with the performance of a musical or a revue.

The area surrounding Sebago Lake in southern Maine, for example, is home to many sleepaway camps, including a number of all-girls, all-around, and non-Orthodox Jewish summer camps.[49] (Androscoggin, the all-boys Jewish camp that Stephen Sondheim attended for years, is also nearby.) Tapawingo, Tripp Lake Camp, Fernwood, and Camp Walden were all founded in the early twentieth century by female Jewish progressive educators, and have a predominantly privileged, predominantly Jewish population of campers, many of whose family members have gone to the camp for generations. Though musical theater is only one activity, all girls are required to participate as they have since the early 1900s, so musicals ultimately shape the girls' experiences in profound ways. Directed and overseen by university-age theater-major counselors, girls aged seven to fifteen present mini versions of Broadway musicals alongside regular activities of swimming, soccer, and arts and crafts. Each week a different age group or bunk works on their show. They produce the show—six musicals per summer, with a few hundred dollars' budget per show—in five days from page to stage.

Summer camp is a special and consciously created community, a home away from home, and the excitement, pressure, and camaraderie of musical theater production create an even more intense bubble in its midst. Whether or not girls are interested in musical theater, their participation inculcates them into a middle-class habitus and gives them a window onto theatrical production. Moreover, musical theater production is intimately tied into the larger project of girls' summer camp: to instill bravery and risk-taking and develop confidence, and to encourage group cohesion and loyalty to the camp. During my visits to camp, I heard over and over, "It's okay if you mess up" and "no one laughs at your mistakes," and "everyone cheers you on."[50] As fourteen-year-old Emma wrote, "Theater at [camp] plays a big role in our day because it is one of the only times the whole camp is together. I think that theater here is much more personal [than at home] because it's imperfect and you know everyone on stage so well."[51] The literal place exchange of actors and audience week by week with few outsiders present makes this occasion more than just a play.

Community theaters

By the time they reach adulthood, many people who have participated in or seen musicals as youth are passionate about the form and elect to dedicate countless hours outside their workday to participate in amateur productions. The label "community theater" applies to the thousands of not-for-profit amateur groups across the country that are typically run by a few paid staff but mostly operate on volunteer labor. Community theaters produce between one and eight shows a season; some have their own space; about half belong to the 7,000-member American Association of Community Theatres.

Every community theater incorporates the quirks and tendencies of that region's theater scene, whether it is the Mormon-inflected practices at the huge family-owned Hale Center in Salt Lake City, Utah, the edgy repertoire of Stillpointe Theatre in Baltimore, Maryland, or the wide-ranging seasons at the Kelsey Theatre in central New Jersey, where a consortium of ten community theaters, some of which have been running since the 1950s, share the space.[52] Community theaters are a locally-flavored national phenomenon. Most rely on ticket sales for income, so they tend to choose shows that appeal to their audience demographic.

Community theaters started in the US in the early twentieth century as a way to engage citizens in their towns, promote patriotism, and instill civic pride through performance. Today, people participate in community theater for various reasons. Some performers, especially in communities closer to big cities like New York, Chicago, or Los Angeles, see community theater as a stepping stone to a professional career. Others did theater as children or teens, and while they make a living doing something else, still enjoy the creative outlet. As Kyrus, a regular director and performer who was 2016 president of the Pennington Players said, "It's a release, we work 9-5, and then we have a choice: go home and watch tv or take the opportunity to be someone else and do something. And a live audience, nothing beats it."[53] Many appreciate the community aspect of musical theater and, as one actor told me, its "forced camaraderie."

Indeed, creating a musical is intense. As Jared, who played Seymour in *Little Shop of Horrors*, said, "It is like a family. We spend so much time together and we're all working for something, for the same goal of making a great show, together. We have to depend on each other and we're very vulnerable. By the end, it's just devastating for it to be over." Another actor, Nikema, added, "Yea, post-partum."[54]

Because acting in a community theater is almost always unpaid (directors occasionally get a small stipend, and musicians, who are fewer and in demand, often do, too), the performers are volunteers, which creates a particular dynamic. Rehearsals must be fun, and the performer's time must be respected. Many community theaters accommodate the presence of children at rehearsals, or choose shows that feature actors of all ages. Directors who succeed in a community theater environment stress the "professionalism" of comportment (it is easier to control than aesthetics), encouraging their cast and crew to be on time, responsible, and to take the production seriously. Directors also need to be teachers and coaches for actors with a broad range of skills and experience. Everyone is expected to pitch in, load in and strike the set and generally help out, and those who can do community theater must have a job that accommodates weeknight or Saturday rehearsals.

In addition to the thousands of year-round community theaters across the country, many cities also support outdoor theaters, typically in unique natural settings, which produce shows in June. Zilker Summer Theatre in Austin, Texas, offers a free musical each summer on a hillside that attracts thousands of spectators, many of whom would not otherwise see a play. The Mountain Play in Mill Valley, California, is a 100-year-old organization that produces six performances of one show each summer in a 4,000-seat amphitheater on the top of Mount Tamalpais. The Open Air Theatre in Washington Crossing State Park in New Jersey, founded in the 1960s, presents thirteen shows (three geared toward children) each summer to more than 18,000 spectators.

The amateur's longevity

Amateur musical theater is at once grassroots, local, hands-on, and inevitably tied to commercial interests and corporations seeking to make money at every turn. This important contradiction tempers the utopian ideals of the nonprofessional who does it for love. Both of the examples that opened this article—the Junior Theatre Festival and BroadwayCon—reveal how corporations support and enable fandom and participation. Both events were organized and created by corporations—iTheatrics, Playbill, MTI, Mischief—yet formed and consolidated an engaged community. There is an interdependence between musical theater fans and corporate capitalism.

In spite of the advent of screens, technology, simulated reality and big data, amateur musical theater's intimate, live, local practices are here to stay. Whether people do it for enjoyment, cultural knowledge, community, or professional aspirations, they gain artistic skills and knowledge of Broadway's repertoire. Amateur theater builds knowledgeable, enthusiastic audiences for professional theater. When amateur artists see *Hamilton*, *Wicked*, or *Shrek* on Broadway, on tour, or at the local high school, they can appreciate how musical theater is made and the labor it requires. Involvement with amateur musical theater as an artist or spectator is a form of civic participation as well. What's happening in your town?

OFF OFF OFF OFF BROADWAY: MUSICAL DEVELOPMENT
OUT OF TOWN AND REGIONALLY
Laura MacDonald

Laura MacDonald is Senior Lecturer in Musical Theatre at the University of Portsmouth in the United Kingdom. Her articles and reviews have appeared in *Studies in Musical Theatre, The Journal of American Drama and Theatre, New England Theatre Journal, Theatre Research International, Theatre Journal,* and *Theatre Survey.* She is preparing a monograph investigating the making and marketing of long-running Broadway musicals. She has held research fellowships at the Shanghai Theatre Academy in China (funded by the Arts and Humanities Research Council) and at Ewha Womans University in Seoul, South Korea (funded by the British Council's Researcher Links program).

In the backstage murder-mystery musical *Curtains* (2007), set in 1959, the company and creative team behind the show-within-a-show *Robbin' Hood* not only have to finish their new musical and prepare it for Broadway, but must also recast a star role when the leading lady is murdered. They are joined at the Colonial Theatre in Boston (where many Broadway hits were first performed) by local detective Frank Cioffi, who investigates the murder but also becomes a show doctor, helping the creative team improve a difficult number. The audience is also introduced to the show's producer, a financial backer, the choreographer, composer, lyricist, director, and a theater critic for *The Boston Globe*—key figures in the development of new musicals. The murder mystery propels the plot of *Curtains*, but during the performance, audiences also witness the rehearsals, writing sessions, casting discussions, and contract negotiations that contribute to the development of any new musical playing "out of town" in preparation for a Broadway run.

Curtains' self-reflexivity showcases the traditional out-of-town tryout, a strategy adhered to for decades. In the past, it was common practice for Broadway musicals to be at least partially written, composed, and cast in New York City, and then dispatched (typically by train) to a tryout city like Boston, New Haven, Washington DC, Detroit, or Philadelphia. The theaters in these cities that hosted Broadway tryouts were otherwise filled with national tours of hit Broadway plays and musicals, and could thus be relied upon to attract audiences for new, untested musicals. As commercial theater in the US struggled from the 1960s onward to compete with film, television, and rock 'n' roll, taking shows out of town became increasingly expensive, and producers keen to economize began previewing their new musicals in New York City. Fewer national tours traveled the country. Megamusicals, imported from Europe in the 1980s, were proven hits, and their spectacular technical elements would only get scaled down for the road *after* opening on Broadway.

At the same time, regional theaters across the US had been growing and developing mandates that increasingly allowed for the development of new musicals. The Goodspeed Opera House in East Haddam, Connecticut, was an early regional developer of musical theater, sending *Man of La Mancha* to Broadway in 1965. Other regional theaters, including the American Repertory Theater in Cambridge, Massachusetts, and the La Jolla Playhouse in San Diego, California, continued the trend when they each presented versions of *Big River* prior to its Broadway opening in 1985. By the early twenty-first century, foreign investment was a well-established source of financing on Broadway, and out-of-town tryouts shifted much, much further out of town: new musicals are now tested in Paris, Hamburg, Tokyo, and Seoul before potentially opening on Broadway. New development models also emerged, such as Off Broadway, regional and festival laboratories, workshops, and productions, as exemplified in *[title of show]*, a post-modern Off Broadway musical that transferred to Broadway in 2008.

[title of show] opens with its songwriters' composition of the show's first notes and includes a conversation with the blank paper they write on. "Broadway?" Blank Paper asks the songwriter Jeff, played by the musical's actual composer and lyricist Jeff Bowen. "Let's start with off or off-off and then you can think about the Great White Way."[55] Jukebox musicals, revivals, or musicals with recognizable stars or source material often have an easier road to Broadway, Blank Paper explains, but original musicals in particular need to be developed and tested in other venues and in front of other audiences before being deemed worthy of Broadway. By staging the writing and rehearsal of the actual musical being performed, *[title of show]* chronicles the development of an original American musical in the twenty first century. During the show's run at the very first New York Musical Festival (NYMF) in 2004, the company sings, "Did we do enough to get someone with money?"[56] As the development process continues, the writers deliberate over casting and writing adjustments in the song "Change It, Don't Change It." *[title of show]* progressed from a festival favorite to further development at the Eugene O'Neill Theater Center, before runs Off, and eventually on Broadway.

Broadway has long been viewed as the site where American musicals are made, but for more than a century, a key portion of the development process for many of the most popular and successful musicals has involved writing, rehearsals, and performances beyond Times Square. Though Jeff and Hunter write *[title of show]* from their New York City apartments, they might as well be in Boston like *Curtains'* tryout company. For while the traditional out-of-town tryout is now exceptional, a new musical's road to Broadway remains a long and difficult one, with new musicals sometimes getting stuck in "development hell." As this chapter explores, and as musicals like *Curtains* and *[title of show]* demonstrate, the places musicals are tried out prior to Broadway openings, and the reasons producers and creative teams conduct their work out of town, have changed over the course of the twentieth century. Pre-Broadway tryouts have become regular features of major regional theaters' seasons, in relationships that have the potential to benefit both the host theater and the musical's Broadway producers. This chapter seeks to establish to what degree these relationships may or may not benefit the contemporary American musical theater.

The out-of-town tryout

In the 1980 Broadway musical *42nd Street*, the company of the show-within-a-show, *Pretty Lady*, sings about "Gettin' Out Of Town" as the performers prepare to travel to Philadelphia to try their show out for audiences and critics before opening on Broadway. Upon their arrival "out of town," the leading lady is injured and the unknown chorus girl Peggy Sawyer is promoted to the star role in order to save the production. In reality, such last-minute casting changes have helped make new Broadway stars: performers like Andrea McArdle (*Annie*, 1977) and Sutton Foster (*Thoroughly Modern Millie*, 2002) were promoted to lead roles while the musicals they performed in were being developed out of town. The short-lived backstage television series *Smash* also depicted an unknown actress, in its show-within-a-show, being promoted to leading lady during an out-of-town tryout in Boston. Along with casting changes, new songs are written, characters are expanded or cut altogether, second acts are completed, and titles are revised during out-of-town tryouts (as was the case when *Away We Go* became *Oklahoma!* in New Haven in 1943).

In the past, tryout cities were traditionally close to New York City (Boston, Baltimore, Washington DC, Philadelphia, and New Haven). The proximity of these cities made it affordable for producers to transport creative teams, performers, and sets after several weeks of rehearsal and construction in New York City. Though *West Side Story* is notable for arriving in Washington DC requiring few revisions or adjustments in 1957, creative teams and performers typically welcome the tryout period as one during which to gain confidence in the project, undertake revisions, rehearse new songs or dialogue, and, most importantly, test a new musical in front of an audience to establish how good it is and what elements might still need work. During the tryout period, union rules traditionally permit some rehearsals of up to ten hours in a twelve-hour period (known as 10 out of 12s). The tryout is often the first time the company rehearses on a completed set, and may also be when the sitzprobe—the first rehearsal with the orchestra—happens.

When tryout performances begin—whether in the past in New Haven or at present in La Jolla, California; Hamburg, Germany; or Seoul, South Korea—performers will typically rehearse during the day, learning new material before implementing it into that evening's performance. Creative teams may be holed up in hotel rooms or the offices of out-of-town theaters, drafting revisions based on the previous evening's performance, while choreographers might be running additional dance rehearsals in hotel ballrooms or the theater's bar, and wardrobe teams might be fitting costumes in the lobby.

Tryout theaters need a seating capacity large enough to carry the cost of taking a musical out of town, and cities need to have a large enough theater scene to lure experienced theatergoers to new musicals. Out-of-town tryout audiences know that they are attending a pre-Broadway performance; the cachet of seeing a potential hit before anyone else does can help sell tickets, though it is not abnormal for tryout tickets to be discounted. Tryout audiences tend to be considered useful but less discriminating than New York theatergoers and critics, and particular cities are chosen by creative teams and producers depending on what they feel they need to accomplish during the tryout. Boston audiences are viewed as intelligent and valuable for tryouts of more serious and challenging musicals, such as Stephen Sondheim's *Company* (1970). Reviewing that tryout, David Sterritt acknowledged, in *Boston After Dark*, the potentially different audiences and mused, "I don't know if New York is ready for *Company* yet, but we in the hinterlands can be grateful for another good opportunity to see where the musical theater is and should be going."[57]

Chicago remains an important commercial theater city, and its audiences are affluent, older, and female in majority, with a good amount of tourists—just like the audience for musicals in New York City. *The Producers* (2001) tried out at the Cadillac Palace Theatre in Chicago, and during the tryout, actor Ron Orbach, cast as Franz Liebkind, had to leave the production and undergo knee surgery. Understudy Brad Oscar went on in his place, was reviewed positively by the Chicago critics, and went on to premiere the role on Broadway. *Kinky Boots* (2013) also benefited from a tryout run in Chicago, at the Bank of America Theatre, where critic Chris Jones concluded: "If the work that needs to be done gets done, 'Kinky Boots,' reviewed Wednesday night, will be a good, solid, highly enjoyable Broadway hit."[58] Jones was not wrong: *Kinky Boots* won the Tony Award for Best Musical and at the time of writing is entering its fifth year on Broadway.

Producers hope for good tryout reviews from the local press, as these can be useful in hyping a musical before it opens on Broadway. Simultaneous with an out-of-town tryout, press and marketing campaigns will be launched in New York to generate word-of-mouth and sell tickets for the opening on Broadway.

Though gossip and buzz often make their way back to the Main Stem, New York City critics generally stay away from tryouts, knowing that if one is successful, they will eventually be invited to assess the finished product on Broadway. The local critics reviewing tryouts are often highly regarded; the Boston critic Elliot Norton (1903–2003) was known as the Dean of American theater critics. Former *Chicago Tribune* critic Richard Christiansen was succeeded in 2002 by Chris Jones; both writers' opinions have been valued by creative teams and producers. In his *Kinky Boots* review, Jones reported, "The other main problem with the show at this juncture is that the stakes are just not high enough for the [shoe factory] workers, who are a likable crew (the ensemble is a huge asset in this show) but who dramaturgically are overly passive. There has to be more at stake for them when the factory nearly goes under; right now, it feels mostly like another day at the office, except drag queens are showing up."[59] By offering such practical advice on how to improve new musicals, many out-of-town critics effectively become play doctors, adding their voices to the team of professional writers, directors, and choreographers called to tryout cities to offer assistance when creative teams struggle to resolve problems in a musical's libretto, songs, or staging.

Aware, perhaps, of the out-of-town critic's function, Jones followed up his review of *Kinky Boots* with an article, "These 'Boots' Are Made for Reworkin'," in which he discussed the show's challenges with its director-choreographer Jerry Mitchell, as well as changes that had already been implemented during the tryout. While in Chicago, the show's book writer, Harvey Fierstein, wrote thirty-seven new pages of script, reordering and intensifying scenes to focus in on the lead character, Charlie Price, "whose trajectory through the story was being eclipsed by the ebullient transvestite Lola, played with great vivacity by Billy Porter."[60] Re-writing scenes and composing new songs can sometimes be easier out of town, because writers and composers, comparatively free from distractions, know the cast and have seen how the director and choreographer are staging a new musical. Stephen Sondheim wrote the opening number "Comedy Tonight" for *A Funny Thing Happened on the Way to the Forum* (1962) at show doctor Jerome Robbins' suggestion, after the musical had been poorly received during its Washington, DC tryout. Robbins recommended a number telling the audience what to expect from the musical, so Sondheim came up with a list song that Robbins built on to physically stage jokes (George Abbott and Jack Cole were the production's director and choreographer).

Critic Elliot Norton once called tryout cities the cutting-room floor for all the discarded songs and rewriting that takes place. But even with ruthless cuts, casting changes, and show doctors, not every musical makes it from a tryout to a Broadway opening. "Bombing in New Haven," despite the loss of investment, may be preferable for producers who would rather lose money than tarnish their reputations and lose even more money by opening a flop on Broadway.

Minimizing these risks has been a major motivation behind commercial producers' partnerships with regional theaters. "Enhancement money" provided to regional theaters guarantees a producer's involvement in any commercial transfer, while providing an opportunity to develop and test a new musical in the relatively safe environment provided by a regional theater's distance from Broadway and its reliable subscriber base as a test audience.

Early regional and Off Broadway development

In 1959, Dale Wasserman adapted Miguel de Cervantes' life and works, the novel *Don Quixote* in particular, as a television play entitled *I, Don Quixote,* to great success. He returned to the material in 1965, this time to write the musical *Man of La Mancha* in collaboration with composer Mitch Leigh and lyricist Joe Darion. Numerous backers' auditions in New York failed to attract any producer except Albert Selden, whose family owned American Express, and who happened to be chairing the committee in charge of restoring the Goodspeed Opera House in East Haddam, Connecticut. Selden offered the creative team the chance to preview the new musical at Goodspeed at the beginning of the summer season, close it for rewrites, and open a revised version at the end of the summer. Broadway performers and designers were hired, and while the initial run was not a huge success, the revised version, with songs cut, set elements redesigned, and the intermission eliminated, generated enough buzz to attract New Yorkers to the small-town theater. *Man of La Mancha* ultimately struggled to secure a Broadway theater; it ended up downtown at the ANTA Washington Square Theatre Off Broadway in 1965 before an eventual move to Broadway in 1968. But the out-of-town development in Connecticut undoubtedly made all the difference in improving the show, and without the costs associated with a traditional out-of-town tryout.

Developed in New York City but relatively far from Broadway both geographically and artistically, *Hair* was inspired by Greenwich Village hippies and war protests observed by the young actors James Rado and Gerome Ragni. While participating in workshops and performing in experimental theater downtown, the actors observed the youth culture around them, making notes and developing their project while performing in the play *Viet Rock* at the experimental Off Off Broadway Open Theatre. Joseph Papp, founder of the Off Broadway Public Theater, selected *Hair* as the inaugural production at his new downtown venue in 1967. The director Tom O'Horgan came aboard and further shaped the musical for its Broadway transfer in 1968. *Two Gentlemen of Verona*, a musical adaptation of Shakespeare's play with music by *Hair* composer Galt MacDermot, also transferred to Broadway, from the Public's New York Shakespeare Festival in Central Park, in 1971. It won the 1972 Tony Award for Best Musical, and its profitable 614 performance run helped subsidize the Public's productions of plays. The same approach was applied to the blockbuster hit *A Chorus Line*, which was developed at the Public and transferred to Broadway in 1975, and again to *Fun Home* and *Hamilton* in 2015. By introducing this relatively new model, in which shows that are transferred to Broadway can help support the Off Broadway theaters in which they are developed, Papp "and his institution had succeeded in doing what no regional theatre had been able to do. They were occupying Broadway as conquerors; they had seized the initiative, and they seemed to be getting (or taking) the power."[61] Navigating the commercial, popular realm of Broadway, Joseph Zeigler suggests, Papp "worked by the rules of the New York game," but was storming the citadel from within.[62] Papp and the Public thus introduced new models of musical theater development that would eventually be taken up at regional theaters across the country.

Zeigler calls regional theaters "an alternative theatre to Broadway,"[63] and points out how much of Broadway's recovery in the mid-1970s could be attributed to the energy and creativity of regional theaters: "These infusions (some see them as *trans*fusions) have played a part in the regeneration of Broadway itself."[64] The Regional Theatre Tony Award, presented annually since 1976, not only indicated that the commercial center and regional institutions had struck a kind of peace accord, but also seemed to confirm the regionals as a new source for new work. "The award symbolized an embrace of the regional theatre by Broadway – and a quick hug back."[65] Unlike the single-direction out-of-town tryout, whereby Broadway-bound productions were polished in a tryout city before returning to the center of production in New York City, these institutional relationships are mutually beneficial, prompting the comparison to a hug.

While regional and Off Broadway theaters have, since the 1960s, independently generated musical theater productions that have caught the eye of commercial producers looking for new shows to produce and successfully transfer, the pre-Broadway development of new musicals, sometimes with more than one regional institution collaborating, has increasingly been negotiated by commercial producers in the very early stages of a new musical's creation. Though funding from the National Endowment for the Arts or the Ford Foundation initially stimulated the development of many regional theaters, enhancement money in the twenty first century typically comes from commercial producers rather than the public or a charitable sector. In turn, the not-for-profit Off Broadway or regional theater provides a fairly sheltered creative environment and a friendly, enthusiastic audience for musicals. The commercial producer supporting the regional or Off Broadway development will likely serve as a lead producer, and will help recruit additional producers and investors to transfer the new production to Broadway. The incubating theater will also serve as a presenter of the production on Broadway, thereby diverting Broadway profits back to the development of new work Off Broadway and in the regions. The institutional theaters benefit from the prestige of Broadway, as well as the talent and reputation of the Broadway-caliber performers and creative teams working on a new musical. These can help recruit ticket buyers and new subscribers. Those who are rewarded with the Regional Theatre Tony Award benefit further from national recognition.

Though this mutually beneficial, typically public–private partnership model has been well established for decades, it has been criticized over the years. Robert Brustein, former artistic director of the American Repertory

Theater (ART) in Cambridge, Massachusetts, has argued that the commercial arena of Broadway should ideally be entirely separate from the work of not-for-profit theaters. "Once you confuse popularity and art, you've effectively muddied important distinctions,"[66] he suggested in 1992. While Brustein acknowledged that not-for-profit theaters might struggle with limited funding, and that it can be tempting to welcome wealthy commercial producers, he believes that to do so is to compromise. "Commercial theaters are looking for tryouts and you can't make New York a final destination ... It's juicy, it's seductive and it's very dangerous indeed. Regional theaters begin to look for that product to bring them more income and into prominence, and it becomes confused about its purpose and why it exists."[67] Counter to Brustein's concerns, the most recent leader of the ART, Diane Paulus, has sent multiple musicals from Cambridge to Broadway, including revivals of *Porgy and Bess* (2011) and *Pippin* (2013), as well as new musicals such as *Finding Neverland* (2015), *Waitress* (2016), and *Natasha, Pierre & the Great Comet of 1812* (2016).

Though her choices to have playwright Suzan-Lori Parks adapt *Porgy and Bess*, and to collaborate with the contemporary circus company Les 7 Doigts de la Main on *Pippin*, were both criticized for diluting iconic musical theater work by George and Ira Gershwin and Bob Fosse, respectively, Paulus's musical productions at ART appeal to a range of theatergoers, which is an essential criteria for a successful Broadway run. *Waitress* has recently followed the trend of conventional film-to-stage musical adaptations such as *Hairspray* and *Kinky Boots*; ART has also further developed the immersive electropop opera, *The Great Comet*, following its Off Broadway premiere in 2012. Such range in musical theater programming and development at the same institution suggests there is scope for musical theater experimentation and innovation to take place in the regions and at not-for-profit theaters Off Broadway, and for these to be circulated to wider audiences through Broadway's commercial apparatus.

Of the twenty-eight musicals running on Broadway at the end of the 2015–16 season, half included productions developed at regional American theaters or Off Broadway not-for-profit theaters: *Aladdin*, *Bright Star*, the revival of *Chicago*, *Finding Neverland*, *Fun Home*, *Hamilton*, *Jersey Boys*, *Tuck Everlasting*, and *Waitress*. A few, as well, have been developed by not-for-profit theaters in Paris and London (*An American in Paris*, *American Psycho*, *Les Misérables*, *Matilda*, and *The Color Purple* revival). Just six musicals were the result of traditional commercial out-of-town tryouts in American cities: *Beautiful: The Carole King Musical*, *The Book of Mormon*, *Kinky Boots*, *On Your Feet!*, *The Lion King*, and *Wicked*. And the long-running *The Phantom of the Opera*, a holdover from the megamusical phenomenon of the 1980s, originally transferred from the West End.[68]

Major regional players and further development

Chicago is now one of the most popular American cities for commercial out-of-town tryouts, with large, well-equipped theaters ready to host new productions, and an enthusiastic audience for musical theater. While the out-of-town tryout is still used—as it was for *Wicked, The Addams Family,* and *The Last Ship*—new Broadway musicals are increasingly being developed at regional theaters across the United States. Washington DC remains a popular tryout city, as much for commercial tryouts as for the excellent development opportunities provided by the local regional theaters Arena Stage and the Signature Theatre. California's La Jolla Playhouse (*Big River, The Who's Tommy, Thoroughly Modern Millie, Jersey Boys*) and Seattle's 5th Avenue Theatre (*Jekyll & Hyde, Hairspray, The Wedding Singer, A Christmas Story*) are both seasoned collaborators with commercial producers, and are regular credited themselves as Broadway producers. La Jolla has even formalized a new musical development program, where audiences are invited to attend early workshops and provide feedback to creative teams. Collaboration also occurs between regionals and not-for-profits, with, for example, La Jolla and 5th Avenue co-producing *Memphis* after an initial development period at the North Shore Music Theatre in Massachusetts. Thus, before reaching Broadway, that new musical had already been tested before three different regional audiences. Chicago's Goodman Theatre and Seattle's Intiman Theatre Company similarly collaborated to develop and produce *The Light in the Piazza* prior to its 2005 Broadway premiere at the not-for-profit Lincoln Center Theater.

Who wins?

While the regional development model provides time, funding, and distance from Broadway, it is not a guarantee of success, as regionally developed musicals continue to flop on Broadway (*Jane Eyre, Cry-Baby, Bonnie & Clyde, Chaplin, Hands on a Hardbody, Catch Me If You Can, Scandalous, The Wedding Singer*). Some do not make it to New York City at all (*First Wives Club, Little Miss Sunshine*). These failures to launch are evidence of the value of pre-Broadway development. But while deciding that a musical's book, score, staging, or cast may not be ready for Broadway, theatergoers are increasingly known to quickly spread reports and bootleg recordings of these productions on the Internet, potentially further jeopardizing a successful Broadway opening.

The regional development of Broadway musicals is exciting for theaters and theatergoers across the United States. It can be a win-win situation for the regional host and Broadway team. But with some regional theaters' increasingly intense focus on landing a Broadway-bound musical, do local and regional musical theater writers and composers lose out on the opportunity to have their own work nurtured? Do regional theater audiences consequently experience less provocative and/or relevant theater because of the commitment to developing a musical with nationwide, if not worldwide, appeal? Or, with the absence of a dedicated national theater in the US, and with so many regional theaters developing Broadway-bound musicals, has the physical grounding of the American musical in their buildings created a kind of national theater circuit? Musicals developed in the regions and Off Broadway have been succeeding far beyond Broadway, on national tours, but also in licensed productions, both amateur and professional.

Conversely, British not-for-profit theaters have been redefining the American musical canon, producing daring revivals of classic American musicals, and transferring these productions to Broadway. Broadway benefits from these theaters' financial and creative resources, but the innovation driving them is not American. The National Theatre (*Carousel*), the Donmar Warehouse (*Cabaret*), and the Menier Chocolate Factory (*Sunday in the Park with George, La Cage aux Folles, A Little Night Music, The Color Purple*) have contributed some of the most exciting reinterpretations of American classics in recent decades. A further shift in musical theater production also has the potential to erode any national, American foundation, as the development of new Broadway musicals begins to be outsourced. After productions in Pasadena and Atlanta, *Sister Act,* produced by a Dutch production company, premiered in London prior to Broadway, despite being developed as an American musical. While written and directed by Americans, *Rocky*, in German, premiered in Hamburg, Germany, and has been embraced by its foreign incubator. It has been branded a "German" musical by its European producers, who launched a "*Rocky* Goes Broadway" marketing campaign once its Broadway opening (or transfer) was confirmed; once on Broadway, the much-hyped production bombed and quickly closed.

Knitting on the bus and truck tour of *[title of show]* is the future one character, Heidi, dreams of. She recognizes that New York City and Broadway are no longer necessarily a musical's final destination. Having been drafted, developed, previewed, and perfected far from Broadway, the most popular and successful musicals go back on the road, whether on national tours or scattered across regional, community, and student-run theaters. At the time of this writing, new companies of five different musicals developed at regional or not-for-profit theaters were being prepared for national tours. While the originating institutional theater and the commercial producers certainly benefit from such national tours, these companies also spread innovation and advances in the musical theater form to an even wider audience—whether it be the multi-ethnic casting and exciting hip-hop score in *Hamilton*, first developed Off Broadway at the Public Theater, or the stunning contemporary ballet created for *An American in Paris* that director-choreographer Christopher Wheeldon first tested before audiences in Paris. Musical theater that is created and tried out miles from Times Square may eventually enjoy a Broadway premiere, but without what has long been seen as crucial development and tryouts conducted Off Broadway, in the regions, or in another country, the musical would likely not be thriving as it is into the twenty-first century.

TODAY, BROADWAY; TOMORROW, THE WORLD: THE "AMERICAN" MUSICAL AND GLOBALIZATION
Jessica Sternfeld

Musicologist Jessica Sternfeld received her PhD at Princeton University in 2002. She is Associate Professor and the Director of the B.A. in Music program at Chapman University. Her book *The Megamusical* (2006) examines hit shows of the 1980s. She has chapters on a wide range of musical theater subjects in *The Cambridge Companion to the Musical* and *The Oxford Handbook of the American Musical* (with Elizabeth Wollman), among others. She has written articles and served as a guest editor for *Studies in Musical Theater*. She contributed a chapter on performativity issues for *Glee* to *Gestures of Music Theater* (2013, ed. Dominic Symonds and Millie Taylor) and another about the musical and disability for *The Oxford Handbook of Music and Disability* (2016, ed. Joseph Straus et al.). She has a chapter in the forthcoming *Palgrave Handbook to Musical Theater Producers*. Her current work focuses on the relationship between musicals, trauma, and societal narratives of disability and overcoming.

In 1987, the co-director of *Les Misérables*, John Caird, who had taken the show from London to Broadway, helped open the "*Les Mis* School" in Japan. At the time, the musical was still quite new; Caird and his fellow director Trevor Nunn had, in conjunction with producer Cameron Mackintosh, taken the score by Schönberg and Boublil from a modest French-language version to British megamusical proportions in 1985, and then restaged it as a record-breaking Broadway hit in 1987. Despite the buzz around the show both in the West End and on Broadway, no one could have known for sure that *Les Misérables* would become the long-running, internationally-accepted cultural mainstay that it did. Mackintosh, fearless impresario that he was, took a chance, and before the show had barely settled in for its sixteen-year run in New York City, he sent it abroad. To put his plan in action, he sent Caird to Japan repeatedly, for a month or so each time, over the course of three years. At the time, there was little interest in Western-style musical theater in Japan. The success of *Les Mis* would, however, change that; Japan has since become an important musical theater center.

The Toho Company, a large entertainment conglomerate, supported the Japanese *Les Mis* production, as well as the "*Les Mis* School." Its goal: to teach promising candidates "the art of musical theatre/rock opera" (Behr 1996, 144). This was no small feat; as Caird reported, "Revolution is not basically a Japanese concept, nor is there a strong Christian tradition. We had to start from absolute grass-roots" (quoted in ibid., 145). The trainees, some of whom would end up in the production, studied religion, the notion of radical protest, and nineteenth-century European history. Caird directed the production through a translator, and worked with a team to translate the libretto into a text that would sound native and comprehensible, while still conveying the story and emotions of *Les Misérables*. The result was a Japanese *Les Mis* that looked—in its sets, costumes, and production elements—just like it did on Broadway, except for its all-Japanese cast, which performed the piece in Japanese. As a result, Japanese audiences had an experience that was simultaneously entirely Broadway and entirely Japanese. This feat was the work of Cameron Mackintosh, and represented the onset of a first wave of Western musicals that were internationalized for audiences across the globe.

Over the next two decades, *Les Mis* went on to Hungary, Poland, the Czech Republic, Israel, Australia, Iceland, Norway, Austria, Sweden, the Netherlands, Denmark, Ireland, Scotland, the Philippines, Singapore, Germany, South Korea, South Africa, Belgium, Finland, Argentina, Brazil, Mexico, Serbia, and France. Curiously, the last was among the least likely countries, since there was virtually no interest in large-scale Broadway-style musicals in France—even those written by native sons. *Les Mis* productions across the world were often enormous successes and major cultural events, while the one in France was only moderately successful. Yet the occasional box office disappointment hardly mattered: as of 2015, the official *Les Mis* website boasts that the musical has been heard in twenty-two languages, and staged in forty-four countries and a whopping 347 cities worldwide.[69]

More international productions of Broadway musicals followed *Les Mis*, though not right away. Mackintosh staged some of his other megamusical properties across Europe and Asia well into the 1990s; Andrew Lloyd Webber's *Cats* and *The Phantom of the Opera* were especially popular. Very few producers were quick to follow Mackintosh's example.[70] Yet around 2000, the global market boomed, and since then, the international audience for American musicals has grown at a rate so fast that some places can barely build theaters or import shows quickly enough to satisfy demand. Leading the way are a handful of cities in Asia.

Asia

In 1992, entrepreneurs Simone Genatt and Marc Routh founded the Broadway Asia Company, which was among the first companies to follow Mackintosh's example by exporting musicals for the Asian market. Genatt and Routh began with shows that relied more on dance and visuals than on lyrics, and thus required little in the way of translation. Their early ventures included *Stomp* and *Swing*, both of which were more dance concerts than musicals. In a reverse of this exporting trend, they also imported the Korean show *Cookin'* (also known as *Nanta*)—in which four chefs cook percussively to pop music—to New York's children's theater, the New Victory, in 2003.

After these dance-based shows allowed Asian audiences to become acquainted with Broadway-style productions, the Broadway Asia Company's focus shifted to book musicals. In 2004 they opened Rodgers and Hammerstein's *The Sound of Music* in Shanghai, and then sent it on tour to five more cities in mainland China, and then to South Korea, Singapore, Taiwan, and Japan over the course of a record-setting twenty-five-week tour. This was the most ambitious tour of a Broadway musical in Asia to date. *Les Mis* had visited several cities by then, but not as many and for much shorter runs in each place (Hofler 2004). Similarly, Disney's *Beauty and the Beast* played in Shanghai in 1999. But the Broadway Asia Company showed that word-heavy musicals—whether classic or more contemporary ones—could generate enough of an audience to support more imports and increasingly extensive tours.

By the mid-2000s, Broadway musicals in Asia—tours, sit-down runs, and an increasing number of home-grown productions—were hugely successful with audiences and were thus reaping enormous financial rewards. A journalist for the *Korea Times* reported in 2005 that for the Korean market— which is currently stronger than Japan, China, or any other Asian country in terms of interest in the genre—the trend began with a production of *The Phantom of the Opera* in 2001. A production of Elton John and Tim Rice's *Aida* arrived in 2005, directed by westerner Keith Batten, featuring a cast of Korean actors who spoke and sang in Korean. Batten told the *Korea Times* that he hoped this sort of production would lead to more musicals not just being performed and directed by local talent, but created by them as well ("Bringing Broadway to Korea" 2005). Yet the transition from imported fare to entertainments developed in Korea has been slow in coming—a vast majority of musical theater in Asia is still imported from Broadway and subsequently translated.

Nevertheless, the popularity of Broadway-style musicals has been growing by leaps and bounds over the course of the last two decades. *Korea Times* gave a rough but telling account of how the Broadway musical has become, with shocking speed, a huge favorite in Korea: in 2002, about 120 musicals were staged around the country. In 2005, an estimate of 462 shows were staged and, in 2006, approximately 670 (ibid.).

The nexus of the Korean musical theater world is Seoul, South Korea. Indeed, it may be safe to declare Seoul one of the most active commercial musical theater cities outside of New York, if for no other reason than its sheer number of theaters—a whopping 300. In contrast, Hamburg, Germany—which is currently the leader of musical theater in Europe outside London—has four. The target audience in Seoul is young people, especially "young women raised on the bombast of Korean pop and the histrionics of television soap operas" (Healy 2013, A1). These young women, often with friends or dates in tow, arrive at theaters early so they can take photos and videos, not just of the cast members, but of the crew and the theater itself, as well. Runs tend to be short by Western standards; often, a hit will run for only a few months, and then close with the aim of reopening a year or two later, once fresh excitement can be generated.

Part of that excitement comes from what Broadway calls "stunt casting": using celebrities from film, television, or the pop music realm to stir interest in a theatrical production. This practice is not occasional in Seoul—it is the norm. A newly reopened production allows new "celebrities to be added to the casts, which fuels repeat business; stars from popular K-pop bands routinely sell out their performances and can earn as much as $50,000 a night in a musical," explains *The New York Times* reporter Patrick Healy (ibid.). The musical theater culture in Korea has eagerly embraced Western stage musicals, whether they be Broadway hits like *Wicked, Grease,* and *Mamma Mia!,* flops like *Ghost* and *Bonnie & Clyde,* or classics like *Guys and Dolls* and *Man of La Mancha.*

Despite what seems to be unabating demand from young Korean audiences, most musicals lose money in Seoul, just as most do in New York. But the industry thrives nevertheless due to those musicals that do particularly well. Marketers have learned very quickly how to sell particular entertainments. Most musicals are marketed as love stories or dramatic family tales, and are aimed squarely at young adults. As a result, the musical version of *The Lion King,* which is the biggest international money-maker of all time, did not fare particularly well in Korea because most target audience members viewed it as a children's show. Though the threat of oversaturation looms, the market shows no signs of flagging. In 2000, sales for musicals in Seoul were estimated at $9 million; by 2013 that number had skyrocketed to $300 million (ibid.).

In 2005, China became a new and very promising—if still somewhat uncertain—market for Broadway musicals. During that year, the Chinese government passed a law granting foreign investors entry into the Chinese entertainment industry. Although the Broadway Asia Company had already established itself in other Asian countries and would quickly venture into China, it was not the first to take advantage of the new law. The first to make the leap was the Nederlander Organization, one of Broadway's largest production companies and theater operators. The Nederlander's international branch, Nederlander Worldwide Entertainment, partnered with a Chinese production group called Beijing Time New Century Entertainment. The joint group, newly named Nederlander New Century, began bringing show after show to China.

In *The New York Times*, theater journalist Campbell Robertson noted that in the past, China had been relatively slow to embrace the Broadway musical trend sweeping Asia. This tentativeness was due in part to the fact that previous ventures, which were granted no government support, had to be produced cheaply and in English. Yet once international investors were permitted to stage live entertainments as they wished, full-scale Broadway productions arrived, and were performed in Mandarin and a variety of other local languages.

Another challenge to staging Broadway musicals in China was a lack of suitable theaters. Elaborate performing arts centers could easily accommodate visiting dance companies and orchestras, but were typically too large for musical theater productions. Other theaters were either too small or did not have appropriate sound systems, or both. When musicals began to boom in China, many theaters were built or hastily converted for use as appropriate venues. The Broadway Asia Company (sometimes called Broadway Asia Entertainment) followed the Nederlanders into China and began building an infrastructure for Broadway-style musical theater there. Also, like the "*Les Mis* School" that established a footing in Japan two decades prior, "theatrical training schools" have grown up in various parts of China. These are designed to help populate casts with Chinese (rather than visiting) talent, so that tours can cast performers who will be understood by Chinese audiences (Robertson 2007, E1).

The Nederlanders opened schools in China, too. In 2008, *Christian Science Monitor* journalist Nancy Pellegrini reported that the Nederlander Organization was partnering with the Central Academy of Drama (CAD) in Beijing to train musical theater performers. Arts training is extensive in China, though in the past focus was typically placed on artistic endeavors that had long been popular there: acrobatics, dance, and especially Chinese opera traditions. Yet the CAD was designed to create musical-theater-style "triple threats" who could sing, dance, and act in Western-style musicals.

Though China has slowly begun to embrace tours of Western musicals, they had, at first, very little incentive to invest in home-grown talent. Generally speaking, the Chinese have often supported artists who could prove their worth through winning contests and prizes. There are international competitions for classical musicians, dance companies, and other art forms, which the country has long supported. But there are no high-profile international prizes for musical theater performers. As Pellegrini notes, "while violinists and ballerinas can return home with competition gold medals, actors have fewer opportunities to win tangible accolades abroad. Without 'international certification,' stars don't get born, audiences don't buy tickets, shows don't get mounted, actors stay unemployed, and the theater industry lies dormant." With this challenge in mind, the Nederlanders developed a three-part plan. First, they would tour Western musicals through China in hopes of developing familiarity with and interest in the form among local audiences. They would then develop Chinese-language versions of said musicals. Finally, they would help develop original, sustainable Chinese musical theater. Step one was, for the most part, successful. As of the mid-2010s, the Nederlander New Century is working on step two, with a Mandarin-language version of the American property *Fame* (ibid.) and plans for other translated shows.

The Nederlander Organization, Broadway Asia, and other similar companies continue their work in China, seeking audiences for tours and building a local culture of performing artists. While the former goal seems to have been met, the latter remains very much in process. Not surprisingly, cultural differences abound. These affect not only the content of the shows (the adaptation of *Fame* mentioned above as the CAD's first venture only barely resembles the 1980 American film or subsequent television series), but the rehearsal process, as well. The Vice Headmaster of the CAD, for example, expressed great surprise about the fact that praising the performers he taught made them work harder and strive to improve—not stop bothering to work. Similarly, Western creative teams quickly discovered that when a performer was late to rehearsal, he or she was accustomed to offering a formal and elaborate apology with numerous bows.

By 2009, with China having fully embraced the imported musical, the demand for theaters became so enormous that Beijing created a brand new theater district, like Broadway or the West End, with thirty-two houses of various sizes, ranging from 300 to 2,000 seats. More musicals in Mandarin and higher ticket prices also made the Chinese market look more like Broadway in terms of catering to a well-off, local audience (Coonan 2009). But the creation of a truly self-sustaining, local musical theater culture in China remains elusive; the Chinese still seem more interested in imported shows than in supporting or training local talent and developing home-grown ones.

As of 2015, this lack of saturation into Chinese culture has led Cameron Mackintosh to back away from the Chinese marketplace. Nick Allott, managing director of Cameron Mackintosh Ltd., told Bloomberg.com that

China seemed more interested in building theaters than training local talent or creating Mandarin-language productions. The Chinese government and private investors alike apparently saw the theaters as sound investments, but without the talent to put on the stage or the audiences to fill the houses, there are no profits to be had. The market is too young, added Allott, and data as to whether or not musical theater will truly catch on in China is not yet conclusive.

The Nederlander Organization, unlike Cameron Mackintosh, has continued to try to make inroads in China. "The level of sophistication is growing significantly," Robert Nederlander Jr. noted in the summer of 2015. "We're confident that the Chinese market will be second only to the American market for musical theater" (Einhorn 2015). Recent statistics support the Nederlanders' conviction that the time is indeed right for supporting the home-grown boom. In 2011, over 300,000 people saw *Mamma Mia!* in Mandarin. *Into the Woods* also had a successful run in Mandarin, and *The Lion King* will soon be opening next door to Shanghai Disneyland, which is still under construction but which promises to be a powerful tie-in to the stage musical. And *The Phantom of the Opera*, a Mackintosh production that has appeared and succeeded in most parts of the world, will arrive in the late 2010s via Andrew Lloyd Webber's company (ibid.). Should these productions succeed commercially and critically in China, a new and increasingly large market for homegrown productions does not seem impossible. Nevertheless, it remains to be seen if China—such a new market with so little infrastructure to support it—will emulate Korea in becoming a lasting home to American and American-style musicals.

Hits and flops in Europe

One unexpected result of the international success of Broadway and Broadway-style musicals is the potential to rework and restage shows in other countries, even if they failed to make an impact on Broadway. Much like Hollywood films that do not become commercial blockbusters in the US but that connect with audiences abroad, Broadway flops—or shows that were mildly, but not wildly, successful—can now find new homes, and more enthusiastic audiences, far beyond Broadway. "Flops on Broadway? Fix Them Overseas" advised a headline in *The New York Times* in 2011, once the trend had become firmly established. Indeed, since the growth of the international market for American stage musicals, productions such as

Shrek The Musical, Legally Blonde, and *Tarzan* have fared better in European cities than they did in New York.

When musicals that do not fare well on Broadway are restaged elsewhere, they are typically reworked, sometimes extensively. Problems that plagued the original productions are addressed and, ideally, fixed. Because production costs on Broadway are so high—typically starting at $10–$15 million, and often costing far more than that—producers are highly motivated to earn their investors' money back, especially if the Broadway production fails to turn even a small profit. Disney's *Tarzan* serves as a good example here. The musical, with a score by Phil Collins and a book by David Henry Hwang, cost $15 million to stage on Broadway in 2006. While it ran for 15 months, it received middling to poor reviews, struggled to connect with audiences, and closed at a loss on Broadway. But the musical found a more loyal audience—and thus more commercial success—in Europe beginning in 2007.

Tarzan first opened abroad in the Netherlands. Before it did, producer Joop van den Ende and his team, with Disney's support, made the staging more immersive, thus covering the entire audience in what appeared to be a dense, leafy jungle. Because Phil Collins remains very popular in western Europe, he heavily promoted the score. Rather than a show for families with children, the Dutch version of *Tarzan* was marketed to adults as the locale for a great date night.

The new approach worked: *Tarzan* ran from 2007 to 2009 in a large 2,000-seat theater, pleasing Dutch audiences and turning a handsome profit. The same production of *Tarzan* opened in 2008 in Hamburg, Germany, where it saw even greater commercial success, due in part to the fact that local excitement was generated with a television tie-in: its original leads were chosen by the German public via a reality show titled *Ich Tarzan, Du Jane.* *Tarzan* ran in Hamburg for an enormously successful five years, closing in 2013 and subsequently moving on to other German cities.

It was likely no coincidence that producers chose to bring *Tarzan* to Hamburg; that city has become something of an important center for musicals in Europe. In some respects, this is surprising: Hamburg is an expensive city, and the costs of doing business there are often as steep as bringing shows to Broadway. Theater rents are expensive, and production crews are traditionally very well-paid. Further, Hamburg is not a capital city that readily draws tourists for a variety of reasons. Nevertheless, Hamburg's status as a musical theater center seems to stem entirely from savvy marketing: it has become promoted unflaggingly as *the* place to see musicals in Europe. In *The New York Times* in 2012, Patrick Healy reported that the connection between Hamburg and musical theater had been steadily "encouraged by 25 years of producers splashing television ads and billboards across Germany, with its population of 82 million, to market Hamburg as the home of Broadway-style shows" (Healy 2012, C1). Similar to the marketing strategies that target young adults (but not children) in Seoul, advertisers in Hamburg now champion musicals as entertainments that are ideal for date nights or getaway weekends.

Hamburg's relationship to the musical theater began earlier than it did in most other cities. The businessman Friedrich Kurz, who was familiar with and fond of megamusicals, brought *Cats* to Hamburg in 1986, and followed it with *The Phantom of the Opera* in 1990. Just as some in the United States have spoken out against the "Disneyfication" of musicals as money-making, middlebrow entertainment, so too did intellectuals and university students protest the coming of "bourgeois musicals" to Hamburg. While Kurz was thrilled by the free publicity, the cultural debate continues in Germany as it does in the US and elsewhere.

At present, there are four commercial theaters that host musicals in Hamburg without government support. There are two government-supported theaters, which tend to stage classic German and English plays instead of American-style musicals. There are also more temporary structures: the sellout production of *The Lion King* is housed in a large tent-like theater that can be seen for miles up and down the Elbe River. "I worry that these musicals aren't producing anything of cultural significance," noted a local government representative (ibid.).[71] Clearly, however, many visitors to Hamburg are not as concerned; the city continues to welcome Broadway shows, whether they made millions or lost their entire investment in New York.

Longtime resident of Hamburg T.J. Hee has been a dancer and dance supervisor in the thriving Hamburg theater community since 1988. He began as a performer in *Cats* (Mr. Mistoffelees), then moved on to *Starlight Express*, *La Cage aux Folles*, *Beauty and the Beast*, *Miss Saigon*, and *The Lion King*. He became the permanent "Resident Dance Supervisor" for *The Lion King* in 2003. His experience verifies that Hamburg's economy partly drives the interest in large-scale shows: "Of course there are other smaller shows around," he notes, but when audiences pay a lot for tickets, they want "spectacle." He considers *The Lion King*'s long-term success to be a result of its broad appeal and the idea that the visual elements are as interesting as the musical ones. After "more than 10 million visitors," he reports, "it becomes kind of like an institution." In his experience, most of the audience is semi-local; they come from Germany, Austria, and Switzerland. Many Germans have seen the show multiple times, he adds; like long-running megamusicals in New York, some of the stability—the institutionalization—comes from life-long fans. When asked about the possible American or British aspects of these hits, he says those elements are generally consumed by a German aesthetic and the simple fact that the shows are performed in German. The shift to a German-feeling tone rather than an imported one may be supported by the increased local talent pool; Hee says in the mid-1980s, when the trend began, most performers came from the US and England, but now there is a large population of German performers.[72]

Long before Hamburg became a musical theater center, there was London's West End, where some shows that fare poorly on Broadway find more enthusiastic audiences. For example, *Legally Blonde* ran for a lackluster eighteen months on Broadway from 2007 to 2008. It was generally disliked by critics and ignored by the Tony Awards, but it succeeded both commercially and critically in London, where it ran from 2009 to 2012. Jerry Mitchell, the director of both productions, did not change anything about the show; he credited its success in the West End to a more receptive audience and a smaller (not larger or more elaborate) theater. It was also helpful, of course, that in the West End, production costs to mount and run the show are a fraction of what they are on Broadway because of steep US union fees and other production factors (including the fact that some West End shows receive government support) (Healy 2011, AR1).

Brazil

Joining the American musical theater import game gradually, but in recent years very enthusiastically, is Brazil, by far the most popular place in South America for musicals. In 2005, *The Los Angeles Times* reported that Brazil supports both imported American products and "home-grown, often quirky Brazilian musical shows" (Johnson 2005). Productions tend to share performers, producers, and directors, and the audience supports both types of theater as well, apparently caring more "about the quality of the finished product than the 'purity' of its pedigree" (ibid.). Brazil has a long-standing interest in musical theater, staging *Follies*-like revue shows in the 1930s and 1940s, and bringing in Broadway standards as early as the 1960s. Politics, including a distinctly anti-American view, squelched the trend for decades; megamusicals like *The Phantom of the Opera*, *Les Misérables*, and *Beauty and the Beast* recently brought interest back. A small handful of impresarios also served as translators, directors, and performers, creating a small but active theater scene.

The boom grew into the 2010s, then hit a severe setback with a national recession around 2014. "Before the recession," *The New York Times* noted in 2015, "producers feverishly licensed musicals, and Brazilian television stars clamored for the prestige of starring in a Broadway import or a Brazilian original" (Wolfe 2015). But thanks to the economic problems, ticket sales plummeted, costs rose, and the industry had to figure out how to cut corners to survive. Performers now often work for no salary, taking a cut of the box office instead. But box office income alone cannot support a show; usually large corporations—now no longer interested—sponsored theater. The *Times* noted that in 2015, *Nice Work If You Can Get It* and *The Full Monty*, both with themes of economic hardship, continued to draw crowds while other spectacle-based shows struggled (ibid.). It remains unclear what will happen to the Brazilian theater scene but if the economy recovers, and interest in American culture continues, it may yet thrive again.

Seoul is expensive but the market is thriving; Hamburg serves a smaller and more captive audience; Brazil supports large-scale entertainment when it can. Yet in all cases, franchising shows makes sense, especially considering the changes that have taken place in the commercial theater realm in the United States. In the 1990s, Times Square was renovated and made more appealing to national and international tourists. To redesign the famously grungy and unwelcoming area, the city invited entertainment conglomerates to develop and stage entertainment properties on Broadway. While this certainly helped Broadway expand its appeal to a global market, the downside has been enormous increases in costs—not only to secure a theater, but to fill bigger and newly renovated houses, pay competitive salaries, and fill thousands of seats. Tickets now cost much more, and producers need to keep shows running for longer and longer stretches just to break even, let alone turn a profit.

In such a hotly competitive and enormously risky field, franchising is logical, if also distressing to some, who have condemned the practice of "'McTheater': a soulless chain of identical productions that destroy local creativity and deprive individual companies of artistic freedom." In response to such concerns, many productions now allow for stagings to be updated and changed. But regardless of whether they are or are not, the musical theater industry continues to thrive, not just on a local level, but newly on a global one that is growing all the time (Sternfeld and Wollman 2011, 118).

At the moment, as we have seen, the global market thrives (or is at least undergoing all sorts of growth and experimentation) in the Netherlands, Hamburg, Seoul, some cities in Japan and China, and Brazil. But international expansion happened remarkably quickly, in only a few decades. Thus, a few decades from now, the global market for American musicals is likely to have shifted entirely, and grown exponentially. Where will new markets develop, and how will they, in turn, influence Broadway? At the moment, Broadway musicals are here to stay—not just in New York City, but across the globe, as a thriving and culturally influential commercial and creative American export.

INTERDISCIPLINARY APPROACHES TO STUDYING THE STAGE MUSICAL

Elizabeth Titrington Craft and Joanna Dee Das

Elizabeth Titrington Craft is Assistant Professor of Music at the University of Utah, where she teaches courses on twentieth-century music, music of the United States, and musical theater. Her research appears in the journal *Studies in Musical Theatre* and the volume *Crosscurrents: American and European Music in Interaction, 1900–2000*, ed. Felix Meyer et al. (2014). She is currently working on a book tentatively titled *Yankee Doodle Dandy: George M. Cohan's Broadway and the Making of American Identity*.

Joanna Dee Das is Assistant Professor of Dance at Washington University in St. Louis, where she teaches dance history, performance studies, and modern dance technique. She received her PhD in history from Columbia University and subsequently held two postdoctoral fellowships in dance studies at Stanford University and Williams College before joining the WU faculty. Her research interests include dance in musical theater, African diasporic dance, and the politics of performance in the twentieth century. She is the author of *Katherine Dunham: Dance and the African Diaspora* (2017). Her writing has also been published in the *Journal of African American History, Journal of American History, Dance Research Journal, Studies in Musical Theatre,* and *TDR.*

What comes to mind when you think of studying a stage musical—say, *The Sound of Music*? To quote from that show, were we to "start at the very beginning," we would turn to the production itself. Yet when it comes to musicals, what constitutes "the production itself" is not immediately clear. The stage musical is a multifaceted form, made up of drama, music, and movement. It is also ephemeral and unfixed, in that one musical can have multiple productions, all of which are different.[73] *The Sound of Music*, for instance, premiered on Broadway in 1959, and since then has toured, been revived both professionally and in student and community theater productions, and been made into a beloved Hollywood film. All of these versions of *The Sound of Music* are different—so which will you choose to investigate? When you decide, you might then want to consult some kind of text or artifact, such as a published script, published score, or sound recording. Yet these sources, too, have limitations. After all, what occurs in a performance may not be precisely what is written in a script and score. The stage musical's openness and multidimensionality make research about the genre a challenging as well as fascinating and creative endeavor.

Until very recently, most scholars dismissed musicals as middlebrow popular entertainments that were not worth serious consideration.[74] At the turn of the twenty-first century, however, scholars from a range of disciplines—including musicology, ethnomusicology, theater, performance studies, dance studies, and American studies—began producing books and articles on the significance of musical theater. This essay introduces some of the approaches scholars have taken. It invites you to consider ways to analyze and interpret the stage musical—in other words, to examine what makes a show work and what questions it raises about our culture.

Analyzing a show: Book, music, movement, and visual elements

Imagine sitting down in a theater for a performance. The usher has just handed you a program, and you have a few minutes to flip through it before the show starts. While doing so, you are likely to see a list of the acts, scenes, and/or musical numbers. Much like the table of contents in a book, the program conveys important information to the spectator about how a musical is structured. When you set out to study a musical production, take note of its form. It may be divided into acts and scenes or organized in some other fashion. Consider also the list of characters, noting how many there are, what roles they play, and how they relate to one another.

Surveying a musical's form is a step toward understanding its message and purpose. Like other types of theatrical productions, the musical's script, frequently called the book, offers the most direct explanation of the show's story, or plot. As you would with a play or another piece of literature, ask yourself how the book writer employs literary elements and techniques to create layers of meaning. What themes emerge? How do the various characters speak, and what does their dialogue say about them? What broader messages does the story seem to offer?

Of course, the musical numbers are the hallmark of a stage musical. Unlike a "straight play," a musical's plot points, character arcs, and emotions are often revealed through song. Musical numbers can bring us into the world being depicted onstage or give us access to the inner realm of a character's thoughts. To study a show's music, musicologists and other scholars might use a written score, along with recordings like a cast album. Those with musical training may turn to techniques like formal analysis, which they apply to examine the musical structure; harmonic analysis, which they apply to chord progressions; or motivic analysis, with which they consider how musical ideas in the score are linked and developed. But one need not have extensive musical training to incorporate musical analysis. We can all make useful observations that help us better understand the functions and importance of a show's music.

To begin, listen to the songs and consider the lyrics. Whether by making the audience chuckle at a witty line or by vividly painting a mental image, musical theater lyricists use rhyme, imagery, and other poetic and literary devices to catch a listener's ear and convey meaning. Listen also for elements of the music. Sound conveys emotions and ideas beyond what can be expressed in words. Can you identify any musical instruments? What effect do they have? Consider what musical styles the show employs overall. It may be a rock musical, for example, with electric guitars and drums, or its music may be influenced by jazz, opera, or other genres. Are the individual songs written in similar or contrasting styles? See what observations you can make about melody (the singable tune), harmony (the different notes or voices that support the melody), tempo (the speed of the music), rhythm (the beats or stresses used), dynamics (the volume of the sound), texture (the number and layering of voices and instruments), timbre (the quality of the sounds), and form (the song's structure). Notice whether there are reprises—musical numbers that repeat and recall earlier ones—and what function they serve. Take note of how many songs there are, who sings them, and the vocal ranges of the different characters. The leading man, for example, may be a tenor with a higher voice, or a baritone or bass with a lower voice, with different implications for how that character is perceived as a result. Ask yourself what decisions the composer made and how they serve the musical's story and themes.

If you are able to compare the written book or score with a cast album or live performance, you might notice differences. Performers often take liberties with musical directions, pitches, or even words as they add their own touches. Stars like Ethel Merman, Nathan Lane, and Audra McDonald have always held great power, both to attract audiences and to shape the meanings of songs and shows through their interpretations. Two stars may deliver the same song very differently. Performance, whether live or on film, provides another realm in which to consider words and music.

Studying a musical's choreography can also shed light on the production as a whole. Thinking about choreography means examining not only the formal dance numbers, but also how people use their bodies throughout the show. Dance and movement can advance the plot, communicate emotion to the audience, and reveal aspects of characters' personalities or relationships. Unlike dialogue, lyrics, and music, however, choreography is rarely written down. So, how do we study the choreography without a textual record?

As you might suspect, attending a live performance of a musical is ideal. When you do, you can see patterns onstage and sense the energy produced by moving bodies. Witnessing a live performance is not always possible, however, so film is another option. Photographs and reviews can also be valuable. Though photographs depict performers in static poses, they often reveal the choreographic style of the show. And some dance and theater critics are good at describing movement and making it come alive on the page.

To analyze movement, begin with description. As you watch a live performance or film, or look at photographs, record your observations about what the performers are doing. Look at the actual steps being performed. Are there lots of turns, kicks, or leaps? What about the shapes the dancers' bodies make—are the movements curved or angular? Do the performers form patterns on the stage? How do the characters interact physically? Think, also, about the tempo of the movement: Do the dancers move slowly, or do they run and jump with excitement? Once you have made your observations, take a step back and reflect on how dance and movement seem to serve the show overall.

The visual elements of a show—sets, lights, costumes, props, and special effects—are also indispensable to telling a musical's story. Sets help establish the time, location, and atmosphere of a show: the small Russian village of Anatevka in *Fiddler on the Roof* (1964); the gritty New York City streets in *West Side Story* (1957); the enormous junkyard in *Cats* (West End, 1981; Broadway, 1982). The lighting design can also help define the space. It concentrates the audience's attention on certain parts of the stage or on certain characters: if one character stands in a spotlight while another crouches in the shadows, we are being told something. Lighting, like a set, indicates something about the mood. Do the lights saturate the stage in warm colors, giving a sense of brightness and happiness? Or are the characters bathed in depressive, dark blue light?

Costume design helps ground the audience in a specific location and historical moment while communicating something about the characters. Whether a character is old-fashioned or a trendsetter, a conformist or a rebel, his clothing will provide clues before he opens his mouth. Special effects serve similar functions to set, lighting, and costume design while also dazzling the audience with spectacle. The falling chandelier in *The Phantom of the Opera* and helicopter in *Miss Saigon* drew attention in the 1980s and early 1990s, while the numerous LED video projection screens and aerial stunts in *Spider-Man: Turn Off the Dark* attempted to take theatrical special effects to a new level in 2011.

Let us take a look at a specific scene to practice analyzing the various elements of a production. *In the Heights* (2008) tells the story of a Latino community in early twenty-first-century New York City. In Act I, the character Abuela Claudia sings "Paciencia y Fe" ("Patience and Faith"), in which she recalls moving from Cuba to New York City in 1943.[75] Visual elements, music, and choreography convey Claudia's experiences as an immigrant and help the audience understand what she means by "patience and faith," a phrase her mother often used. As Claudia begins the song, the lighting changes. A spotlight focuses exclusively on her, making the background set, a cityscape of Washington Heights, disappear from view. The new lighting also shows the audience that this scene takes place not in the present, but instead in Claudia's memory.

As Claudia sings, the chorus enters, donning period costume to signal a shift to this earlier era. They occupy the shadows: they are ghosts of Claudia's past, not live characters. Music and dance aid in setting the scene. The song is a mambo—a musical style originally from Cuba—and it is punctuated with harsh brass chords when Claudia sings of the discrimination she experienced as a newcomer to the US. The dance chorus mixes mambo steps with aggressive, sharp gestures symbolizing the unwelcoming culture she encountered. Using more than just words, the scene shows how "paciencia y fe" helped Claudia bridge old and new worlds in 1943, and how they help her face new challenges in the present.[76]

Charting a show's development

Although the analytic tools discussed so far focus on a musical's final product, many scholars have studied a show by focusing on its creation and development. Entire books have been written about how specific musicals made it to the stage.[77] Most musicals go through extensive development and revision before the official premiere, whether on Broadway, in London's West End, or elsewhere. Looking at how a musical evolves can help you understand it not only as a finished product, but also as a creative process where many factors must be balanced and compromises made to achieve a single, coherent vision. You might trace a show's trajectory from early drafts, readings, workshops, or "out-of-town tryouts" through to a later stage.

The business of musical theater is also important to a show's development. You might investigate, for example, how a show was financed, or which entertainment company was behind it. The stories of many musicals come from another medium—novels, plays, or movies—and the process of adaptation offers yet another area for study. For example, how did *La Bohème*, a nineteenth-century Italian opera by Giacomo Puccini, become Jonathan Larson's 1996 rock musical *Rent*? What changes were made when Disney's 1994 animated movie *The Lion King* was adapted for Broadway in 1997? A musical's backstory can shed light on both the musical itself and, more broadly, the commercial theater industry.

You can further understand a musical by studying the people who created it, including the composer, lyricist, director, choreographer, and designers. Composer George Gershwin started out as a song plugger for a Tin Pan Alley music publishing company—that is, he would promote songs by playing and singing them for buyers and performers looking for material. Knowing this bit of personal history not only gives us insight into Gershwin's biography but also might spur us to look for stylistic elements of Tin Pan Alley in the scores of his shows. You may also want to take into account the education and training of members of the creative team. A set designer with a background in architecture, for example, may bring a different sensibility than one trained in visual art. The lives of performers also reveal much about a musical. Their accounts of the rehearsal process and the experience of performing onstage bring the vibrancy of human experience to the story, making the musical come alive in our imaginations.

Researching individual lives is perhaps the easiest way to learn about a musical's development. Several composers, directors, choreographers, and performers have written memoirs or have had biographies written about them. Online websites contain biographical information and photographs. Newspapers and magazines often publish profiles of artists. Some more prominent figures, such as Richard Rodgers or Jerome Robbins, even have their own archives, where you can view their notes, letters, and other material from their lives and careers.

Analyzing consumption and reception

Thus far, we have looked at approaches to studying the musical that focus on the show itself and the processes that developed it. By analyzing consumption and reception, you can also consider the relationship between a show and its audiences. This approach helps you learn more about how stage musicals function as commercial enterprises and fit into the broader culture.

In consumption studies, scholars analyze how a show is marketed and how people "consume" a show as a commodity. As the term "show business" implies, musical theater is not only an art form but also a business venture that needs a paying audience to survive. Though not all musicals are for profit, even those performed in not-for-profit or community theaters must appeal to audiences. Producers and members of the creative team frequently consider how their show will appeal to audiences and develop marketing strategies to convince potential theatergoers to buy tickets.

How a show is marketed can tell you more about to whom a particular musical appeals and why. The 2009 show *Memphis*, which centered on an interracial romance between a white man and a black woman in the 1950s, made deliberate attempts to attract a black audience. The marketing team played clips of the female lead singing the number "Colored Woman" at sites in predominantly black neighborhoods in New York City, including street fairs, beauty salons, churches, and community centers. The producers also created the "Inspire Change" program, which brought students from city public schools to the musical, and encouraged their parents to attend as well (Healy 2010, A1).

Images or graphics featured in advertisements can be informative. A poster for the 1996 revival of *Chicago* showed six women in fishnet stockings and cleavage-revealing black tops, suggesting that the musical had an erotic element and was geared toward adults. The posters for 2008's *Shrek The Musical*, on the other hand, featured characters from the family-friendly Dreamworks film, signaling that the musical was appropriate for all ages.[78] The rise of social media in the early twenty-first century has given marketers a new promotion tool. When the musical *Next to Normal*, a show about mental illness, opened on Broadway in 2009, the topic initially seemed to scare off audiences. After six weeks, the box office was only filling about 72 percent of seats. In a daring move, the producers hired a digital marketing agency to start a Twitter campaign, and an adapted version of the show was "tweeted," 140 characters at a time, over the course of 35 days. By the end of the campaign, *Next to Normal* had over a million followers on Twitter and was filling 90 percent of its seats on a regular basis (Newman 2009, B4).

Reception studies address how various audiences receive and interpret a musical within their own social contexts. Theater critics form the first line of reception, evaluating productions for their readers. Examining reviews is thus an important way to understand a show's popularity and how well (or poorly) it captures the zeitgeist of the era. Opinions may vary: one writer might extol a musical for its depiction of contemporary gender dynamics, while another might focus instead on the unoriginality of a musical's choreography.

It is important to balance critical reviews with other aspects of reception, such as statistics on ticket sales. While the financial records of many shows have been lost or discarded, magazines such as *Variety* report on sales figures. Similarly, you can learn the number of weeks a show played in a Broadway theater through the Internet Broadway Database (IBDB.com) or Playbill Vault (playbill.com/vault). Critics might dislike a show that audiences absolutely love, as was the case with the 2003 musical *Wicked* (Dvoskin 2011, 374–6). In such cases, you may seek to understand the reasons for the disparity.

You can also attempt to gauge consumption and reception by studying audience demographics. By looking at ticket prices for a particular show, for example, you may be able to estimate the audience's average income level.

Producers and theater owners have adopted techniques to help them learn about the age, gender, race, income, educational background, ethnicity, and other characteristics of a show's audience. There are challenges to be aware of when trying to analyze demographics, however. The Broadway League (the trade association for the Broadway theater industry) only began collecting and studying audience data in the 1990s (Lyman 1998, E7). Previously, musical productions had few ways to learn about their audiences. Furthermore, the Broadway League publishes data for Broadway as a whole, not for particular plays or musicals, and it relies on voluntary audience surveys to learn such information (Hauser 2013, 52).[79] Therefore, it may not be entirely accurate or comprehensive. Beyond Broadway, it can be difficult to glean information about audience demographics, but reviews in local newspapers are often at least a starting point.

Ultimately, studying reviews, financial figures, marketing materials, and demographics can tell you only so much about why a musical succeeded or failed and what kind of impact it made more broadly. In order to answer these questions, you may want to follow the lead of scholars who have studied shows' historical and social contexts.

Evaluating historical, social, and cultural contexts

Musicals speak to their times, whether directly or indirectly, and thus a show's historical context is critical to understanding its meanings. *Oklahoma!* and *On the Town*, for example, both opened on Broadway during the Second World War. *On the Town* told of Navy sailors on wartime leave in New York. The context of the Second World War was equally important, though, for *Oklahoma!* Even though its early twentieth-century frontier setting was far removed from the global conflict raging outside the theater walls, *Oklahoma!* promoted homespun values in the heartland, and many spectators viewed it with wartime concerns in mind.[80] As you study a musical, ask yourself what was happening around the time of its performance that might have affected its creation and reception. This can be true for revivals as well as original productions: the 2002 revival of *Oklahoma!* carried new resonances in the wake of 9/11.

In addition to considering the historical context, you may delve into a musical's treatment of social issues such as race, class, or gender. Many musical theater scholars use social and cultural analysis, in which they apply a particular critical lens—such as feminism or literary criticism—to the study of a musical. Because musicals often respond to the concerns of contemporary society, they are fertile ground for such approaches.

When looking at musical theater through a sociocultural lens, consider who has had access to the industry through its history and which roles they have occupied on both sides of the footlights. Race and ethnicity, critical issues in twentieth-century history, are important to musical theater history. It is a telling coincidence that another name for Broadway is the "Great White Way," as Caucasian Americans have long held positions of power in the industry and filled seats in the theaters. Other groups, however, have played important roles. Jewish American creators and performers have been prominent in the history of the American stage musical since its inception.[81] There is a rich tradition of African American musicals, despite the fact that they were relegated to segregated spheres of creation, production, and reception for much of their history.[82] And vital traditions of ethnic theater— productions by and for immigrants, in their native languages—flourished from the nineteenth century well into the twentieth alongside the "mainstream" stage.[83]

Consider also the gender identities of a musical's creators and performers. Like Jewish Americans, gay men have been disproportionately represented among musical theater's creators, performers, and audiences, and several scholars have looked at musicals through the lens of gay culture.[84] Class is a less studied but important barrier to participation in musical theater, especially as ticket prices have increased throughout the twentieth century and into the twenty first.

In addition to thinking about participation and access, you might also consider issues of representation—how characters and groups of different races, ethnicities, genders, or other modes of identity are depicted onstage. What messages does a particular musical send regarding contemporary societal debates? How might those messages differ for audience members of different backgrounds and identities? Minorities are often depicted through stereotypes, whether positive or negative, and musicals tend to reflect the limitations of the era in which they were created. When *Show Boat* first premiered in 1927, it was considered progressive, but from a twenty-first-century perspective, its depictions of African Americans are mired in stereotypes. Whiteness has historically been considered a default—stories about white characters are seen as universal rather than as being about a particular racial or ethnic group—but recent scholarship shows that whiteness, too, is represented in significant ways through particular strategies.[85] Issues of gender and sexuality offer another fruitful realm of study, especially given the musical's traditionally strong emphasis on heterosexual romance.[86] How does a musical reinforce or challenge social norms?

Finally, you might consider alternative readings of a musical. One book on the American musical, for example, explores the genre's potential for queer affinity for lesbians.[87] Other scholarship describes how early twentieth-century African American musicals spoke to black and white audiences in different, even coded ways. The 1921 show *Shuffle Along*, for example, reproduced many egregious stereotypes of minstrelsy, including the use of blackface, but also included satirical or "signifyin(g)" commentary on white American culture through jokes that only African American audiences understood (Johnson 1987, 133).[88] If you adopt different perspectives, you will likely find varying, subtle meanings beneath a show's surface.

You need not limit yourself to the issues listed here. While race, ethnicity, class, gender, and sexuality are tremendously important lenses, so too are depictions of disability, age, religion, region, and politics. Follow your own observations and instincts.

Collecting evidence

As you have probably noticed, studying a musical's many facets involves a wide range of types of evidence. Further, sometimes even basic texts and evidence are not readily available. Carrying out research on musicals requires ingenuity, flexibility, and determination.

Viewing a performance is an important way to gather evidence about a musical. A live performance gives you a sense of the show's style and mood. You can see and hear how all of the elements—visual, choreographic, musical, verbal—come together. You can observe an audience's reaction to the show and get at least a sense of the demographics represented.

Yet there are some problems with relying on live performance as your only source of analysis. One is obvious: the performance disappears as soon as it is over. You have to hold tight to your memories as you write about a show after the fact, and memory can be notoriously fickle. In addition, directors and performers often make different decisions about how to interpret and perform a musical. Dance, costumes, lighting, and even elements of the music and script may vary widely from production to production. Further, if you write about a show solely based on your one-time observation, you may miss how the show comes across overall. Perhaps the performers were having an off night the evening you attended, and the songs fell flat. Maybe a snowstorm prevented more people from attending, and so the theater seemed empty.

Watching a film of a stage musical, whether a glossy Hollywood movie or an unauthorized fan video posted online, eliminates some issues with live performance and creates new ones. Because you can watch a film repeatedly, you do not have to rely on your memory as much. This may allow you to write a more precise analysis of a choreographic sequence or correctly copy down the lyrics of a song. Yet films cannot capture the energy of a stage musical, because a crucial element is missing: the audience. A stage musical involves give-and-take with audience members; as mentioned above, stage performers will sometimes improvise lyrics, dialogue, or movement based on the mood in the theater. Also, a film musical can differ dramatically from a stage version. The 1972 movie *Cabaret*, based on the 1966 Broadway production, changed the nationality of the main character, Sally Bowles; eliminated a subplot about a budding romance between an elderly couple, Herr Schultz and Fräulein Schneider; and cut several song-and-dance numbers. Finally, viewing a film cannot solve one of the main problems with viewing a live show: you only see one iteration of the performance. Whether you examine a stage or movie version, you must balance the authority of your analysis with the knowledge that other versions of the show exist.

Along with performances, published scripts, scores, and cast albums are indispensable sources. Still, keep in mind that performances may not follow published scripts and scores precisely, and a studio-produced cast album has been edited for audio-based circulation and only captures one particular performance. Moreover, the published score is usually a piano-vocal score that condenses the full score, performed by a variety of instruments in the pit orchestra, to one that can be played on a piano. Delving into a musical entails creative use of both published and unpublished materials.

When studying contemporary musicals or those in the relatively recent past, ethnographic approaches and oral history can be valuable sources of evidence. Ethnography involves the study of a human society or culture, usually through some kind of firsthand, experiential research. You might use participant-observation fieldwork to learn about the practices and culture surrounding musical theater, watching and taking notes on rehearsals and performances, conducting interviews with people involved in the production, and even participating as you research (a fun excuse to sing along to your favorite show tunes!). Oral history similarly involves interviews. You might talk with members of a musical's creative team, cast, or audience to learn about a production. Audio recording equipment can help you preserve interviews. Ethnographic practices involve ethical responsibilities, especially obtaining the permission of those to be observed or interviewed ahead of time.

Archival sources, generally taken to mean unpublished or out-of-print historical documents and objects, also give insight into a musical. Whether contained in an official archive or a shoebox in someone's garage, materials such as letters between members of a creative team, pieces of original sets and costumes, program booklets, or reviews in a local newspaper provide a road map through the world of a show. Archival sources are particularly valuable for studying the creative process. A published score or cast recording tells you about the final product, but the archive tells you how the musical was made: it might include lyrics that were dropped, a sketch of a costume idea that was discarded, or a photograph of a performer doing a dance that the choreographer cut before opening night. Archival documents can aid you in studying elements of a musical such as lighting design, which may be difficult to chart from viewing a performance alone. And if a musical's score or script was never published, archival research may be the only way to obtain a written record of what audiences saw and heard.

The digital revolution has changed the nature of research. Many archives have been digitized, making their materials widely accessible for the first time. One such archive, ProQuest Historical Newspapers, includes the collections of over forty newspapers dating back to the eighteenth century, including many African American newspapers as well as *The New York Times*, *The Washington Post*, and *The Christian Science Monitor*. Websites like Playbill.com, Broadway.com, and BroadwayLeague.com offer news and information on current and past Broadway productions.

With all of these sources, you must keep in mind whose history is being told and what other stories are overlooked given the current limitations of scholarly evidence. The voices of the creative team ring loudest in published materials and archives; we have few records of the stagehands and crew members who made the production happen. We have memoirs of star performers, but not of chorus-line dancers. We rarely know individual stories of audience members—what their motivations were for attending and how they felt about a performance. Musicals that made it to Broadway and had successful runs are more documented than those in smaller venues or those that "flopped."

Conclusion

The interdisciplinary nature of the stage musical and range of available approaches makes musical theater research a challenging, exciting field of study. There are countless ways to "read" a musical. The subject invites creative, wide-ranging, or even collaborative scholarship—like this essay, co-written by scholars trained in music and dance history.

The ways of studying stage musicals continue to expand as new sources and approaches emerge. Although this art form is predicated on live performance, the digital revolution has transformed the art, business, and scholarship surrounding musical theater. Technicians can mix sound in a theater in real time, affecting the audience's aural experience. Motion-capture technology promises new options for documenting choreography. Technology has also allowed for new types of spectacle, even as it has shown its limitations. Websites like YouTube.com and social media platforms like Facebook have opened new avenues for marketing and research, while tools like ProQuest Historical Newspapers have transformed the landscape for studying older musicals. Scholars in the twenty-first century have more options than ever for combining and creating approaches to make new contributions to this thriving field of inquiry.

NOTES

Chapter 1

1. The terms "Broadway," "Times Square," and "New York's Theater District" are often used interchangeably, but there are geographical distinctions to all three. A small segment of the avenue named Broadway cuts through Times Square, a neighborhood located in midtown Manhattan. Many of the large commercial theaters that have been built in or near this neighborhood are not, in fact, located on Broadway proper, but instead on various side streets to the east or west of the avenue; they are nonetheless referred to, both collectively and individually, as Broadway theaters. The "Broadway theater" designation has been assigned to any theater in New York that has more than 500 seats and hosts productions eligible for Tony awards. While the majority of so-called "Broadway theaters" are located in or near the Times Square neighborhood, some are not. The Vivian Beaumont Theater, for example, is located at Lincoln Center on West 65th Street, far north of Times Square.

2. http://www.theatrehistory.com/american/hornblow01.html (accessed July 30, 2013).

3. The first census in the United States was not taken until 1790, and estimates vary widely regarding the population of New York in the mid-eighteenth century, especially since some take into consideration the entire metropolitan area and some, like the one offered here, only include New York County. The population of the entire metropolitan area in 1849—including New York, Kings, Queens, Richmond, and Westchester counties—was, by Jackson's estimation, approximately 36,000 people.

4. http://www.granburyisd.org/cms/lib/TX01000552/Centricity/Domain/287/Fact_Sheet_U5_Growth_in_Population.pdf (accessed August 1, 2013).

5. These figures are for Manhattan only; the five boroughs that currently comprise contemporary New York City were not consolidated until 1898.

6. Mates notes that there was "no stigma . . . attached to a lady seen at a play" in the early years of American theater, and that women in fact contributed to the code of conduct within the theater through behavior and particularly flamboyant dress (1962, 64–7).

Notes

Chapter 2

1. My thanks to Gillian Rodger for her advice and assistance on this section. For a more in-depth discussion of nineteenth-century burlesque in the US, see http://www.oxfordreference.com/view/10.1093/acref/9780195314281.001.0001/acref-9780195314281-e-1270?rskey=uYIhbW&result=38.

2. Pastor's early life is inconsistently documented. Some sources list his birthdate as 1834, others as 1835 or 1837. His father was either a Spanish or Italian immigrant who worked either as a barber, a musician, a grocer, or a perfumer. All early biographical details about Pastor should be taken with a grain of salt.

3. http://www.digitalhistory.uh.edu/era.cfm?eraid=9.

4. In the first decades of the twentieth century, during the onset of the Great Migration, the population of black New Yorkers in the five boroughs nearly tripled, growing from approximately 60,000 in 1910 to approximately 152,000 by 1920. The population more than doubled in the next decade, leaping to approximately 328,000 by 1930.

5. Charles Hamm notes that musically and stylistically, coon songs are difficult to distinguish from ragtime songs, since both were "brash, spirited, slightly syncopated, breezy [and] almost always humorous," though coon songs were written and performed in dialect, "with a text somewhat less than complimentary to blacks" (1979, 321).

Chapter 3

1. Seasons on Broadway begin in the fall and continue through the spring of the following year.

2. Special, star-studded editions of the *Follies* appeared on Broadway as well in 1927, 1931, 1936, 1943, and 1957.

3. The Shubert Organization controls seventeen of the forty Broadway theaters currently in operation; several that the Shubert brothers did not build were acquired later in the twentieth century.

4. http://www.ascap.com/100.aspx#1914

5. http://www.actorsequity.org/aboutequity/timeline/timeline_1919.html

6. http://archives.nypl.org/scm/20858#bioghist.

7. http://lcweb2.loc.gov/diglib/ihas/loc.natlib.ihas.200038853/default.html.

8. Contemporary demographic breakdown courtesy of the Broadway League's 2013–14 audience study: http://www.broadwayleague.com/index.php?url_identifier=the-demographics-of-the-broadway-audience.

9. Cinderella musicals focused on working-class female characters who—as the result of hard work, optimism, and gumption—succeed in love and business by the end of the show. Often named for their female protagonists, Cinderella musicals were enormously popular through the 1920s, and are seen to reflect both the country's robust economy and the changing roles for American women during that decade.

Chapter 4

1. http://www.history.com/topics/great-depression. (accessed October 27, 2015).

2. The Hippodrome itself proved too big to sustain during the Depression era, and was razed in 1939.

3. http://www.broadwayleague.com/index.php?url_identifier=season-by-season-stats-1 (accessed November 5, 2015).

4. All statistics culled from ibdb.com (accessed November 5, 2015).

5. Show titles and dates all from Woll 1989, 135–53.

6. My thanks to Ryan Donovan for his input on the subject of dance in 1930s Broadway musicals.

7. Like many American folk tunes, "Frankie and Johnny" was based on actual events. In the song, Frankie learns that her man has been sleeping with another woman, so she kills him. In Gershwin's adaptation, she does so in error.

8. Founded in 1918, the Theatre Guild was an organization run by a board of directors, which selected and produced "high quality, noncommercial American and foreign plays." http://thetheatreguild.com/about/ (accessed December 7, 2015).

9. A new wave of controversy began after the composer Stephen Sondheim wrote a letter to *The New York Times* arguing that the changes playwright Suzan-Lori Parks and the director Diane Paulus made to *Porgy and Bess* were foolish and condescending to audiences. http://artsbeat.blogs.nytimes.com/2011/08/10/stephen-sondheim-takes-issue-with-plan-for-revamped-porgy-and-bess/ (accessed January 20, 2016).

10. http://www.kwf.org/foundation/marc-blitzstein/50-foundation/blitzstein/641-the-cradle-will-rock (accessed December 10, 2015).

11. http://www.loc.gov/teachers/classroommaterials/presentationsandactivities/presentations/timeline/depwwii/unions/ (accessed December 21, 2015).

12. http://www.illinoislaborhistory.org/labor-history-articles/memorial-day-massacre?rq=memorial=20day=20massacre (accessed December 21, 2015).

13. http://www.coleporter.org/bio.html

14. http://www.capitalnewyork.com/article/culture/2012/07/6132084/lorenz-hart-inside-out (accessed January 13, 2016).

Notes

Chapter 5

1. For more information on Hollywood's response to the Second World War, see *Hollywood Goes to War: How Politics, Profits, and Propaganda Shaped World War II Movies* (Koppes and Black 2000). For more information on the radio during the Second World War see *Radio Goes to War: The Cultural Politics of Propaganda During World War II* (Horton 2002).
2. http://www.shmoop.com/civil-rights-desegregation/timeline.html (accessed February 23, 2016).
3. http://www.archives.gov/publications/prologue/1996/summer/irving-berlin-1.html (accessed February 24, 2016).
4. Ibid.

Chapter 6

1. http://www.oed.com/view/Entry/198559?redirectedFrom=teenager#eid (accessed April 12, 2016).
2. Information provided in this section is drawn from my previous work on Off and Off Off Broadway's contributions to the American stage musical in the postwar era, in my books *The Theater Will Rock* (2006) and *Hard Times* (2013).
3. Much of the material in this section is adapted from my book *The Theater Will Rock*, as well as my article "Busted for Her Beauty: *Hair*'s Female Characters," which can be accessed at: http://www.brooklyn.cuny.edu/web/academics/centers/hitchcock/publications/amr/v43-2/wollman.php (accessed May 3, 2016).
4. This section is adapted from the introduction to the article "Women in the Music Industry in the 1970s," which can be accessed at: https://www.gilderlehrman.org/history-by-era/seventies/essays/women-and-music-industry-1970s (accessed May 3, 2016).
5. Material from this section is drawn from chapter two of my book *Hard Times* (2013).
6. This lyric has been changed by Sondheim in revivals to "I could understand a person / If he said to go away / I could understand a person / If he happened to be gay."
7. The material about the city's fiscal crisis is drawn from chapter nine of my book *Hard Times*.
8. For more on the departure of craft and industry workers from Times Square in the 1960s and 1970s, please see chapter six of Timothy R. White's book *Blue Collar Broadway: The Craft and Industry of American Theater* (2015, 162–200).

Chapter 7

1. http://www.nycgo.com/articles/nyc-statistics-page (accessed June 2, 2016).

2. Statistics courtesy of the Broadway League: https://www.broadwayleague.com/research/grosses-broadway-nyc/ (accessed July 12, 2016).

3. For more on the reception history of *Wicked*, see chapters six and seven of Stacy Wolf's *Changed for Good: A Feminist History of the Broadway Musical* (2011).

4. http://thehill.com/blogs/in-the-know/in-the-know/272964-obama-hamilton-is-the-only-thing-dick-cheney-and-i-agree-on (accessed July 14, 2016).

Chapter 8

1. Some of this material appears in a different form in my chapter, "Broadway Junior," in *Childhood and the Child in Musical Theatre* (Leve and Ruwe, forthcoming).

2. http://itheatrics.com/jtf/ (accessed July 26, 2016). The Junior Theatre Festival has proven to be so successful that they are launching a West Coast version in 2017.

3. http://www.nytimes.com/2016/01/22/theater/a-multitude-of-fans-with-a-high-regard-for-broadway.html?_r=0 (accessed July 26, 2016). http://www.nytimes.com/2016/01/25/theater/broadwaycon-carried-on-even-as-broadway-went-dark.html (accessed July 26, 2016). http://www.nytimes.com/2016/04/08/theater/broadwaycon-to-expand-to-javits-center-next-year.html (accessed July 26, 2016).

4. BroadwayCon surpassed all expectations and moved to the Javits Center in 2017 to accommodate more attendees. http://www.broadwaycon.com/ (accessed July 26, 2016).

5. http://www.oxforddictionaries.com/us/definition/american_english/amateur (accessed July 24, 2016).

6. Ibid.

7. Tim MacDonald, personal email, April 24, 2013.

8. Putnam 2000, 402.

9. See Cerniglia and Mitchell 2014, 129–45.

10. Carlson 2003, 2.

11. Ibid., 66.

12. http://www.samuelfrench.com/; http://www.tamswitmark.com/about/; http://www.dramatists.com/text/contact.asp; http://www.rnh.com/our_history.html (accessed August 31, 2015).

Notes

13. Riis 2008, 245.

14. http://www.mtishows.com/content.asp?id=1_2_0 (accessed August 31, 2015). Also see Riis 2008.

15. http://www.tamswitmark.com/shows/ (accessed August 31, 2015).

16. Carol Edelson, personal interview, New York, October 19, 2012. The other half is professional productions.

17. See Chapman 2011, 392–407. The National Public Radio analysis of *Dramatics* magazine estimates 12,000 high schools have theater programs. See http://www.npr.org/sections/ed/2015/07/30/427138970/the-most-popular-high-school-plays-and-musicals (accessed July 26, 2016).

18. https://www.nhsmta.com/pages/participating-theaters (accessed July 26, 2016).

19. http://www.npr.org/sections/ed/2015/07/30/427138970/the-most-popular-high-school-plays-and-musicals (accessed July 26, 2016).

20. Commentator Howard Sherman has been on the front lines of these issues. See, for example, http://www.americantheater.org/2015/01/06/why-i-care-about-censorship-on-school-stages/; http://www.splc.org/article/2014/08/censorship-takes-the-stage-topical-plays-draw-criticism-from-officials; http://www.broadwayworld.com/article/Two-High-School-Theater-Controversies-Make-National-Coalition-Against-Censorshipss-List-of-Top-40-Free-Speech-Defenders-of-2014-20141027 (all accessed July 26, 2016).

21. http://www.marilynizdebskiproductions.com/past-shows (accessed July 16, 2015). I thank Marilyn for her generosity in speaking to me and allowing me to observe auditions and rehearsals.

22. http://www.marilynizdebskiproductions.com/marilyn-short-film-sam-stoich (accessed July 1, 2015).

23. Ibid.

24. "Who Is Freddie Gershon?" (June 2012). http://www.freddiegershon.com/FreddiePrintBioJune2012.pdf (accessed June 10, 2013).

25. Quoted in Papatola 2005, 13–14. Also see Perlov 2009, 6–7.

26. Robert Lee, personal phone interview, August 27, 2015.

27. Ibid.

28. Ibid.

29. http://schools.nyc.gov/offices/teachlearn/arts/Bway%20JR/Why_We_Tell_FINAL-LD.pdf (accessed August 23, 2015); http://itheatricals.com/bio_pdfs/Cynthiabio.pdf (accessed August 23, 2015); http://www.itheatricals.com/history.html (accessed August 24, 2015).

30. MTI has also developed School Editions of some titles—full-length, cleaned-up versions for high schools. These include *Rent* and *Les Misérables*, for example. On the pilot production *Rent School Edition* at Stagedoor Manor summer camp, see Rapkin 2010.

31. http://www.educationupdate.com/archives/2006/May/html/mad-lettheshow. html (accessed November 29, 2015).

32. Though MTI licenses and sells the product, Disney creates their own JR. and KIDS' scripts as well and their "ShowKit" materials. See my article, "Not Only on Broadway: Disney JR. and Disney KIDS Across the US," in *The Disney Musical: Stage, Screen, and Beyond* (Rodosthenous 2017).

33. Papatola 2005, 13.

34. Gershon, personal interview, December 11, 2014. I thank Freddie Gershon for his generosity in speaking to me and Carol Edelson at MTI for her help.

35. http://itheatrics.com/adapting-broadway-musicals/ (accessed August 27, 2015).

36. For a description of the process, see http://itheatrics.com/adapting-broadway-musicals/ (accessed August 28, 2015).

37. I also discuss the difference between full-length and JR. musicals in my article on Disney JR. and Disney KIDS.

38. Robert Lee, personal interview, August 27, 2015.

39. http://www.mtishows.com/show_detail.asp?showid=000223 (accessed August 30, 2015).

40. Some of this material appears differently framed in "Not Only on Broadway: Disney Junior Across the US," in *The Disney Musical: Stage, Screen, and Beyond* (Rodosthenous 2017).

41. http://www.opendurham.org/buildings/west-durham-graded-school-no-2-ek-powe-school-elementary-school; http://museumofdurhamhistory.org/ beneathourfeet/landmarks/EKPowe (accessed July 27, 2016).

42. Lia Pachino, phone interview, July 27, 2016.

43. DMIS resembles another successful NYC-based musical theater outreach program: Broadway Junior. Supported by the Shubert Foundation, Music Theater International, and the New York City Department of Education, Broadway Junior was the brainchild of MTI Cofounder and CEO Freddie Gershon and supports the production of Broadway Junior titles, including some Disney shows, at a handful of NYC public middle schools each year.

44. Cerniglia and Mitchell 2014, 140.

45. Kristin Horsley, personal communication, May 5, 2015.

46. J. Ashby, personal communication, May 29, 2015.

47. The Tennessee Performing Arts Center sponsors school visits to its theaters for kids to see a professional play, but some schools lack the resources to organize permission slips, bus rental, and so on to get the children downtown. Joe Ashby, personal communication, May 7, 2015. I thank TPAC and DMIS participating teachers for their generosity in welcoming me to Nashville, and Lisa Mitchell for her help and advice.

Notes

48. Buena Vista Enhanced Option Elementary 2015, personal communication, May 7, 2015.

49. Some of this material appears differently framed in my article " 'The Hills Are Alive with the Sound of Music': Musical Theater at Girls' Jewish Summer Camps in Maine, USA," *Contemporary Theatre Review* (forthcoming).

50. Personal correspondence, July 2012. I want to thank the camps' directors for welcoming me to observe rehearsals and performances.

51. Emma, personal correspondence, July 2012. Most of the girls to whom I spoke and who wrote me notes did not share their last names.

52. https://www.hct.org/online/; http://www.stillpointetheatre.com/; http://www.kelseytheatre.net/ (all accessed July 27, 2016).

53. Kyrus, personal interview, January 23, 2015. I thank the community of artists at Kelsey for their time and generosity, and for welcoming me and allowing me to observe auditions and rehearsals.

54. Jared, Nikema, personal interviews, October 2012.

55. Jeff Bowen and Hunter Bell, *[title of show] Original Cast Recording* (New York: Ghostlight Records, 2006); https://www.amazon.co.uk/gp/dmusic/cloudplayer/web?ie=UTF8&albumAsin=B002O4W9G8&playNow=1&ref_=dm_ws_pm_bb_pa_xx_xx#albumDetail/%5Btitle+of+show%5D+-+Original+Cast+Recording/TITLE+OF+SHOW+ORIGINAL+CAST+RECORDING/TITLE+OF+SHOW+ORIGINAL+CAST (accessed March 6, 2016).

56. Ibid.

57. David Sterritt, " 'Company': Amusing, Inventive, Hummable," *Boston After Dark*, April 1, 1970, 4.

58. Chris Jones, "REVIEW: 'Kinky Boots' at Bank of America Theatre," *Chicagotribune.com*, October 17, 2012. http://www.chicagotribune.com/entertainment/chi-kinky-boots-review-chicago-column.html (accessed March 10, 2016).

59. Ibid.

60. Chris Jones, "These 'Boots' Are Made for Reworkin'," *Chicagotribune.com*, November 1, 2012. http://www.chicagotribune.com/entertainment/ct-ott-1102-jones-loop-20121101-story.html (accessed March 10, 2016).

61. Zeigler 1977, 229–30.

62. Ibid, 231.

63. Ibid, 1.

64. Ibid, 268.

65. Ibid, 269.

66. Alvin Klein, "State Is a Testing Ground for Broadway," *The New York Times*, April 19, 1992, sec. N.Y. / Region. http://www.nytimes.com/1992/04/19/nyregion/state-is-a-testing-ground-for-broadway.html (accessed March 10, 2016).

67. Ibid.

68. Two not-for-profit theaters—Lincoln Center Theater and Roundabout Theatre Company—each had a revival running on Broadway, and five musicals had opened cold on Broadway.

69. http://www.lesmis.com/uk/history/facts-and-figures/ (accessed October 13, 2015).

70. For more on the early days of sending identically staged copies of shows abroad, see Joe Brown, "McMiz: Mass Marketing the 'Musical Sensation,'" *Washington Post*, July 3, 1988; and Prece and Everett 2008.

71. Michiko Kakutani, in an editorial for *The New York Times*, agrees. She laments that where we once sent the world our best cultural material, like *My Fair Lady* and plays by Eugene O'Neill, we now export *Cats* and *Baywatch*, and myriad "trash." She makes no room for the notion that anything contemporary (she writes in 1997) has artistic merit. See "America Used to Put Its Best Cultural Foot Forward . . ." *The New York Times*, June 8, 1997.

72. Hee, personal communication.

73. We would like to thank Elizabeth Wollman for inviting us to co-author this essay and Ryan Bañagale for his thoughtful feedback on an earlier draft. On the unfixed nature of musicals, see Kirle 2005, xx, 1–20, 125; and Lovensheimer 2011, 20–31.

74. "Highbrow," "lowbrow," and "middlebrow" are terms describing cultural levels with both class and racial connotations. "Highbrow" refers to the purported taste of the intellectual and cultural elite for arts such as the opera, symphony, or classic works of literature. "Lowbrow" refers to cultural products associated with the working classes, or the masses, like comic books, professional wrestling, and tabloids. "Middlebrow" culture falls in between. The term "middlebrow," which like "lowbrow" is generally considered derogatory, arose in the mid-twentieth century to refer to cultural products that enjoyed widespread popularity, such as musicals and Book-of-the-Month clubs. For more information, see Levine 1988 and Rubin.

75. "Abuela" is Spanish for "grandmother," and Abuela Claudia is a grandmotherly figure for several characters in the musical. You can view a short clip of "Paciencia y Fe" from the Broadway production of *In the Heights*, posted by "In the Heights Broadway," May 19, 2009, at https://www.youtube.com/watch?v=qo911wdE3rk

76. For further discussion of themes of immigration in this scene and *In the Heights* as a whole, see Craft 2014, 274–303.

77. Examples include bruce mcclung, *Lady in the Dark: Biography of a Musical* (2007); Tim Carter, *Oklahoma! The Making of an American Musical* (2007); Dominic McHugh, *Loverly: The Life and Times of My Fair Lady* (2012); and Paul R. Laird, *Wicked: A Musical Biography* (2011).

78. "*Chicago* Broadway Revival (1996)," accessed January 27, 2017, ovrtur.com/production/2882788, "*Shrek The Musical* images," accessed January 27, 2017,

http://www.fanpop.com/clubs/shrek-the-musical/images/18754962/title/
shrek-musical-poster-photo.

79. In addition to publishing on the demographics of the Broadway audience, the
League publishes reports on audience demographics for touring Broadway
productions, Broadway's economic impact on New York City, and the economic
impact of touring Broadway. "Research Reports," The Broadway League, http://
www.broadwayleague.com/index.php?url_identifier=research-reports-1,
accessed July 24, 2014.

80. Many discussions of *Oklahoma!* comment on its historical context. Scholarship
focusing especially on how it spoke to wartime concerns includes Wilsch Case
2006; Kirle 2003; and Schiff 2014.

81. See for example Bial 2005 and Most 2004.

82. See for example Riis 1989 and Woll 1989.

83. See for example Haenni 2008 and Koegel 2009.

84. See for example Miller 1998 and Clum 1999.

85. See for example Hoffman 2014.

86. See for example Wolf 2011.

87. Wolf 2002.

88. See also Krasner 2002, 239–88. For more on Henry Louis Gates's term
"signifyin(g)" as it applies to African American performance, see Dagel Caponi
1999, 22–3.

BIBLIOGRAPHY

Allen, Robert C. *Horrible Prettiness: Burlesque and American Culture*. Chapel Hill and London: University of North Carolina Press, 1991.

Atkinson, Brooks. "The Play: Design and Dance in an 'American Revue' That Represents Modern Taste in Artistry." *The New York Times*, October 6, 1932, p. 19.

Bagli, Charles V. "After 30 Years, a Rebirth Is Complete." *The New York Times*, December 4, 2010, P.A17.

Baldinger, Scott. "Marketing Broadway as a Cool Spot." *The New York Times*, April 14, 1996, H5.

Barnes, Clive. "'Hair'—It's Fresh and Frank." *The New York Times*, April 30, 1968, p. 40.

Barron, James. "100 Years Ago, an Intersection's New Name: Times Square." *The New York Times*, April 8, 2004. http://www.nytimes.com/2004/04/08/nyregion/100-years-ago-an-intersection-s-new-name-times-square.html?pagewanted=print

Beckert, Sven. *The Monied Metropolis: New York City and the Consolidation of the American Bourgeoisie, 1850–1896*. Cambridge and New York: Cambridge University Press, 2001.

Behr, Edward. *Les Misérables: History in the Making* (New York: Arcade Publishing, 1996).

Bernheim, Alfred L. *The Business of the Theatre: An Economic History of the American Theatre, 1750–1932*. New York: Benjamin Blom, [1932] 1964.

Bernstein, Iver. *The New York City Draft Riots: Their Significance for American Society and Politics in the Age of the Civil War*. New York: Oxford University Press, 1990.

Bial, Henry. *Acting Jewish: Negotiating Ethnicity on the American Stage and Screen*. Ann Arbor: University of Michigan Press, 2005.

Bianco, Anthony. *Ghosts of 42nd Street: A History of America's Most Famous Block*. New York: HarperCollins, 2004.

Block, Geoffrey. "The Melody (and the Words) Linger On: American Musical Comedies of the 1920s and 1930s." In *The Cambridge Companion to the Musical*, edited by William A. Everett and Paul R. Laird. Second edition. Cambridge and New York: Cambridge University Press, 2008, pp. 103–23.

Block, Geoffrey. *Enchanted Evenings: The Broadway Musical from* Show Boat *to Sondheim and Lloyd Webber*. Second edition. New York: Oxford University Press, 2009.

Bohlen, Celestine. "Broadway Shows Rebound, But With Fewer Tourists." *The New York Times*, October 11, 2001, p. E1.

Bordman, Gerald. *American Musical Theatre: A Chronicle*. Third edition. New York: Oxford University Press, 2001.

Bibliography

Bowen, Jeff and Hunter Bell. *[title of show] Original Cast Recording*. New York: Ghostlight Records, 2006. https://www.amazon.co.uk/gp/dmusic/cloudplayer/web?ie=UTF8&albumAsin=B002O4W9G8&playNow=1&ref_=dm_ws_pm_bb_pa_xx_xx#albumDetail/%5Btitle+of+show%5D+-+Original+Cast+Recording/TITLE+OF+SHOW+ORIGINAL+CAST+RECORDING/TITLE+OF+SHOW+ORIGINAL+CAST (accessed March 6, 2016).

"Bringing Broadway to Korea," *Korea Times*, September 1, 2005.

Brinkley, Alan. "The Legacies of World War II." In *Major Problems in American History Since 1945*, edited by Robert Griffith and Paula Baker. Third edition. Boston: Wadsworth, Cengage Learning, 2007, pp. 16–24.

Bristow, Eugene K. and J. Kevin Butler. "*Company*, About Face! The Show That Revolutionized the American Musical." *American Music* 5, no. 3 (Autumn 1987): 241–54.

Brown, Thomas Allston. *A History of the New York Stage, From the First Performance in 1732 to 1901*. Volume I. New York: Dodd, Mead, 1903. https://play.google.com/books/reader?id=CDALAAAAIAAJ&printsec=frontcover&output=reader&authuser=0&hl=en&pg=GBS.PR2

Burrows, Edwin G. and Mike Wallace. *Gotham: A History of New York City to 1898*. New York and London: Oxford University Press, 1999.

Burston, Jonathan. "Theatre Space as Virtual Place: Audio Technology, the Reconfigured Singing Body, and the Megamusical." *Popular Music* 17, no. 2 (1998).

Carlson, Marvin. *The Haunted Stage: Theater as Memory Machine*. Ann Arbor: University of Michigan Press, 2003.

Carter, Tim. *Oklahoma! The Making of an American Musical*. New Haven: Yale University Press, 2007.

Cerniglia, Ken, and Lisa Mitchell. "The Business of Children in Disney's Theater." In *Entertaining Children: The Participation of Youth in the Entertainment Industry*, edited by Gillian Arrighi and Victor Emeljanow. London: Palgrave Macmillan, 2014, pp. 129–45.

Caulfield, Keith. "Hamilton's Historic Chart Debut: By the Numbers." *Billboard*, October 7, 2015. http://www.billboard.com/articles/columns/chart-beat/6722015/hamilton-cast-album-billboard-200 (accessed January 9, 2017).

Chapman, Jennifer. "Knowing Your Audience." In *The Oxford Handbook of the American Musical*, edited by Raymond Knapp, Mitchell Morris, and Stacy Wolf. New York: Oxford University Press, 2011, pp. 392–407.

Charyn, Jerome. *Gangsters and Gold Diggers: Old New York, the Jazz Age, and the Birth of Broadway*. New York: Thunder's Mouth, 2003.

Chesluk, Benjamin. *Money Jungle: Imagining the New Times Square*. New Brunswick, NJ: Rutgers University Press, 2008.

Clum, John. *Something for the Boys: Musical Theater and Gay Culture*. New York: Palgrave, 1999.

Coonan, Clifford. "Beijing Seeks a Broadway of Its Own; $686-Million Project Will Feature 32 Theatres," *Edmonton Journal* (Alberta, Canada), January 8, 2009.

Covach, John and Andrew Flory. *What's That Sound? An Introduction to Rock and Its History*. Fourth edition. New York and London: WW Norton, 2015.

Cox, Gordon. "Broadway's *The Lion King* Becomes Top Grossing Title of All Time." *Variety*, September 22, 2014. http://variety.com/2014/legit/news/broadwayslion-king-box-office-top-title-1201310676/ (accessed June 23, 2016).

Craft, Elizabeth Titrington. "Becoming American Onstage: Broadway Narratives of Immigrant Experiences in the United States". PhD dissertation, Harvard University, 2014.

Dagel Caponi, Gena. "Introduction: The Case for an African American Aesthetic." In *Signifyin(g), Sanctifyin', & Slam Dunking: A Reader in African American Expressive Culture*, edited by Gena Dagel Caponi. Amherst: University of Massachusetts Press, 1999.

"*Dahomey* on Broadway: Williams and Walker Make an Opening at the New York Theatre and Hold It." *The New York Times*, February 19, 1903.

Dalzell, Rebecca. "The Gilded Age Origins of New York City's Rooftop Gardens." *Curbed*, July 16, 2014. http://ny.curbed.com/archives/2014/07/16/the_gilded_age_origins_of_new_york_citys_rooftop_gardens.php (accessed June 8, 2015).

Decker, Todd. Show Boat: *Performing Race in an American Musical*. New York: Oxford University Press, 2013.

Domosh, Mona. "Those 'Gorgeous Incongruities': Polite Politics and Public Space on the Streets of Nineteenth-Century New York City." *Annals of the Association of American Geographers* 88, no. 2 (June 1998): 209–26.

Dorbian, Iris. *Great Producers: Visionaries of the American Theater*. New York: Allworth Press, 2008.

Dorman, James H. "Shaping the Popular Image of Post-Reconstruction American Blacks: The 'Coon Song' Phenomenon of the Gilded Age." *American Quarterly*, 40, no. 4 (December 1998): 450–71.

Douglas, Ann. *Terrible Honesty: Mongrel Manhattan in the 1920s*. New York: Farrar, Straus and Giroux, 1995.

Dvoskin, Michelle. "Audiences and Critics." In *The Oxford Handbook of the American Musical*, edited by Raymond Knapp, Mitchell Morris, and Stacy Wolf. New York: Oxford University Press, 2011, pp. 365–77.

Einhorn, Bruce. "Broadway in China! It's a Mess!" BloombergBusiness, Bloomberg. com, June 9, 2015. http://www.bloomberg.com/news/articles/2015-06-09/broadway-in-china-it-s-a-mess-

Erenberg, Lewis A. *Steppin' Out: New York Nightlife and the Transformation of American Culture 1890–1930*. Chicago: University of Chicago Press, 1981.

Farber, David. "Introduction." In *The Sixties: From Memory to History*, edited by David Farber. Chapel Hill and London: University of North Carolina Press, 1994, pp. 1–10.

Fass, Paula S. Review of *A Cycle of Outrage: America's Reaction to the Juvenile Delinquent in the 1950s* by James Gilbert. *History of Education Quarterly* 27, no. 1 (1987): 152–22.

Forbes, Camille. *Introducing Bert Williams: Burnt Cork, Broadway, and the Story of America's First Black Star*. New York: Basic Books, 2008.

Freeman, John W. "Opera." In *The Encyclopedia of New York City*, edited by Kenneth T. Jackson. New Haven and London: Yale University Press, 1995, pp. 865–6.

Bibliography

Frick, John W. and Martha S. LoMonaco. "Theater." In *The Encyclopedia of New York City*, edited by Kenneth T. Jackson. New Haven and London: Yale University Press, 1995, pp. 1165–76.

Friedman, Andrea. *Prurient Interests: Gender, Democracy, and Obscenity in New York City, 1909–1945.* New York: Columbia University Press, 2000.

"George M. Cohan, 64, Dies at Home Here." *The New York Times*, November 6, 1942, p. 20.

Graebner, William. "The 'Containment' of Juvenile Delinquency: Social Engineering and American Youth Culture in the Postwar Era." *American Studies* 27, no. 1 (1986): 81–97.

Gray, Christopher. "Streetscapes/Astor Place: It's Only Two Blocks, But It's Full of Literary History." *The New York Times,* March 2, 2003. http://www.nytimes.com/2003/03/02/realestate/streetscapes-astor-place-it-s-only-two-blocks-but-it-s-full-of-literary-history.html

Graziano, John. "Images of African Americans: African American Musical Theatre, *Show Boat* and *Porgy and Bess.*" In *The Cambridge Companion to the Musical,* edited by William A. Everett and Paul R. Laird. Second edition. Cambridge and New York: Cambridge University Press, 2008, pp. 89–102.

Great Migration. http://www.history.com/topics/black-history/great-migration (accessed May 28, 2015).

Green, Stanley. *Broadway Musicals of the 30s.* New York: Da Capo Press, 1971.

Green, William. "Burlesque." In *The Encyclopedia of New York City*, edited by Kenneth T. Jackson. New Haven and London: Yale University Press, 1995, pp. 168–9.

Greher, Gena R. "Night & Day: Cole Porter, Hip Hop, Their Shared Sensibilities and Their Teachable Moments." *College Music Symposium* 49/50 (2009/10), pp. 158–63.

Griffith, Robert and Paula Baker, eds. *Major Problems in American History Since 1945.* Third edition. Boston: Wadsworth, Cengage Learning, 2007.

Grimes, William. "Ezra Stone, 76, Henry Aldrich on the Radio." *The New York Times*, March 5, 1994, p. 12.

Haenni, Sabine. *The Immigrant Scene: Ethnic Amusements in New York, 1880–1920.* Minneapolis: University of Minnesota Press, 2008.

Hamm, Charles. *Yesterdays: Popular Song in America.* New York and London: WW Norton and Company, 1979.

Hammack, David C. "Consolidation." In *The Encyclopedia of New York City*, edited by Kenneth T. Jackson. New Haven and London: Yale University Press, 1995, pp. 277–8.

Hardy, Camille. "Bringing Bourrées to Broadway: George Balanchine's Career in the Commercial Theater." *World Literature Today* 80, no. 2 (March–April 2006), pp. 16–18.

Hauser, Karen. *The Demographics of the Broadway Audience 2012–2013.* New York: Broadway League, 2013.

Healy, Patrick. "Broadway on the Elbe." *New York Times*, December 9, 2012, p. C1.

Healy, Patrick. "Broadway Sees Benefits of Building Black Audience," *New York Times*, June 28, 2010, p. A1. http://www.nytimes.com/2010/06/28/theater/28diverse.html

Healy, Patrick. "Musicals Couldn't Be Hotter Off Broadway (by 7,000 Miles)," *The New York Times*, December 8, 2013, p. A1.

Healy, Patrick. "Flops on Broadway? Fix Them Overseas," *The New York Times*, July 31, 2011, RAR1.

Heroux, Gerard H. "George M. Cohan." *Rhode Island Music Hall of Fame Historical Archive*. http://www.ripopmusic.org/musical-artists/composers/george-m-cohan/ (accessed March 19, 2015).

Hirsch, Foster. *The Boys from Syracuse: The Shuberts' Theatrical Empire*. Carbondale and Edwardsville: Southern Illinois University Press, 1998.

Hischak, Thomas. *Off-Broadway Musicals Since 1919: From* Greenwich Village Follies *to* The Toxic Avenger. Lanham, Toronto, and Plymouth, UK: Scarecrow Press, 2011.

Hischak, Thomas. *The Oxford Companion to the American Musical: Theatre, Film, and Television*. New York: Oxford University Press, 2008.

Hoffman, Warren. *The Great White Way: Race and the Broadway Musical*. New Brunswick and London: Rutgers University Press, 2014.

Hofler, Robert. "B'way's 2-Way Street," *Variety*, March 14, 2004. http://variety.com/2004/legit/news/b-way-s-2-way-street-1117901255/

Holland, Bernard. "Court Permits Shuberts to Buy More Theaters." *The New York Times*, September 5, 1981, p. 12.

Holmes, Sean P. "All the World's a Stage! The Actors' Strike of 1919." *The Journal of American History* 91, no. 4 (March 2005): 1291–1317.

Horn, Barbara Lee. *The Age of* Hair: *Evolution and Impact of Broadway's First Rock Musical*. New York: Greenwood Press, 1991.

Hornblow, Arthur. *A History of the Theatre in America*, volume I. Philadelphia: JB Lipincott and Company, 1919. http://www.theatrehistory.com/american/hornblow01.html (accessed March 10, 2016).

Horton, Gerd. *Radio Goes to War: The Cultural Politics of Propaganda During World War II*. Berkeley and Los Angeles: University of California Press, 2002.

Jackson, Kenneth T. "Bowery." In *The Encyclopedia of New York City*, edited by Kenneth T. Jackson. New Haven and London: Yale University Press, 1995, pp. 131–2.

Jasen, David A. *Tin Pan Alley: An Encyclopedia of the Golden Age of American Song*. New York and London: Routledge, 2003.

Jasen, David A. and Gene Jones. *Spreadin' Rhythm Around: Black Popular Songwriters, 1880–1930*. New York: Routledge, 2005.

Johnson, Helen Armstead. "*Shuffle Along*: Keynote of the Harlem Renaissance." In *The Theater of Black Americans: A Collection of Critical Essays*, edited by Errol Hill. New York: Applause Theatre, 1987.

Johnson, James Weldon. *Black Manhattan*. New York: Da Capo Press, 1991.

Johnson, Reed. "Brazil Goes Broadway Yet Keeps Its Own Beat," *Los Angeles Times*, July 31, 2005.

Jones, Chris. "'Kinky Boots' at Bank of America Theatre," *Chicagotribune.com*, October 17, 2012. http://www.chicagotribune.com/entertainment/chi-kinky-boots-review-chicago-column.html (accessed March 10, 2016).

Bibliography

Jones, Chris. "These 'Boots' Are Made for Reworkin'," *Chicagotribune.com*, November 1, 2012. http://www.chicagotribune.com/entertainment/ct-ott-1102-jones-loop-20121101-story.html (accessed March 10, 2016).

Jones, Douglas A., Jr. "Slavery, Performance, and the Design of African American Theatre." In *The Cambridge Companion to African American Theatre*, edited by Harvey Young. New York: Cambridge University Press, 2013, pp. 15–33.

Jones, John Bush. *Our Musicals, Ourselves: A Social History of the American Musical Theatre*. Hanover and London: Brandeis University Press, 2003.

Kantrowitz, Nathan. "Population." In *The Encyclopedia of New York City*, edited by Kenneth T. Jackson. New Haven and London: Yale University Press, 1995, pp. 920–3.

Kennedy, John A. "The Concert Saloons: Report of the Superintendent of Police." *The New York Times*, January 5, 1862, p. 5.

Kennedy, Shawn G. "Disney and Developer are Chosen to Build 42nd Street Hotel Complex." *The New York Times*, May 12, 1995, p. B2.

Kenrick, John. *Musical Theatre: A History*. New York: Continuum International, 2008.

King, Bobbi. "A Legend in His Own Lifetime: Conversation with Eubie Blake." *The Black Perspective in Music* 1, no. 2 (Autumn 1973), pp. 151–6.

Kirle, Bruce. "Reconciliation, Resolution, and the Political Role of *Oklahoma!* in American Consciousness." *Theatre Journal* 55, no. 2 (2003), 251–74.

Kirle, Bruce. *Unfinished Show Business: Broadway Musicals As Works-In-Progress*. Carbondale: Southern Illinois University Press, 2005.

Kissel, Howard. *David Merrick: The Abominable Showman*. New York and London: Applause, 1993.

Klein, Alvin. "State Is a Testing Ground for Broadway." *The New York Times*, April 19, 1992, sec. N.Y. / Region. http://www.nytimes.com/1992/04/19/nyregion/state-is-a-testing-ground-for-broadway.html (accessed March 10, 2016).

Klein, Milton M., ed. *The Empire State: A History of New York*. Ithaca and London: Cornell University Press, 2001.

Knapp, Raymond. *The American Musical and the Formation of National Identity*. Princeton and Oxford: Princeton University Press, 2005.

Knapp, Raymond. *The American Musical and the Performance of Personal Identity*. Princeton and Oxford: Princeton University Press, 2006.

Koegel, John. *Music in German Immigrant Theater: New York City, 1840–1940*. Rochester, NY: University of Rochester Press, 2009.

Koppes, Clayton R., and Gregory D. Black. *Hollywood Goes to War: How Politics, Profits, and Propaganda Shaped World War II Movies*. London: Tauris Parke, 2000.

Krasner, David. *A Beautiful Pageant: African American Theatre, Drama, and Performance in the Harlem Renaissance, 1910–1927*. New York: Palgrave MacMillan, 2002.

Krasner, Orly Leah. "Birth Pangs, Growing Pains and Sibling Rivalry: Musical Theatre in New York, 1900–1920." In *The Cambridge Companion to the Musical*, edited by William A. Everett and Paul R. Laird. Second edition. Cambridge and New York: Cambridge University Press, 2008, pp. 54–71.

Laird, Paul R. *Wicked: A Musical Biography*. Lanham, MD: Scarecrow Press, 2011.

LeMoyne, James. "New York City Reports '83 Tourism Windfall." *The New York Times*, January 9, 1984, p. D11.

Leonard, W. T. *Broadway Bound: A Guide to Shows that Died Aborning*. Metuchen, NJ: Scarecrow Press, 1983.

Leve, James. *American Musical Theater*. New York: Oxford University Press, 2016.

Leve, James, and Donelle Ruwe, eds. *Childhood and the Child in Musical Theatre*. New York: Ashgate, forthcoming.

Levine, Lawrence W. *Highbrow/Lowbrow: The Emergence of Cultural Hierarchy in America*. Cambridge and London: Harvard University Press, 1988.

Lewis, Robert M. *From Traveling Show to Vaudeville: Theatrical Spectacle in America, 1830–1910*. Baltimore and London: Johns Hopkins University Press, 2003.

Lott, Eric. *Love and Theft: Blackface Minstrelsy and the American Working Class*. New York: Oxford University Press, 1993.

Lovensheimer, Jim. *South Pacific: Paradise Rewritten*. New York: Oxford University Press, 2010.

Lovensheimer, Jim. "Texts and Authors." In *The Oxford Handbook of the American Musical*, edited by Raymond Knapp, Mitchell Morris, and Stacy Wolf. New York: Oxford University Press, 2011, pp. 20–31.

Lundskaer-Nielsen, Miranda. "The Prince-Sondheim Legacy." In *The Oxford Handbook of Sondheim Studies*, edited by Robert Gordon. New York: Oxford University Press, 2014.

Lyman, Rick. "Under-18 Crowd Doubles, Broadway Study Finds," *New York Times*, March 3, 1998, P.E7. http://www.nytimes.com/1998/03/03/theater/under-18-crowd-doubles-broadway-study-finds.html

Magee, Jeffrey. *Irving Berlin's American Musical Theater*. New York: Oxford University Press, 2012.

Marchand, Roland. "Visions of Classlessness." In *Major Problems in American History Since 1945*, edited by Robert Griffith and Paula Baker. Third edition. Boston: Wadsworth, Cengage Learning, 2007, pp. 97–109.

Marcosson, Isaac F. and Daniel Frohman. *Charles Frohman: Manager and Man*. New York and London: Harper and Brothers, 1916.

Marks, Peter. "Laughing Away the Tears and Fears." *New York Times*, October 28, 2001, p. AR5.

Mast, Gerald. *Can't Help Singin': The American Musical on Stage and Screen*. New York: Overlook Press, 1987.

Mates, Julian. *America's Musical Stage: Two Hundred Years of Musical Theatre*. Westport: Greenwood Press, 1985.

Mates, Julian. *The American Musical Stage Before 1800*. New Brunswick: Rutgers University Press, 1962.

mcclung, bruce. *Lady in the Dark: Biography of a Musical*. Oxford: Oxford University Press, 2007.

McHugh, Dominic. *Loverly: The Life and Times of My Fair Lady*. New York: Oxford University Press, 2012.

McKinley, Jesse. "Sales Plummet As Broadway Posts Losses." *The New York Times*, September 19, 2001, p. E1.

Bibliography

McNamara, Brooks. *The New York Concert Saloon: The Devil's Own Nights*. New York and Cambridge: Cambridge University Press, 2002.

Miller, D.A. *Place for Us: Essay on the Broadway Musical*. Cambridge, MA: Harvard University Press, 1998.

Miller, Tom. "The Lost 1882 Casino Theatre—39th Street and Broadway." *Daytonian in Manhattan: The Stories Behind the Buildings, Statues and Other Points of Interest that Make Manhattan Fascinating*, June 2013. http://daytoninmanhattan. blogspot.com/2013/06/the-lost-1882-casino-theatre-39th.html (accessed June 8, 2015).

Most, Andrea. *Making Americans: Jews and the Broadway Musical*. Cambridge: Harvard University Press, 2004.

Ndounou, Monica White. "Early Black Americans on Broadway." In *The Cambridge Companion to African American Theatre*, edited by Harvey Young. New York: Cambridge University Press, 2013, pp 59–84.

Newman, Andrew Adam. "It's Broadway Gone Viral, With a Musical Meted Out via Twitter." *The New York Times*, August 17, 2009, p. B4. http://www.nytimes. com/2009/08/17/technology/internet/ 17normal.html

Oja, Carol. "*West Side Story* and *The Music Man*: Whiteness, Immigration, and Race in the US During the Late 1950s." *Studies in Musical Theatre* 3, no. 1 (2009), 13–30.

Oja, Carol. *Bernstein Meets Broadway: Collaborative Art in a Time of War*. New York: Oxford University Press, 2014.

Papatola, Dominic P. "Children Will Listen: Juniorized: Sondheim Provided the Impetus for Smaller-Scale Versions of Shows." *The Sondheim Review* 12, no. 2 (Winter 2005), 13–14.

Paulson, Michael. "Broadway Sets Sales and Attendance Records With Tourist Boom." *The New York Times,* May 26, 2015. http://www.nytimes. com/2015/05/27/theater/broadway-sets-sales-and-attendance-records-with-tourist-boom.html (accessed June 30, 2016).

Pellegrini, Nancy. "In China, a Taste of Broadway's 'Fame.'" *Christian Science Monitor*, December 19, 2008. http://www.csmonitor.com/The-Culture/ Music/2008/1219/p13s04-almp.html

Perlov, Barbara. *Why We Tell the Story: A Report on The Shubert Foundation/MTI Broadway Junior Program in the New York City Public Schools*. November 2009.

Prece, Paul and William A. Everett. "The Megamusical: The Creation, Internationalisation and Impact of a Genre." In *The Cambridge Companion to the Musical,* edited by William A. Everett and Paul R. Laird. Second edition. Cambridge and New York: Cambridge University Press, 2008, pp. 250–69.

Preston, Katherine K. "American Musical Theatre Before the Twentieth Century." In *The Cambridge Companion to the Musical,* edited by William A. Everett and Paul R. Laird. Second edition. Cambridge and New York: Cambridge University Press, 2008, pp. 3–28.

"Pursuit of Merriment: It Will Be Attended with Difficulty at the Casino." *The New York Times*, September 22, 1896.

Putnam, Robert D. *Bowling Alone: The Collapse and Revival of American Community*. New York: Simon and Schuster, 2000.

Rapkin, Mickey. *Theater Geek: The Real Life Drama of a Summer at Stagedoor Manor, the Famous Performing Arts Camp* (New York: Simon and Schuster, 2010).

Rich, Frank. *Hot Seat: Theater Criticism for* The New York Times, *1980–1993*. New York: Random House, 1998.

Richards, David. "*Beauty and the Beast:* Disney Does Broadway, Dancing Spoons and All." *The New York Times*, April 19, 1994, p. C15.

Riis, Thomas L. *Just Before Jazz: Black Musical Theater in New York, 1890–1915*. Washington: Smithsonian Institution Press, 1989.

Riis, Thomas L. II. *Frank Loesser*. New Haven: Yale University Press, 2008.

Riis, Thomas L. and Ann Sears, "The Successors of Rodgers and Hammerstein from the 1940s to the 1960s." In *The Cambridge Companion to the Musical*, edited by William A. Everett and Paul R. Laird. Second edition. Cambridge and New York: Cambridge University Press, 2008, pp. 164–89.

Robertson, Campbell. "Ballyhoo of Broadway Shuffles Off to China." *The New York Times*, March 14, 2007, p. E1.

Rodger, Gillian. *Champagne Charlie and Pretty Jemima: Variety Theater in the Nineteenth Century*. Urbana, Chicago and Springfield: University of Illinois Press, 2010.

Rodosthenous, George, ed. *The Disney Musical: Stage, Screen, and Beyond*. London: Bloomsbury Methuen Drama, 2017.

Rosenberg, Bernard and Ernest Harburg. *The Broadway Musical: Collaboration in Commerce and Art*. New York: New York University Press, 1993.

Rothstein, Mervyn. "Equity Reverses 'Saigon' Vote and Welcomes English Star." *The New York Times*, http://www.nytimes.com/1990/08/17/theater/equity-reverses-saigon-vote-and-welcomes-english-star.html (accessed June 20, 2016).

Rubin, Joan Shelley. *The Making of Middlebrow Culture*. Chapel Hill: University of North Carolina Press, 1992.

Sampson, Henry T. *Blacks in Blackface: A Sourcebook on Early Black Musical Shows*. Second edition. Lanham, MD and Plymouth, UK: Scarecrow Press, 2014.

Savran, David. *Highbrow/Lowdown: Theater, Jazz, and the Making of the New Middle Class*. Ann Arbor: University of Michigan Press, 2009.

Schiff, David. "*Oklahoma!* and the Nazi Threat." In *Crosscurrents: American and European Music in Interaction, 1900–2000*, edited by Felix Meyer, Carol J. Oja, Wolfgang Rathert, and Anne Shreffler. Woodbridge: Boydell Press, 2014, pp. 275–83.

Schumach, Murray. "Shuberts Seek to Widen Theater Chain." *The New York Times*, August 27, 1975, p. 32.

Sears, Ann. "The Coming of the Musical Play: Rodgers and Hammerstein." In *The Cambridge Companion to the Musical*, edited by William A. Everett and Paul R. Laird. Second edition. Cambridge and New York: Cambridge University Press, 2008, pp. 147–89.

Shafer, Yvonne. "Black Actors in the Nineteenth Century American Theatre." *College Language Association Journal* XX (March 1977): 387–400.

Shandell, Jonathan. "The Negro Little Theatre Movement." In *The Cambridge Companion to African American Theatre*, edited by Harvey Young. New York: Cambridge University Press, 2013, pp. 103–17.

Bibliography

"*Shuffle Along* Premiere: Negro Production Opens at Sixty-Third Street Music Hall." *The New York Times*, May 23, 1921, p. 20.

Smith, Eric Ledell. *Bert Williams: A Biography of the Pioneer Black Comedian.* Jefferson, NC: McFarland and Company, 1992.

Snyder, Robert W. "Concert Saloons" and "Vaudeville." In *The Encyclopedia of New York City*, edited by Kenneth T. Jackson. New Haven and London: Yale University Press, 1995, pp. 271-2 and 1226.

Snyder, Robert W. *The Voice of the City: Vaudeville and Popular Culture in New York.* New York and Oxford: Oxford University Press, 1989.

Sotiropoulos, Karen. *Staging Race: Black Peformers in Turn of the Century America.* Cambridge: Harvard University Press, 2006.

Stempel, Larry. *Showtime: A History of the Broadway Musical Theatre.* New York: WW Norton, 2010.

Sternfeld, Jessica. *The Megamusical.* Bloomington and Indianapolis: Indiana University Press, 2006.

Sternfeld, Jessica and Elizabeth L. Wollman, "After the 'Golden Age.'" In *The Oxford Handbook of the American Musical*, edited by Raymond Knapp, Mitchell Morris, and Stacy Wolf. New York: Oxford University Press, 2011.

Sterritt, D. "'Company': Amusing, Inventive, Hummable." *Boston After Dark*, April 1, 1970, 4.

Symonds, Dominic. *We'll Have Manhattan: The Early Work of Rodgers and Hart.* New York: Oxford University Press, 2015.

"The Great Fire—Details of the Disaster." *The New York Times*, May 23, 1866, p. 8.

"The Week at the Theatres." *The New York Times*, May 14, 1893, p. 13.

Toll, Robert C. *Blacking Up: The Minstrel Show in Nineteenth-Century America.* New York: Oxford University Press, 1974.

Toll, Robert. *On with the Show! The First Century of Show Business in America.* New York: Oxford University Press, 1976.

"Tony Pastor and His Sixty Years on the Stage." *The New York Times*, August 16, 1908, p. SM3.

"'Tony' Pastor Dead in His 77th Year: Famous Theatrical Man Expires After a Long Illness at His Elmhurst, L.I. Home." *The New York Times*, August 27, 1908, p. 7.

Traub, James. *The Devil's Playground: A Century of Pleasure and Profit in Times Square.* New York: Random House, 2005.

Trav, S.D. *No Applause—Just Throw Money: The Book That Made Vaudeville Famous.* New York: Faber and Faber, 2005.

Travis, Steve. "The Rise and Fall of the Theatrical Syndicate." *Educational Theatre Journal* 10, no. 1 (March 1958), 35-40.

Turan, Kenneth and Joseph Papp. *Free for All: Joe Papp, the Public, and the Greatest Theater Story Ever Told.* New York: Anchor Books, 2010.

Vacha, J.E. "The Case of the Runaway Opera: The Federal Theatre and Marc Blitzstein's 'The Cradle Will Rock.'" *New York History* 62, no. 2 (April 1981), 133-52.

Wall, Carey. "There's No Business Like Show Business: A Speculative Reading of the Broadway Musical." In *Approaches to the American Musical*, edited by Robert Lawson-Peebles. Exeter: University of Exeter Press, 1996, pp 24-43.

Walsh, Michael. "Andrew Lloyd Webber: Now, but Forever? Measuring the Impact, Other Than Commercial, of a Broadway Giant." *The New York Times*, April 9, 2000, p. AR1.

Weinstein, Deena. *Rock'n America: A Social and Cultural History*. Toronto: University of Toronto Press, 2015.

White, Timothy R. *Blue Collar Broadway: The Craft and Industry of American Theater*. Philadelphia: University of Pennsylvania Press, 2015.

Wilsch Case, Claudia. "Inventing the Heartland: The Theatre Guild, *Oklahoma!* and World War II." *Theatre Symposium: A Journal of the Southeastern Theatre Conference* 14 (2006), 35–47.

Wilmeth, Don B. *The Cambridge Guide to American Theatre*. Cambdrige: Cambridge University Press, 2007.

Wolf, Stacy. A *Problem Like Maria: Gender and Sexuality in the American Musial*. Ann Arbor: University of Michigan Press, 2002.

Wolf, Stacy. *Changed for Good: A Feminist History of the Broadway Musical*. New York: Oxford University Press, 2011.

Wolfe, Jonathan. "Broadway Stumbles in Brazil," *The New York Times*, October 17, 2015.

Woll, Allen. *Black Musical Theatre from* Coontown *to* Dreamgirls. New York: Da Capo, 1989.

Wollman, Elizabeth L. *Hard Times: The Adult Musical in 1970s New York City*. New York: Oxford University Press, 2013.

Wollman, Elizabeth L. *The Theater Will Rock: A History of the Rock Musical, From* Hair *to* Hedwig. Ann Arbor: University of Michigan Press, 2006.

Zeigler, Joseph Wesley. *Regional Theatre: The Revolutionary Stage*. New York: Da Capo Press, 1977.

Zellers, Parker R. "The Cradle of Variety: The Concert Saloon." *Education Theatre Journal* 20, no. 4 (December 1968): 578–85.

INDEX

Index

Aspects of Love (Lloyd Webber), 171

Astaire, Adele, 89

Astaire, Fred, 89, 98, 99, 103

Astor Place riots (1849), 8–9

Astor, Henry, 7

Atkinson, Brooks, 86, 106

Avenue Q (Lopez, Marx), 188

Babes in Arms (Rodgers, Hart), 102, 104

Bailey, Pearl, 117, 157, see also Hello, Dolly!;
    St. Louis Woman

Baker, Joséphine, 53, 68

Balanchine, George, 88, 103–4, see also
    Ziegfeld Follies of 1936

    "Princess Zenobia" (ballet from On Your
        Toes), 104

    "Slaughter on Tenth Avenue" (ballet from
        On Your Toes), 104

Baline, Izzy. See Berlin, Irving

Ballroom (Goldenburg, M. Bergman, A.
    Bergman), 196

Bandanna Land (Cook, Shipp, Rogers), 48

Barnes, Clive, 149

Barras, Charles M., 18

    Black Crook, The, 17, 18–21, 20, 23, 24,
        36, 88

Bartholomae, Philip, 61, see also Bolton, Guy;
    Kern, Jerome; Princess musicals;
    Wodehouse, P.G.

Batten, Keith, 228, see also Aida

Beautiful (King), 181, 222

Beauty and the Beast (Disney animated film),
    174

Beauty and the Beast (Menken, Ashman,
    Rice), 175, 177, 204, 228, 236

    Disney animated film version, 174

Bechdel, Alison, 184

    Fun Home (graphic novel), 184, see also
        Fun Home (Tesori, Kron)

Beck, Martin, 30, see also Orpheum Circuit;
    Walter, Gustav

Beggar's Opera, The (Gay), 3

Belasco, David, 35, 54

Bell, Hunter, 182, 216

    [title of show] (with Bowen), 182, 215–16

Bells Are Ringing (Styne, Comden, Green),
    190

Bennett, Michael, 145, 152, 153, 156, 164, 196,
    see also Ballroom; Chorus Line, A;
    Company; Dreamgirls

Berkeley, Busby, 83, 182

Berlin Stories, The (Isherwood), 147

Berlin, Irving, 27, 53, 57, 59, 84, 86–7,
    113

    Annie Get Your Gun, 113

    As Thousands Cheer (with Hart),
        86–7

    This Is the Army, 119–20

    Yip Yip Yaphank, 119

Bernstein, Leonard, 133–4

    Fancy Free (with Robbins), 120

    On the Town (with Comden, Green),
        120–1, 245

    West Side Story (with Sondheim,
        Laurents, Robbins), 132–5, 136, 147,
        193, 217, 241

"Bewitched, Bothered, and Bewildered" (Pal
    Joey), 105, 106

Big River (Miller), 215, 223

"Bill" (Show Boat), 72

Billy Elliot (John, Hall), 193

Bishop, Andrew, 194, see also Falsettos;
    Light in the Piazza, The; Lincoln
    Center Theatre; Once on This Island
    (Flaherty, Ahrens); Playwrights
    Horizons; Sunday in the Park with
    George; Weitzman, Ira

Black Crook, The (Barras), 17, 18–21, 20, 23,
    24, 36, 88

    critical reception, 19–20

    New York Times review, 19

    synopsis, 19

Black, Don, 180

    Bombay Dreams (with Black), 180

Black Lives Matter, 179

Black Manhattan (Johnson), 49

Black Patti's Troubadours (Isham touring
    company), 43

black performers, 42–50, 53, 63, 65–70, 72–4,
    84–7, 91–4, 117–21, 157–9, 164–5,
    243–4, 247, 250

Blackberries of 1932 (Heywood, Peluso,
    etc.), 85

blackface minstrelsy, xii, 9–15, 23, 24, 26, 28,
    39, 42, 44, 45, 48, 70, 92, 119–20, 247,
    see also minstrelsy

Blake, James Hubert "Eubie," 66, 67, 68

    Shuffle Along (with Sissle, Miller, Lyles),
        65–70, 84, 85, 247

Blinn, Holbrook, 60

Index

Index

Index

Index

Hirson, Roger O., 154, *see also* Fosse, Bob; *Pippin*
Hitler, Adolf, 87, 91
Hoffman, Warren, 116, 250
Hogan, Ernest, 44, 49, *see also Clorindy, or the Origin of the Cake Walk*
Holder, Geoffrey, 158, *see also Wiz, The*
Holm, Celeste, 119
Holzman, Winnie, 183, *see also Wicked*
Hoover, Herbert, 77, 86
Hope, Bob, 53
Houseman, John, 96–8, *see also* Blitzstein, Marc; *Cradle Will Rock, The*; Federal Theatre Project (FTP); Welles, Orson
Hoyt, Charles
    Trip to Chinatown, A, 37, 43, 72
Hughes, Langston, 118
    Street Scene (with Weill), 118
Humphry, Doris, 85
Hupfield, Herman, 85
Hurtig, Benjamin, 46, 47
Hurtig, Jules, 46, 47
Hwang, David Henry, 233
    Tarzan (with Collins), 233
Hytner, Nicholas, 180, *see also Carousel*

I Am a Camera (Van Druten), 147, *see also Cabaret*; Isherwood, Christopher
"I Could Write a Book" (*Pal Joey*), 105
"I Love New York" campaign, 161, 163
I Married an Angel (Rodgers, Hart), 104
Idle, Eric, 182
    Monty Python's Spamalot, 182, 204
In Dahomey (Cook, Dunbar, Shipp), 46–7
In the Heights (Miranda), 185, 188, 201, 241–2
"Pacienca y Fe," 241
Internet, xi, 1, 134, 175, 186, 224, 250
Into the Woods (Sondheim, Lapine), 188, 190, 204, 206
Irish immigration, 39, 41–2, 58
Irwin, May, 38
Isham, John W., 43–4, *see also Black Patti's Troubadours*; Octoroons; *Oriental America*
Isherwood, Christopher, 147, *see also Cabaret*; *I Am a Camera*
    Berlin Stories, The, 147
iTheatrics, 201, 206, 207, 213

Izdebski, Marilyn, 205, 210, *see also* musicals in schools, middle schools

Jane Eyre (Paul Gordon, John Caird), 223
Jarrett, Henry, 18–19, *see also Black Crook, The*
jazz, xii, 57, 63, 68, 72, 88, 89, 91, 93, 95, 103, 104, 120, 239
Jazz Singer, The (film), 78–9
Jekyll & Hyde (Wildhorn, Bricusse), 223
Jerry and Nellie, 40, *see also* Cohan, George M.; Four Cohans
Jersey Boys (Gaudio, Crewe, Brickman, Elice), 181, 188, 194, 222, 223
Jesus Christ Superstar (Lloyd Webber, Rice), 150, 167, 168, 188
Joel, Billy, 181–2
    Movin' Out (with Tharp), 181–2
John, Elton, 228, *see also Billy Elliott*
    Aida (with Rice), 228
    Lion King, The (with Rice), 177, 179, 184, 207, 208, 222, 229, 232, 234, 242
Johnson, Billy, 43
    Trip to Coontown, A (with Cole), 43
Johnson, James Weldon, 48–49, 50
    Black Manhattan, 49
    Red Moon, The (with J.R. Johnson, Cole), 48
    Shoo Fly Regiment, The (with J.R. Johnson, Cole), 48
Johnson, J. Rosamond, 48, 49
    Mr. Lode of Koal (with Shipp, etc.), 48, 49
    Red Moon, The (with Weldon, Cole), 48
    Shoo Fly Regiment, The (with Weldon, Cole), 48
Jolson, Al, 38, 89, 92, 102
    Hallelujah, I'm a Bum! (film), 102
Jones, Chris, 218
Jones, John Bush, xiii, 167
    Our Musicals, Ourselves: A Social History of the American Musical Theatre, xiii
Judson Poets' Theater, 144
Jujamcyn Organization, 160, 179
jukebox musicals, 181–2, 215
"Jump Jim Crow" (Rice), 10
Junior Theatre Festival, 198–99

Kander, John, 147, 190
    Cabaret (with Ebb), 145, 147–8, 224, 248
    Chicago (with Ebb), 154–55, 179, 222, 244
    Curtains (with Ebb), 214, 216

281

Index

Index

Index

Index

Index

Index

"Why Can't the World Go and Leave Us
    Alone?" (*Dance a Little Closer*), 166
Wicked (Maguire novel), 188
Wicked (Schwartz), 183–4, 188, 194, 195,
    197–8, 213, 222, 223, 229, 244
Wilder, Thornton, 157, 188
    Matchmaker, The, 157, 188, *see also Hello,
    Dolly!*
Williams, Bert, 44–50, 53, 63, 66, 67, 155,
    see also Bandanna Land; Cook, Will
    Marion; Dunbar, Paul Laurence; *Gold
    Bug, The*; Hurtig, Benjamin; Hurtig,
    Jules; *In Dahomey*; Koster and Bials;
    Mr. Lode of Koal; Seamon, Harry;
    Shipp, Jesse; Walker, George; Ziegfeld,
    Florence, Jr.; *Ziegfeld Follies of 1910*
Willson, Meredith, 135
    Music Man, The, 132, 135–6, 207
Winter Garden Theatre, 54, 136, 169, 193
Wiz, The (Smalls), 158
Wizard of Oz, The (film), 85, 103, 158, 183,
    207, *see also* Bolger, Ray; Harburg,
    E.Y. "Yip"; *Wicked*; *Wiz, The*
Wodehouse, P.G., 61, 72, 100, *see also*
    Bartholomae, Philip; Bolton, Guy;
    Kern, Jerome; Princess musicals
    "Bill" (*Show Boat*), 72
Wolf, Stacy, xiii
    *Changed for Good: A Feminist History of
    the Broadway Musical*, xiii
women's movement, 63–4, 110, 119, 122, 150,
    151–2, 183
Woodhull, Caleb Smith, 9
Woods, Albert H., 80

WPA (Works Progress Administration), 94,
    96, 97, 103, 110
Wynn, Ed, 53, *see also* Ziegfeld, Florenz, Jr.

Yeah Man (Wilson, Weinberg, etc.), 85
Yeston, Maury, 195
Yip Yip Yaphank (Berlin), 119
"You Could Drive a Person Crazy"
    (*Company*), 153
"You've Got to Be Carefully Taught" (*South
    Pacific*), 127
Youmans, Vincent, 84
Young Performers' Editions, 207, *see also*
    Broadway JR.; Disney Musicals
    in Schools (DMIS); Getting to
    Know Collections; Music Theatre
    International; musicals in schools
youth culture, 122, 139, 173
YouTube, 199, 201, 208, 210

Zeigler, Joseph, 220–1
Ziegfeld Follies, 50, 52–3, 56, 62, 63, 64, 84, 88,
    174, 182
    Ziegfeld Follies of 1910, 50
    Ziegfeld Follies of 1936, 103
    Ziegfeld Follies of 1957, 142
Ziegfeld, Florenz, Jr., 50, 52–4, 62, 72, 79–80,
    81
Ziegfeld Theater, 70
Zimmerman, John Frederick, 31, 55, 56,
    see also Erlanger, Abraham L.;
    Frohman, Charles; Hayman, Al; Klaw,
    Marc; Nixon, Samuel F.; Theatrical
    Syndicate

CPSIA information can be obtained
at www.ICGtesting.com
Printed in the USA
LVHW012251110723
752230LV00029B/663